PUPPETS OF NOSTALGIA

PUPPETS OF NOSTALGIA

THE LIFE, DEATH,
AND REBIRTH OF THE JAPANESE
AWAJI NINGYŌ TRADITION

Jane Marie Law

PRINCETON UNIVERSITY PRESS　PRINCETON, NEW JERSEY

Copyright © 1997 by Princeton University Press
Published by Princeton University Press, 41 William Street,
Princeton, New Jersey 08540
In the United Kingdom: Princeton University Press,
Chichester, West Sussex
All Rights Reserved

Library of Congress Cataloging-in-Publication Data

Law, Jane Marie.
Puppets of nostalgia : the life, death, and rebirth of the
Japanese Awaji ningyō tradition / Jane Marie Law.
Includes bibliographical references and indexes.
ISBN 0-691-02894-X (alk. paper)
1. Puppet theater—Japan—Awaji Island.   2. Performing arts—
Religious aspects.   3. Japan—Religious life and customs.
I. Title.
PN1978.J3L39   1997
791.5'3'0952187—dc20   96-33487

Publication of this book has been aided by a subvention
from the Hull Memorial Publication Fund Committee

This book has been composed in Galliard

Princeton University Press books are printed
on acid-free paper and meet the guidelines
for permanence and durability of the Committee
on Production Guidelines for Book Longevity
of the Council on Library Resources

Printed in the United States of America
by Princeton Academic Press

10 9 8 7 6 5 4 3 2 1

For Adam, Samuel, and Tamar
with love

If we should laugh at and insult the memory of the Puppet, we should be laughing at the fall that we have brought about in ourselves, laughing at the Beliefs and Images we have broken.

—E. Gordon Craig (1912)

Contents

Acknowledgments _____

FROM THE first time I walked into the Awaji Puppet Theater in Fukura in 1978 until this final manuscript was prepared for publication, I have been indebted to many agencies, teachers, and friends in both Japan and the United States for support, guidance, and assistance.

On Awaji, my first thanks go to Fujimoto Yasurō and his family—Seiko, Hatsuho and Mizuho—for being my home during many extended periods of fieldwork. The people of their neighborhood of Nakanochō in Fukura all became a special part of this project, and I will never forget their kindness and interest in my work. At the theater, the Awaji Ningyō Jōruri Kan, the puppeteers, chanters, and musicians were most generous with their time and knowledge. Naniwa Ayako and Matsuyama Mitsuyo took care of endless details with equally endless good spirits. Nakanishi Hideo, director of the high school puppetry club at Mihara High School and a scholar of Awaji puppetry, was always helpful and patient, and I acknowledge his many contributions to this work. Fudō Satoshi, an avid *Awaji ningyō* enthusiast, grandson of a puppeteer and son of the first "revivalist" of the tradition, was always available to drive me to new locations and discuss ideas. He also generously gave me permission to use rare photos from his father's collection in this book. Mori Masaru, president of the Awaji Puppetry Preservation Society, was most generous with financial support during many stages of my research. Tamura Shōji of the Awaji Historical Archives in Sumoto was always gracious in giving me access to rare documents.

Two very special people merit a separate accolade. Umazume Masaru, director of the Awaji Ningyō Jōruri Kan, and Naniwa Kunie, its resident grandmother and spirit, gave me more inspiration and assistance than I can ever acknowledge. I doubt I shall ever again have such enchanting experiences in field research as I had working with these two fine people.

For assistance in setting up my research trips to Usa, I am grateful to the Shingon priest Iwatsubo-sensei on Awaji and the Andō family in Usa at Dairakuji. Kabata Yoshimizu of the Oita Prefecture Buraku History Study Group gave me an excellent historical and thematic overview of the issues relating to puppetry and status in the Oita area.

Research for this project was funded by different agencies. From 1987–89, I was a Mombushō scholar with affiliation at Tsukuba University in the Division of Philosophy. During my stays at Tsukuba, Professor Araki

Michio and Miyata Noboru were most supportive. Also at Tsukuba, I was assisted with many aspects of this research by Komatsu Kayoko, Yoshimine Kazu, and Miyamoto Yōtarō. After I came to Cornell in 1989, I received summer subsidies from the Cornell East Asia Program to conduct the research for the final chapter of this work.

Many teachers at the University of Chicago had a major influence on this project. Mircea Eliade's enthusiasm for the religious dimensions of puppets and his interest in my research helped form the early stages of my work. Lawrence Sullivan and David Tracy were both careful and critical readers, and I acknowledge their assistance and support.

My deepest gratitude for my teachers goes to Professor Joseph Mitsuo Kitagawa. He was a model of humane academic integrity, and I can never express all he has done for my educational development. I miss him greatly, and although my research has gone in different directions, his voice informs all my reflections on the history of religions, reminding me to look for the subtle and gentle gestures of people.

At Cornell, many colleagues and friends gave me much help. John McRae read parts of this work and offered helpful criticism and advice. Kyoko Selden's careful attention deserves a special note of thanks, and I am deeply grateful for her endless support and assistance over the years. Leslie Peirce, Rachel Weil, and Chris Franquemont read early drafts of chapters and helped me find my own voice in this writing process. I am particularly grateful to Chris for reading through the entire penultimate draft and making many helpful stylistic suggestions. Diane Kubarek of Cornell Information Technologies was especially helpful in showing me how to digitize the drawings included in this book.

Preparing a manuscript for publication and being a working mother with two tiny children requires more than the ability to do several things at once. One needs special friends who can step in and help out. To Karen Davison, Uemura Yasuko, and Peng Chenna, I extend gratitude for kindness and assistance I can never repay in full. Ivy Mauser, Kay Reynolds, Amelia Massi, Louise Raimando, Rebecca Schwed, and Bettina Ehrmann were a great support to me as I juggled my several roles.

I owe a special thank you to my copyeditor, John LeRoy, who liberated many of my cumbersome sentences from the clenched fists of verbosity. At the Princeton University Press, I thank Helen Hsu for her careful attention to endless details, and Ann Wald, my editor, for her support and clarity. Janet Snoyer prepared the index.

My father-in-law, Ron Law, read chapters of the book, and made many helpful stylistic suggestions. My own parents, Alfred and Delores Swanberg, were also a great support along the way. My husband, Adam, and my two children, Sam and Tamar, have earned the dedication of this book many times over. I could not have written this book without their support, and I owe them my love and gratitude.

While all of these people made many contributions to this work, it goes without saying that any errors are my own. I have given surnames first in Japanese, unless referring to works by Japanese authors published first in English. Any photographs in the work, unless otherwise noted, are my own.

PUPPETS OF NOSTALGIA

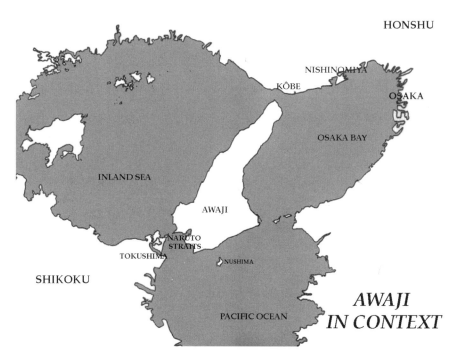

HONSHU

NISHINOMIYA

KÔBE

OSAKA

OSAKA BAY

INLAND SEA

AWAJI

NARUTO
STRAITS

TOKUSHIMA

NUSHIMA

SHIKOKU

*AWAJI
IN CONTEXT*

PACIFIC OCEAN

Map of Awaji as situated in Japan.

Introduction

Of Stories and Fragments

Place and Time: The Man with the Pictures

The man was in his sixties, going bald, with bits of gray hair around his temples. He sat on the bench outside the Awaji puppet theater, on the promenade overlooking the swirling Naruto Straits. On the other side of the enormous whirlpools, the island of Shikoku could be seen through the bright sunshine. It was late afternoon, and the direction of the whirlpools indicated the water of the Pacific Ocean was flowing into the Inland Sea of Japan. In several hours, it would flow back out once again. The cape at the southern tip of the small island of Awaji, where we sat, formed one side of the opening of the *Setonaikai*.

On his lap, the man held a pile of old black and white photographs, a tattered and yellowed handwritten manuscript, and a collection of papers. These were documents collected by his father in the 1940s when he had tried to save the tradition of Awaji puppetry from extinction. This man had come to the theater to show me the documents, and as he did so, he told me the following story:

"My grandfather [on my father's side] was a *Dōkumbō mawashi*—he manipulated sacred puppets at New Year, weddings, and sometimes at other small festivals. Of course, this wasn't his only occupation. We were poor, and so he opened up a little store. You could call it a mini supermarket, I guess.

"I was about ten when the war started. I remember that time clearly. Like so many other people in Japan, we were soon starving as Japan moved further into the war. No one had any money to spend in the store. Things were really tough. So one day, to feed the family, Grandfather decided to sell his puppets. No sooner had he made the decision, it seemed, than several men from Osaka showed up in the courtyard to look them over. His puppets were really beautiful. He had Sanbasō, Okina, Senzai, Ebisu, all the little flutes and drums and hand rattles—the whole bit. He even had nice little costumes for all of them—in pretty good shape, too.

"The men from Osaka paid my grandfather a small amount of money, packed the puppets into the car, and drove away.

"I can see that day like it happened yesterday. I was watching the transaction from a little bit behind my grandfather. He stood in the courtyard and looked down the road until long after the car with the men in it had rounded the corner and the dust it raised on the road had settled. He just kept standing there and standing there. In my mind, I remember him standing there all day, until the sun went down.

"Then he came inside, and I tell you, he never said another word about those puppets. They were never mentioned again.

"I was only a kid, but I felt really sad. I didn't know what made me sad then. But thinking back on it now, I guess I felt like a part of Awaji had been packed into the back of a car and stolen away to Osaka. Or maybe I felt something had died. I don't know what I felt, really.

"Many years later, after my grandfather died, we were going through his things, and we found all these little sketches he had made of Sanbasō. They were quite detailed—they showed the puppet's eyes, his costume, how his mouth worked, his hands and feet. They were just lovely. Do you suppose he was trying to remember the puppets he had sold away to the collectors from Osaka? I don't know, but I still have the sketches."

This story was told to me in July 1988, while I was conducting fieldwork on the island of Awaji concerning the history of *Awaji ningyō shibai* (the Awaji puppetry tradition). Far from being a puppet theater for children, Awaji puppeteers performed rituals that maintained rigid ritual purity codes and kept dangerous spiritual forces properly channeled and appeased. Out of these ritual roots, a rich dramatic *jōruri* (ballad) tradition developed.[1] This form of puppet theater later became the classical Bunraku for which Japan is famous.

This book, based primarily on my fieldwork on Awaji in the village of Fukura in 1984, from 1987 through 1989, in the summers of 1990 and 1991, and in the fall of 1993, is a study of the dynamics of tradition formation and revival in Awaji ningyō shibai. Most studies of Japanese puppetry by Japanese and foreign scholars focus on ningyō jōruri, the ballad tradition, giving only passing attention to the ritual underpinnings of this strong theatrical tradition. I have chosen to take a different approach. I am most interested in what is called *shinji* (or *kamigoto*, an alternate reading, for "sacred matters"), the ritual use of puppetry in this tradition. In the following chapters, I explore the history, development, and meanings of rites performed by itinerant puppeteers in Awaji. I show how these rites used beings once removed from the human realm—puppets—to mediate the dichotomies of order and chaos, purity and pollution, danger and safety, good and evil, the human and the divine, and in recent years, the ordinary and the exotic. The existence of this ritual system carried out by outcast itinerant puppeteers challenges common assumptions in ritual theory that posit "a shared system of meaning" as the basis for ritual efficacy and significance.

The man who told me the above story, whose grandfather sold his puppets to survive, was also the son of the man who started the movement to preserve Awaji ningyō in the 1940s. I open this work with this particular story because it succinctly expresses the paradox contained in almost any study of a Japanese "folk performing art" (*minzoku geinō*) in the 1990s: While one may be trying to study the past of a tradition, any understanding of that past is refracted through two powerful lenses: the threatened extinction of these folk performing arts and the nostalgic discourse supporting their revival. When I began my preliminary fieldwork on Awaji puppetry in 1984, my initial interest was in how Awaji ritual puppetry developed and how its formation and dynamics could shed light on larger issues in Japanese nonecclesiastical religious practice and worship. I went to the village of Fukura in southern Awaji not only because it was the home of the only surviving troupe on Awaji, the Awaji Ningyō Jōruri Kan, but also because this was the best base from which to access archives relating to Awaji puppetry's past and because it was close to where most of the surviving puppeteers from the pre–World War II period lived. But studying the past of Awaji puppets during the 1980s meant that I was also witnessing the coincidence in time and place of numerous currents in what could only be described as the dusk of this once vital performance tradition: grief many people felt over the passing of Awaji as a vital center for puppetry performances and life on Awaji, public expressions of nostalgia for the "good old days" when visits by ritual performers and puppet festivals were common, manipulations of these strong sentiments of nostalgia and sadness for various political and economic ends, and in the late 1980s and early 1990s, the subsequent "revival" of this tradition as a lucrative financial endeavor. People working at revival of Awaji ningyō took what appeared to be a trajectory toward extinction and rerouted it into something else. My fieldwork coincided with—and in some strange and ironic ways contributed to—the revival of this tradition.

In a very real sense, this study begins with the crisis of the tradition's threatened extinction. The man in this particular story clearly expressed how he felt an essential part of his identity had been lost when the Awaji puppets of his childhood were sold to collectors from Osaka. I heard many stories with this same theme. One woman told me that near the end of the war, when she was desperate, malnourished, and suffering from disease, she and her husband took the puppet heads that her father, like his father before him, had handled as a Dōkumbō mawashi and burned them to heat bath water to wash their sick, dirty children. She laughed wryly when she thought of how much one of those *kashira* (puppet heads) would bring today as an example of "folk art."

Discussions of Awaji puppetry often became narratives about where people were when the last performances took place and how they felt about the demise of the tradition. I have heard this same man tell his story about the collectors from Osaka many times, and in each telling the story changed considerably, becoming more concise and affecting. Initially I was tempted to dismiss this continuous transformation of the narrative as the fabrications of an unreliable informant, but I came to see that reviving a tradition entails reworking life stories. Stories are more than just data. For people on Awaji, telling stories about one's grief over the threatened death of the tradition becomes a way of legitimating one's right to partic-ipate in its revival. Revival constitutes a retelling of the past, including the tradition's "near death experiences." Because these stories reveal so much of the feelings that people on Awaji have for their puppetry tradition, careful sculpting and constructing of narratives becomes a way of process-ing conflicting feelings of grief, loss, confusion, and guilt. They have seen their island change dramatically in the last few decades, and they know that they have been unable to hold on to what they feel made Awaji a unique place in Japan: Awaji ningyō. Something about Awaji puppets has captured the imaginations of many people living on the island, and for them Awaji ningyō has become deeply synonymous with a certain part of their identity, tied up with what they have come to regard as a collective and intricate system of meaning, which, they insist, people on the island all share. To tell the story of the death and rebirth of Awaji puppets is to tell a story about a part of themselves and their relationship to both the present and the past.

Awaji has been a center for puppetry from at least the sixteenth century, when documents describe the activities of puppeteers living in the district of Sanjo in present-day Mihara-gun. Stories involving a puppet or a pup-petry performance included striking human experiences, often told with a charged sense of nostalgia or a strain of grief. These stories seem as much a part of the traditions as the facts about performances and puppets in the historical texts. What memories was the old grandfather seeking to recap-ture when he made his tiny sketches of the ritual puppets that he had sold to the collectors from Osaka? What emotions was the old man who told me the story trying to express when he continually revised this poignant event from his childhood into an ever tighter story? This story and others like it convey, in a way that accounts of troupes being revived today in Japan cannot, the emotion and sense of attachment people feel about puppetry performances, ritual or dramatic.

A Series of Questions, an Integration of Sources

The Awaji ningyō tradition as a whole raises a range of historical and structural questions in the history of Japanese religions: (1) the significance of the use of effigies of the human form in ritual appeasement and purification rites; (2) the ritual dynamics of itinerant performance and the significance of the "outsider" in the maintenance of the ritual purity codes of medieval and early modern Japan; (3) the social status problems of Japan's "outcasts," the category to which puppeteers belonged and from which their descendants have struggled to free themselves; (4) the significance of Sanjo districts as "geographies of otherness"; (5) the history and development of the *kugutsu* groups (wandering performers, both male and female), mentioned in literary texts from the middle of the Heian period on; (6) the movement from sacred rites (shinji or kamigoto) to "secular" entertainment (in this case, jōruri ballad recitation enacted by puppets) and the continued interaction of the two; and (7) the rediscovery of the ritual origins of this tradition and the political implications of the revival of Japanese "folk performing arts" with its ironic retrieval of outcast arts as expressions of the "authentic and the valuable." While it is readily apparent that each of these important issues is inherent in the Awaji tradition, written sources for a comprehensive study of each issue are either fragmented or nonexistent. In preparing this book, I have combined textual studies of primary and secondary sources relating to both Awaji puppetry and other forms of ritual and entertainment in Japanese history with extensive fieldwork on Awaji and around Japan. Doing so has led me to question the facile distinction drawn between "primary" and "secondary" sources. Every performance, every personal story about the past and the present, and every recorded interview becomes a new and different primary source, as do supposedly secondhand accounts from people living on Awaji.

I first studied Awaji puppetry while preparing a doctoral dissertation on Awaji puppetry as it relates to Japanese folk religion. After I finished my doctoral studies, I continued to visit Awaji and participate firsthand in discussions about the extended revival of puppetry throughout Japan. This book is a result of both periods of research, and although it draws on some of the research of my doctoral dissertation,[2] it addresses decidedly different questions. My earlier concern was with how a study of Awaji ningyō revealed larger dynamics in Japanese folk religion, an enterprise for which I admit a declining enthusiasm. In this study, I am interested in how ritual puppetry in Japanese history has continually been in a process of tradition formation, attempting to forge a tradition for itself, even as that very tradition was continually being absorbed and appropriated by the larger dynamics of Japanese religious and political life.

During my predoctoral research on Awaji, conducted for one month in 1984 and again for several extended periods from 1987 to 1989,[3] I engaged in four very different types of research. First, for nearly two months I spent every day at the Awaji Ningyō Jōruri Kan watching rehearsals, performances, and daily activities at the theater, and talking with visitors who would come by to chat, see what was happening, and ask questions. This theater continues to be the hub of both contemporary Awaji puppetry activities and ongoing scholarship into the history of the tradition. In lengthy talks with performers and the director, Umazume Masaru, I learned about the training experiences they had undergone and about how they understood puppetry's uniqueness as a dramatic and ritual medium. I also interviewed the younger members of the theater separately, to understand how they perceived the tradition from the perspective of the next generation. For them, Awaji puppetry was about the present and the future, and I was curious how they related to the tradition's past. While at the theater, I interviewed audiences who came to the Awaji Ningyō Jōruri Kan on tours to see the brief performances. Often I handed out questionnaires prior to performances. This work gave me a healthy distrust of questionnaires as an exclusive fieldwork methodology in Japan. Although the questionnaires provided me with the occasion to converse with people in the audiences, the answers I received were largely polite attempts to second-guess what I wanted to hear: "Lovely performance." "Very nice dolls." "What a lovely setting." "*Gambatte ne!*" (Good luck!) I used conversations with the audience, the occasional helpful questionnaire, discussions with members of the theater and the community, and my own observations of performances to reconstruct how people understood the genre of puppetry as a ritual and theatrical medium.

Second, during this period and on numerous other lengthy research trips in 1988 and 1989, I talked with people directly connected with puppetry today. In 1987, members of the Awaji Ningyō Hozonkai (Awaji Puppetry Preservation Society) were just beginning a new wave of activity to revive the numerous arts relating to puppetry, particularly puppet head carving, and costume and stage prop production. I was able to meet with Oe Minosuke, the famous puppet-head carver for the Bunraku theater and the last master of kashira carving alive today, in his home in Naruto, across the Naruto Straits from Awaji on the island of Shikoku. Local scholars on Awaji were also starting new collaborations in research to revive Awaji ningyō and understand its history.

Third, on several trips to Awaji from 1984 through 1989, I spent mornings at the ceremonial center of Awaji ningyō, the Omidō Hachiman Daibosatsu shrine in Sanjo. This shrine claims to be the birthplace of

Awaji ningyō, and in the past all itinerant puppeteers setting out from Awaji would present themselves before it to venerate the patrons of puppetry enshrined here: Hyakudayū, Dōkumbō, Ebisu, and Akiba. Today, every morning at about ten o'clock local people from Sanjo (mostly elderly farmers) take a break from their work and play gateball, a game not unlike croquet, under the shady trees at the shrine. These leisurely mornings afforded me the opportunity to talk at length with people who had grown up in a small village that less than fifty years ago had been the home of several active puppetry troupes. No one ever wanted me on their gateball team, but I heard a lot of stories, most of them told more than once and with great embellishment over the years.

Finally, I spent time at the Awaji Rekishi Shiryōkan (Awaji Historical Archives) in Sumoto, using manuscripts and secondary sources difficult if not impossible to get elsewhere in Japan. Through each of these research strategies, I intended to observe the local response to the tradition, to understand how people on Awaji understood the meanings of Awaji puppetry, and to get some picture, through both historical research and studies of the present situation, of what prewar Awaji puppetry was like.

My concern at that time was one of retrieval and reconstruction of the religious rites performed by itinerant puppeteers, particularly the *Sanbasō* rite. Sanbasō ritual is the most sacred rite in the Awaji tradition. Derived from the larger Okina tradition in earlier Japanese performing arts such as Noh and Kagura, this rite represents the direct manifestation in the human realm of visiting deities ("old men") from the other world, and is performed to purify homes, remove pollution, and bring blessing from the sacred realm at the period right after the New Year. This ritual forms the main pillar in the religious use of puppetry in Japan, and so the focus of my study was on this rite before its demise in the twentieth century. Awaji puppeteers had traveled all over Japan performing these rites, and many of them had settled in other regions and started their own puppetry troupes, considering themselves to still be "Awaji puppeteers." Some of those Awaji lineage centers still have remnant performances presented at shrines as part of a ritual calendar. I was interested in using the Sanbasō performances of these other Awaji lineage theaters to reconstruct a picture of the Sanbasō ritual on Awaji at an earlier time. In 1988, I traveled to Nagano prefecture and attended the International Puppetry Festival in Iida-shi. Then I watched puppetry performances at the Kuroda Ningyō Za (presented outdoors in the precincts of the Hachiman shrine), and interviewed the puppeteers at that theater and at the Waseda Ningyō Za nearby. The puppetry traditions in both of these shrines were started by an Awaji puppeteer in the early eighteenth century.

In the midst of my studies, an exciting discovery in the town of Morioka in Iwate prefecture brought to light puppets, texts, and ritual implements from the Awaji tradition. An Awaji puppeteer by the name of Suzue Shirobe had performed in Morioka around 1641 and had established an Awaji lineage theater in the area, manipulating his puppets for the Lord of Nanbu and even the Emperor. There has not been an active theater in Morioka since before the Meiji Restoration in 1868, but I wanted to examine the puppets and documents found there as a reference point in reconstructing the types of puppets used in the early Awaji tradition. In February 1989 I spent several days in Morioka examining the findings.

At the end of my fieldwork on Awaji in 1988, I spent nearly two months traveling throughout the Inland Sea and around Kyushu, examining references to the mythical founder of Awaji puppetry, Hyakudayū, and trying to unravel the relationship between this name, ritual puppetry, appeasement of malevolent spirits, and worship of the deity Hachiman.

This period of focused fieldwork prior to writing my doctoral dissertation impressed upon me the need to understand the "local knowledge" about religious activities, to listen to the stories of the people involved, and to attend to their issues. Research trips from the northernmost part of Honshu in Iwate to the tip of Kyushu indicated the wide scope of this important puppetry tradition in Japan. This perspective impressed on me the importance of understanding *the road* as sacred geography in this tradition.

As I was involved in the research of reconstructing Awaji puppetry's past, I had a series of persistent questions that I consider hermeneutically significant. First, I was continually interested in the activity of memories, even painful memories, as a lens through which this tradition is reconstructed. While I viewed nostalgic discourse with some suspicion, I was interested in understanding what kind of creative and even healing process was being served by this "painful longing" for the past and by the effort to retrieve what was rapidly vanishing. How are we to understand this revival of a ritual and dramatic tradition? My second question was, What was I doing working alongside people for whom this tradition was part of their past, trying to sort through fragments of evidence to piece together a coherent history? Why Awaji and not Kalispell, Montana (or Silver Spring, Maryland, or Hampstead, England or wherever we are from)? Why their past and not my own? Nostalgic discourse and the telling of stories about the past is a multitextured field. The interplay of nostalgic discourse and tradition formation is perhaps best seen initially in someone else's tradition, but it is capable of being generalized to shed light on activities closer to home. This book addresses these fundamental issues and confronts the related problem of fragmented evidence and the fabrication of seamless "histories" by scholars for a variety of ends.

Although the first several chapters are about the history of ritual puppetry in Japan and the rise of Awaji as a center for ritual puppetry in the early seventeenth century, my focus in these studies has shifted from my earlier interests. I am less interested in reconstructing the past of ritual puppetry in Japan than in showing how the traditions of ritual puppetry and worship have been continually reconstructing the past and forging new identities and traditions. My studies on Awaji in the summers of 1990 and 1991, and again in the autumn of 1993, have provided the opportunity to explore these issues more directly, since during those trips I was fortunate to participate in the discussions and development of the forum for reviving puppetry around Japan, the triennial All Japan Puppetry Summits (Zenkoku Ningyō Shibai Samitto), which occurred from 1990 to 1993.

This book directly addresses the issue of nostalgia and the revival of folk culture in Japan today. Far from being a modern phenomenon, nostalgic discourse is part and parcel of the formation of tradition throughout history, even in the case of ritual puppetry. Finding a past and making it coherent is at one level a most fundamental human activity. Appropriating the past is part of the narrative process, and narration is a special kind of knowledge that people can have about themselves. Narrative construction, almost by definition nostalgic at some level, can even have a healing effect.[4]

In chapter 1 I lay the groundwork for a discussion of ritual puppetry in Japan by considering puppetry as a ritual medium and by exploring the threads of influence from various magical uses of dolls, effigies, and puppets that find expression in Japanese ritual. This discussion shows the variety of ritual uses of puppets in Japanese religions and also indicates how it is not possible to argue for a single tradition of Japanese puppetry. I point out the multivalence of the term *ningyō*, which I translate as "puppet." I suggest that in each case of ritual use of dolls, effigies, and puppets, there is a concretization of a narrative event in the life of a person or a community.

Chapter 2 is a study of the issues of sameness and difference in Japanese ritual. It reveals the need to have outsiders, in this case outcasts, to perform certain ritual functions in Japanese society. The discussion explores the development of the ritual specialist as Other, and the nature of the *kadozuke* (literally, "attached to the gate") performance tradition, in which itinerant specialists were responsible for mediating order and chaos, the realms of the human and the divine, and pollution and purity through ritual performance. I explore the history of two forms of itinerant performance, *Senzu manzai* and *Matsu-bayashi*, to reveal the structure of itinerant performance appropriated by nonecclesiastical specialists discussed later. Since the Awaji ningyō tradition was based upon itinerant ritual performance, this chapter lays the groundwork for those that follow.

Chapter 3 turns to a discussion of clearly manipulated ningyō as opposed to ningyō as static objects. I take up the issue of the late Heian *kugutsu* groups (itinerant ritual puppeteers). The discussion presents the major evidence we have about these groups, as well as a thorough discussion of the activities of ritual specialists several hundred years later, also called kugutsu, attached to the Nishinomiya Ebisu shrine. The deity Ebisu, usually represented as a fat, happy-go-lucky deity with a fish under his arm, is in fact understood to be capable of causing epidemics, disasters at sea, and other natural calamities. Ritual puppeteers were understood to mediate and transform the spiritual powers of this enigmatic and dangerous deity into a deity of luck *(fukushin)* as Ebisu is commonly understood today. These Nishinomiya *Ebisu-kaki* (bearers or carriers of Ebisu) traveled the countryside disseminating the power of the Nishinomiya center and performing ritual appeasement for Ebisu by using a puppet understood to be its spirit vessel *(goshintai)*. Since this is the ceremonial center from which Awaji puppeteers broke away, and against which the Awaji tradition comes to define itself, understanding the Nishinomiya kugutsu and Ebisu's liminal nature is a necessary step in appreciating the formation of the Awaji ningyō tradition.

It is clear that by the middle of the sixteenth century, the ties that bound the Nishinomiya kugutsu to this ceremonial center were weakening as these puppeteers struck out on their own, engaged in more dramatic styles of entertainment, and became increasingly popular. Chapter 4 studies the rise of Awaji puppetry as a distinct tradition developing out of its Nishinomiya origins. While puppeteers may have been active on Awaji prior to the sixteenth century, only then did Awaji puppetry develop a unique identity in contrast to the Nishinomiya kugutsu. The discussion focuses on how one text, *Dōkumbō Denki*, became a central work in the formation of the Awaji ningyō tradition. Being a tradition means having a common story about the past. I present evidence showing how this narrative gave the Awaji tradition a coherent center and thereby encouraged the spread of Awaji puppetry throughout Japan.

Chapter 5 presents an in-depth study of the two sacred performances Shiki Sanbasō and Ebisu-mai, their use in itinerant performance, and their inclusion in larger puppetry events on Awaji called *ningyō matsuri*. The discussion includes a translation of each piece along with a detailed discussion and an interpretation of its content. I focus on the multitextured alterity of these rites. Puppets, puppeteers, and deities are all "outsiders" in the Japanese order of meaning, and these rites become powerful invocations of these forces from outside the everyday realm, capable of revitalizing and purifying communities. I show the interaction between the developed jōruri performances and the ritual performances, and I also discuss a theatrical spectacle unique to the Awaji tradition known as *dōgu-*

gaeshi (literally, "changing stage sets"). Ningyō matsuri, presented either in the spring right after planting or in the fall right after harvest, were understood to be festivals for the *kami* (deities) of agriculture. We explore the dynamics of these elaborate ritual and theatrical events, performed over several days on temporary stages or in shrine precincts.

The final chapter is a discussion of the contemporary state of Awaji puppetry. Today, Awaji ningyō appears to have made a comeback, and the Awaji Ningyō Jōruri Kan has become a successful financial venture, with the troupe making overseas tours at least once a year and giving daily performances at the new, specially built indoor Fukura theater. In this discussion, I trace the history of this comeback and discuss the coincidence of regionalism, revivalism, and nostalgia in Japanese society in the last two decades. I discuss the status of Awaji ningyō's ritual tradition in this retrieval process, and the irony of its initial exclusion and later inclusion in the revival. Finally, I explore the role of the foreign scholar in this process.

Metanarratives in the Study of Japanese Religious History

This book deals with an expression of nonecclesiastical, popular religion in Japanese history. It is centered on the activities of a group of people who occupied the margins of Japanese religious life and society, while performing ritually integral activities to keep the central systems of meaning functioning. This study adds to the growing number of monographs that argue against a singularity of experience in Japanese popular religious life and ask us to see Japanese history as radically heterogeneous, even though there have been strong attempts both within and outside Japan to posit a notion of a singular identity.

Until recently, most scholarship on Japanese folk religion has posited a unity of experience at the popular level. This idea of a uniform "folk culture," articulated in the United States by the work of Robert Redfield, was in Japan most ardently advocated by the folklorist Yanagita Kunio. Yanagita argued that people shared a unified experience, half conscious at times, parallel to and equally as important as the Japanese imperial line. "The folk" in Hokkaido shared a strata of consciousness with "the folk" in Kyushu. Yanagita constructed what has become the rudimentary framework of all studies of Japanese folk religion, although it ignores groups such as Korean immigrants living in Japan, outcasts, and other people whose experiences somehow deviated from his norm. Yanagita, hoped to give voice and identity to people who could not speak for themselves, and to invest the everyday life (*nichijō seikatsu*) of "folk culture" with a prestige it had previously not enjoyed. To a certain extent, had it not been for the ethnographic enterprise spawned by Yanagita's agenda and his enthusiasm for it, much of the data used in this study would have been permanently missing from the historical record. But another result of his enterprise was the construction of an identity for the imagined masses in Japan, and a metanarrative of Japanese religious history that has become hegemonic and oppressive. According to Yanagita, the folk were rural and to a certain extent ahistorical. They shared a common heritage and set of concerns and religious sensibilities. His imagination of the folk transcended description and became a prescription for an authentic Japanese identity.

Yanagita's view of folk religion was expanded upon and systematized most directly by his son-in-law, the folklorist Hori Ichirō. Hori argued for a unity of Japanese religious experience: "In this context we may point out that there is good reason to speak of Japanese religion as an entity."[5] He identified six "common tendencies" he claimed could be considered continuous in Japanese folk religion:

> emphasis on filial piety *(kō)* and ancestor worship connected with the Japanese family system; emphasis on *on* (debts and favors given by superiors) and *hōon* (the return of *on*); mutual borrowing and mixing of different religious traditions (or syncretic tendency); belief in the continuity between man and deity, or easy deification of human beings; coexistence of different religions in one family or even in one person; strong belief in spirits of the dead in connection with ancestor worship as well as with more animistic conceptions of malevolent or benevolent soul activities.[6]

This approach to Japanese popular religion was echoed by Joseph Kitagawa, who also proposed that Japanese religions shared a unity of consciousness. While he never addressed the issue of "folk religion" directly, he maintained that it is possible to speak about Japanese religion in the singular (just as he would maintain that one can learn a great deal about various data by understanding Japanese religions in the plural). As well, Kitagawa identified a series of common tendencies: (1) a nonsymbolic understanding of symbols, or the tendency for the represented to participate in its representation (he writes that "the meaning of each being was sought not in itself but in it mutual participation, continuity and correspondence to and with others within the total framework of the monistic world of meaning");[7] (2) viewing past, present, and future in a fluid relationship to one another, evidenced by the tendency to interpret past events in terms of present realities, or what Kitagawa calls (inverting the Augustinian axiom) "a past of things present"; and 3) the tendency to view the given world as the ultimate world, and the Japanese nation "as the measure of all things."[8]

Kitagawa goes one step further than Hori in maintaining that these tendencies all point toward a Japanese sensibility of "seamlessness." This seamlessness, demonstrated in the Japanese conception of the human relationship to the natural world, matter, symbols, and sacredness, comprises what Kitagawa calls a "unitary meaning structure": "As far as one can tell, one of the basic features of the early Japanese religious universe was its unitary meaning structure, a structure which affirmed the belief that the natural world was the original world, and which revolved around the notion that the total cosmos was permeated by sacred or *kami* nature. Everybody and everything in the early Japanese monistic universe, including physical elements such as fire, water, wood and stone, as well as animals and celestial bodies, were believed to be endowed with kami nature."[9]

Yanagita, Hori, and Kitagawa can be seen as representative of a particular approach to Japanese popular religion which, though often insightful, posits a continuity across consciousness (Yanagita), geography (Hori), and time (Kitagawa). One wonders just what tattered seams in society are concealed by such an adamant insistence on a single piece of fabric.

Such an approach is problematic, particularly in our discussion of ritual puppetry, in that it tends to blur differences and exclude persons and data that do not fit with the currents of the grand narrative of "Japan" as an idea.[10] Recent scholarship guided by the zealous instincts of postmodernism has directed our gaze toward those people who for different reasons have stood outside the grand narrative of Japanese history. This same current of scholarship also warns us not to be too strident in our claim to speak for those who have not been spoken for in history. H. D. Harootunian writes as follows about Yanagita's agenda to give voices to the "folk": "He committed himself to the impossible task of trying to speak for the folk outside the language of power and reason that had concealed them from view. He misrecognized his task, failing to see the misfortune of the folk—the interminable misfortune of their silence and their failure to secure representation for themselves—lay precisely in the fact that as soon as a person attempted to convey their silence, he passed over to the side of the enemy, the side of history and reason, even if, at the same time, he puts the claims of the enemy into question."[11]

In this study, I do not claim that a unitary structure of meaning undergirds the various and widespread uses of puppets in ritual practice in Japan. Nor do I claim to have somehow given voice to the unvoiced "outsiders" of Japanese religious history. My claim is more humble: to present the fragments of evidence we have for a study of a particular case in Japanese religious history, and in the process provide insight into a recurring dynamic in Japanese religious history—the interaction between the central religious authorities, for whom a unified structure of meaning is a useful device, and those people on the margins, whose very ritual actions both challenge and maintain the power of the center.

This study of ritual puppetry is about one group of "others" in Japanese religious history. To a large extent, the lives and stories of ritual puppeteers and their activities have been left out of the historical record. Often all we have are relics (even icons) from the past, pieces of physical or textual evidence with few clues about how they were used or understood or what they meant. It is not possible to tell their story for no one knows what it is. This book, however, presents the evidence that we do have. By putting it in one place and examining it, perhaps we will hear other voices in the history of Japanese religious life, telling stories otherwise lost to us. I situate this concern within a larger intellectual movement of breaking away from grand narratives of the center, a movement that demands we "activate the differences" and promises to reflect a more textured picture of Japanese religious histories.[12]

1

In the Shape of a Person: The Varieties of Ritual Uses of Effigy in Japan

I FIRST SAW a performance of Awaji ningyō in the fall of 1978, when I happened into the dilapidated theater on the waterfront of Fukura Bay, in a small fishing village in the southern part of the island. The theater was in a large hall located over a souvenir shop. A few dozen folding chairs were set up in rows for the audience. Downstairs, one could buy seaweed from the nearby Inland Sea, and trinkets with a regional flair.

That day I saw the pilgrimage scene from *Keisei Awa no Naruto*, the story of a young girl who, separated from her parents since the age of three, goes looking for them wearing the garb of a pilgrim on the Saikoku Pilgrimage route. In the scene, she arrives at the home of a woman who quickly recognizes the child's story and realizes that she is her daughter. A heart-wrenching drama unfolds as we learn of the events that led to the separation of the parent and child. For political reasons, the woman is forced to conceal her identity as the girl's mother, and in the end sends her away to continue her search for her parents.

The manipulation of symbols imparted a tragic feeling to the performance. The audience became aware that at some level both mother and child know they have been reunited, but must experience their separation all over again as the child is thrown out the door and it is slammed shut behind her.

It was a powerful performance. Like the Bunraku theater for which Japan is famous, the puppets used in the performance were each manipulated by three people.[1] The puppeteers were clothed in black and covered with hoods, called *kuroko*. Unlike the Bunraku puppets, the puppets used in this performance stood well over a meter high, giving them an eerie quality as they were moved through their paces by shadowy figures who controlled their destinies in this tragic drama. The large size of Awaji puppets, one of their distinguishing features, developed from their roots as rural drama presented in outdoor theaters and makeshift spaces. Bigger puppets are easier to see. The smaller, delicate dolls of the Bunraku theater were developed to suit the aesthetics of an indoor theater.

Concerning the large size of Awaji ningyō, the scholar of Japanese puppetry Nagata Kōkichi commented, "You know that Awaji ningyō are a little larger than Bunraku puppets. The reason is that Awaji puppets aren't

meant to be stage puppets primarily. They are puppets of the road, meant
to be performed in people's entryways and courtyards, by the sides of
roads, in shrines, wherever there is enough space and people to put on a
show. Bunraku puppets are lovely, but those are puppets of the stage. If
you take Awaji puppets and stick them only inside a theater, it is like putting a wild animal in a zoo. It loses all its wildness. I like Awaji puppets
because as they have developed they have maintained their *yaseimi* [innate
wild nature]."[2]

The story of this girl and her mother was in the jōruri ballad style. Because the action was presented with puppets, the text was recited by a single
chanter, whose forceful interpretation was punctuated by the sharp notes of
a *shamisen*, a three-stringed instrument played by an accompanist. Although the piece I saw had only two characters, there were eight performers on stage throughout, with of course the unseen crew backstage managing the backdrops. While the performance was undeniably lovely, there
seemed to be something intentionally inconvenient about using puppets.

I was struck by a very basic question about this theatrical medium:
Why go to all this trouble? Surely having three people manipulate one
large doll with the characters' lines and even stage asides recited by a
chanter is more costly and cumbersome than using human actors. (How
much more cumbersome it must be when a performer is itinerant and has
to haul these puppets around, as was the case in the purification rituals of
the Awaji tradition!) What is it that a puppet can express that a human
performer cannot?

This book is in part an exploration of that question. On the one hand,
I have been interested in the general phenomenology of puppetry as a
theatrical medium and in the discussions by theater specialists, puppeteers, and ritualists around the world who struggle with this same question: why puppets? On the other hand, I have tried to discover how these
large figures made of paulownia wood and fabric are understood in Japan.
Clearly a broader understanding of the power of effigies, dolls, and body
substitutes in Japanese religion has contributed to the development of this
ritual tradition.

In Japanese *ningyō* is written with two characters meaning "person"
and "shape." I have chosen to translate this term as "puppet" although in
other contexts it could as easily be translated as "doll" or even "effigy."
My decision to translate this term this way was uncomplicated: In the first
place, most scholars writing in western languages about Japanese *ningyō*
shibai (drama using ningyō) translate the term this way, or see an affinity
between this type of performance and other puppetry forms around the
world. Second, I maintain that the abstract idea of the puppet as a descriptive category goes the furthest toward helping us understand the decision
to use these nearly life-size beings in rituals of appeasement and purifica-

tion, and eventually dramatic theater. Throughout the world, the decisions to use effigies rather than human actors in ritual share some common religious concerns.

In this chapter I want to set Awaji ningyō in its larger context. First, I explore what a comparative study of puppetry can do for our understanding of this particular case. Second, I survey other ritual uses of ningyō that inform the rise of ningyō shibai, particularly on Awaji, in the mid-sixteenth century. Inherent in the following discussion is an abstraction: in different effigies of the human form in a variety of cultural contexts around the world, there is a category we have come to regard as "puppet." Although in this book I present materials concerning the realities of puppets in one region, I must begin by talking about "puppets" in general. By looking at the category of puppet "bracketed" (as phenomenologists say) out of its context, I feel it is possible to become sensitized to the deeper meanings inherent in specific cultural cases. While I am not looking for the "essential puppet," I think a preliminary phenomenological approach lays the groundwork for a descriptive understanding of the specific Awaji materials of later chapters. This methodology, though unable to account for specific meanings of one cultural context, can train our eyes to see important aspects of the data.

Studying ritual puppetry in Japan, I am continually amazed by the provincialism of American theater audiences and even scholars when it comes to the issue of puppets. Because in our own culture puppets have been relegated to the playroom and because gifted puppeteers must ply their trade presenting poorly developed skits for children (who, one can only assume, must be partly offended by adult assumptions about their tastes), it is often difficult for Americans to realize that in other cultures puppets are used to stage serious dramas for mature audiences. I cannot count the times I have had to defend the legitimate right of a historian of religions to take Japanese puppets seriously. A large part of studying puppetry is spent apologizing, justifying and continually explaining this choice to otherwise broad-minded and intelligent people.

Most scholars of puppetry are forced to mention this problem at the outset. Confronting this bias as I studied Japanese puppetry, I found myself in a strange sort of kinship with the sentiments of the flamboyant early twentieth-century British playwright and director E. Gordon Craig. He considered the puppet an example of true and total theater (while suggesting actors could be done away with). In his famous essay "The Actor and the Übermarionette" he expressed this most vehemently:

> To speak of a puppet with most men and women is to cause them to giggle. They think at once of the wires; they think of the stiff hands and the jerky movements; they tell me it is "a funny little doll." But let me tell them a

few things about these Puppets. Let me repeat again that they are the descendants of a great and noble family of Images, Images which were made in the likeness of God; and that many centuries ago these figures had a rhythmical movement and not a jerky one; had no need for wires to support them, nor did they speak through the nose of the hidden manipulator. (Poor Punch, I mean no slight to you! You stand alone, dignified in your despair, as you look back across the centuries with painted tears still wet upon your ancient cheeks, and you seem to cry out appealingly to your dog, "Sister Anne, Sister Anne, is *nobody* coming?" And then with that superb bravado of yours, you turn the force of your laughter [and my tears] upon yourself with the heartrending shriek of "Oh my nose! Oh my nose! Oh my nose!") Did you think, ladies and gentlemen, that those puppets were always little things of but a foot high? . . . If we should laugh at and insult the memory of the Puppet, we should be laughing at the fall that we have brought about in ourselves, laughing at the Beliefs and Images we have broken.[3]

Overwrought though his prose may be, Craig's comments point to an important element of puppetry traditions around the world. Not infrequently puppets have been used in religious rites to represent and embody what are seen as divine forces. The discussion that follows—of puppetry as it is viewed around the world and of the wide range of ritual and dramatic uses of puppets in Japan—will properly contextualize the unfortunate cultural bias of recent American audiences and scholars, which reduces puppets to pathetic comedians in a second-rate theater.

What Is a Puppet?

In common usage, the word English word "puppet" has a wide variety of referents. *Webster's Third International Dictionary* provides the following information:

> [ME *popet*, fr. MF *poupette*,] 1a. little doll, dim. of assumed *poupée*, doll, fr. assumed VL *puppa*, alter scale figure of a human or other living being often constructed with jointed limbs appropriately painted and costumed and usually moved on a small stage by a rod or hand from below, or by strings or wires from above—see marionette, 1b. an actor in a play or a pantomime, 2. archaic: IDOL, 3. archaic: a vain, gaudily dressed person, 4. one who acts or is controlled by an outside force or agent and is no longer the arbiter of his own situation.

While this dictionary definition gives us the common uses of the word, it provides no criteria to justify grouping the many kinds of puppetlike objects under one heading. In Japan, what in English we would translate as "puppets" can be nearly life-size dolls, with elegantly carved and carefully lacquered heads having moving eyes, mouths, and even eyebrows, exquisitely costumed and realistically manipulated by as many as three persons. In the Tōhoku district, small heads of horses or women are attached to the ends of sticks and manipulated by shamans. On Sado Island tiny dolls act out comical skits between more serious pieces, always peeing on someone in the audience and drawing a few laughs before the performance returns to the stuffier highbrow drama. Or puppets may be small jointed dolls said to be entered by deities in a sacred sumo match conducted to appease malevolent spirits.

In Indonesia, Turkey, Southeast Asia, and China, words commonly translated as "puppet" refer to flat pieces of leather cut and painted in the likeness of any number of characters, held up in front of a lamp to cast shadows on a cloth screen. A "puppet" can also be a doll held by a rod or moved by hand. The word also refers to the marionette, a doll manipulated by a complicated series of strings or wires. A glove with a face painted on it is also a puppet. In theaters in the Soviet Union during the 1960s, the word referred to the chairs and tables moved about by actors as part of a performance. In West Germany's experimental theater in the late 1960s, the word was given to a series of geometric shapes which danced to music, joined in the final act by the cello—also a puppet. Theater directors in the Soviet Union and West Germany consciously intended these examples as deconstructions of the common assumptions the audience had about puppetry as representations of the human. They thereby hoped to move the theatrical medium to a new level of vitality.

Each of these examples has a special name in its own cultural context, yet we have come to call them all puppets in English. Likewise, scholars in Japanese performance would consider them all of ningyō shibai, the puppetry tradition. Our unconscious categories are divorced from the issue of mechanical complexity. How have we come to take this step? What is common to all these examples?

The American puppeteer Bil Baird had an answer: "A puppet," he wrote, "is an inanimate figure that is made to move by human effort before an audience."[4] According to this definition, a puppet is not merely a doll. If a child begins to move a doll and give it speech, the doll is still not a puppet. But if this child moves the doll to animate it and presents the performance before an audience of parents or friends, he or she is participating in a basic form of puppetry. In this same vein, a puppet is not the mechanized man or bird that pops out of a clock at the strike of an hour. Such animation lacks the element of human effort behind the movement. Puppetry, according to Baird's widely accepted definition, must simultaneously contain an inanimate object, a human effort, and an audience. According to this helpful definition, the context of performance is an essential element in what constitutes puppetry.

Although Baird's definition does provide limiting criteria for the category, it is still inadequate. If one waves a pencil in the face of a spectator, does the pencil then become a puppet? Such action conforms to his definition. Two more ingredients are necessary: the intention to communicate something meaningful (even if that meaning is the meaninglessness of life) and some idea of representation. Our linguistic usage of the word *puppet* in such a wide variety of contexts indicates a general awareness of this schema. What is fascinating about the ritual use of puppetry in the Awaji case is how this tradition's formulation of each of these points—inanimate object, human effort, audience, intentionality, and representation—challenges many of our assumptions about ritual and theater.

The Appeal of Puppets: Five Perspectives

I have always been interested in how people who have seen serious puppet theater feel about the medium. Responses tend to be polarized: people either love or hate puppets. Among those who hate them, the reason most commonly given is that puppets give people the creeps. There is something unsettling about imagining that inanimate humanlike figures are actually human and then being brought back to the awareness that these effigies are in fact nothing more than wood and paint. For others, this is precisely what is powerfully appealing about puppetry. Seeing a good puppetry performance is like watching magic at work. A puppet theater presents an apprehension of the boundaries between reality and illusion, body and soul, human and nonhuman, the living and the dead, and the material and immaterial worlds. Puppets, I argue, elicit an intensity of response in an audience precisely because the use of an inanimate object allows for an exploration of the hidden processes of the imagination, and in the case of ritual puppetry, the inner workings of the spiritual life.

Below, I present five different perspectives describing the appeal of puppets as a ritual or theatrical medium, drawn primarily from Western language sources. Each reveals something of the experience that people have of puppets as a theatrical medium. (1) Puppets have allowed for a particular freedom of expression not possible with human actors (until the advent of special effects in film). (2) The use of puppets enables human beings to imagine an escape from a seemingly inescapable fate, and to create beyond the constraints of the human condition. A person can assume the role of the creator and controller of beings. (3) The transformation of an innate, material object into a living and breathing character satisfies a creative spiritual and psychological need. (4) Puppets are more convincing because they remain what they are—they do not "represent" their part and then revert to someone else when they walk off stage. Through the intentional inconvenience of having to "represent" the human being, puppets metaphorically figure the human condition. (5) Puppets represent an awareness of the relationship between the material and spiritual realms and are able to become vessels for visiting spiritual forces.

Puppets and the Freedom of Expression

A dominant feature of a theater using puppets instead of human actors is the possibility of greater freedom of expression. Puppets can be made to do things with ease that human actors can do only with great effort and elaborate theatrical devices. Puppets can fly, change into animals, ghosts, and demons, dismember themselves and one another, and enact terrific physical transformations. A beautiful maiden can reveal herself to be an ugly demon or a terrifying fox spirit, and suddenly change again into the maiden—a device common in the classical jōruri puppet theater, using a *gabu* (trick head). Just as a person may have flashes of insight into some- one else's true nature, so too puppet theater audiences gain fleeting reve- lations through the use of gabu.

In puppet theater all over the world, furthermore, although extensive speaking parts may be given to child characters, the actions of a plot are narrated by an adult (such as the *dhalang* in Javanese shadow theater or the *tayū* in Japan). Human child actors may have difficulty remembering many lines, and their delivery may lack the performative force demanded by a mature audience of serious drama.

There is also the appeal to the playwright that his or her work will not be tampered with extensively by haughty actors. It is often noted that the great playwright Chikamatsu Monzaemon, who wrote many of the great dramas of the Japanese puppet theater, much preferred this medium. He did not have to contend with the extravagant egos of actors insisting on their own interpretations of characters. Chikamatsu's alleged attitude, perhaps apocryphal, is part of the understanding people working with puppets have about the appeal of their work.

The art of the classical puppet theater in Japan consists of three inter- dependent arts: dramatic recitation of the jōruri, or ballad, by a *tayū* (chanter), shamisen accompaniment (*shamisen hiki*), and puppet manipu- lation (*ayatsuri*) by a puppeteer (*ningyō tsukai*). Within the art of jōruri recitation, there is a level of artistic force called *hakusei* (white voice). This term refers to the chanter's voice that is said to transcend the chanter's individual character or personality, allowing the spirits of the jōruri char- acters to appear in the performance. This aesthetic ideal expresses the view

This fox spirit *kashira* (puppet head) is concealed in the head of a specially crafted female ka-shira. When a string is pulled on the kashira, this fox appears.

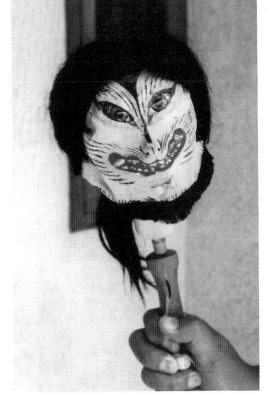

This demon head (*gabu*) works the same way as the fox spirit *kashira*.

西國三十三寺
同行二人

The child character from *Keisei Awa no Naruto: Junrei no Dan* at the Awaji Theater. Using puppets rather than human actors makes it possible to give major dramatic roles to child characters, as the lines are recited by the *tayū* (chanter). This puppet is manipulated by three people.

that sometimes the personality of a particular artist can be a hindrance to the depth of a performance, and the artist's transparency (if not outright invisibility) becomes necessary.

Last, a theater with puppets can present horror in a way that is at once abstract and concrete. In the Japanese theater, examples abound of what can only be considered scenes of gratuitous violence. Dismemberment, with body parts being thrown about as a jilted lover flies into a murderous rage, decapitation, and the grizzly scenes of warriors hungry for blood on the battlefield were often presented on the puppet stage. They were popular partly because they allowed for a cathartic release of tensions in a society where civil war was a recent part of its history. According to a convention developed in the theater, those in the audience who found particularly violent scenes upsetting would avert their eyes from the stage, look toward the tayū's platform, and watch his face while he chanted the lines. Tayū came to use these scenes, during which they receive much attention from the audience, to further their own careers. This convention developed from the realization that staging violence with puppets can be highly affecting.

In the same vein, working with puppets may allow for a distancing from the realities of violence and horror. Precisely because puppets are not actual human bodies, they allow for an exploration of the realities of horror and violence and for an abstract consideration of the basic ideas of finitude, aversion, and tolerance.

Recent avant-garde theater in London and New York has explored the use of exacting realism using human actors. The directors of these pieces discuss their work differently, but they seek to make the audience experience a performance as if they were actually present at a murder, a rape, or even a mass killing. People attending these performances have often found them to be so upsetting that they have required counseling. For the directors, this is evidence of the success of their productions. Good theater, they maintain, should tear asunder the boundaries people erect between art and life.

The use of puppetry in scenes of violence argues for a diametrically opposite notion of theatrical experience. Using puppets as a device makes the scenes of violence less immediate, allowing people to explore their emotions without feeling as if they they were themselves the victims—to have experiences without feeling overwhelmed.

In short, the puppet theater enables staging a full range of imaginative experiences, which may exceed the boundaries of actuality, possibility, and even tolerance. With the advent of film and special effects, it is true, human actors have a new freedom; puppetry no longer has the great advantage it did during the many millennia before the invention of celluloid.

A Human Being as an All-Powerful God

It has also been suggested that part of the urge to create and use puppets arises from the desire to become the master of one's own destiny, even if only within the confines of a performance space. The puppet theater director and playwright Andrei Sokoloff wrote: "Out of an urge for the artistic freedom of his creative will, man invented puppetry. By this invention, man freed himself from his belief in an inescapable fate; he created a world of figures determined by himself and thus consolidated his will, his logic and his aesthetic—in short, he became a little god ruling his own world."[5]

Ironically, the prominence of tragedies in the puppet theater in the end tells us that even when given the chance to become God, human beings repeat God's mistakes (and, one could argue, God's sadism). What kind of god would drive its creations to the tragic ends often staged in puppetry? Perhaps through the irony of the puppet, this question of theodicy is repeatedly being asked at some level.

The classical Japanese puppet theater, Bunraku, is famous for its elaborate puppets, each manipulated by three people. This style of manipulation, developed in the late seventeenth century, was a response to the demands of theater audiences who wanted more stylized and subtle movement. The heyday of puppetry in Japan coincided with a period of rigid social control by a top-heavy military government, which literally stripped away most social freedoms. It is tempting to argue that the popularity of puppetry during this period was in part due to the identification many audiences felt with the wood and lacquered beings on the stage. Just like the audiences, these puppets were moved through tragic events by shadowy or invisible forces.[6] There is an awareness in a theater with puppets that one is witnessing a metaphor for real life on the stage, and in the case of Tokugawa Japan, this metaphor could have been one of maximal social restriction and manipulation of the person in society.

The Triumph of Life over Death in Creation

Perhaps one of the most compelling reasons why puppet theater is so appealing is the human need to see and participate in the reversal of death. What is death but the transformation of the animate into the inanimate? In puppetry, this direction is reversed. This point was made by the director of the Budapest Puppet Theatre, Dezsö Szilágyi, when he wrote:

> The audience at a puppet show witnesses action which satisfies an urge present since time immemorial. On the puppet stage, before the spectator's eyes, the supreme act of creation is taking place—lifeless dead matter is turned into life. In his own activity man, as a rule, achieves the opposite. In order to create anything, he has to watch part of his living environment suffer death. To clothe himself, to make a chair, to put his ideas down on paper, to represent the world with brush and paint—to do any of these things, he must turn living organisms into lifeless minerals. At the same time his yearning and wish to create life are in fact far stronger than the compulsion of his destructive instinct. This creative urge is translated into other spheres and satisfied by the puppet bought to life.[7]

Myths about the origins of puppetry reflect this motivation. One of the myths from the Chinese shadow puppet theater narrates the origins of puppetry as a magical response to the iron clad finitude of death. Here is the story:[8]

An emperor and his beloved wife were deeply in love and spent many hours in each other's company. One day, the wife fell ill. Her husband tended her day and night, but a short time later, she died. The emperor could not be consoled. Day after day and night after night he grieved the loss of his love and companion. He grew pale and thin. He was despondent. Affairs of state were neglected. One day, a sorcerer arrived at court and told the emperor that he could bring his wife back. The emperor's heart quickened. "What must I do to have her back?" he implored. "You must promise me three things," responded the sorcerer. "I must have a cotton screen, a lamp, and your promise that you will stay on your side of the screen. You must never try to look at your wife's face." The emperor agreed. And so, with the help of the sorcerer, the loving wife returned to her husband night after night. They spent long hours in conversation—the emperor on one side of the screen and his wife on the other. They discussed their love for one another, events of the day, and their past and future. The emperor was at last consoled. His strength returned. He was once again able to see to the duties of his office. But one night, in a moment of passion, the emperor could contain himself no longer. He rushed to the screen and tore it down. To his great horror and anguish, he found not his wife but the sorcerer. Now he discovered the truth: The sorcerer had been imitating his wife's voice all along during those long and intimate nights, and casting her shadow from the lamp on the screen with a leather puppet intricately carved in the likeness of her profile.

The Chinese sources provide two endings to the story. They are always presented together, and the reader can choose which one is more fulfilling. In one ending, the emperor is so outraged that he orders his guards to put the sorcerer to death. The other ending tells us that the emperor is so grateful to have his wife back, even if only "behind the screen," that he promotes the sorcerer to marshal and gives him a fortune.

And this, so the sources tell us, is the origin of Chinese shadow puppet theater. Even today the cotton screen in the theater is commonly called "the veil of death."

This myth reveals a potential in puppetry to enact symbolically one of the deepest (and most hopeless) of human yearnings: that the finality of death can be undone. By insisting on the double perspective through both endings, the story suggests the hope that puppetry can magically accomplish the impossible, provided one can live with the illusion.

Puppetry and the Power of Generalization

Another appeal of puppets is their ability to stay what they are: puppets do not have real lives offstage. An audience may have to suspend its disbelief to transform a wooden puppet into a character, but that is all. It does not have to suspend its awareness that the stage character has an offstage life, as is true for a human actor. While the transformation of a person into a stage character is magical, there is always the sense of "representation," or worse, a sort of "pretending" inherent in role-playing.

Craig made this point most dramatically at the turn of the century. Appalled by what he thought was the decay of the British theater through an obsession with the particular talents of individual artists over the total-ity of theater as an art form, he called for a radical reinvention of theater. His discussion was intended to focus attention on the problem of inter-pretation and what he called a debased realism running amuck in the thea-ter and ruining performance. At the heart of his argument was the (hugely hyperbolic and rhetorical) insistence that actors must be replaced by pup-pets, a stance that so radically distanced him from the theater that he was never able to reclaim a place in the very art form he sought to revitalize. His championing of the puppet as an "ideal actor" is revealing of a certain aesthetic sensibility:

> As I have written elsewhere, the theater will continue its growth and actors will continue for some years to hinder its development. But I see a loophole by which in time actors can escape from the bondage they are in. They must create for themselves a new form of acting, consisting for the main part of symbolic gesture. Today they impersonate and interpret; tomorrow they must represent and interpret; and on the third day, they must create. By this means style may return. Today the actor impersonates a certain being. He cries to the audience, "Watch me! I am now pretending to be so and so, and I am now pretending to do so and so," and then he proceeds to imitate as exactly as possible, that which he has announced he will indicate. For instance, he is Romeo. He tells the audience that he is in love, and he proceeds to show it, by kissing Juliet. This, it is claimed, is a work of art; it is claimed for this that it is an intelligent way of suggesting thought. . . . The actor looks upon life as a photo-machine looks upon life; and he attempts to make a picture to rival a photograph. He never dreams of his art as being such an art for instance as music. He tries to reproduce Nature. As I have said, the best he can do when he wants to catch and convey the poetry of a kiss, the heat of a fight, or the calm of death, is to slavishly copy, photographically—he kisses—he fights—he lies back and mimics death—and when you think of it, is not all this dreadfully stupid?
>
> . . . The actor must go, and in his place comes the inanimate figure—the Über-marionette, we may call him, until he has won for himself a better name. . . . Today in his least happy period many people have come to regard him as rather a superior doll—and to think he has developed from the doll. This is correct. He is a descendent of the stone images of the old temples—he is today a rather degenerate form of a God. Always the close friend of children, he still knows how to select and attract his devotees.

When anyone designs a puppet on paper, he draws a stiff and comic looking thing. Such a one has not even perceived what is contained in the idea which we now call Marionette. He mistakes gravity of face and calmness of body for blank stupidity and angular deformity. Yet even modern puppets are extraordinary things. The applause may thunder or dribble, their hearts beat no faster, no slower, their signals do not grow hurried or confused; and though drenched in a torrent of bouquets and love, the face of the leading lady remains as solemn, as beautiful and as remote as ever.

There is something more than the flash of genius in the marionette, and there is something in him more than the flashiness of displayed personality. The marionette appears to me to be the last echo of some noble and beautiful art of a past civilization.[9]

Craig's comments about the human stage may be overstated, but his insight into the potential of the puppetry stage is valid: the puppet has a unique power of generalization capable of transcending the finitude of any one person's experience. It can portray a human being in general because it is in fact no single human being. The famous Soviet puppeteer and theater critic Sergei Obraztsov of the State Central Puppet Theatre in Moscow echoes this sensibility:

What is it then, that an inanimate puppet can express that a flesh and blood actor cannot? What is its power? Strange as it may seem, its very power lies in the fact that it is inanimate. If an actor on a stage sits down in an armchair and hitches up his trouser leg so that his knees do not spoil the crease, the audience may well not notice it. But if the same movement is made by a puppet, the audience is likely to burst into applause because the puppet has made fun of all the men who make this movement.

On the stage, a man may portray another man, but he cannot portray man in general because he is a man himself. The puppet is not a man and for that very reason it can give a living portrayal of man in general. . . .

The puppet is a plastic generalization of a living being: man, reindeer, dove. The puppet is a sculpture, the puppeteer creates a dramatic generalization of a living being; man, reindeer, dove. The process by which this inanimate becomes animate seems to the audience to be a real miracle.[10]

Human actors can certainly portray "the human being in general" on stage. But what is compelling about Obraztsov's comment is the fact that puppets spare us from the awareness of the representational and imitative quality of ritual and theatrical performance.

Puppets as Vessels for Other Forces

The Japanese religious use of puppets carries the representational capacity of puppets to a higher level. In some cases, puppets are understood to become actual abodes for visiting deities and wandering spirits. While actual human sacred specialists sometimes assume this role, human beings are able to enter into such altered states only through a radical break with their human personae. A puppet, however, has no other persona to shed and can serve as a temporary residence for sacred forces repeatedly. Such puppets, through their continual contact with sacred forces, become sacred objects in their own right. The puppets used in the Sanbasō ritual (discussed in later chapters) are an example of these sacred objects.

An example from Indian mythology, often cited as an origin tale, reveals the mythical use of puppets as vessels for supernatural forces: A long time ago, when Indian dolls were crude blocks made of wood with painted faces, there was a certain doll maker who made dolls with movable limbs and lovely carved heads. The deity Shiva and his wife Parvati loved to go to this doll maker's shop to see his various creations. One day Parvati happened to see some beautiful dolls fashioned with exquisite detail. She was so enchanted by them that she begged Shiva to allow the two of them—Shiva and Parvati—to enter the dolls and bring them to life. Shiva granted her request, and soon the dolls were dancing about the shop, much to the joy of their creator. Finally after much fun and dancing, both Shiva and Parvati became tired. They withdrew themselves from the dolls and were about to leave, when the doll maker grabbed them by the arm and pleaded, "Having given life to my dolls, how can you bear to leave them lifeless and just go away?" To this Parvati responded, "Since you made these dolls, it is for you to give them life." And then the deities left the doll maker alone with his wooden creations. He was so determined to bring them back to life that he attached strings to their limbs to help them dance. And so, it is told, the marionette was born.[11]

The religious motif that this story elaborates—divine beings enter inanimate objects and bring them to life—is a central element of Japanese ritual puppetry. Puppet bodies become spirit vessels for divine spirits, spirits of the dead, and even souls of those still alive. Nagata Kōkichi discusses this aspect of Japanese puppetry as one of the origins of the strong tradition of using effigies in Japanese ritual:

> Essentially, the human body is vacant. Empty. The *Man'yōshu* abounds with such references, indicating this early Japanese sense about the human body. We find a poem that asks, "Would that we were only able to borrow the discarded shell of the cicada as a body." Further, the classic the *Konjaku* includes the lines, "the shell of the locust is empty." This empty human body becomes the dynamic lodging place for the soul. In other words, the human being is that essence inhabiting the carcass of the "material" body. Spirit and flesh are two.[12]

A discussion of the phenomenology of puppets leads us immediately into the perception of the relationship between the body and the soul, the material and the spiritual. A study of Japanese puppets reveals various

Japanese understandings of the spirit world and human souls (*tamashii*) and the power of a human agent to harness and control these forces. This was a pronounced feature of the Awaji tradition. Rituals using puppets were designed to invoke, manipulate, and contain spiritual forces in the bodies of puppets.

In the Shape of a Person: Meanings of the Word *Ningyō*

The Japanese word ningyō has a wide variety of referents, and can not simply be translated as puppet. Ningyō is the sinicized reading of a two-character compound, and it can also be read *hitogata* when using indigenous Japanese pronunciation. In the context of the Awaji tradition, ningyō is best translated as puppet, according to the above five-part definition in which a puppet is an inanimate object moved by a human agent before an audience with the intention of communicating something through the process of representation. In the larger context of Japanese ritual, however, ningyō encompasses a wide range of objects, including both static and manipulated ritual objects. Here I present materials which argue for a Japan-specific reading of the term.

As a general category using the Chinese readings for the two characters "person" and "shape," the word ningyō appears in the Japanese language relatively late, toward the end of the Heian period. Prior to this, all the cases considered below that can be considered examples of ningyō had specific names in their own contexts: *haniwa, hitogata, kokeshi, kugutsu,* etc.

The connotations of this general term ningyō and the phenomena to which it refers have undergone a great deal of transformation throughout Japanese history. A number of elements, however, seem to recur. Most apparent is the simultaneity of ningyō and shamanic magic and the use of ningyō as mediators between the human and divine worlds. Within this general shamanistic tendency, we see a number of recurring motifs: (1) ningyō are used as spirit vessels for deities or spirits summoned by a shamanic figure; (2) ningyō are tangible references to a particular person or animal used as representational equals; (3) ningyō are understood to have the power to ward off danger when placed at the entrance to tombs or other strategic places; (4) ningyō can serve as surrogates for human beings in rites of purification and healing; (5) ningyō are understood to be substitutes for unborn children and small infants, protecting them from epidemics and sickness, and appeasing their spirits should they reach an untimely end; (6) ningyō are used in appeasement rites to reenact the calamities that brought about the malevolent actions of a spirit, or to serve as vessels for the malevolent spirits when they are summoned to the rite; (7) ningyō serve as substitute bodies for possession when the power of the spirit being invoked is too powerful to enter a living human being. Here, I survey some of these uses of ningyō in Japanese religious history.

Haniwa *Figurines: Surrogacy and Protection*

One of the most ubiquitous images to stare mutely at us from the history of Japanese archaeology is that of the *haniwa* figurines. Clay effigies of animals (boars, dogs, birds, horses, etc.), ornamented women, musicians, and soldiers have been exhumed from tombs throughout Japan, and the styles of these objects vary from the most simple and abstract to the highly detailed.

As with other data from the archaeological record, we can only speculate about how they were used and understood. Perhaps the haniwa mediated for the deceased while in the tomb. Many of the figurines were fashioned after what appear to be female shamans.[13] They wear the regalia of possession seen in later religious practice and appear to be in a trance. Perhaps these shamanic figures were understood to serve as points of connection between the living and the dead. Perhaps they were ancient guardians, embodying the sacred powers to ward off evil from the tomb. Perhaps the presence of haniwa suggests a conception of surrogacy—the figurine took the place of an actual person in the tomb. Wives, children, and even pets and dwellings may have followed the deceased to the other world in the form of an effigy. These three possibilities—incarnate mediumship, guardianship, and surrogacy—reveal a powerful and magical understanding of representation. The represented form *participates* in the power of that which it represents.

Ritual Substitutes and the Removal of Ritual Pollution: Hitogata *from the Nara Period*

The concern with ritual purity has been a remarkable feature of Japanese religiosity since the earliest records describing the Japanese people. Death, illness, elimination of bodily fluids, blood, pus, childbirth, and menstruation were, and to some extent still are, considered to be polluted states requiring purification rites. The state of pollution was a difficult issue that needed to be symbolically expressed and ritually resolved. It was in this context that another use of effigies arose.

The use of some sort of substitute to remove pollution from persons, homes, spaces, and even the head of the nation is a dominant theme in ningyō from all over Japan. An effigy or body substitute was understood to be capable of attracting dangerous forces and even becoming possessed by them. A ningyō could literally absorb pollution. When the ningyō was destroyed or allowed to float away, it carried with it the evil spirit or pollution from the person against whose body it had been rubbed or in whose honor it was created. Such an understanding of the ritual efficacy of the represented human form depends on three ideas: a represented form participates in the reality of that which it represents and vice versa; inanimate matter can be possessed by spiritual forces; and pollution can be absorbed (and subsequently removed) through contact with the polluted source. The study of itinerant puppetry rites in later chapters show how this religious idea developed.

One of the most pronounced uses of human representation in Japan began in the Nara imperial court and continued up through the Muromachi period. According to documents scattered over several hundred years, there was a monthly practice using a kind of ningyō called *nademono*, from the characters meaning "a thing one caresses or pets," or *hitogata*, the characters meaning "in the shape of a human." The ceremony was referred to as *nanase o-harai*, or "purification at the seven shallows."[14] On the first night of each month, according to the lunar calendar, a Taoist diviner (*onmyōji*) would make a small doll, which would then be sent to the imperial court. Here, the ladies of the court would admire, fondle, and dress it in fancy costume. It would be presented to the emperor, who would then rub it all over his body. The doll would absorb all of the emperor's ritual pollution (*kegare*) and various and assorted sins and transgressions (*wazawai*). Next, the doll was placed in a special box and floated downriver to the sea, taking with it the assorted pollutions. There were said to be seven locations from which the effigy could be sent to the sea, hence the name *nanase o-harai*.[15]

Yamagami Izumo, in his article "'Nanase no harai' no genryū" (The Origins of the Seven Shallows Purification) provides a thorough evaluation of the extant sources that mention the rite.[16] His reading of the materials suggests another interpretation which has a bearing on our understanding of the use of an effigy in this rite. He maintains that a part of the emperor's soul was actually externalized and entered the effigy. This "externalized spirit" (*gaikon*) was sealed in a box and carried to the seashore, where it was purified. The ritual thus enacted a sort of spirit pacification through the emperor's detached spirit. This interpretation, although not conclusive, suggests that rather than understanding the ningyō as only a body substitute, it should be understood as a vessel for a detached spirit. Yamagami sees this rite as evidence for the belief in the detachability of spirits during the ancient period in Japan.[17]

The ability of an effigy to serve both as a substitute and as a spirit vessel is reflected in other examples from early Japan. Like the practice of placing haniwa of family members in tombs mentioned above, wives, children and siblings of a deceased noble would place effigies of themselves, called *hito-gata* in the coffin of the deceased as a way of accompanying their beloved beyond the grave. These effigies were understood to contain part of a living person's spirit, detached from the person's human form and able to travel with a dead loved one to the world beyond the grave.[18]

Nagata Kōkichi has suggested that hitogata were also used to curse people.[19] Since most hitogata were made of paper, straw, or wood, the survival of ancient examples is most rare. In the Imperial Treasury in Nara, there is one ancient example from the Nara period which seems to be a hitogata. It is a simple wooden stick-shaped person, with a head, legs, and a torso, about fifteen centimeters high, upon which is painted a crude face.[20] It is believed that this figure, and types like it, were used in magical curses.[21] These uses suggest that effigies not only served as ritual substitutes but also had the power to capture a living human spirit and take it to the afterworld.

Although we have few surviving examples of hitogata, the practice seems to have been widespread. References too numerous to mention from ancient Japanese literature tell of people making effigies of friends and loved ones and of themselves.

Amagatsu *and* Hōko (Bōko)

Beginning in Heian Japan and continuing until the present, various dolls or effigies have been widely used as substitutes for fetuses, infants, and children to protect them from evil influences and disease. A reference in *The Tale of Genji* notes in passing that when the child of Genji's lover, Lady Akashi, is taken from her so that she can be raised in the capital, her *amagatsu* (heavenly infants) are put into the carriage with her.[22]

Amagatsu were dolls or effigies used to protect children by serving as their ritual substitutes. Sometimes they were called *hōko* (*bōko*). They are also generically called *o-san ningyō* (birthing dolls). Sources mentioning these dolls appear in the Heian period but become more numerous during the Muromachi period. A text entitled "Ise ke hisho tanjō no ki" (Secret chronicles of the births in the Ise family), records that at the birth of an infant, the doll was dressed simply, taken to the shrine, offered on the altar, and then prayed to for the health and longevity of the child. *Hōko* are simple stuffed dolls, shaped like an infant. According to the ningyō scholar Kitamura Tetsuro, although this text refers to these dolls by another name, the description is of objects from the more general category of amagatsu or *hōko*. He further suggests that the main difference is that

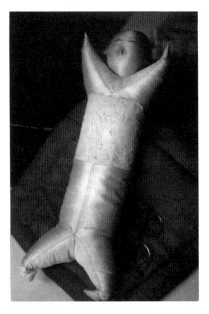

This *amagatsu* from Morioka-shi in Iwate Prefecture is an example of an effigy used to protect children by serving as a spirit vessel for their souls.

the amagatsu is a spirit substitute (*katashiro*) for a boy, while the latter is for a girl.[23]

This practice, though considered only of historical interest to Kitamura, seems to have survived until recently in Iwate-ken. On a research trip to Morioka in February 1989, I was shown two hōko by a woman who ran the inn where I stayed. She said they had been in her family for generations and were passed down matrilineally. She also had the old clothes used to dress the dolls. Apparently, as soon as a woman was pregnant, a doll was set up on the family altar, unclothed (like the unborn child). When the child was born, the doll was dressed and taken to the shrine, where it was presented to the tutelary deities of the family (*ujigami*). It was believed, she told me, that the ningyō would confuse supernatural forces who might come to take the child. For example, epidemic spirits (*ekibyōshin*) would come and possess the effigy, sparing the child an untimely death.[24]

Kokeshi *as Effigy*

One of the best known Japanese folk arts in the west is the *kokeshi*, the almost shapeless cylinders made of wood on which are painted faces, costumes, and various designs, made in the rugged and poorer northeastern part of Japan (Tōhoku District). Kokeshi have become one of the most standard tourist items in Japan and are found in gift shops throughout the country. The diverse styles of Tōhoku kokeshi can be classified into ten major types, each with its own characteristics and shapes.[25] The most pronounced aspect of kokeshi, which range in size from a few centimeters to nearly a meter, is their shapelessness.

All over the world, in agricultural societies where famine was a real threat, too large a family often meant that some family members would not survive, whereas a well-spaced and manageable size ensured that a family would not only survive but do well. In Japan, family size was controlled through a practice called *mabiki* (thinning or pulling of seedlings). This was an infanticide carried out by a midwife, who "returned" the child to the other world, perhaps to be reborn again at a later time.[26] One Tokugawa period opponent of this practice writing in the early nineteenth century estimated that 60,000 to 70,000 infants were "returned" in Mutsu and Dewa Provinces alone, two areas where the growing season is short and families tended to be exceedingly poor.[27]

It is possible that the practice of carving these cylindrical objects derived from the need to somehow concretize the grief and guilt families felt when faced with the choice between an unwanted child's slow starvation and it's quick death.[28] Kokeshi, lightly decorated with painted flowers and serene and undeveloped facial features, may have served as ritual substitutes for the dead child. The amorphous quality of these figures is one of their outstanding characteristics, suggesting the formlessness of the unborn or newly born.

Another interpretation of kokeshi holds that they resemble phalluses and that they were perhaps used as fertility symbols to invoke the deities responsible for a good harvest. Today they are carved as art objects, and are bought and sold without any religious connection.

Mizuko Jizō: *Effigies of the Aborted Fetus*

If objects said to be "in the shape of the human" are indeed used to concretize inner emotions or spiritual states, it is likely that effigies will be used in situations that give rise to difficult and often conflicting emotions. One of the most extensive uses of effigies in Japan today is the practice of *mizuko kuyō* (rites for aborted or miscarried children). While in the United States and other Western countries a miscarried or intentionally aborted fetus is rarely the object of burial and mourning rites, in Japan there is a practice of using small stone *mizuko jizō* (water child Jizō, ("water child" referring to a child *in utero*) to represent the dead fetus.[29] These small effigies of the bodhisattva Jizō (Ksitigharba in Sanskrit) are purchased at temples after one has had a funerary service conducted for an aborted fetus. The mizuko jizō is then placed in a specific spot in the temple grounds and serves as a mourning site for the parents. Many temples throughout Japan have a small place of worship dedicated to mizuko jizō, and recently this service has developed as a business for many temples—a practice that has been the object of outcry by Buddhist clergy who feel that to advertise for clients is to take advantage of people's emotions.

The Hase Kannon in Kamakura, a famous Kannon temple in eastern Japan and the fifth site on the Bantō Pilgrimage route, is the most commonly visited mizuko jizō site. Here, the steps leading up to the main worship hall are covered with thousands of stone statues of Jizō, the average size being about fifteen centimeters. These small statues are decorated and dressed with baby clothes and bibs, and most of them have offerings placed in front of them: food, juice, snacks that children enjoy, pacifiers, rattles, or toys—pinwheels and cupie dolls are very common. Here and there one sees a bib with a mother's words to her unborn child written on it, frequently apologizing, or asking for forgiveness. The votive offerings (*ema*) hanging at the Inari worship hall in the complex also express such sentiments. Some of the stone statues have small piles of baby shoes and baby clothes in front of them. One can not go to Hase Kannon without being deeply moved by the human grief concretized in the thousands of stone mizuko jizō.

This practice, seen all over Japan, gives us some additional understanding of the Japanese perception of things "in the shape of the human:" First, we see the continuation into the present of the pattern of amagatsu, namely that a doll or puppet can become the spirit vessel for a child, in this case an unborn child. Second, mizuko jizō indicate the role of dolls, however unconscious, in taking away pollution or "sin," in this case the transgression of having an abortion or a miscarriage. Like the ritual objects in the *nanase harai* from the ancient period, these jizō statues remove the pollution and are then placed in a special zone outside the profane world in which people dwell—in the precincts of the temple. Third, these small statues provide a mourning site for Japanese women, where they can grieve the child they have lost, a place where an inner process can become externalized and ritually resolved over time. The small stones become a sort of grave marker to which the women can return periodically to make offerings and recite prayers. When one makes a visit to Hase Kannon, one notices that some of the mizuko jizō are being carefully tended by some woman or family, while many others appear to have accomplished their task of healing, and now their bibs and toys fade in the weather and fall apart, leaving only the slowly eroding stone effigy standing in the midst of hundreds of thousands of others just like it.

Stone and Paper Bodies of Bodhisattvas: Healing Rites at the Togenuki Jizō

In the temple of the Togenuki Jizō (the "thorn-pulling Jizō," so named because this bodhisattva pulls out the thorns of human suffering) in the Sugamo district of Tokyo, there is a large festival every spring around the end of May. The festival is intended for healing, and many ill people come on this day from as far away as Hokkaido and Kyushu. *Shugendō* practitioners, people selling dried snake powder (made on the spot by putting cured and dried snakes in a Cuisinart), fortune-tellers, and palm readers set up booths inside or adjacent to the temple precincts. The major attraction of the shrine is the Arai Kannon, or "washing Kannon." Kannon (Avalokitesvara in Sanskrit) is the bodhisattva who (according to the *Lotus Sutra*) regards the cries of the suffering world, and can perform miracles for those who call upon this name.

At Togenuki Jizō, a petitioner takes a small brush and washes the part of a stone statue of Kannon corresponding to the part of the body he or she wishes to have healed. People stand in line for several hours to scrub the body of the bodhisattva, whose body is now featureless, scrubbed smooth by so many petitioners and prayers. The operative religious idea in this practice is that the body of the bodhisattva in effigy is the body of the devotee. The act of washing the effigy is an act of pious devotion, performed while one recites the Kannon chapter of the *Lotus Sutra*. The merit of this action can be transferred to the practitioner in the form of a healing.

At the same temple people also swallow small paper Jizō, said to help in curing cancer and other illnesses. After reciting a number of sutras, the ill person ingests a piece of paper on which the figure of Jizō is inscribed. This practice is repeated daily for several weeks during a course of treatment that consists of meditation, prayer, and recitation of sutras. Both of these practices, Arai Kannon and ingestion of Jizō, indicate an understanding that objects "in the shape of the human" can embody powerful transcendent forces that have a beneficial effect on the human body.

Imitative Magic: Sexual Puppets of the Island of Sado

The island of Sado, located in the Sea of Japan, is about two hours by ship from the port of Niigata. Until the end of the Tokugawa period, Sado was used as a penal colony. Many important figures in Japanese history were exiled there, including the Buddhist figure Nichiren and the dramatist

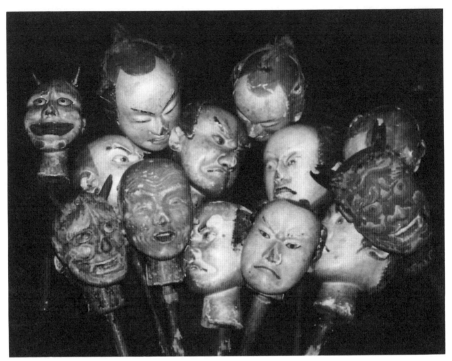

Kashira from the island of Sado, in the collection of Yamamoto Shūnosuke.

Zeami. The island is also famous for its mines, where prisoners were forced to work, sometimes to death.

Another feature distinguishing this island is the prevalence of ritual and dramatic performances using puppetry. One of the most unusual features of Sado puppetry is the prevalence of explicit genitalia on the puppets. The sexually explicit nature of Sado puppetry comes in two forms: the anatomically correct male and female puppets, about which little is known, and the bawdy humor of the Noroma ningyō.[30]

The former, no longer presented in performances, were originally used in a ritual in local shrines on Sado during the spring planting. According to one elderly man who was active in the local *miyaza* (shrine guild) when he was a child, the puppets were used in a ritual conducted by the local Shinto priest at night in the main inner sanctuary of the shrine. No one witnessed the rite, although the naked puppets were displayed to people gathered at the shrine for the festivities. I was able to photograph an old pair of puppets with genitalia when I visited the home of Yamamoto Shūnosuke, the leading authority on Sado puppetry.[31]

"Noroma ningyō" designates four puppets used together to present short, humorous skits, usually derived from *kyōgen* (skits performed in

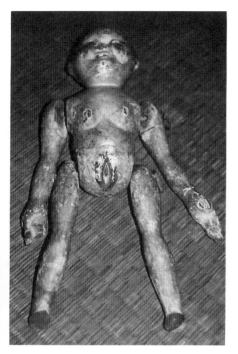 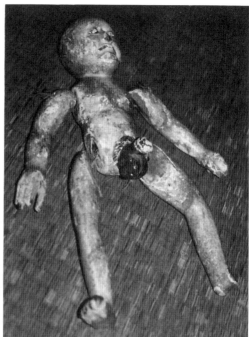

Male and female puppets from the island of Sado, in the collection of Yamamoto Shūnosuke.

Noh). These pieces are presented as light entertainment between long dramatic performances. Noroma ningyō have made Sado puppetry famous, even though they were intended as minor attractions in longer puppetry events. There are numerous plots used in Noroma pieces, but unfailingly at the end of each piece, the protagonist of the Noroma ningyō, Kinosuke, opens his clothes, extends his rather sizable penis, and urinates on the audience. The "urine" is water, and it is blown through a hole carved into his paulownia-wood penis by the puppeteer. This final scene usually has nothing intrinsically to do with the performance of a humorous kyōgen to which it is attached, and sometimes it gets introduced by the character simply announcing near the end of the piece, "I need a piss." But it is this risqué moment that has made the Noroma skits so popular. Concerning this aspect of the Noroma ningyō, Yamamoto Shūnosuke writes: "It is said that if showered with this urine, barren women will be blessed with children. It is also used to shower newlywed brides. This type of gesture is one example of a felicitous rite for the blessing of descendants and prosperous crops seen all over Japan."[32]

I saw a day-long performance of puppetry on Sado in July of 1991. It was presented at a senior citizens center, and everyone in the audience was

Four puppets used in Noroma *ningyō*. Notice that the main puppet is in his underwear. In many plays, he exposes himself and urinates on the audience through a large penis.

retired. In the course of the day, we saw two long jōruri pieces, but four Noroma skits. Since the jōruri pieces were all tragedies, the humor of the peeing Kinosuke gave everyone some comic relief, which perhaps left them more receptive to the profundity of the longer plays.

Sexual effigies used in fertility rites are a common feature of Tōhoku shrine practice, and such dolls and effigies can be seen all over northeastern Japan. The Sado puppets are most likely a Sado expression of a larger regional practice. Perhaps Noroma ningyō's pronounced use of a "puppet with a penis" gag at the end of a performance grew out of the larger ritual use of sex puppets. The Noroma ningyō may be the popular and "dramatic" expression of this ritual form of imitated sexual intercourse.

It seems obvious that the exposure of genitals in a ritual setting would in some way indicate a concern with fertility. But what other meanings

This wooden penis, about four inches long, is used in the Noroma performance. It has a tube in it, through which the puppet sprays water ("urinates") on the audience.

could be attached to such a gesture? If we consider the most famous case of "genital flashing" in Japanese mythology—the dance performed by Ame-no-Uzume-no-Mikoto before the heavenly cave door in order to draw the goddess Amaterasu out of her concealment—we can tentatively suggest another level of meaning to this act.

According to a Japanese myth, recounted in Book One, Chapter 17 of the *Kojiki*,[33] the sun goddess concealed herself in a cave because her unruly brother Susanoo defiled her heavenly weaving chamber by defecating on the walls and tearing down the dikes between the rice paddies. When she tried to placate him through gentle speech, he defiled her further by throwing a flayed heavenly piebald colt on her through an opening in the ceiling while she was weaving. In shock, she struck her genitals with the shuttle of her loom and died. Thereupon, she went into a cave, and the Plain of High Heaven was plunged into darkness. To lure her out, elaborate preparations were made by the other deities, which involved the creation of ritual implements to be used in what is considered to be a reflection of a shamanic rite of spirit pacification, a *chinkonsai*. Finally, the deity Ame-no-Uzume-no-Mikoto turned a wooden bucket over and began to dance. Becoming more and more frenzied, she finally pushed down her waistband to reveal her genitals. The other deities laughed at this. Hearing this laughter outside the cave door, Amaterasu peeked out, and was pulled back into the Plain of High Heaven by other deities.

This particular event has been extensively interpreted, but for the purposes of this discussion, two interpretations seem particularly seminal.

Chiri Mashiho has suggested that the exposure of the genitals can be used to drive away evil spirits, and he has noted a similar ritual among the Ainu, called *hoparata*.[34] Matsumura suggests that this gesture is an act of entertainment for deities, used in rites intended for divine rather than human audiences.[35] So, while the exposure of genitals certainly argues for a concern with fertility, it may also be a remnant of an earlier shamanic use of ecstatic and erotic dance to lure and entertain deities and drive away evil spirits.[36]

One obvious reason why a puppet is used on Sado as opposed to a human being concerns modesty. People, even those working for shrines, can not go around flashing their genitals. But at another level, the use of a puppet makes it clear that the concern is with fertility in an abstract sense. The wooden penis of the male doll and the long member of Kino-suke are reminders that these objects are symbols of something else. A penis on a real human being is a penis. On a puppet it is the generalized sense of fertility, bravado, and even transgression of social boundaries and propriety.

Bodies at the Edge, Bodies In-Between: *Ningyō* in the Awaji Context

At the start of this chapter, I suggested that there may be something intentionally inconvenient about using puppets rather than human actors, and the preceding discussion has shown that in Japan the use of represented human beings reveals a complex underlying religious structure. The survey of objects in the shape of the human has shown that far from being merely decorative items, ningyō (under many different aliases) have served important religious purposes in Japanese history. Representational objects having a human shape were used to concretize and localize otherwise abstract dimensions of life, providing a focal point for ritual actions that explore and resolve difficult spiritual issues.

The remainder of this chapter examines how the puppet body was constructed, manipulated, and understood in the Awaji case, a tradition that developed in the sixteenth century. As we shall see in more detail later, this tradition was divided into two distinct aspects. The earliest use of puppets, called *shinji* (sacred matters), and consisted of appeasement rites for the deity Ebisu and purification rites for visiting deities of agriculture. Out of these ritual origins, there developed a dramatic tradition, ningyō jōruri. Artists in this later tradition influenced and interacted with performing arts in urban centers, and developments parallel to those of classical Bunraku can also be seen. While the performance that first stirred my interest in Awaji puppetry came from the jōruri part of the tradition, the questions this performance generated about the use of puppets are even more to the point in the study of ritual puppetry. In this book, as I have already noted, I am leaving aside a discussion of the dramatic jōruri tradition and am focusing solely on ritual puppetry. This focus has two implications for a discussion of puppet bodies and manipulation. First, ritual puppets were lighter, smaller, and simpler than their dramatic counterparts, and so in this work we will not have a detailed description of the inner workings of a puppet head, nor of the subtle art of puppet manipulation which fascinates audiences of Japanese classical puppetry and tends to dominate discussions of this subject. Second, manipulation of ritual puppets was decidedly less developed, which means that the impact of these rites depended on other, context-specific nuances of ritual performance. But much of what can be said about ritual puppets can also be said of the early jōruri puppets, before the development of the three-person manipulation. Here we will examine the important components of a ritual puppet body, the methods of manipulation, and the understanding of puppets as beings once removed from the human realm.

The Sum of Its Parts: A Puppet Body

The earliest puppets of the Awaji tradition appear to have been small, handheld stick puppets in which the head was the most important feature. The puppeteer presented his puppets from a box hung around his neck. This style of carrying puppets was called *kubi-kake* (hung from the neck), and the box gave puppeteers the nickname *hako-mawashi*. The box was open at the back and served as a sort of stage. This method of manipulation was also seen among the Nishinomiya kugutsu, discussed in chapter 3. These boxes were a natural choice for an itinerant performer, as they could serve the dual purpose of carrying case and portable stage. The puppets themselves were held by inserting one's hands into the pant legs of the puppet, a method of manipulation called *sashikomi ningyō*. Because these puppets were light and simple, it was possible to carry several around as one moved from place to place, and concerns about staging and special effects were to come later.

By the beginning of the eighteenth century, Awaji puppeteers had made larger puppets for their rituals, which led to more specialization in their arts and also to more detailed attention to the puppet body. Puppeteers then began to carry their puppets in boxes on their backs, which they would unpack before performances. Unpacking puppets and making them come alive as they moved out of a "sleeping position" was made a part of the ritual process. The method of manipulation changed slightly from the earlier *sashikomi ningyō*; the puppets were held through a hole

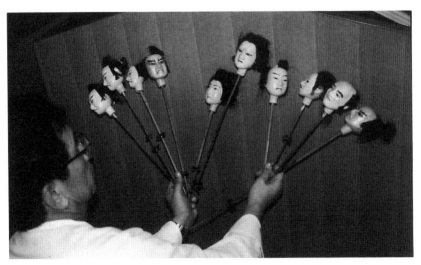

Umazume Masaru holds examples of small stick puppets. These small puppets were widely used by itinerant performers because they were lightweight and easy to carry and manipulate.

in the back of their costume. Furthermore, due to their larger size and weight, the only way they could be manipulated gracefully was to hold them at waist level. The puppeteers performed in full view of the audiences, holding the puppets in front of them. This added a new dimension to the performances. Puppets, nearly half the size of the puppeteer and held in front, appeared to be almost second selves for the puppeteer. The puppeteer held them like shields between himself and the world as he ritually controlled dangerous deities and absorbed noxious forces and pollution.

These larger puppets consisted mostly of a head attached to a long stick, with a fabric body draped about it. The most important part of a puppet was its kashira, or head. Early kashira were made of paulownia or cypress wood, and features were painted onto the face. The puppets used in Sanbasō rituals, however, had moving eyes and mouths, features that were used to indicate that the puppet was going into trance and was about to be entered by a deity.

Carving kashira became an art related to the practice of puppetry, and techniques for making subtle kashira were handed down from master to disciple. The most famous puppet-head carver (ningyō-shi) of the Awaji tradition was a man named Tengu Hisa, who lived in the middle of the nineteenth century. Today, kashira carved by this artist are rare and are worth hundreds of thousands of dollars. Puppet-head carvers were understood to be liberating spirits from the wood they carved. They spoke of themselves as midwives to the process, and of kashira as being either "born well" or "not born well." A well-born kashira was one with a spirit in it.[37]

Ritual puppets have hands and feet, and objects they need to carry or hold are inserted into small holes in the hands of the puppets. The illusion of a body is constructed by draping an outer garment over the assembled body parts, which then must be held gracefully by a skilled puppeteer.[38] A puppeteer is considered a failure if the parts appear unconnected when he or she manipulates them (sometimes in conjunction with other puppeteers). If the puppeteer is skilled, this collection of bodily parts is transformed into a living, moving, and even ecstatic being. When a puppet is put down in a performance, it must be set down face first with its sleeves folded in front of it in the proper "sleeping" position.

Body parts of puppets come alive through manipulation. Coming alive is the key analogical event giving these puppet rituals their force. This transformation of assorted body parts into a body with a being inside it belies the close relationship between puppetry, fertility, and life and death. This relationship seems to be an issue of ritual concern. Sometimes life does not happen when it should, and the world—whether seeds or human wombs or fish from the sea—remain nonproductive, unyielding, and dead. With every gesture, the puppet indicates the other side of life, for as soon as the puppeteer puts it down in its proper sleeping position, the puppet is again no more than the sum of its parts: a dead body. Display of the inert puppet body before and after the manipulation is a part of the performance.

Puppets: Beings Once Removed

As we have seen, the use of puppets rather than human actors raises a number of interesting questions. In chapters to come we shall deepen our understanding of this ritual preference for puppets in the Awaji tradition.

The most important feature of the rites under discussion in this volume is that sacred beings, Ebisu, the deity of the rice fields, or any number of assorted kami are being summoned and made manifest in the human community through a ritual context. Herein lies a problem of representation. Inherent in the conception of sacred (and dangerous) beings undergirding this ritual tradition is the idea that the sacred can be made present in the human realm, and yet no mode of manifestation can fully convey its sacredness. In some shamanic contexts, a shaman may summon a sacred force to enter his or her body. This activity creates a coincidence of opposites, since the shaman's body becomes at once human and divine. Here, the puppet can stand between the puppeteer and the sacred forces and serve as the receptacle for the summoned deity. The puppet then is the physical object which enables (*yosasu*) the manifestation of the sacred force. In these rituals, puppets are often referred to as the *yorishiro* (possession vessel), *goshintai* (deity body), or *tamashiro* (spirit vessel) of the deity—all these terms referring to physical objects that become temporary abodes for the deity—the most important ritual use of puppets.

The status of the puppet in the ritual events examined in subsequent chapters is that of a bridge between the two separate but interdependent worlds of human and divine beings. The puppet, however, belongs to neither. Removed from the realm of human beings, the puppet occupies a world of its own. Although the shape of the puppet is modeled on the human body, the content of its spirit when fully possessed is supplied by sacred forces.

While there is clearly a religious awareness of the power of ningyō in the Awaji choice to use puppets rather than human actors, there is also another reading of the ritual form. The use of puppets intensifies an important social and religious metaphor of power, control, and interdependence. The puppeteer controls, even invents his puppet as he puts it together, and yet he is dependent on it for his livelihood. The forces that enter the puppet are greater than the puppeteer, and because of the ability of the puppet body to attract and contain these forces, the human community is able to survive and avoid calamities. The puppeteer and the puppet, working together in a carefully scripted ritual space, are able to control those spiritual forces. This triangular relationship of shifting power relations reveals a subtle awareness of the connection between human and divine beings. In the following chapters, we shall see how the ritual use of puppets has posed and resolved these relationships.

2

Kadozuke: The Outsider at the Gates

IT IS THE third day of the first month of the year. In a small village facing the Inland Sea, an elderly man makes his way through the narrow streets carrying on his shoulder a small bag and on his back a box wrapped in a black cloth. He wears short trousers, a *haori* belted at the waist, and straw sandals. The bag on his shoulder holds a small hand drum and a flute, and in the box on his back are puppets, each almost a meter in length, with their costumes and implements. As he walks through the village, he stops at the gate of each house and blows a few sharp notes on his flute to announce his arrival. He is expected this time of year. He is the Dōkumbō-mawashi, the ritual puppeteer who has come to perform a purification ritual and utter felicitous words and blessings for the new year.

Shortly, a householder appears at the gate, greets the puppeteer, and grants him permission to perform. At some homes the puppeteer is invited no further than the gate and must set up his performance space while still half in the street. At others, he is invited into the courtyard or the entryway. Sometimes, his host escorts him up into the *zashiki*, the main room of the house, where the family *kamidana* (Shinto altar) is located. At this house, the householder invites him up inside and then rushes ahead to inform the others in his family that the Dōkumbō-mawashi has arrived.

The puppeteer pauses at the entryway of house and bows to the householder. He then removes his sandals and steps up into the zashiki. The host indicates the location of the kamidana and the puppeteer seats himself in front of it. The host leaves the room briefly and the puppeteer spreads a cloth on the tatami before the altar, sets down his packages, and carefully unpacks his musical instruments. He places the box containing the puppets in front of him, where he can easily remove them one at a time. Momentarily, the host reappears with a small tray containing a dish with polished rice and a cup of sake. These he places in front of the puppeteer. The puppeteer takes from his bag some white paper and a pair of scissors and cuts the paper into zigzag strips, called *gohei*, which serve as markers for a sacralized space. He arranges these strips on the tray with the rice and sake, lifts the tray as an offering to the deities in the kamidana, and then sets it in front of his small performance space.

Now, seated carefully on the floor with his puppets before him, he claps his hands and bows his head to the floor in prayer before the deities in the kamidana. Then, he picks up his flute and plays a short, shrill melody to invite the deities to watch his performance. He then takes up a drum and beats it rhythmically for a few moments to set the cadence for his performance.

With meticulous care, the puppeteer performs his short ritual, manipulating three puppets in succession. Had his host let him no further than the gate, he would have been quicker and finished in a few minutes. But since he is in the main room of the family home, he can take his time. To show his gratitude for the honor of being invited inside, he gives a more elaborate performance. His opening notes on the flute and the drum cadence have attracted the dangerous spirit forces in the house, and shortly, when he begins to manipulate his puppets, these forces will be so fascinated by the performance that they will enter the puppets. The puppets perform a solemn and then frenzied dance, and the puppeteer recites a nuanced chant full of images of longevity, time, and nature. The spirits are soothed by the poetry and dancing.

When the puppeteer finishes his ritual, he packs up his puppets and instruments and leaves the house, taking with him the spirit forces that have entered his puppets. As he departs, the householder presents him with a token payment on a tray—a few coins or notes wrapped in paper perhaps, or a small bag of rice. At the doorway to the house and again at the gate, the puppeteer bows to the householder and moves on to the next house.

As he makes his rounds through the village, he will not meet any competitors, for ritual puppeteers have already agreed to work in different neighborhoods, lest they drive one another out of business or annoy their patrons. Toward the end of the day, a householder will offer the puppeteer a meal and lodgings for the night in exchange for the performance. If no such offer is forthcoming, he can always sleep in the local shrine or camp at the edge of the village or on the bank of a nearby river.

This routine continues every day until the close of O-shōgatsu, the New Year period from the 1st to the 15th of the first month. Then the puppeteer will head back to the Sanjo district on the island of Awaji, where he lives for the part of the year when he is not performing. Perhaps he will present a different kind of puppet performance in local shrines or along the fishing docks on his way home. Perhaps a wedding or a new house will need blessing along the way.

Maybe next year when he sets forth again, he will take on a partner to play the musical instruments and help carry his gear—some puppeteers do this. A partner would provide a little company on his travels. But then he would have to share his earnings, so perhaps it is better to stay on his own. A solitary Dōkumbō-mawashi works harder but can keep all his earnings.

Back in the village, the New Year period winds down. The Dōkumbō-mawashi has come and gone. His appearance, announced by the shrill flute call from the street, is as much part of New Year as the pine branches decorating the gate and the pounded rice cakes eaten for the first fifteen days of the year. But like these markers of the season, the puppeteer is far from everyone's minds for the rest of the year. The year draws to a close then and it is *O-Shōgatsu* again. Then he would be noticed only if he failed to appear. It just wouldn't be New Year without this visit.

This vignette, based on oral histories, old films, and written sources, describes the seasonal visit of a ritual puppeteer, a common feature of fishing and farming villages surrounding the Inland Sea or scattered throughout central and western Japan from as early as the sixteenth century until about 1947 or 1948.[1] Court diaries from the late sixteenth century note in passing the arrival of these visitors at New Year, and people I interviewed on Awaji remembered the regular visits of the seasonal puppeteer in the early twentieth century. While itinerant puppet performers' styles differed, the events described above could just as easily have happened in the late sixteenth century as in 1938. These wandering puppeteers, known by a number of different names—*kugutsu, Dōkumbō-mawashi, deko-mawashi, hako-mawashi, Sanbasō-mawashi, Ebisu-mawashi, Ebisu-kaki,* or simply *ningyō-mawashi*[2]—performed an essential ritual function. They mediated the boundaries between the distinct but sometimes overlapping worlds of sacred forces and human beings, order and chaos, life and death, and fertility and infertility. Their ritual performance served to usher in the new year, purify dwellings for another season, and revitalize sacred forces in communities. On occasion their rituals were used to bring rain, drive away noxious insects, prevent epidemics, and ensure safe travel. They performed before audiences in all levels of society, from the emperor, lords, and ladies at court to merchants and farmers. A study of ritual puppetry in Japan reveals the boundaries of the cosmological convictions of Japanese society, the structures of social hierarchy and ritual purity, and the understandings of the power of ritual to generate meaning, cope with disorder, and mediate difference.

An essential element of puppeteers' ritual function was their status as outsiders to communities where they performed. Their itinerancy and otherness were as much a part of the power and fascination they generated as the eerie puppets they made dance, and as the potentially dangerous and otherworldly beings they summoned to the human realm.

Although ritual puppetry has a long and complicated history in Japanese religion, one feature stands out: puppeteers and puppets shared a world set apart from the everyday realm. As performers sharing this territory, puppeteers and puppets enjoyed a unique freedom of movement in society and throughout the cosmos. They carried the responsibility for generating order out of chaos and purity out of defilement, and consequently suffered from shifting assessments of their status and worth.

In this chapter, we explore the meanings of the ambiguous relationship of the puppeteers to their audiences and hosts by examining two interrelated issues: the role of the stranger or outsider in Japanese religious performances and the dominant ritual purity system of medieval and early modern Japan, which led to the symbolic exclusion of these ritual performers and the formation of outcast strata of society, contained within special areas called Sanjo districts. I will show how puppeteers as outsiders were inhabitants of a symbolic space reserved for ritual specialists who maintained social boundaries. Precisely because the performers were unknown to their audience and came from the potentially disordered world beyond village boundaries, they were regarded as effective ritual practitioners. Their otherness meant that they embodied the power of the unknown. Their rituals made that power available. The unknown from which they came also had a location in the Japanese ritual map: special precincts attached to shrines and along the edges of towns. The generation and manipulation of this symbolic authority over the other realm was essential for their rituals to work.

This specific discussion of Japanese ritual puppeteers as outsiders can be best understood by situating it within a series of larger intellectual concerns. Theoretical discussions of the Other as both a fundamental category in the history of religions and as a highly nuanced cultural construct have revealed the tensions and dynamics in ritual puppeteers's performances from late medieval and early modern Japan. Following a general discussion of these dynamics, I examine one specific element, that of the stranger in Japanese religions. I investigate how this concept of the stranger/outsider is encoded in Japanese cosmology, solidified in the Japanese ritual purity codes and symbolic geographies, and presented in a series of ritual practices and understandings pertaining to the role of ancestors in Japanese religions. I then turn my attention to one specific type of ritual puppetry—kadozuke, "rites at the gate." To appreciate the itinerant context of kadozuke rites, I discuss two important itinerant performance traditions, *Senzu manzai* and *Matsu-bayashi*, both from late Heian and medieval Japan, which can be regarded as important prototypes of the later kadozuke context.

In kadozuke performances, two levels of otherness shaped how people perceived puppeteers: the puppeteers' geographical and symbolic relationship to the people for whom they performed and the puppets' status as beings removed from the human realm. The itinerant context of these rites, the relationship between host and performer, the perception of puppets as special beings in between two worlds, and the fluid idea of the Other collectively impart meanings to these ritual actions.

The Other: A General Issue in the Study of Religion, Cultures, and Identity

The category of the Other in all its guises—the sacred, the unconscious, the foreigner, the outsider—has become a central focus of scholarship and discourse in the twentieth century. At once posited to be an ontological category of experience, a necessary device of all knowing and perception[3] and a highly constructed aspect of identity formation, it is possible to argue that because of the idea of an other we have such disciplines as anthropology (dependent on the culturally other to supply its data) or history of religions (dependent on the claim that people live their lives in some sort of relationship to some other order of reality). Michael Theunissen notes the ubiquitous quality of the category of otherness in the opening lines of his study of alterity, *The Other*:

> Few issues have exercised as powerful a hold over the thought of this century as that of "the other." It is difficult to think of a second theme, even one that might be of more substantial significance, that has provoked as widespread an interest as this one; it is difficult to think of a second theme that so sharply marks off the present—admittedly a present growing out of the nineteenth century and reaching back into it—from its historical roots in the tradition. To be sure, the problem of the Other has been thought through in former times and has at times been accorded a prominent place in ethics and anthropology, in legal and political philosophy. But the problem of the Other has certainly never penetrated as deeply as today into the foundations of philosophical thought. It is no longer the simple object of a specific discipline but has already become the topic of first philosophy. The question of the Other cannot be separated from the most primordial questions raised by modern thought.[4]

The idea of the other has been a major theme in the history of religions, anthropology, and literary criticism. While it is beyond the scope of this work to survey the history of this theoretical concept in nineteenth- and twentieth-century anthropology, it is possible to delineate three general approaches to the idea of the Other: the perspectives of religiosity, anthropology, and critical studies of hegemonic discourse. These three approaches reveal a complexity of attitudes and appropriations of this term within academia. On the one hand, scholars such as Rudolf Otto and Mircea Eliade have considered the category of a wholly other, distinct order of being and meaning, set apart from human life as "the sacred" (the "numinous" in Otto's nomenclature), to be a necessary component of a religious life. For Otto and Eliade, the *perception* of this otherness is removed from and even prior to the development of constructions of "good" and "evil." This focus has many limitations, but, it remains that both Otto and Eliade were recognizing a fundamental fact of the data in religious studies: people talk about, organize their lives around, and seek to maintain relationships with what they regard as an *other* order of meaning. While the historian of religions is not in a position to validate or invalidate the existence of this other order of meaning, the conviction that it exists is a central component of religious experience in many religious traditions, and for this reason the historian of religions considers it a datum to be studied and understood.[5] For the purposes of this discussion, what is significant about the category of the sacred (or the numinous) is the way it is described as an *other* order of reality. This very otherness becomes the focus of religious life and the center for orientation of meaning and action. For scholars in the history of religions following the tradition of Otto and Eliade, then, constructions of otherness participate in a religious structure.

Early studies of "primitives and savages" often noted the "fear of strangers" as a component of the "savage mind."[6] The field of anthropology has widened in the last century, however, and studies of societies closer to home reveal that alterity (and its signification, production, and manipulation) is a component of a wider range of human activity. Strangers and Others are as much a part of the generation of social meanings in upstate New York as they are in Papua New Guinea. Furthermore, scholars have explored how the ethnographic Other reflects a need within western academic anthropology to develop through a continually renewed contact with actual Others in the field.

Within contemporary mainstream anthropological discourse and later literary critical studies, the Other as a construct and idea has been studied as a central feature of two interrelated (though often competing) types of ideology: identity and oppression. In both of these constructs, some outsider becomes a screen against which a conception of group or self-identity is constructed. The outsider may be someone living in one's midst, as the case of Jews, gypsies, gays and lesbians, and the disabled in the Third Reich; or an other "out there," as in the case of Muslims as they were imagined and invented in European religious and cultural studies in the latter nineteenth century;[7] or an imagined idea of alterity infecting society, as in the case of the Tokugawa nativists' invocation of Chinese elements in Japanese religion, literature, and aesthetics.[8]

Recent scholarship on the issue of otherness has focused on the manipulation of the category of the Other in the construction of identities. These studies reveal that who Others are in any society varies dramatically, depending on how the issues of identity are formulated. For example, if the concern is with constructing an identity of nationality, otherness will be determined by one's ethnicity and roots. If the concern is with a gender identity, sexual preference, behavior, and gender assignment determine one's otherness. If the concern is with constructing an idea of mainstream identity ("the folk," "the middle class," etc.), rendering certain groups of people exotic serves to reinforce the image of the mainstream.[9] The only constant seems to be the endless need for an Other against which an identity can be constructed. The social construction of otherness has everything to do with social rules and the generation of power relationships, order, and meaning in society. Others are often symbolically constituted by images of disorder, chaos, danger, and the exotic.

One of the most haunting, menacing, and frequently cited images in studies of otherness is Foucault's specter of the ship of fools, the *Narrenschiff*, an actual phenomenon in medieval Europe embellished in literature and the popular imagination of the time. A Narrenschiff was a ship that traveled from port to port, carrying the insane or otherwise mentally disabled who had been expelled from towns and villages. "They did exist, these boats that conveyed their insane cargo from town to town. Madmen then led an easy wandering existence. The towns drove them outside their limits; they were allowed to wander in the open countryside, when not entrusted to a group of merchants and pilgrims. . . . Frequently they were handed over to boatmen. . . . It is possible that these ships of fools, which haunted the imagination of the entire early Renaissance, were pilgrimage boats, highly symbolic cargoes of madmen in search of their reason."[10]

Foucault's image of the insane floating about the ports of Europe and the imaginations of the Renaissance has become the watershed case for a study of otherness during the past thirty years. His key point is embodied in one word from this passage: "reason." Although of course the lack of a fixed abode, the travel at sea, and the foreigner status of these *ships'* cargo contributed to how they were imagined, what was important (at least as Foucault imagines it) was that their very madness, real or otherwise, was a perfect point of reference against which a Europe seeking to give birth to the Enlightenment (a celebration of reason par excellence) could define itself. The operative dyad in this case was between reason and madness, and the social construction of madness allowed culture to maintain its allegiance to reason.

In her book *Purity and Danger*, Mary Douglas explores another level of otherness by presenting a theoretical framework for pollution and taboo. Douglas's study marks an important early step in appreciating the manipulation of otherness in the creation of social order and the symbolism of pollution often attached to marginalized people. While defilement is not necessarily an attribute of the Other, it is not uncommon for persons who are marginal, placeless, without status, or in any way ambiguous to be considered potentially defiling. Douglas notes the common tendency to view marginal people as potentially dangerous. This, she writes, is due to the fact that a marginal person in a ritual process is understood to be in a dangerous situation, and this danger is communicable to others. While her cases are drawn from ritual processes where a person is only temporarily marginal as part of the move to a new status, her examples well describe the imagination of people who are permanently marginal.[11]

In her discussion of ritual purity systems Douglas focuses on the human body as a powerful metaphor for society. If the body is a locus of ritual action, this means that the dominant metaphor of society is readily available to everyone. In this study, I will show how both the puppeteer and the puppet are implicated in the ritual purity system, and the puppet serves as a body substitute for the puppeteer, absorbing spirit forces and embodying disorder and ambiguity. The equation of the body and society, then, is an example of a total ideology, one with the power to be all inclusive, while at the same time remaining abstract enough to resist attempts to challenge it. Douglas writes,

> The idea of society is a powerful image. It is potent in its own right to control or to stir men to action. This image has form; it has external boundaries, margins, internal structure. Its outlines contain power to reward conformity and repulse attack. There is energy in its margins and unstructured areas. For symbols of society any human experience of structures, margins, or boundaries is ready to hand. . . . The body is a model which can stand for any bounded system. . . . The functions of its different parts and their relation afford a source of symbols for other complex structures. We cannot possibly interpret rituals concerning excreta, breast milk, saliva and the rest unless we are prepared to see in the body a symbol of society, and to see the powers and dangers credited to social structure reproduced in small on the human body.[12]

Douglas notes that closed societies (of which Tokugawa Japan is a premier example) are, like the human body, concerned with balance. One of the primary goals of a social system is the maintenance of stability, and this requires minute attention to those areas that could negatively affect this balance, places where an other or otherness could manifest itself. These areas she terms types of contradictions and she maintains that the way these concerns get expressed within society are usually encoded upon the body and its orifices. She identifies four threats to balance and stasis: (1) threats to external boundaries, such as foreign invasion, etc., (2) threats to internal boundaries, such as social revolt, (3) danger in the margins of society's internal lines, and (4) the danger of internal contradiction, such as ambiguously classified items within the system—people who fall into more than one social category or into a place that serves contradictory purposes.[13]

Douglas's discussion is useful on a number of levels, many of which will become apparent later in our discussion of ritual puppeteers and the purity system they helped to maintain. I mention her work here because any view of a bounded system implies an Other against which the system is bounded. Just as diseases and contagion (real or imagined) are thought to violate the body from the outside and then work within it, so too are outsiders and marginal people feared as sources of some kind of threat to the integrity of social categories and order. This, in short, is the stigma suffered by strangers in cultures around the world. Furthermore, there are the forces of the darker side of consciousness, frequently formulated in mythology as aborted, deformed, or half-developed deities, which inhabit the boundaries, paradoxes, and interstices of this bounded social system— and occasionally have to be reckoned with. In Japan, the handling of such forces becomes the work of specialists in impurity.

The World out There Comes in Here: The Dangerous Stranger and the Manipulation of Power

What happens to a society's sense of order, boundaries, and purity when the unknown world out there comes in here, into society, violating its boundaries and sense of itself? This is what a stranger—in any number of guises—does. Numerous examples in ethnographic literature illustrate how the unknown person who arrives at a village or home from some undesignated and unformed place (the road, the wilderness, the forests, the sea) is treated according to a special set of rules of conduct. The reader can readily supply examples from folk tales, religious texts, and contemporary literature of this powerful motif. Although the social identity of this person may vary—the homeless, the saint, the leper, the beggar, the insane, the healer, the witch, the aged—the range of responses to the outsider are few: (1) the outsider is treated with utmost caution and respect, and banquets, ceremonies, and entertainment are frequently presented for his or her benefit; (2) initially the outsider is treated in this manner but after a brief period of time is expelled or killed; (3) the outsider is treated in this manner but after a period of time is assimilated as a "resident other" and occupies an ambiguous status within the confines of a given world of meaning; (4) the outsider is treated well and is assimilated into the community as a resident outsider, but when problems arise, this new person becomes the focus of negative attention, prejudice, violence, and even murder, ritual or otherwise; (5) the outsider or stranger is either expelled or killed (or perhaps first tortured and then killed) immediately upon appearing at the village or home. Of note here is how a particular person, or type of person—an outsider—becomes a symbol for an entire order of meaning. The stranger comes to symbolize all that is unknown, unseen, hidden, mysterious, and potentially capable of bestowing blessings or calamity. An itinerant puppeteer, for example, whose role is to unleash spiritual powers for revitalizing and cleansing the home and handle those forces that are potentially dangerous to society, comes to symbolize these frightening aspects of sacredness and pollution, and is regarded with the very dread and abjection that pollution engenders.

Ritual puppetry is an example of a multi-textured alterity. Ritual puppeteers, outsiders to the communities in which they performed, manipulated beings once removed from the human realm—puppets—to handle forces from outside the human realm. Amorphous deities such as Ebisu and the equally enigmatic *yama no kami* (mountain deities) traverse the cosmos at will and have at times adverse affects on the human condition in the form of bad harvests, disasters, and even epidemics.

Ritual handling of puppets expresses not only alterity but also the control of power. Just as mainstream society must control and manage the arrivals and departures of puppeteers, so too did the puppeteers manage the arrival and departure of other beings—particularly the deity Ebisu who, as we shall see, is the outsider deity par excellence: unformed, ambiguous, unseen, unpredictable and potentially dangerous. In short, puppeteers did with Ebisu and the other deities they contacted what society did with puppeteers—channeled the forces represented by this alterity for their own benefit. Controlling the outsider and manipulating the symbolic significance of this status (be it occupied by a person or a deity) was not only necessary but ritually desirable.

The outsider can be used ritually as the representative of that which is difficult to represent symbolically. How does one bring the unknown to life and make it present? Rituals involving outsiders are dependent on the very alterity of the performers; they arise out of a need to periodically recreate and renew the cosmos by inviting the unknown into the realm of the known for purposes of purification, revitalization, and protection. Conversely, these rituals also depend on the ability to expel the outsider, so that a distinction between the known and unknown can be maintained.

All of these studies point to a common apprehension: Outsiders possess a great deal of symbolic power. It is not enough to keep these outsiders perpetually at bay, although people may try to do so. Rather, it is necessary to periodically manipulate and even invoke their power, for a variety of ends. In the case we are studying here, otherness is encoded and manipulated through itinerant ritual to achieve symbolic authority over an entire order of meaning. Outsiders have at once the power both to destroy a closed system of meaning and to revitalize and purify that system. Maybe the outsider will do what is desired, or maybe the outsider will refuse to cooperate. This dual potentiality creates yet another level of power, born of the fear of not knowing how an exchange will come out. How the many layers of this symbolic power is handled makes the difference between these two very different outcomes of contact with the world beyond the known. There is an implied tyranny in the textures of the unknown.

Now, we turn to a discussion of the formulation of this problem in Japanese history by looking at the dominant categories of order that ritual puppeteers maintained. As we shall see, society recognized the need for a ritually and semantically separate group of people who could be responsible for taking care of the world of the unknown—pollution, chaos, death, and perhaps most important, the sacred. These people were isolated from the rest of society physically and symbolically into a multitiered pariah group, and yet it was their very otherness that made it possible for mainstream society to maintain its vision of order and purity.

By the Muromachi period (1333–1573), many of the rituals conducted by itinerant performers were those performed to remove pollution and defilement from homes and even entire villages. What ideological system underlay this practice of itinerant performance? Here we must look at a dominant ideological system in Japan during the medieval period, the corpus of meanings, attitudes and practices relating to purity and pollution.[14] This complex, body-based ritual purity system, which has gone through great transformations throughout Japanese history, was expressed in an early and mythical form in the redacted Japanese creation myths, recorded in the eighth century the *Kojiki* and *Nihongi*. While this ritual purity system was articulated with reference to the physical body, its excreta, and gender, these referents must be read as a complex symbolic language describing the relationships between different levels of the cosmos. These mythical references to the body and pollution indicate that a concern with ritual purity has a long history. In fact, most scholars of Japanese society would agree that the concern with ritual purity continues to be a strong preoccupation even today. Yokoi Kiyoshi, a scholar of medieval Japanese history, writes, "The concept of being contaminated by ritual pollution was not limited to people living in ancient or medieval Japan, but is something which, deeply rooted in our consciousness, continues to move us [even today]."[15] After an overview of this system and its transformations in Japanese history, we examine how puppeteers and other ritual performers were implicated in these ideas of the pure and the polluted.

Pure and Impure: A Shinto Dyad

It can be argued that the most fundamental and long-abiding distinction in Shinto practice is that between purity and impurity. A great deal of Shinto practice is devoted to periodically ridding space, time, and bodies of the pollution that time and living in the world generate. Perhaps the most pronounced example of this process of ritual purification is the periodic rebuilding of the ceremonial center at Ise. Every twenty years (until the recent controversy over lumber) this large ceremonial center was completely torn down, burned, and reconstructed. The significance of this act was that without a periodic and total destruction of the site, the center could not be spiritually regenerated. Time itself in this case has generated the pollution that requires the destruction of the sacred architecture. The new structure, built on the alternate site next to the previous structure, is understood to have been purified and revitalized. In this gigantic and costly example, we see an important principle of the Japanese ritual purity system. Ritual action of a purifying nature is understood to produce spiritual revitalization and rebirth. The very process of purification is a highly generative act.[16]

While the most coherent formulation of the Japanese ritual purity system can be found in texts considered today to be Shinto, most of these texts are drawing on a wider, pre-Buddhist religious ethos. As Ohnuki-Tierney points out, "The Japanese concepts of purity and impurity are usually labeled as Shinto concepts. However, since the early historical records included oral traditions, it appears that Shinto simply gave an official stamp to already well-established values."[17]

What exactly counts as pure and polluted, and what words are used to denote these orders of meaning? Two terms are most commonly used: *hare*, meaning bright, clear, or pure, and *kegare*, meaning polluted, defiled, or filthy. While these two terms and the states of being they represent stand in clear juxtaposition to one another, we must resist the temptation to view purity as sacred and impurity as profane. As Namihira Emiko and others have rightly pointed out, and as our examination of Japanese sources will show, both states are highly sacred, extremely powerful, and potentially dangerous. In contrast to the sacredness of both purity and pollution, there stands a third category, *ke*, which can be best understood simply as neither pure nor polluted but merely profane.

Events that create pollution are often potentially dangerous situations involving passage from one stage of physical development to another, such as childbirth, menstruation, recovery from illness, and of course death, funerary rites, and acts of mourning. Controlling the movement between states of purity and pollution becomes a matter of extreme importance in the Shinto ritual system.

Hare can be most easily defined as that which enhances life and is creative. A number of items in Japan are understood to be inherently *hare*, and these reveal something of the substance of this order of meaning: new rice seedlings, clear sunny days, festival days, sites where a sacred presence has manifested itself, and waterfalls are a few of the most pressing examples. Ritual purity, however, is not a static or permanent state. One moves into and out of states of pollution in varying degrees throughout the day, the week, the month, the year, and one's lifetime.

Kegare can best be understood as that which undoes life and leads to death and destruction. It is a principle in the cosmos that works against creation. In the understanding of medieval Japan, the most obvious examples of sources of pollution were actual death and decomposition of the body, but a number of other states and objects were also considered polluting and polluted: the death or birth of domestic animals, miscarriage, ingestion of meat, reburial (*kaisō*), injuries that break the flesh, pregnancy, menstruation, handling and extinguishing of fire, and directly touching a woman. Within this list, there was a hierarchy, and also a set number of days during which a polluted person was excluded from appearing in general public.[18] *Hare* exists in a constant dialectical relationship with its opposite, *kegare*, and this movement constitutes one of the most important acts of spiritual development within this system of meaning.[19]

Further division of kinds of pollution into two categories indicates the complexity of this system. Red pollution (*akafujo*) generally referred to menstruation and childbirth; it also extended to all letting of blood, including wounds. Black pollution (*kurofujo*) referred to death and included both the physical body of the deceased, the family of mourners, and of course all acts involving murder, killing, or death of human beings or animals. In between all these categories, contact with bodily excreta—blood, semen, mucous or secretions from any orifice, pus, urine, feces, and vomit—was understood to be polluting. Both broad categories of pollution, red and black, carried a limited power of contagion (called *shokue*, literally, "touching pollution").[20] Coming into contact with any of these substances or states (death, mourning, childbirth, or menstruation), whether directly or indirectly, was understood to be polluting and required ritual purification. Fear of contagious pollution gave rise to the practice of separating people directly affected by pollution from society—either temporarily or permanently.

Yokoi notes that understandings of pollution in medieval Japan were organized into a system of primary, secondary, and tertiary pollutions. Primary pollution was the original place or person who was polluted (for example, a corpse or a menstruating woman). Secondary pollution was coming in contact with the original pollution (touching a corpse or a menstruating woman), and tertiary pollution was coming in contact with a second-level pollution (meeting someone who has just come from a funeral, someone who had touched a corpse, etc.).[21]

Ordinarily, any individual will come in contact with these pollution in the process of being alive. Daily emissions, sexual relations, menstruation and childbirth, and deaths in the family are common occurrences, so a

ritual purity system must provide ways for a person to be cleansed of a
temporary pollution. According to this system, there were basically four
ways a person could be cleansed, and each had its appropriate application.
The different methods of purification varied regionally. The earliest
method of ritual purification, widespread in ancient Japan but used today
only in certain areas, and then only in the cases of menstruation, childbirth, or death in the immediate family, is the immersion in either a running body of water or the ocean. This practice is recorded in the earliest
records describing the Japanese by Chinese writers, dating from the
fourth century C.E. The *Gishi Wajiden* describes the following: "When
there is a death, they mourn for ten days, during which period they do not
eat meat. The chief mourners wail and weep, and the others sing, dance,
and drink liquor. After the burial, the whole family goes into the water to
bathe, like the Chinese sack-cloth ablutions."[22]

The most common method is daily bathing, and this cleanses one from
the pollution of contact with the world outside the home (the contagion
of coming into contact with persons or places of undetermined purity),
and the pollution of daily bodily emissions. This kind of bathing takes
place in a tub of pure water (either at home or at a public bath), which one
enters only after having completely washed the body. Yokoi suggests that
this method of immersion probably grew from the practice of immersion
in natural flowing rivers, and that tub bathing as a method of purification
is rather late, perhaps dating from the medieval period when the intensifi-
cation of the concern with ritual purity required making it more con-
venient.[23] The third method of purification uses salt, and this method is
most commonly used to purify someone who has come into contact with
a death outside the family, usually through attending a funeral. Upon
returning home, a person who has attended a funeral is met at the gateway of the house and salt is dusted over his or her shoulders (and sometimes hair). Finally, the use of fire (and sometimes merely smoke) to
purify objects that have come in contact with a major pollution is not
uncommon. These four methods—immersion in natural bodies of water,
bathing in a tub, salt, and fire—are widespread even today in Japanese
ritual purity practices.

The concern with this fundamental distinction between purity and pollution is apparent in the Japanese creation myths, recorded in the eighth-
century *Kojiki* and *Nihongi* texts. The first book of the *Kojiki*, consisting
of forty-six chapters, is widely considered to be a highly redacted narrative
which incorporates various myth cycles, including those from people
living in the Inland Sea of Japan around the beginning of the historical
period—people usually lumped under the general category of *amazoku*
(literally "sea people"). Many of the myths reflect a strong maritime influence. Here we follow the redacted myth's treatment of essential physio-

logical events: sexual foreplay and union, illness, vomiting, defecation and urination, death, weeping in grief, murder and bloodletting, and bathing. These events, we shall see, all create substances of ambiguous status that must somehow be appropriated into the cosmic system. What happens to the bodily excreta of divine beings? How do these mythical substances become symbols for larger meanings in society? How does this creation myth define these categories and paradigms for human beings?

The first six chapters of this mythical narrative describe the coming into existence of five heavenly deities called the Separate Heavenly Deities and the Seven Generations of the Ages of the Gods. The Separate Heavenly Deities are without form. The text uses the words "they hid their bodies" to express their invisibility and formlessness, but, as we shall see, this also denotes their complete purity, for having a body becomes the source of all pollution.[24] In these first few chapters, we are told that two of the deities who are part of the Seven Generations of the Ages of the Gods, Izanagi and Izanami, are ordered to consolidate a shifting and unformed land. To do this, they lower a jeweled spear into the unformed primordial brine and create an island (*Onogorojima*, literally "the self-curdling island")[25] from the substance that drips off the end of it. They then descend to this island and erect a heavenly pillar and a palace.

Having found a place on which to stand, the discussion moves immediately to bodies. Izanagi asks his wife, "How is your body formed?" and she replies, "My body, formed though it be formed, has one place which is formed insufficiently," to which Izanagi responds, "My body, formed though it be formed, has one place which is formed to excess. Therefore I would like to take that place in my body which is formed to excess and insert it into that place in your body which is formed insufficiently and [thus] give birth to the land. How would this be."

While possibly one of the least romantic and most technical allusions to foreplay in world mythology, the end result of this exchange does not go well, for after the initial movements around the heavenly pillar, the woman speaks first before they have sexual relations. Because of this, their creation is a leech, an amorphous blob, which even at the age of three cannot walk. (Hereafter in mythology this child is referred to as Hiruko, the Leech Child.) The deities, realizing that something has gone wrong, abandon the failed offspring in a reed boat onto the ocean and try again. They fail again when they create the island of Awa, literally "foam," not the stuff of which firm land is made.[26]

Some scholars have read these failed creations as mythical expressions of miscarriages (spontaneous abortions), abandoned to the waters. While the physiological experience of a miscarriage may have inspired the formulation of the symbolism, it would seem that the idea of a failed creation is a larger idea, of which miscarriage (along with failed crops, bad fishing, and disorder) is but one dramatic example. The motif of the failed creation is not uncommon in world mythology and does not always get interpreted as a direct reference to human beings. In this case, the tale of the Leech Child gets resurrected at various times in Japanese history as a symbol of the outcast. In the following chapter, we shall see that the legless Leech Child is identified with Ebisu and becomes a deity embodying disorder, destruction, and epidemics. He must be entertained and appeased by puppeteers lest he cause terrible calamities in the human realm.

The creation myth continues through the successful creation of numerous islands by Izanagi and Izanami in chapter 6, and in chapter 7 we see the beginnings of the outlines of a ritual purity system emerging. In this chapter, Izanami gives birth to a deity called Hi no Kaga Hiko no Kami, the fire deity.[27] "Because Izanami no Mikoto bore this child," the myth relates, "her genitals were burned and she lay down sick. In her vomit, there came into existence the deity Kana-yama hiko no kami; next Kana yama hime no kami. Next, in her feces there came into existence the deity Pani yasu hiko no kami; next Pani yasu bime no kami. Next, in her urine there came into existence the deity Mitu-pa-no-me-no-kami; next, Waku musubi no kami. The child of this deity is Toyo uke bime no kami. Thus at last, Izanami no kami, because she had borne the fire-deity, divinely passed away."[28]

This piece of Japanese mythology has been interpreted in a number of ways, with most interpretations viewing the myth as a narrational explanation of natural phenomena of nature.[29] What is outstanding in this myth is the intense focus on a number of physiological processes: vomiting, defecation, urination, parturition, and in the end, death. All of these bodily events result in a physical product. What is the status of the physical excreta (and finally the corpse) of a goddess? In this case, these body products are highly creative: deities literally spring from them. Once they were part of a divine body, but now they have been expelled. The status of these physical substances is ambiguous and therefore they are regarded as highly polluted.

The next stage in the saga of this creation myth concerns the death of Izanami. The myth tells us: "At this time Izanagi no Mikoto said, 'Alas, I have given my beloved spouse in exchange for a mere child!' Then he crawled around her head and around her feet, weeping. At this time, in his tears there came into existence the deity who dwells at the foot of the trees in the foothills of Mount Kagu, named Naki Sapa Me no Kami."[30] In this section of the myth, another type of bodily excreta, tears, is understood to be potent enough to create deities.

The next section of the myth describes how divine blood likewise engenders deities. In his grief and rage that his wife has died in childbirth, the father Izanagi unsheathes his sword and cuts off the head of his son, the fire deity. Blood from various parts of his sword—the tip, the guard, and the hilt—all turn into deities, eight altogether.[31] Eight more deities spring from the body of the slain child, from his head, chest, belly, genitals, and left and right hands and feet.[32]

Up to this point in the myth, products of the body, far from being merely profane, are regarded as powerful and creative. This is a point to be kept in mind as we see the later manifestations of a more abstract ritual purity system. The world of pollution is far from profane. It is highly generative when properly handled.

The climax of this creation myth is in the journey of the grieving Izanagi to meet his wife in the land of the dead.[33] Although Izanami asks her husband not to look upon her form, Izanagi cannot contain himself; he breaks one of his combs and lights it so he can look at her. What he sees is this: "At this time, maggots were squirming and roaring in the corpse of Izanami no Mikoto. In her head was Great-Thunder; In her breast was Fire-Thunder, In her belly was Black Thunder; In her genitals was Crack-Thunder; In her left hand was Young-Thunder; In her right hand was Earth-Thunder; In her left foot was Sounding-Thunder; In her right foot was Reclining-Thunder."[34]

With this vision of his wife's rotting corpse, Izanagi flees from the land of the dead, pursued by his furious wife and the hags of the realm. At the pass dividing the land of the living and the dead, the two deities finally face each other and announce their divorce. Izanami vows to strangle a thousand people per day, and Izanagi vows to build five thousand parturition huts, or places for birth, per day.

After this ordeal, Izanagi is in need of purification. He says, "I have been to a most unpleasant land, a horrible, unclean land. Therefore I shall purify myself."[35] He then purifies himself in a river. Deities arise from his polluted articles of clothing and various parts of his body. Washing his left eye, he creates the sun goddess Amaterasu; washing his right eye, he creates the moon, Tsuku Yomi. From his nose comes the turbulent Susanoō. In all, fourteen deities are born.[36]

This elaborate creation of the Japanese pantheon out of the body products of deities' illness, childbirth, death, grief, murder, decomposition, and washing could not be more emphatic: the products of the body (and we can argue, what the body symbolizes) are generative sacred substances. This mythical tradition casts the later dominant medieval Japanese ritual purity system in a different light. It is not possible to argue that this ritual purity system is a misguided code to ensure hygiene. As Dumont points out, "Hygiene is often invoked to justify ideas about impurity. In reality, even though the notion may be found to contain hygienic associations, these cannot account for it, as it is a religious notion."[37]

Using the ancient Israelite case as a model from which to interpret the concern bordering on obsession with the body in ritual purity systems in other parts of the world, Mary Douglas suggests that a concern and obsession with the excreta of the body reflects a deeper analogical process. She maintains that in cases where there is a deep concern over the excreta of the body, there is also a concern with guarding the boundaries of the social group. The body is an intimate symbol of society itself, capable of being generalized to the experience of every living person within the group.

Yokoi presents a parallel case arguing from Japanese materials. He maintains that the rigid ritual purity codes of medieval Japan were really about social control of the population and maintenance of social class distinctions. He cites a fifteenth-century document indicating the problem which arose when an outcast visited a home on business, such as bringing wood or delivering stone. The outcast in this case was a *kawara mono*, or "person of the riverbed," a term that the text extends to people who lived in the Sanjo districts attached to shrines since both were domiciles of outcasts. Their very presence was defiling to anyone who came in contact with them, and one needed to consider this in one's daily life. Such a system guaranteed a rigid social hierarchy. [38]

When the ruling class is concerned with its hegemony and with the clarity and purity of its identity, and when moreover it wishes to enforce at all costs its right to rule, the margins of that society must be carefully watched for threats. Likewise, the body, with its many orifices and ambiguous products (tears, feces, blood) must be carefully guarded. A body-based ritual purity system extends the symbolism of social control to every single person in the society, at once making the symbolism real, everyday, and immediate. It is also not hard to imagine how the maintenance of a system such as this can serve as a suitable pseudoconcern for people, for it is all pervasive and demanding. The proper handling of these products is of the greatest ritual as well as practical concern. Put more directly, how we relate to what goes into and comes out of the body determines the purity of that body. You are what you eat and touch and how you treat what you expel, just as your village (or nation) is what it allows in and assimilates and what it forces out.

The Personification of Defilement and the Systematization of Discrimination

With a ritual purity system such as the one described above, a number of logistical problems arise for society. How can the products of pollution, both physical and spiritual, be safely contained and removed from society without infecting everyone around with their potency? It is the job of culture to mediate experience for people and to safeguard order and classifications. Pure and polluted, sacred and profane, inside and outside, this and that, must be allowed to interact only according to a prescribed set of rules. The job of handling those aspects of society which by definition will be polluting becomes the domain of specialists, whom Louis Dumont calls "the specialists in impurity."[39] What is the status of those whose job it is to come around and purify the neighborhood? What is the role of those people who must permanently traffic in the realm of the metaphorical equivalents of bodily excreta? Any analysis of Japanese ritual purity systems must begin by recognizing the impact such a system has on those required to maintain it. At what cost is this system maintained?[40]

Burakumin: *Nomenclature and Unconscious Associations*

In the last several decades, scholars in the United States and Europe have become aware of the civil rights struggle of Japan's historically discriminated class, called today *burakumin* (meaning simply "settlement or village people," a label adopted by the people themselves to replace derogatory labels).[41] In central and western Japan, where most of these people live, being a person from a village designated as the domain of outcasts (*hisabetsu buraku*) is still a highly charged issue. References to their struggle for equal rights are on public buses and street signs throughout the Kansai area, calling for an end to social discrimination.[42]

It is important to see puppeteers both as included in a larger group of social outcasts and as distinct from some of the associations of this group. From the perspective of mainstream Japanese society, contact with anyone considered polluted was itself potentially polluting. From within the outcast communities, however, one had to distinguish between different types of specialists of impurity. There was not only a rigorous hierarchy but also great variation in specialization. There were those who cleaned latrines and temple grounds, those who prepared the dead for cremation, and those who specialized in the care of the sick and the delivery of children. There were also sacred specialists who removed invisible pollution—spiritual transgressions and the pollution brought about by the passage of time; and there were ritual specialists who contacted the dead and delivered their oracles and messages to the human community. What all of these cases have in common is that they deal with the *margins of the human condition*: death and sickness, body orifices, or margins between the human and sacred realms. They cross boundaries that others do not, and come back to tell about it.

The rituals we will look at in the following chapters involved negotiations with the forces capable of ensuring safety, abundant harvests and good fishing catches, and the health of the community. Negotiating with these forces meant crossing a line out of the everyday human condition into a liminal plane where two realms meet. The task of conducting these negotiations fell to certain sacred specialists who used beings once removed from themselves—puppets—as receptacles for the forces they summoned.

The *burakumin* of Japan are historically from several different groups. On Awaji, many are the descendants of puppeteers.[43] To understand some of the forces creating their outcast status, we can look at a larger dynamic in Japanese religious history. From the Heian period, the office of sacred specialist divided into two distinct and to some degree competitive professions. One was the *kannushi* (sacred specialists attached to shrines). The other was the *waza bito* (performers), who presented nonecclesiastical sacred performances, of which puppetry was one type. This group included *onmyōji* diviners, *nembutsu* dancers, performers of *banzairaku* (felicitations and blessings), and *kugutsu-mawashi* (puppeteers) to name a few. They tended, from about the late Heian period on, to congregate in areas connected to major Sanjo shrine complexes, discussed below. The waza bito came to be regarded as outcasts for what seems to be two overlapping reasons. First, they were sacred specialists, and their power to make divinations, perform exorcisms and purifications, and bring back spirits of the dead—in short, to "cross the bridge out of this world"—gave them an aura of sacredness and power that was frightening. They performed a necessary function in society, but they were kept at a distance. Second, it appears that they were partially or totally itinerant. These two features of their lifestyle turned them into the powerful Other from another plane—although often just another village. As Yoshida has pointed out, "The attribution of mystical evil qualities to newcomers may be a reflection of the Japanese villagers' traditional fears and suspicions of outsiders and strangers. . . . Newcomers and strangers . . . are regarded as dangerous for some reason. In this we see the underlying pattern of ambiguity."[44]

A third, related issue in the case of puppeteers concerns the puppets themselves. This aspect of the perception of the otherness of puppeteers has been overlooked by scholars. It is not just that puppeteers come from outside, nonagricultural spaces that they are other. As we saw in chapter 1, puppets challenge the boundaries of what it means to be human. Puppets, which exist "in the shape of the human," are not simply metaphors for the human but actually comprise a world of their own, a parallel world bridging the domains of the human and the divine. The puppet, as an intersection of these two worlds, is powerful and frightening, eliciting both fear and fascination. They have the capacity to draw sacred forces and can become vessels (*yorishiro*) in which the sacred comes to dwell. Furthermore, they can embody the souls of human beings, both living and dead. Something about puppets is grotesque. They draw their greatest power when they are not merely mimetic devices depicting human activity (a task at which they invariably fail) but when they occupy their own parallel world. Since this parallel world is powerful and frightening, the people who contact it are to be kept at a distance.

Awaji ritual puppeteers were indeed specialists in impurity, as we shall see in subsequent chapters. But the impurity they dealt with was not that of the physical, tangible world but rather that generated through contact with the realm of ambiguous deities, particularly the deity Ebisu. What certain specialists of impurity were to corpses, puppeteers were to the spiritual world. They were integral players in the "spiritual cleanup" crew. Their role in society, often highly negative, was regarded within the same system of meaning. They took away *waza-wai* (assorted pollutions) and made sure that a most liminal deity, Ebisu, was kept under control.[45] The deities handled by puppeteers and the bodily products discussed above had this in common: both were ambiguous entities within the larger structure of the cosmos.

The Localization of Pollution: Riverbeds and *Sanjo* Districts in Medieval Japan

The ideology of the ritual purity system defined certain groups of people as permanently ritually polluted. The status of these outcasts changed over time. By the Tokugawa period, when most of the rituals discussed later were presented, their place in society was rigidly fixed by laws of domicile, dress, and occupation. In medieval Japan, when social movement was not so rigorously restricted, the place of outcasts was maintained through a symbolic mapping of the landscape into restricted zones where they could congregate and live. We turn now to a discussion of two of these special geographical zones where pollution became localized: riverbeds and Sanjo districts.

Kawara: *When Rivers Run Low*

The first of these special zones in medieval and Tokugawa Japan was the *kawara* (riverbed or riverbank). Japanese rivers tend to run fast and full for certain periods of the year, particularly during the rainy season, and so the channels of major rivers have two levels. The deeper level remains wet or at least muddy when the river is not high. The higher level is a floodplain that the river covers when it is flowing at its fullest in the spring and early summer, at least in unusually wet years. Although this area usually remains dry, is not a predictable area for agriculture, since any serious rainy spell can send the river up into its higher level. Since this kawara land could not reliably be put to productive use, they were not taxed. They were legally as well as symbolically outside the Japanese authority system. Marginal groups of people made their temporary homes on this land and were able to live a life somewhat outside the law.

The occupations of people living in these riverbed districts reveals an interesting localization of pollution. Gravediggers, road cleaners, haulers of night soil, comb makers,[46] ritual puppeteers, and midwives all made their homes in kawara, and hence were referred to as *kawaramono* (riverbed people). More derogatory was the term *kawara kojiki* (riverbed beggars).

The most famous of these riverbeds is that of the Kamogawa in Kyoto, particularly the area called Shijō Gawara (The Fourth Street Riverbed). A large number of people living in this area were engaged in the business of performing. In fact, the popular performing art Kabuki is said to have been started by a shrine attendant from the Izumo shrine named Okuni, who is said to have performed a dance at Shijō Gawara in 1603. This area later became a major center for Kabuki, with many actual theater buildings lining the riverbanks, a reminder of this relationship between specialized geography and the development of performance in Japan. Shijō Gawara was also the location of the first formal puppet theater, started by a puppeteer who had left the Nishinomiya shrine, a center for puppetry to be discussed in the following chapter.

A second point to note in a discussion of kawara is how people who were regarded as permanently polluted were geographically isolated into the margins of society. According to a Japanese-Dutch dictionary published in Nagasaki in 1603, the following definition can be found under the heading "kawara no mono": "Also called *kawaya*. People responsible for removing the hides off dead beasts and managing lepers."[47] This definition is interesting because it suggests that by the early seventeenth century, the nomenclature of the riverbed was already rigidly fixed on the idea of these zones as places of physical pollution—the abodes of tanners and lepers—even though the people who lived there were doing a wider variety of jobs.

Riverbed districts were marginal in almost every respect—legally, geographically, agriculturally, and socially. People living there could literally slip through the cracks of society. They floated on their boats throughout Japanese society tying up at a riverbank and staying on land for extended periods of time only when the rivers got too dry. It is not hard to imagine how such a phenomenon could become embellished in the popular imagination. One is reminded of the image of Foucault's Narrenschiffen. But whereas the European dyad was reason and madness, here it was the polluted and the pure, the settled and the itinerant.

Sanjo *Districts: Setting the Margins*

The symbolic geography of Japan located the mediation of disorder, transgression, and pollution elsewhere: in Sanjo districts. Sanjo districts offer another vantage point for understanding the shifting significance of ritual puppeteers from the late Heian period through late Tokugawa. Three major shrines where ritual puppetry has been prominent—the Usa Hachiman shrine, the Nishinomiya Ebisu shrine, and the ceremonial center of Awaji puppetry, Omidō Hachiman Daibosatsu—are adjacent to or located within districts called Sanjo. These districts, and the people who lived in them, were part of the imagination of otherness, expressed in this case not in the lives of people but in geography. During medieval Japanese history, many ritual puppeteers were predominantly affiliated formally or loosely with these special districts and ceremonial centers.

What is important in studying these districts is not just the activities of the people who lived there and their roles within Japanese religious life. Rather, the very existence of special districts of divination and pollution suggests that they were important in the Japanese imagination of landscape. Meaning and value were literally transposed onto the geography of Japan. Ceremonial centers ordered the practice, ideology, and politics of Japanese ecclesiastical religious life, and districts at the margins of these centers formed a locus for all that did not fit within the realm of the commonplace. What Eliade has called "boundary situations" of the human condition—death, birth, extreme sickness, epidemics, delivery of oracles, and longing to make contact with spirits—these aspects of life were contained within certain physical spaces, so that the meanings these situations engendered could be contained, controlled, and channeled. What a study of Sanjo districts discloses is a medieval symbolization of the cosmos and a means for contending with disorder, ambiguity, and ruptures in planes of meaning.[48] While most studies of cosmos in the history of religions focus on the problem of finding a center (à la Eliade), what Sanjo districts tell us is that an essential aspect of a cosmic order is its margins. This, in large part, is what the gradual ostracization of puppeteers in Japanese history is all about. The Sanjo cases provide a clear expression of this task of world building and spatial organization in medieval Japan. We shall discuss below the general history of these districts, and in subsequent chapters look specifically at those Sanjo districts famous for puppeteers.

Sanjo: *History and Meaning*

What exactly were Sanjo districts and what can be known about them? The exact connotation of the term is difficult to determine, because the term has been written using different characters throughout Japanese history. The variety of character compounds used to write "Sanjo" provoke some interesting speculations as to how these districts were imagined and signified throughout Japanese history: "scattered place" (as opposed to central place or real place),[49] "place of divination," "birthing place," "mountaintop," and "third district" are all characters that have been used to write Sanjo. Most scholars attempt to find the meaning of these sites by insisting that one reading of these characters is correct and developing an interpretation along these lines. But even the same Sanjo district can be written differently at different times. This variety and confusion tells us something not only about the range of meanings that these places had but also about the confusion and even the hysteria that signifying the unsignifiable has generated in Japanese society over time.

Sanjo districts are decidedly a medieval phenomenon, and their existence reveals a great deal about the medieval vision of place. Nagahara Keiji presents a list of textual references to Sanjo districts and persons, including twenty two references dating from 1045 to 1246.[50] The question of the nature and existence of Sanjo districts before Muromachi is complex, but the earliest document using this term writes the name with the characters "scattered place."

There were at least two lines of development for these places called Sanjo. Most of them originated as special compounds for ritual performers (musicians, diviners and deity pacifiers, etc.) attached to major ceremonial centers. During the medieval period, such people were the dominant residents of Sanjo districts. In this context, it is important to note that in premodern Japan, performance was primarily intended for divine entertainment. Frequently, performances had a shamanic element, and beings from other realms were regularly contacted through the medium of performance.

Referring to Sanjo districts and the performers who live in them, Hayashiya has noted that ritual performers attached to Tennōji (located in present-day Osaka) lived in a Sanjo district attached to the shrine; and he suggests that these performers had a large impact on ritual performance in other areas of Japan. As the demand for ritual performers specializing in shamanic activities (delivering oracles, curing, calling back the dead, invoking divine beings, etc.) began to decline and residents of these districts suffered the inevitable fall from status, they dispersed throughout Japan, and specialists originating in the Tennōji Sanjo district could be found as far away as Tōhoku. Hayashiya cites a selection from *Chūyūki* (dated 1114) which discusses the performance of dances at Byōdōin in Uji (near present-day Kyoto). It seems that at the end of this performance, when payment and praise were being distributed to the performers, those from the Tennōji Sanjo district were denied equal reward.[51] The passage clearly shows that even from this early date, Sanjo residents were discriminated against. Although residents of Sanjo districts had clear religious duties at the shrines and temples to which they were attached, otherwise they were a pariah group.

Throughout the Muromachi period, Sanjo districts appear to have been fluid spaces of pollution, and so references around Japan describe these sites differently. While they may have originated as the domiciles of performers and diviners, by the Tokugawa period they were often associated with blood pollution. A look at perceptions of these sites during the Tokugawa period reveals the results of Sanjo districts acting as a catch-all for various members of outcast groups for several hundred years.

According to Kida Teikichi, the main inhabitants of Sanjo districts were diviners who put sacred chants (*tonaegoto*) to song and dance and who, on the side, "couldn't resist" becoming performers as well.[52] A text dated 1734 lists a number of districts called Sanjo throughout the country and indicates that these districts were places where menstruating women would go. According to this list, by the mid-eighteenth century there were twenty-five Sanjo districts throughout the country. As the list is relatively late, many of the sites were at the time of compilation nothing more than place-names. Of the twenty five, three were primarily the domiciles of Taoist diviners (*onmyōji*), two of gate chanters (*shōmon hōshi*), two of puppeteers, one of a female shaman (*miko*), and one of ritual purifiers (*harae-mono*); four were place-names only, two belonged to farmers, and in over ten the origins of the site were unclear since descendants of the original district were no longer living there.[53]

These districts called Sanjo shared several basic characteristics: (1) they were affiliated with or attached to major ceremonial centers or manors; (2) they were restricted zones, and access was discouraged lest one come in contact with pollution; (3) they were frequently places where women would give birth and spend the postpartum period of pollution; (4) they were occupied by Taoist diviners, performers, and other specialists who made contact with spirits and deities; (5) the dead were frequently prepared for cremation in these places; (6) lepers, animal skinners and leather workers, and people engaged in menial work at temples and shrines would reside in these districts; (7) they are most prevalent in the Kansai area, where the imperial family resided for most of Japanese history, and are frequently though not always in close proximity to an imperial tomb; and (8) they were not taxed. Itinerant performers who traveled around Japan could come and go freely through these districts, and Sanjo districts may have become common stopping off places for marginalized people during the medieval period. The fluid movement into and out of these districts is a sharp contrast to the lack of social mobility outcasts suffer under the Tokugawa shogunate government.

These places of exorcism, divination, magical healing, childbirth, puppetry performances, ecstatic dancing, and treatment and burial of the dead constituted both a physical and imaginary landscape of otherness. It is unlikely that the average Japanese would have ventured into a Sanjo area except on business of a highly pressing spiritual nature. These districts participated in the power and dangerous potential of the sacred, which the itinerant sacred specialists who issued from Sanjo embodied and took on the road. By the late medieval period, traveling papers always indicated a person's name and type of business. Because performers from these districts often had the name "Sanjo" (or "Sanjo hōshi") affixed to their name (as in "the Dōkumbō from the Sanjo on Awaji"), a performer who resided in such a district carried a signification of otherness with him when he traveled. Sanjo was not simply an address, it was a mode of being.

Unusual Beings: Others in Japanese Cosmologies

The outsider at once encodes symbolism of the dead, the polluted, the banished, the unseen. A large part of the Japanese ritual calendar is organized around the idea of beings from other realms visiting the human realm to bring blessings and fecundity. Inherent in the outsider's entry into the established order is the conviction that the everyday world will be in some way revitalized by contact with outside modalities. The symbolically controlled movement of the outside, which constituted a fundamental ritual complex in Japanese nonecclesiastical religion, is predicated on an understanding of the power of outsiders. Japanese scholars refer to it as *marebito shinkō* (belief in *marebito*).[54] *Marebito* is the word given to the sacred person who visits on special occasions, and is usually written with the two-character compound meaning "the rare person," implying the phenomenal nature of the visit.

The category of marebito has been most widely discussed by the Japanese folklorist and poet Origuchi Shinobu (1887–1953), who is credited with creating the term to describe a wide ranging phenomenon in Japanese religious practice.[55] The basic premise of *marebito* is that at certain times of the year, and in particular the period between the harvest and the new year, the entire cosmos is in a state of negative capability and potentiality. That is to say, whether or not the cosmos will spring to life in the new year is undetermined. The entire realm of human existence is dependent upon the forces from the other realms—sacred beings and an-cestors—to regenerate the cosmos, revitalize life, release fish for the com-ing year's catch, and germinate rice seeds. During this period of time, therefore, the visit of these sacred beings is ritually actualized. Certain beings come not just into a village but into each house, where they recite words of blessing and perform magical rites to purify the home and revi-talize the sacred forces upon which existence depends. These beings are understood, ritually if not literally, to be forces from other realms, and they are treated with special care while they are present. Dressed for travel, they are given food, money, and lodgings. Banquets are held in their honor, and they and are welcomed into homes and village places. Their arrival and departure are highly marked moments in these ritual visits. At the end of their visit, just as at the beginning, they are carefully escorted back to the margins of the village, so that they can return to the world from which they came and life in the human realm can return to its bal-ance. Too much sacredness would threaten to change the very nature of the human realm, which requires a carefully guarded economy of sacred forces mixed with the activities of daily life—fishing, agriculture, sericul-ture, tending children, and living and dying.

Inherent in the pattern of marebito is the possibility that a stranger or beggar could be a visiting ancestor or kami in disguise. The traveler partic-ipates in this symbolic structure, which equates the unknown with the potential to generate renewal (or threaten destruction). Consequently, notes Origuchi, Japanese attitudes toward beggars and travelers can be seen as a veiled expression of this underlying religious sensibility.[56]

One of the only studies in English of the practice of the visiting stranger at New Year in Japan is Yoshiko Yamamoto's thorough work, *The Nama-hage*.[57] This excellent ethnographic study is based on fieldwork by the author on the Oga Peninsula, the small finger of land jutting out into the Japan Sea in northern Japan, where the practice of New Year visitors (young men from the village dressed as "other beings" in straw coats and hats) was, until the postwar period, a dominant ritual event. These visi-tors, called *Namahage*, went from door to door on New Year's Eve and threatened and terrorized young wives and children so that they would be obedient in the coming year. During their visit, they made frightening noises, and broke rules of propriety by searching the house for their hid-den victims, pinching and chastising them when they were discovered. The purpose of the visit was not to entertain but to terrify: to safeguard order and hierarchy, in gender and age, during the coming year. In return for their visit, Namahage were given sake and food, becoming increasingly more intoxicated with each household visit.

Yamamoto's study rightly points out that belief in these visitors had little to do with the ritual event. Most people (even some children) knew these people actually were members of the community dressed as "outsiders." Nevertheless, people found the visits terrifying. What her study makes clear is that a visit from the outside—even if only in a constructed and symbolic way—is an important element in the transition from the old year to the new.

As Yamamoto's case material points out, the Namahage were part of a larger practice of the "New Year's visitor." A map in her book shows that in the prewar period, examples of visiting outsiders coming around at New Year, like the Dōkumbō-mawashi described at the start of this chapter, were quite widespread, particularly in the northeast and in the area around the Inland Sea.[58] The visitors were either friendly or terrifying. But in all cases the visits were connected with the transition from the old year to the new and the visits were at a fixed time, usually the lunar new year (the sixteenth of the first month); the visitors were always marked in some way, through costume and dress, as Others; their arrival was announced by noise-making or music; and their departure was effected through a transfer of gifts of goods (sake, rice, money, etc.).

Another aspect of the marebito matrix can be seen in the Japanese practice of the festival of the dead (o-bon), held every summer during the seventh or eighth month (depending on what part of Japan one is in). While ostensibly conducted within the domain of Buddhist practice, the view of ancestors is clearly influenced by other traditions in Japanese religious life, including the matrix of marebito shinkō. During this rite, family members go to the cemetery—that physical space symbolically serving as a link between the worlds of the living and the dead—and bring the spirits of their ancestors back to the house with them for several days of festivities. Rites punctuate the arrival and departure of the spirits. During this interval, the family members can receive the benefits of the presence of these beings while at the same time serve their ancestors to strengthen their spiritual power. The interdependence of these two realms is most apparent during the rites of o-bon. At the end of the festival, an elaborate dance is held.

I participated in the o-bon rites in a Japanese family living in the village of Fukura on Awaji in 1988, and this year was the first o-bon after the death of the grandmother in this family. The afternoon of the first day of the festival a number of us went to the graveyard and built a ritual fire on the family tombstone, all the while reciting the *Heart Sutra*. We then invited the grandmother to come home with us, and to bring all the other ancestors with her. When we returned home, the father of the house jokingly asked, "Did you bring Grandma back with you?"

For the days that the festival lasted, we set a place at the table for Grandmother, and each evening spent our time looking at old photo albums and discussing her personality while members of the family recalled events from her life. This event impressed upon me the shallowness and simplicity of insisting on "belief" in events as the primary category to assess their religious validity and potency. Did members of this family "believe" that the grandmother's spirit was back with them? Perhaps, and perhaps not. But her memory was being ritually revitalized through this intimate and coded annual practice, and a sense of her presence was generated out of our daily activities designed to focus on her life.

On the final night of the festival, a dance was held on the beach near the ocean, and the spirits of the ancestors were sent out on small boats with candles in them back to the realm from which they came. Arrival and departure are the most elaborate moments in this "visit" from another realm.

In both of these cases of marebito shinkō, a number of key features are worth underscoring. First, although it is possible for beings from other realms to visit unannounced, the ritual system controls the timing of these visits, so that they come during the period of the year when the presence of sacred forces is required. Second, these visits from sacred beings are temporary, and the ritual system ensures that the visits come to an end. Controlling the timing and the duration of sacred visits ensures that a balance and economy is maintained between the two orders of meaning. This is accomplished through the elaborate symbolization of arrival and departure, and the careful marking of the visitor as outsider (whether through strange clothing, noises, musical instruments, or ritual processions). Third, sacred beings are understood to bring blessings and have the magical power to revitalize the communities and homes they enter. These blessings are made possible through elaborate ritual events in which song, dance, and mime ritually actualize the bestowing of blessings and good fortune.

It is clear that the ritual context of itinerant performance appropriates this system of meaning. We now turn to a discussion of this context.

Kadozuke: Rites at the Gate

Itinerant performers have been a common feature throughout the history of Japanese performing arts. A number of words are used to denote itinerant performance: *hyōhaku no gei* (drifting arts), *yugyō no gei* (itinerant arts), and *kadozuke no gei* (arts attached to the gate). All three terms situate a wide range of ritual performances in the context of the relationship between performers and the people for whom they perform. Quite simply, the performers are outsiders, coming from the road to perform in the shrines, gateways, and even the zashiki of private homes and manors, at street crossroads, and even in the gardens and rooms of the Imperial Palace before the imperial family.

Performances presented by itinerant performers were one of the main forms of entertainment in Muromachi Japan. The most common term used to describe performances presented in this way is *kadozuke*.[59] The word literally means "attached to the gate" or "at the gate," but it also refers to rites, skits, acrobatics, and dramatic performances at shrines, crossroads, and marketplaces or "on the road." An important group of such itinerant performers were puppeteers, whose drifting lifestyle was a source of fascination, fear, ritual renewal, and even political expediency for people in medieval and early modern Japan.

Locus and Meaning: The Significance of Itinerant Performance

As noted above, the visit of strangers at certain times of the year was associated with the arrival of sacred forces from beyond the human realm. Because of the way that the world "out there" beyond the settled and defined parameters of village life was perceived, strangers who arrived from unknown places were clearly associated with the power of the unknown. Add to this general perception the abilities of these performers to enact all kinds of fanciful theatrical transformations, and it is not hard to imagine how itinerant performers could be perceived as magical and powerful. Jugglers, contortionists, sword swallowers, storytellers, and ventriloquists were among the magical performers whose originally religious art forms were slowly popularized outside of their strict ritual settings.

The term *kadozuke* arises from a common understanding of the gate as a boundary between two orders of meaning. Gates figure prominently in Japanese domestic and ecclesiastical architecture. Large Japanese manors have always had large covered gates as entryways into the inner area surrounding the house itself, and this part of the architectural design of a home (which was seen in a less elaborate form) had, and continues to have, special symbolic significance. It is a barrier between the world inside the home and the world outside. The distinction between "inside" and "outside" as an important element of Japanese order has been widely discussed.[60]

Gates of homes, temples, or cities as symbolic spaces have figured prominently in depictions of important shifts in Japanese society. For example, many readers will be familiar with Kurosawa Akira's famous film *Rashōmon* (Rashō Gate). The entire eerie narrative of the film is framed by the large gate of Rashō, as two speakers meet under the shelter it provides and discuss the strange times they are experiencing. In using the gate as the setting for this film, the director is appealing to a common Japanese perception of gates as liminal places.

The character "gate" in *kadozuke* refers not to a particular gate but rather to a metaphorical quality of space. Neither inside the house nor part of the street itself, the gate is the no-man's-land to which all meanings can be attached and onto which all projections of potentiality and danger can be projected. It is tempting to assume that the term *kadozuke* arises because performers presented their rites moving from gate to gate, and most interpreters of the term suggest this, but most likely the term refers to the domicile of itinerant performers during the medieval period, when they frequently congregated and even lived under the large gates of temple complexes. These gates were more than mere doors to temples. They had huge roofs and were architecturally imposing, forcing worshippers to a temple to consider the issue of passage from one realm to another. In Pure Land Buddhism the temple gate symbolized the doorway to Amida's paradise itself. They were also shelters for people, a place to escape the elements for beggars, lepers, and other liminal people.[61] The gate was a feature of the urban imagination of space that embodied otherness by being neither here nor there, neither inside nor outside.

The history of kadozuke performance reveals a subtle manipulation of this quality of space to generate and enhance notions of sacredness. Two early performance forms, *Senzu* (or *senshu*)[62] *manzai* and *Matsu-bayashi*, can be considered prototypical and paradigmatic examples of kadozuke, and in fact it can be argued that much of the success and popularity of kadozuke performers arose from the popularity of these earlier performance forms, which prepared the way for a wider use of this performance context. In both forms, the arrival of an outsider at the gate to recite magical incantations and bless the home is a central feature. A review of the two will give us an understanding of how the kadozuke context and sensibility was formed.

Senzu manzai

Senzu manzai, literally "a thousand autumns and ten thousand years,"[63] refers to a performance presented by itinerant performers, popular from the late Heian period through early Tokugawa, in which the performers would dance and intone felicitous magical incantations for blessing and longevity. The name is taken from the refrains sung by the performers during their rite: "Senzu manzai" or "manzairaku, manzairaku, manzairaku!"[64] The performers were referred to as *Senzu manzai hōshi*. The term *hōshi*, which literally means priest, was commonly used in medieval Japan to denote religious specialists who may or may not have had formal ecclesiastical affiliations.[65] A dictionary from the mid thirteen century entitled *Myōgoki* defines senzu manzai hōshi as follows (note the residence of these performers): "*Senzu manzai* is a celebration of the first day of the year seen these days on O-Shōgatsu. Beggar priests from Sanjo wearing the clothes of mountain people and holding in their hands a small pine, make their rounds, reciting various words of blessing, and recording things down."[66]

Other sources from Heian through Muromachi reflect this Kamakura definition, and common elements of the Senzu manzai hōshi were as follows: At New Year performers dressed as priests would proceed from gate to gate reciting magical blessings for longevity and prosperity and performing ritual dances. They carried in their hands a small pine branch. These performers were understood to bring sacred forces with them, and the branch in their hands was understood to be the *torimono*, a receptacle for the sacred seen in many Japanese shamanic practices.[67] Their performance, a combination of song, dance, and magical incantation, was understood to bring the blessings of the sacred to everyone present. Although they were dressed in ecclesiastical attire, they were in fact not proper monks or priests, but many received food and lodgings from particular temples, much like indentured servants. Frequently they were residents of the Sanjo districts. On occasion, these hōshi would perform certain roles in the temples and perform divinations and healings in towns and villages. In this way, notes Misumi Haruo, these Senzu manzai hōshi were part ecclesiastical and part nonecclesiastical religious specialists of very low rank.[68]

The standard theory as to the origin of this performance form is that it developed out of Japanese *tōka*, a type of dance that involved stamping and tripping the feet upon the ground while singing and dancing. The tripping and stamping, while stylistic, also suggests the practice of driving out evil spirits and demons. The dance form is said to have come from T'ang China, and was popular at court, where it was used at New Year for blessing rites.

Originally tōka were performed in the Chinese style, on the first day of the new year at night under the light of the moon. The practice began in about the middle of the seventh century as a New Year ritual in the imperial court, presented every year by naturalized Chinese in Japan to pray for good things in the year. Tōka were performed on the fourteenth and fifteenth of the new year by men and on the sixteenth by women performers. Beginnings of the songs included T'ang poetry, but the others parts often used *saibara*, a popular if at times bawdy song style in Japan during the

Nara period. Some of the references may have had sexual overtones, but invariably the songs would conclude with references to ten thousand years, a set expression implying longevity. The words "Senzu manzai" were part of the chants and poems in these tōka performances. The oldest record describing tōka is in the thirtieth book of the *Nihonshoki.* In this chapter of the text, which deals with events during the reign of Empress Jitō (r. 690–697) we find several references to performances of *arare-bashiri*[69] performed by men on the sixteenth day of the new year. At the end of each stanza of these performances, the words "man nen arare" were repeated, meaning roughly "may you live for 10,000 years!"[70]

Gradually, tōka performances became familiar to a larger group of people in the capital as well. The popularity of this ritual form caused no small amount of agitation, and things got so out of hand that the singing of tōka in public was prohibited by a decree.[71] Due to the popularity of these tōka forms, the expression "Senzu manzai" became very widespread as a felicitous phrase. Hence, many scholars have argued that the later practice of Senzu manzai is derived from these tōka origins.[72]

By the early Heian period, it appears that itinerant performers not connected to the court were engaged in activities now recognizable as Senzu manzai itinerant performances. These performers would travel from gate to gate reciting blessings and songs for the benefit of wealthy land owners. A number of features of this context for Senzu manzai performances attract our attention: First, there is the itinerant nature of the performer. In his study of Senzu manzai, Morita discusses the probable origins of New Year rites presented by "others" who come from outside the village or family unit. His discussion is reminiscent of the marebito shinkō interpretation of the role of outsiders. "Among Japanese people," he notes, "it is believed that at certain prescribed times, divine spirits come to visit, particularly at the start of the year, bringing blessings for the new spring to each household. This belief that deities who bestow blessings on people come to visit exerts a great deal of influence even today. A person called a *shinnin*—divine person) dressed in strange clothes (to indicate that he or she is a deity) visits the gate of each house and recites magical words as blessings. . . . *Senshumanzai* is a performing art with its origins in this practice of a sacred person visiting each gate."[73] Second, the performers were marked as outsiders by their attire and the fact that they held a pine branch in their hands. In subsequent chapters, I show how this marking of the outsider and the transformations in meaning of this person become major components of these performances. Third, we note their loose ties to ecclesiastical centers and their somewhat ambiguous status as "unordained" or not fully recognized priests, although they are called hōshi. In this way, part of the role of these performers was to mediate a number of dichotomies on society, including the tension between ecclesiastical versus nonecclesiastical religious authority. Fourth, the relatively low status of these performers as "religious specialists for hire" suggests that while their services were necessary during certain seasonal events, they were relegated to the margins of everday life for large parts of the year—but it is not uncommon for sacred specialists to be irrelevant for long periods. Mediating between different orders of meaning is necessarily highly irregular employment. Fifth, we note periodic involvement of these performers in magic and divination, as well as occasional healing rites. Last, as the standard definition of a Senzu manzai in the mid-Kamakura period points out, these performers were often from Sanjo districts. This origin was commonplace enough to make it into the dictionary definition.

In summary, a special set of agreed upon codes and symbols marked the Senzu manzai as set apart from the rest of society. Not only did their attire tie them to ceremonial centers, but the fact that they carried branches with them indicated that they were possessed by, or at least messengers for, deities. As we shall see, these features of the Senzu manzai are all common to the later kadozuke context and shaped people's understanding of it.

Matsu-bayashi

Matsu-bayashi, a term which can be literally translated as "pine players," "pine bearers," or "pine noisy (or merrymaking)," refers to a practice common in Japan during the Muromachi period in which strangers from mountain villages would travel to the homes of wealthy landowners before New Year, carrying pine branches and reciting magical blessings for the coming new year. According to Misumi Haruo, they provided a service by presenting people with the pine branches used to decorate entryways, but the branches were also torimono, or receptacles he sacred. Misumi refers to the still common practice in Japan of decorating one's home with a small pine branch for New Year, not dissimilar to the way wreaths decorate homes around the holiday season in the United States. He argues that this custom in Japan, now seen as merely decorative, probably has its roots in a religious practice of marking one's home after the mysterious visitor had arrived during New Year.[74] These Matsu-bayashi would leave a pine branch at the gate to ward off evil forces and show that the house has been blessed and purified for the coming year. Inherent in this visit, however, was an additional dimension not readily apparent in the Senzu manzai case. By merely visiting the house, these Matsu-bayashi were also carrying away the pollution that had been generated in the previous year. In exchange for their services, they were given food and money. Then they were sent on their way, lest the pollution they attracted should remain within the area.

Zeami is said to have mentioned Matsu-bayashi. In his son's record of his comments, *Zeshi Rokujō Igo Sarugaku Dangi* (1430), we find this observation:

> Nowadays there are no families specialized in *Matsubayashi*. What is performed during the Gion festival is probably an example of it. Nevertheless, in the first month of the second year of Eikyō, as there was no family at all to perform the Matsubayashi of the palace, they asked Zeshi a few things. The opening melody is a congratulatory song and should be plain. It should be like this: "In the pine tress the wind dropped and the clouds are motionless on Mount Inari, dropped and the clouds are motionless on Mount Inari, the flower dress of this reign that becomes more and more prosperous . . . oh, spring is splendid." But this time it was a little long.[75]

This brief reference affirms what we know about Matsu-bayashi. It also dates the practice, showing that it was already in decline by 1430, and indicates that the singing of felicitous words was a central part of the performance, much like the Senzu manzai performers.

It is a common understanding in Japan that the deities responsible for generating rice seedlings (*ta no kami*) come from the tops of mountains in the springtime and return to the mountains in the fall after the harvest. These performers, dressed in strange attire and clearly coming from the mountains, were seen as the bearers of these sacred forces. They served the dual purpose of purifying the village and revitalizing the forces of life.

The case of Matsu-bayashi resembles Senzu manzai on a number of counts. The performers are outsiders, itinerant, visit at New Year, recite magical blessings, and are perceived as having a sacred status. Furthermore, the role of the itinerant performer as part of a divine distribution system is apparent. When the Matsu-bayashi came to one's home, he was literally delivering the sacred to one's door along with a recognized insignia for the sacred, a pine branch. In the next chapter, I show that this was also a common activity of ritual puppeteers from the ceremonial center called Nishinomiya for they, too, distributed protective talismans and placards for this major shrine famous for puppeteers.

By the end of the Muromachi period, the practices of Matsu-bayashi and Senzu manzai were being absorbed into the broader context of kadozuke rites. The popular performance that developed in this loosely structured setting were, like those elsewhere in the world, highly syncretic. But the basic religious structure—the visiting outsider bringing sacred forces to the human community—became a part of the perception, half conscious at times, of kadozuke performers. Inherent in the Japanese popular conceptions of the sacred is the idea that sacredness, in its raw, unchanneled state, is undifferentiated and potentially dangerous. As kadozuke performers became less formally tied to religious centers and Sanjo districts, and as their duties became less prescribed, this negative potential was projected onto the performers themselves, and this led in no small part to the heavy discrimination they suffered during the Tokugawa period.

Kadozuke: *A General Pattern of Arrival and Departure*

Not all kadozuke performances are of an overtly ritual or religious nature. Some are merely humorous skits and short scenes from famous ballads. Nevertheless, the context of gate-to-gate performance absorbed much of the highly religious prototypical performance traditions. While the list is somewhat redundant, here are what can be considered the major features of the kadozuke context.[76] First, kadozuke performances were presented by itinerant artists. Second, because they were not members of the communities in which they were performing and were not situated in a familiar social setting, their nature was a mystery, and thus a number of attributes of radical negativity were projected upon them. Third, as outsiders, these performers were regarded with a certain degree of ambivalence and even fear or loathing. The itinerant performer represented an unassimilable dimension of life—the realm beyond ordered space and meaning—and was hence potentially dangerous. Expressions of this can be seen in the claims that these people were part human and part animal. The fundamental human/animal distinction cannot be broken in the normal order of things, but people from the margins were thought to transgress it routinely.[77] Fourth, the ambiguity of itinerant performers led to their being perceived as having special magical powers to cure illness, bring or ward off epidemics, cause or prevent calamities, and so on. Fifth, because itinerant performers aroused apprehension, their arrivals and departures were carefully mediated. Arrivals were timed and announced, and departures were noted with exchange of gifts. Usually, the host in the village where the artist performed would give the performer either food, money, or temporary lodgings. Far from being merely payment for services rendered, this exchange of money or goods must be understood as a ritual exchange between two realms of existence: the settled realm of everyday, profane life and the realm of the sacred, represented by the itinerant ritual artist. Those living in the settled and established world of everyday meanings (villages and towns) had need of the services of the ritual performers but were also afraid of them. The payment of goods was in part a gift to send the performers away. Sixth, elaborate systems of marking the performers as outsiders developed through time, and the style by which these outsiders announced their arrivals became highly stylized. For example, a ritual puppeteer became identifiable by the manner in which he carried puppets in a box and the way he announced his arrival with a flute or a call. Other types of performers had a series of codified signs marking them as *yosomono* (outsiders). This process of marking became incorporated into the signs and symbols of the ritual performances, as I show in subsequent chapters.

Last, the arrival of these performers was usually seasonal in nature. The period between the harvest and the new year, when the future of the cosmos was in question, was the most common time for their visits. This was a marginal time when the new year was not yet fully formed and the order of the cosmos was being recreated. Hence these days were regarded as powerful and sacred. The rites presented by these visitors served to harness this sacredness and channel it for the benefit of the community or home, thereby revitalizing life forces, instilling good health and prosperity, promising large fishing catches, and so forth. In addition to the New Year period, there were also appearances at other moments during the ritual calendar. For example, ritual puppeteers presented the Shiki San-basō rite at weddings and boat launchings, or when rice seedlings were transplanted to the paddies in the spring. What all these moments share—New Year, weddings, boat launchings, planting time—is the quality of transformation and transition.

The kadozuke performance context challenges our usual assumptions about ritual. As Gerd Baumann has pointed out, "We tend to take it as a given, on the whole, that rituals are symbolic performances which unite the members of a category of people in a shared pursuit that speaks of, and to, their basic values, or that creates or confirms worlds of meanings shared by all of them alike."[78] As Baumann argues, our understanding of ritual carries on the tradition of Durkheim, in which rituals assume homogeneity. Leach echoes this notion of homogeneity: "The performers and the listeners are the same people. We engage in rituals in order to transmit collective messages to ourselves."[79] Baumann's point raises an interesting problem in our view of Japanese rituals. The standard interpretation of Japanese ritual is likewise predicated on the notion of homogeneity: specifically, the constructed notion of a seamless people, undivided and living as "one family" with the emperor as father. As the case of *kadozuke* clearly shows, however, for a significant period of Japanese religious history, and at a very popular level, a central ritual context in Japanese religions was driven by a rigidly maintained distinction between the performer and the host. They were seen not simply as socially different; they were ontologically distinct. The kadozuke performer (Senzu manzai, Matsu-bayashi, Dōkumbō-mawashi, etc.), precisely because he was an outsider, was able to make the ritual context work. The dominant ideological system was dependent on the existence of this other not only as an entity against which to define itself, but as the symbolic nexus of power capable of keeping the system viable, pure, and whole. Nowhere else could the ideological function of the outsider be more apparent. The signification of the puppeteer as visitor, outsider, and other is more than just one aspect of this ritual context. *It is the essential sign.*

How is this otherness generated and maintained in the ritual? As we shall see in later chapters, the levels of otherness go deeper than the social context and status of the performer. The beings represented in the rites and the puppets themselves layer this alterity in a complex and multivalent fashion.

The Demise of the *Kadozuke* Context

The ritual context described in this chapter was widespread throughout Japan until it began to gradually decline at the start of the Meiji period. By the late 1940s, kadozuke rituals were almost completely defunct.[80] As I shall show later, some of these itinerant rituals were highly developed both aesthetically and dramatically. I was often told during my fieldwork that the "visits" of ritual puppeteers were an important component of the festivities of the New Year period. In fact, so common was the appearance of Sanbasō-mawashi and Ebisu-kaki during this time that one informant noted, "It just isn't New Year's anymore without Sanbasō."[81] Nevertheless, immediately following the war, there was a campaign throughout Japan to obliterate itinerant performance, including puppetry rites.

One reason these practices were discredited was that people regarded them as a kind of begging, an activity which for a number of reasons came to mean many things in the postwar period. Because the daily life of most people was terribly difficult for a number of years after the war, any activity that looked like asking for handouts was immediately discouraged and even violently put down. I was told the story of one elderly man on Awaji who was beaten one New Year after the war when, at the request of some people near his home, he made the rounds of the village to present the Sanbasō ritual. According to my source, he was told he was just looking for a free handout. That was the last time he performed.

The exchange of goods (food, money, lodgings) was an important component of the ritual action being accomplished. A highly negative attitude toward the exchange of goods at the end of these rituals came up in my fieldwork during 1984. While on Awaji conducting the preliminary segment of my fieldwork, I had the opportunity to interview an elderly man shortly before his death that same year. He had been famous shamisen player of the Awaji theater. In the course of the interview, he mentioned that in the prewar period, he had worked for a while with a Sanbasō-mawashi as a musician. As he was telling me this story, he simply said in passing, "Tokidoki, monomorai wo shita." (Sometimes we did *monomorai*). *Monomorai* means "begging." At the time, it did not strike me as at all odd that a performer should be given something in exchange for his performance, even if it was done from door to door. The old man who told me this saw this as perfectly normal. Later that evening, however, my host on Awaji (who had been present at the interview) was deeply troubled by the fact that this man had said he did monomorai. "This makes Awaji puppetry look terrible," he insisted. This anecdote reflects a certain attitude toward itinerant performers, even in the village they called home. In the postwar period, when all religious activity had to be rationalized, ritual exchange of goods for services was considered to be simply begging, and therefore it was necessary to wipe it out.

There was another serious concern (underscored by attitudes and policies of the occupation forces) that contributed to the demise of the kadozuke context. Many people regarded such ritual practices as superstitious and primitive. Summoning spirits and appeasing deities was not compatible with a newer, more rational view of religion as ethical behavior. This general attitude toward religious life in Japan was expressed at both a popular and scholarly level. The highly influential work of Nakamura Hajime, *Ways of Thinking of Eastern Peoples* (a metanarrative of history if ever there was one!), written in Japanese in 1948–49 and published in English in 1964, can be seen as a reflection of the zeitgeist among scholars. Referring to the entire magical tendencies expressed in shamanic practices in Japan, he writes that "such shamanistic or magical tendencies will, with the diffusion of scientific knowledge, disappear sooner or later. A fuller investigation is required concerning the problem of the post-war growth of heretical religions of this sort."[82]

This comment of Professor Nakamura's is indicative of the construction of a new, postwar vision of a rationalized religious world in Japan. Chief targets for elimination on the grounds that they were "irrational and barbaric" were any rites with shamanic overtones. Professor Nakamura was expressing a cultural tendency of the times, but the success of his work as a whole, which argues throughout for a purer Buddhism than is found in actual practice in Japan, suggests that both the denial and suppression of nonecclesiastical forms of religious expression was a powerful force in postwar Japan. The construction of a new identity in the postwar years demanded a denial of all religious behaviors that did not agree with Japan's new and reformed image as a rational democracy.

This general negative attitude toward ritual practices in the postwar period is noted by Robert J. Smith in his introduction to Yamamoto's study of the Namahage festival:

It seems that during and after the war village officials waged a campaign against the masked visitors of New Year's Eve, urging the people to abandon this supposedly barbaric and childish custom that had no place in wartime Japan or in the new Japan of the post-surrender period. No doubt the ceremony was denounced as a remnant of the feudal past—an epithet routinely directed at any Japanese practice, belief, or custom that anyone wanted to discredit. Although the campaign against the observance was successful, and the villagers were persuaded to give up their festival, it was clear that they remembered it fondly as an occasion when everyone had a good time and no harm was done to anyone.[83]

In short, the renewed "protestantization" of religious life in postwar Japan meant that the intentions, contexts, and styles of kadozuke rituals were no longer deemed worthy of the effort needed to maintain them.

There is an irony in these campaigns to wipe out seasonal rituals with shamanic overtones such as kadozuke puppetry rites. Less than forty years later, the very activities which were discouraged and even flatly outlawed are now being reclaimed as part of an "authentic religious past" and "folkways." In the last chapter of this book, I shall show how the Awaji people's decision to revive their past—and embrace their very otherness as evidence that they are "truly Japanese"—created an unusual mixture of nostalgia, guilt, and healing.

3

A Crippled Deity, a Priest, and a Puppet: *Kugutsu* and *Ebisu-kaki* of the Nishinomiya Shrine

A Fragmented History

In this chapter, we turn to a discussion of the early puppeteers in Japan commonly called *kugutsu*, and examine the fragmented evidence from the Heian period through early Tokugawa describing their activities. This term is the earliest in Japanese which specifically refers to manipulated dolls, as opposed to static ritual objects such as the examples of various kinds of ningyō discussed in chapter 1.

Ideally, a history of these ritual puppeteers could begin in the early period of state formation in Japan and unravel as a rich narrative spanning nearly fifteen hundred years, linking up the scattered references to kugutsu into one long story and showing in exhaustive detail the ritual roles they played for the state, for villages and collective concerns, and for individuals. In such an idealized history, we would know people's names and be able to document how they interacted, and we would have detailed descriptions of the puppets and their ritual uses.

Sadly, references to ritual puppeteers are usually made in passing and seemingly refer to something so commonplace that a description is seen as unnecessary. We have many examples of puppets but few records of the people who manipulated them or what they did with them when they "made them dance." Passing references, vignettes in poetry and song, brief mentions in journals and travelogues—these tell us little. Like many marginalized groups in Japanese history, puppeteers have not always been recorded or remembered. Ritual puppetry has suffered from being at once too commonplace and too marginal to gain the attention of historiographers.

Having only fragmented evidence in the history of religions is not an uncommon predicament. The work of an historian of religions is not unlike that of an archaeologist trying to excavate the past. Sometimes one finds a whole pot, but sometimes one recovers only shards, which may possibly reveal a pattern or a motif but are fractured nevertheless. Usually there is a mixture of both. But we must resist the tendency to assume that the fragmented evidence accurately depicts a world. I am reminded of a cartoon I once saw. The caption was something like "A British schoolboy imagines ancient Greece and Rome," and in the cartoon, people were walking round with incomplete torsos—the odd arm, leg, or head missing—conducting their business in incomplete buildings.

I must admit that the evidence for a history of ritual puppetry is fragmented. What are we to do with the shattered bits of clay that we have? We can only hope that they may give hints of a much more complex reality of which they are remnants. As Jonathan Z. Smith wrote, "The historian in his work detects clues, symptoms, exemplars. He provides us with hints that remain too fragile to bear the burden of being solutions."[1] So it is with much of the evidence in the study of ritual puppetry. They give hints and clues but do not yield a fluent narrative, perhaps because one never existed in the first place. Fragments may be able to whisper stories to us, but are too often silenced by the larger, more fluid, constructed narratives of metahistories which give us the false impression of seamlessness.

A study of ritual puppetry must try and make sense out of these fragmented pieces, fitting them end to end, trying to find which pieces make sense together and are most likely to yield some understanding of puppetry in Japanese religious life. We must resist the temptation to make ritual puppetry in Japan into one single story, for the evidence in chapter 1 demonstrated that there are numerous sources for the ritual use of effigies and dolls in Japan, and many of these religious and magical ideas clearly continued to influence one another throughout Japanese history. Nowhere is the hermeneutical axiom that "all history is interpretation" ever more clearly evidenced. Nevertheless, the religious and performance idioms of ritual puppetry reveal a great deal about Japanese religious life and performance. In this chapter, I present and interpret some fragments of evidence, and I try to understand the forces that led to fragmentation.

Although ritual puppetry was widespread throughout Japanese religious history, the status of puppeteers has fluctuated between respect and esteem and the perception that puppeteers are, because of the nature of the work they do, *hinin* (nonhuman). In documents relating to kugutsu, we can see evidence—sometimes faint and obscured—of the signification of puppeteers as outcasts. The occupation of puppeteers in religious rites for deities, especially Ebisu, has a direct bearing on how they were perceived and treated at different times in Japanese history.

Our discussion begins in the late Nara period (based on Heian and Kamakura period sources) with the earliest sources describing puppeteers. First we look at the role of ritual puppeteers in a decisive battle (at least from a mythical perspective) in early Japanese history, the defeat of the Hayato by the centralized government in the early eighth century. Next, Ōe Masafusa's often cited twelfth-century source, *Kairaishi-ki*, provides us with evidence of how puppeteers were imagined in Japanese literary discourses of "otherness." The process of depicting these people as exotic and exaggerating their nomadic lifestyle served to define Japanese notions of "the good people" (*ryōmin*).[2] Next, we explore the evidence from the Nishinomiya Ebisu shrine, the center where kugutsu groups began to congregate during the medieval period.

Magicians in Battle: The Usa Shrine and the Hayato Rebellion of 720

In the early eighth century, the centralized government of Japan was involved in an ongoing struggle to secure a stronghold on the major island of Kyushu. One of the problems in the government's campaign for hegemony was a strong tribal resistance particularly among the Hayato tribes of the Ōsumi and Hyōga Districts. According to sources from the Usa Hachiman shrine in what is now Oita Prefecture, in 720 a major military effort was launched to bring these tribes into submission, and the Usa Hachiman shrine played an important role in this campaign. Sources from the shrine tell of battles being led by "warrior priests" from the shrine who, in the name of Hachiman, sought the subjugation (and even annihilation) of the Hayato. Shrine records tell us that the Hayato were "subjugated" through a violent and protracted battle. Because of its role in this important campaign (along with the famous Usa Hachiman oracles, which stabilized the imperial line by dictating that only members of the imperial family could ascend the throne), the Usa center began to rise in power.

Of interest for our discussion is the role of magician shamans using puppets in the battle. A key source, from the Usa Hachiman shrine *Usa Hachimangū Hōjō-e Engi*, tells us that during the battle the Hayato sequestered themselves in seven castles, and it was not possible to break through their defenses until ritual magicians using puppeteers from the Usa shrine staged a puppet performance on the walls of the castles. The Hayato inside became so enamored with the performances that they let their guard down and were successfully attacked. In the words of the text, "They also made little male puppets dance. The puppet performance was so interesting that the Hayato forgot about their hostilities and came out of the castle to see the performance. They all surrendered and were subjugated."[3]

According to this tradition, then, ritual puppetry played a part in the subjugation of the Hayato. It is possible to interpret these Usa shrine materials as later glosses on an event that happened during Yōrō (717–724). Given that such ritual magic was commonplace in early Japanese battle, however, it seems likely that these texts reflect some degree of historical fact. For our purposes, what is most important is not whether or not puppets were actually used, but rather the conviction, mentioned time and again in these sources, that ritual puppetry was powerful enough to bring an entire tribe of separatists unwittingly and magically into submission. Ritual puppetry, far from being trivial or despised, was regarded as an extremely powerful force. Presenting puppetry in this light was part of the emerging tradition of ritual performance at Usa.

The Hachiman cult, although clearly a strategic ritual outpost for the Yamato state, created its own set of ideological problems for the government when it was used to legitimate violence. Hachiman was by this time already a major figure in amalgamated Shinto (or at this time, "proto-Shintō") and Buddhist practice and doctrine, so the fact that the center was involved in an outright slaughter created a discrepancy between Hachiman as a deity protecting the nation and Hachiman as a bodhisattva. Usa sources claim that Hachiman was the reincarnation of Emperor Ōjin and that Hachiman had been tonsured, become a bodhisattva, and was practicing austerities in the Kunisaki region of Kyushu. Put simply, the question is how can a bodhisattva condone and even legitimate slaughter? What happened after the battle is of even deeper interest for a study of Japanese puppetry. Following the defeat of the Hayato, Usa sources claim, an epidemic raged in the area of Kyushu.[4] Attributing this epidemic to the malevolent spirits of the defeated Hayato, priests of the Usa Hachiman shrine began an appeasement rite based on oracles and revelations from the deity Hachiman himself. In this rite, puppeteers were again active. They ritually reenacted the battle and performed a sacred dance and stylized sumo match in which major Japanese deities battled one another. This was intended as entertainment for the souls of the defeated Hayato.

A Hōjō-e (literally, "Rite for the release of sentient beings") is primarily a Buddhist rite, but in this context it shows signs of being more of an appeasement rite. In the rite, puppetry again plays a central role, but this time as a reenactment of the original events. It appears that the emperor, when invited to travel down to the region to get a better understanding of what happened, heard how the puppeteers had played a role in the Hayato defeat. He wanted that reenactment to be a part of the ritual appeasement. Its purpose, I would maintain, was to legitimate the centralized government and to consolidate its ritual relationship with the Hachiman center. Acting out that alliance was at one level the work of ritual puppeteers. Again, the *Usa Hachimangū Hōjō-e Engi*:

> In the next year, in the reign of Shōmu in the first year of Jinki [724 C.E.], there was an oracle: "I, the god, as the retribution for killing many of the Hayato, on separate years will do a Hōjō-e. To lead the dead spirits to nirvana, and for

repentance of our sins, we do the Hōjō-e." So, following this oracle, in the reign of Emperor Shōmu in Tempyō 16 [745] on the fifteenth day of the eighth month, the emperor gave the official tablet and for the first time the Hōjō-e was performed. (Actually, it was first performed following an oracle in the first year of Jinki, twenty one years before.)[5] Even though the great bodhisattva [Hachiman] kills countless people, because he has an enlightened status, and does good, there is a lot of merit in his killing. The internal proof is that no ray is hidden, each gets brighter and brighter and there is no hiding the bright light [presumably a reference to Hachiman again].

As a result of that oracle they began to perform *Hōjō-e* in all the provinces. When the emperor journeyed to Wamahama from the temporary palace to the floating palace, and he learned how the ritual performers had performed when they attacked the Hayato, *he had them reenact those performances*. So that is why in the rite, various dances—dragon's head, bird's head, lions, puppets, etc., are presented. The performers go out to the front of the floating shrine and present music and dances. Everything is done just as it was in the ancient times [i.e., when the *hōshi* performed to distract the Hayato]. As for the Hayato, they are released as snails under the floating worship hall.

The case of the Usa Hachiman Hōjō-e provides two examples of the ritual use of puppets: First, it presents a case (possibly mythical) in which ritual puppeteers use their magic to assist in battle itself. Such cases are not uncommon in early Japanese history.[6] It has been argued by a number of Japanese archaeologists that ritual specialists worked in battles with the Yamato military campaigns in the early stages of "state formation" in Japan.[7] Magicians, including those using puppets, were commonly employed in battle to strengthen warriors or to fascinate, control, and confuse the enemy.[8] Ritual performers also helped legitimate the central government by performing purification and land-calming rituals. This text suggests that the magicians were Shūgendō practitioners from the Kyushu center on Mt. Hiko, a center with strong ties to the Usa ceremonial complex.

Puppeteers still participate in the Hōjō-e rite held every four years in a revived "traditional folk performing art" that has been resuscitated in the last decade. Puppeteers from two subsidiary shrines, Koyō and Kohyō, presented the puppetry ritual until the turn of the century. There are no records indicating how early these two centers came to be affiliated with the Usa center as ritual centers. It seems possible, however, that their ritual specialization in puppetry may date from the Nara period around the time of the Hayato Rebellion.

This case is strong evidence that puppeteers were held in high regard and were used as ritual magicians in military campaigns. It also indicates that the role of ritual puppeteers in appeasement rites was considered im-

portant enough to merit their inclusion in Japan's oldest Hōjō-e, the Usa
Hachimangū Hōjō-e. During this early period, puppeteers were equated
with powers capable of controlling enemies in battle, sacred forces, and
even epidemic spirits.

A number of scholars, including Suzuka Chiyono, have looked to the
Usa Hachiman case and the puppets of the Koyō and Kohyō shrines as an
origin of the late Heian and medieval kugutsu groups. There is clearly a
relationship between the spread of Hachiman worship throughout the
Inland Sea during the early Heian period and the proliferation of religious
rites with puppets as a medium. Ebisu rites, examined in detail in chapter
5, most likely have strong ties to the early Hachiman cult. Ebisu is a maritime deity, and it is possible that the worship of this deity was incorporated into the Usa complex when confederated tribes formed the power
base in the Buzen region in the protohistorical period. One of the hereditary lines in the Usa center, the Usa clan, was thought to have been originally made up of maritime peoples, called by the generic term *ama* (sea
people). Perhaps the attributes of the deity we now know as Ebisu were
absorbed from their religious tradition.[9] Our concern here, however, is
not to unravel this impossible question of origins. Not only is such an
inquiry impossible to prove, but determining the origins of ritual puppeteers in medieval Japan does not go far toward accounting for their significance and role in society. Our question is of an entirely different nature:
we are concerned with how the valuation of puppeteers in society changed
over time, how puppeteers have had traditions of meaning ascribed to
them in Japanese history, how they have struggled to name traditions for
themselves, what puppeteers are said to have done, and what the scanty
historical evidence shows.

Heian Period Puppetry: Sources and Meanings

As we noted in the opening chapter of this work, the practice of using
hitogata, or body substitutes, to represent an individual for purposes of
purification was a widespread phenomenon during the early Heian period. Here, we will look at a later development in the history of Japanese
uses of the represented human form, the kugutsu groups. These people
manipulated effigies to create the illusion that they were coming alive,
rather than regarding them as static ritual objects.

Before looking at one of the key texts thought to describe the early
activities of puppeteers, let us consider the term *kugutsu* and its possible
derivations. The first appearance of the word is in a gloss on a Chinese
Buddhist text in the eighth century. Interpretations the word's meaning

and significance for understanding the origins of Japanese puppetry are basically of two types: the nativist theory, which insists on the uniqueness of Japanese puppetry, and the foreign origin theory, which seeks to locate the origins of Japanese puppetry abroad.[10] Many scholars suggest that the characters used to write this word were attached to an indigenous word pronounced "kugutsu," and the key to understanding the history of kugutsu can be found by looking at the derivation of this pronunciation. Representative of this approach is the work of Origuchi Shinobu, whose theories maintain a nativist interpretation.

According to Origuchi, *kugutsu* originally referred to a kind of basket called *kugu* carried by the early sea people (*amazoku*) to collect seaweed and shellfish. Sacred specialists would carry their puppets in these same baskets when they presented their performances describing the events of deities. Later the word for these baskets came to be attached to the puppets. These puppets were, according to Origuchi, sacred vehicles or residences for the deities (*goshintai*) of these amazoku.[11] This theory seems to have no evidence to support it, save the desire to construct a grand narrative that would account for the amazoku as a "lost tribe."[12]

A contrasting interpretive strategy suggests foreign origins and argues that the etymology of the word can be traced as far as Greece, suggesting diffusion not only for the practice of puppetry but for the very word *kugutsu* as well. Tsunoda, perhaps the most widely used and least cited scholar writing on Japanese puppetry, has pointed out the similarity between the words for puppet and puppeteer in China and Eastern Europe. In China, the word for puppet is pronounced *kuirui*, and the word for puppetry is *kuorong*, or *kuotu*. Among the "gypsies" the word for puppet is *kuki* or *kukli*, puppet theater is *kukiengēro* or *khēlēpen*, and puppeteer is *kukienrengēro* or *khēlēpaskēro*.[13] Compared with the Japanese word *kugutsu*, this seems evidence enough to suggest some Altaic contact in this word derivation. Donald Keene, probably basing his discussion on Tsunoda, argues this:

> The earliest Japanese name for "puppet" was *kugutsu*, a word found in an eighth-century gloss on a Chinese Buddhist text. This mysterious name has intrigued scholars for centuries; it has variously been traced to a Chinese word for puppet, pronounced approximately *kuai-luai-tzu* in the same period, or to *kuki* or *kukli*, gypsy words which some claim were probably the origin of both Chinese and Japanese terms. The Turkish *kukla*, and the late Greek *koukla* have also been cited as proof of the transmission of the art of puppetry from Asia Minor across the vast Central Asian regions to China, Korea, and eventually Japan. . . . The possibility of foreign origins is intriguing, but the evidence is by no means conclusive.[14]

One small problem has to do with what part of the word means puppet. In some sources, *kugutsu* is used to refer to puppet, while *kugutsu-mawashi* (one who makes puppets dance) is used to refer to puppeteer. In other sources, *kugutsu* means both puppet and puppeteer.

Regardless of the conclusions which could be drawn from inquiries of this sort, such philological research is not without its problems, for it is easy to invent linguistic evidence to support a theory. Beyond raising the possibility of a foreign influence on Japanese puppetry expressed in etymology, it seems futile to argue the point further. Perhaps it is best to play it safe, along with Keene, and avoid a nativist quagmire. He writes what should be the last word on this matter: "The early history of Japanese puppetry might be interpreted entirely in terms of a spontaneous, native development, but probably continental influence was present even in the earliest stages."[15]

Although the term *kugutsu* (and the characters with which it is written) referred to puppetry throughout the Heian period, it frequently referred to traveling women who were entertainers and frequently prostitutes.[16] Consequently, we can not assume that every time we see this term that it is a reference to puppeteers. It does seem that many of these women were involved with itinerant performers of some sort and were themselves itinerant. Six verses about kugutsu dating from the mid-twelfth century (exactly when Ōe Masafusa was writing his text) explored the lives of these women. Only his one text, *Kairaishi-ki*, mentions puppets specifically, however.

By the late Heian period, perhaps because of the popularity of this text (to be discussed shortly), *kugutsu* became the common word for a wandering puppeteer. Just what these wandering performers did and just how they lived is greatly open to question. We have no reliable textual evidence describing the lives or activities of these marginal people. Scholars have tended to build an edifice based on one eleventh-century text, to which we now turn.

Ōe no Masafusa and the Signification of Otherness

The eleventh-century court scholar Ōe no Masafusa (1041–1111) wrote a brief description of the kugutsu groups of his day, called *Kairaishi-ki* (also pronounced "Kugutsu no Ki," alternate readings for the same characters).[17] The document, thought to be dated about 1070, is a mere 320 characters in length, yet is perhaps the source that Japanese scholars cite most often when describing the history of itinerant performance and puppetry in Japan. Here is my translation of the text:

Kairaishi-ki (Kugutsu no Ki)

("A Record of the *Kugutsu*")

The kugutsu are those who have no fixed abodes, no proper homes. They pitch their rug tents under the sky, following water and grass, rather like the customs of the northern barbarians [of China].

As for the men, they all use arrows and horses to hunt game. Some juggle two swords or seven or balls or make peachwood puppets wrestle. They can make it look as if the puppets were live human beings. These performances come close to those of the Chinese transformation artists.[18] They can change sand and stones into gold coins, and grasses and wood into birds and beasts, (dazzling)[19] people's eyes.

As for the women, they make up their eyebrows to appear sad and grievous. They wiggle their hips when they walk, flash devilish teeth when they smile, and use vermilion powder on their cheeks. They act and sing of licentious pleasures, and lure you with their sorcery and magic. Their fathers, mothers, and husbands know this and do not admonish them, yet help them in their meetings with travelers. The travelers do not hate to spend a night in beautiful union with them. If they find the women's charms agreeable, they give them lots of money, clothes sewn of brocade fabric, gold ornamental hairpins and lacquered boxes. There is no one who would not accept this as worth cherishing.

They do not cultivate a single section of land, nor gather a single branch of mulberry.[20] Consequently, they have no connections with the government and are all landless people. They are strictly drifters. Moreover, they do not know who the sovereign is. The emperor does not know of them either, and they enjoy an entire life of not being taxed. At night, they worship a lot of deities[21] with drumming and dancing and a great deal of boisterousness. They pray to a large-headed male doll for good luck.[22]

In the eastern provinces, their groups are very powerful and daring around Mino, Mikawa, and Tōtōmi. In the south of the mountains (in Sanyō) Harima and along to the west of the mountains (in San'in) Tajima bands are next and the Saikai bands are regarded as lowest.

Some of the known women among them are: Komi, Nichihyaku, San'zensai Manzai, Kogimi, Magogimi, etc. [23] They kick up the dust when they sing, and all the noise they make permeates the rafters. The listeners soak the very tassels of their hats and are unable to calm themselves. Imayō, Furukawayō,[24] Ashigara, Kata-oroshi, Saibara, Kurotoriko, rice planting songs,[25] sacred songs,[26] boatmen's songs[27] roadside songs,[28] mikata, folk songs,[29] magical Buddhist chants[30]—It isn't possible to list all the methods they use.

The kugutsu are one of the things under heaven. How could one not be moved by them?

Uses of Kairaishi-ki *by Japanese Scholars*

This text has been used in two ways. Most scholars of ritual performance and folk performing arts in both Japan and the West use this document as a reliable historical record describing the puppeteers of the Heian period (even though the text was using the term *kugutsu* in a much looser way, referring also to female performers). They allow for a "coherent" moment in the history of ritual puppetry that looks just like what Ōe no Masafusa wrote. The skimpy descriptions of the puppeteers in the text are read as ethnographic accounts, usually with little suspicion as to any other agenda the author may have had in mind when preparing the piece or how this text may have participated in a wider discourse. This optimistic and naive use of this text is probably due to the dearth of other reliable sources, and most scholars turn to this short piece with relief after expressing their lament that other sources are not available. Often scholars mention *Kairaishi-ki* in passing as a source for more information in discussions that shortchange early puppetry altogether. Inoura and Kawatake, for example, simply mention in their two pages on "The Origin and Development of Puppeteering" that "accounts of [puppeteers'] manner of living are to be found in a late eleventh-century document, *Kairaishi-ki* or *Kugutsu-mawashi no Ki*, written by Ōe no Masafusa."[31] Hayashiya Tatsusaburō, in his *Chūsei Geinōshi no Kenkyū*, is representative of this approach to the text: "As performance artists of the late ancient period, it is truly the *kugutsu* who show an extremely unique existence. And, fortunately, we have the work of Ōe Masafusa, *Kairaishi-ki, concretely describing the lifestyle of these people*."[32] Hayashiya's next several pages discuss each section of the short text and summarize the historical realities expressed, raising no suspicions about the reliability of the content.

To see where we would end up were we to accept the methodology of Hayashiya and other folk performing arts scholars, let us consider a reference in the text that Hayashiya does not discuss: Ōe no Masafusa's reference to "the Chinese transformation artists" (*yulong manyan zhixi*). Ōe tells us that the kugutsu greatly resemble these artists of Han China. What did these artists actually do? According to Wu Hung, a Chinese art historian, their performances "began with one actor dressed as a lynx, dancing in a courtyard. When the lynx reached the front of the palace it jumped into a pool and transformed itself into a flounder. Clouds burst from the mouth of the fish, obscuring the sun. By the time the clouds had dispersed, the fish had changed into a dancing yellow dragon eighty feet long, whose scales gleamed and flashed more brightly than the sunlight."[33] All this, and in Japan, with peachwood puppets! Exciting stuff, to be sure, but if we read this text literally, we would have to wonder why such great theater is not mentioned elsewhere in Japanese records. This is but one example of why Ōe no Masafusa's references cannot be taken at face value, however tempting it may be to imagine feline-fish-dragon transmutations in ancient Japanese performances. Hayashiya's interpretation must be attributed to the desperation and wishful thinking that a dearth of sources may provoke in a researcher.

On the other hand, we have those scholars, mostly Japanese, who raise objections to what are regarded not as ideological uses of poetic license but rather as errors of fact introduced by Ōe no Masafusa. Scholars using this line of interpretation point to two types of errors. First, they contend that the author relied too heavily on fixed poetic forms and stock phrases from Chinese histories of the period, in part to show his familiarity with these literary traditions and in part to play insider word games with his equally savvy audience (much the way we scholars today sprinkle our prose with French terms or references to current theories to show that we are both clever and part of an in-group). Ōe no Masafusa appears to have borrowed heavily from a motif of the "wandering nomad" in Chinese ethnographic poetry. Some of the lines in the text are lifted directly from popular Chinese chronicles and may not accurately describe eleventh-century Japanese realities. As Tsunoda Ichirō has noted, at least one motif in the text is taken directly from Chinese texts: the reference to "people without fixed abodes following grass and water." This exact same reference occurs a number of times in popular Chinese texts—the *Sui Shu* and the *Hou Han Shu*—with which Ōe was undoubtedly familiar.[34] Yamaji Kōzō raises this objection: "In summary, the text describes a group of itinerant performers. But, in this text, there is the influence of Chinese poetry, and thus it cannot be thought of as a simple description of the realities of the *kugutsu* as they really were."[35]

Donald Keene has also raised this concern, following such Japanese scholars as Tsunoda: "No other record indicates the existence of such nomads in Japan, and some scholars have therefore asserted that Ōe Masafusa merely used stock phraseology borrowed from Chinese accounts of foreign tribes to decorate his brief account of the puppeteers. Undoubtedly the choice of words was influenced by Chinese examples, but we cannot disregard Ōe's general implication that the puppeteers led lives so unlike those of the sedentary Japanese that they were taken for foreigners."[36]

The second type of error of fact scholars point out concerns the relationship of the kugutsu groups to government forces. The text, the reader will recall, claims that kugutsu do not cultivate land or gather mulberry, that they have no connections with the government, and are untaxed landless drifters unaware of who the sovereign is. Yamaji Kōzō argues against these lines of the text, pointing out Ōe's poetic license. "Even if there were groups of *kugutsu* who did not follow the existing tax laws, those were the *kugutsu* of a period prior to the late Heian (i.e., when the text was written)."[37] He backs this up with sources from the same period. Several documents from around the twelfth century show kugutsu groups in litigation over labor and tax disputes. In Fujiwara no Munetada's document *Chūyūki* (which spans the period from 1032–1114) from Eikyū 2, (1114), there is a lawsuit dated the sixth day of the fourth month in which a *kugutsu-shi* had taken horses and cotton from some conscripted shrine servants (*kodoneri*). Further, the diary *Meigetsuki*, dated 1121, describes kugutsu being brought to trial for disturbing the peace. In both of these cases, Yamaji points out, they requested what amounts to some sort of legal council or were within the jurisdiction of the law. This pattern seemed to continue, since as late as 1249, on the twenty third of the seventh month, there was a lawsuit against Minamoto no Yoritomo by the kugutsu concerning conscripted labor or taxes for a ceremony. The case was brought before the Kamakura government. The kugutsu won the litigation.[38] While these exceptions to Ōe's description do not commend the kugutsu as the most neighborly sort, they do raise a question about the text's insistence on the legal liminality of the kugutsu groups. It is not entirely possible to say that they had no access whatsoever to the legal system at the time, that they did not appeal to it when necessary, and that they were quite apart from established authority.

This second way of dealing with the text, namely, calling its flights of fancy and "facts" into question, leads us to wonder if these scholars would suggest that other areas of the text can be used as they stand. Can we trust descriptions of the performances? Were their puppets really made of peachwood? Are his discussions of the coquetry of the women reliable? Is it safe to assume his lists of performances and places of residence he assigns to these people are factual? These two strains of scholarship on this text, one bordering on blind historicism and the other, arguing at the level of factual error on two counts, leave us with two options: either we use the text as a reliable description of the kugutsu or we pick from it the data that we want to use. Both seem to be based on an assumed translucence of the text as a historical document, something it probably was never intended to be.

A Third Alternative: Ōe no Masafusa's Signification of Otherness

I propose a third way to read this text. While Ōe's poem had to have enough basis in a recognizable reality to catch people's attention, it is best read as a piece of fanciful "exotica." I suggest that this text created a discourse that cast the itinerant puppeteer as Other in the Japanese imagination, and in so doing helped to define the meaning of being mainstream

Japanese. The reader will recall how the ships of fools of medieval Europe were embellished in literary reference. Such texts should be read not as reliable descriptions of the treatment of the insane in Europe at the time but rather as reflections of how these marginal people were appropriated by dominant discourses of identity. Our reading of the kugutsu text should therefore not simply ask, "Is it factual?" but rather, "How did it participate in the marginalization of these people in subsequent Japanese history and what purposes did it serve?" All texts, in some way or another, are highly constructed descriptions of phenomena, and one must bring the usual "hermeneutics of suspicion" to bear on them. This case is no exception. The specific of this text reconfirm our view that it is not simply an ethnographic description of a particular strain of the Japanese performing arts. What then is this text all about?

This short 320-character text creates a fantastic world of beautiful, seductive women, who exert power over the men who happen upon them, and virile, horse-riding, bow-and-arrow-wielding men, "noble savages" who command the powerful transformation of matter using wooden puppets. Perhaps Ōe's kugutsu tell us more about what a noble court scholar (such as Ōe) was *not* (and perhaps what he secretly at times wished he could be) than what a puppeteer was. This pattern of *signifying otherness* seems to be an important dynamic in the movement toward the social discrimination that kugutsu groups suffered later.

Ōe seems intent on impressing his eleventh-century readers with the following features of the kugutsu's otherness. They are not agrarian but resemble hunters and gatherers. They entertain themselves with exotic, shamanic types of entertainment using peachwood puppets, which indicate a connection with spiritual forces. Both the men and the women, in different ways, are able to enact strange transformations and weave webs of mystery and fantasy that entrap people who come into contact with them—the men through performances with puppets, the women through songs and overt sexuality. Their families do not follow established moral codes of behavior as regards the proper activities of daughters and wives. They are outside the law and have no responsibilities to the government. Lastly, they live in out-of-the-way places scattered along the water and land routes of Japan. Everything about them suggests the margins of society.

"What is special about peachwood?" the reader may ask. Scholars of ritual puppetry in Japan are always looking for peachwood puppets. When I traveled in Japan doing research and looking at lots of different puppets, I was incessantly asked, "Have you found any puppets made out of peachwood?" Behind this question, it seems to me, is the desire to find the validation of Ōe no Masafusa's description, almost so that we can breath a sigh of relief that in fact this text can be used as evidence *sans* interpretation of its intentions. Peachwood, as we know, was a wood used in ancient China in purification rites; this use of peachwood was introduced into Japan in the Nara period and is recorded in *Engi-shiki*. Book 16, item 8 lists peachwood staffs as a requisite substance for the Na festival of driving out noxious vapors from the country.[39] The English translator of this text, Felicia Bock, notes that "the bows and staffs of peachwood demonstrates the Chinese belief in the efficacy of the wood of the peach tree for warding off evil."[40] I have yet to come across a peachwood puppet in my research, and although this lack of evidence may simply mean that no puppets from the Heian period have survived, it is also possible that they were never made of peachwood in the first place. Issues such as choice of wood are likely to remain fairly consistent among artisans, and we would expect to find some puppet heads made of peachwood had this been a significant feature of the puppets. It is possible that Ōe no Masafusa was familiar with the association of peachwood with divination and purification, and mentioned it to add mystery and otherness to his description.[41]

If this text was on one level part of a genre of fantastic literature, something like Ripley's Believe It or Not, what was its purpose? It calls to mind the stories out of the urban legends genres, which tell of fast women and wild men who usually meet terrifying ends. While this text spares the terrifying ends, it could be read on another level with attention to two dominant features of the text. In one sense the text can serve as a mirror held up to polite Japanese society. It can be read somewhat loosely as a "what nice people (*ryōmin*) don't do" sort of text. I propose that a playful, subtext in mirror opposite of the *Kairaishi-ki* might look something like this:

> The ryōmin are those who have fixed abodes, proper homes. They sleep under roofs, stay where their crops and jobs are, and are decidedly unlike northern barbarians.
>
> As for the men, they use *soroban* and brushes to write out accounts and literature. Their activities involve no slight of hand, no tricks. They dazzle no one with their activities. (They are honest, hardworking people.)
>
> The women do not overly alter their appearance with makeup. They walk in a polite manner and cover their mouths when they smile. They discuss polite matters, and their fathers and mothers are aware of what they do. They don't spend the night with strangers and never receive extravagant gifts from men. This is the normal way things go.
>
> Ryōmin work the land and grow silkworms for cloth. They have connections with the government and are tied to the land. They stay put. They know who the sovereign is, and the emperor is aware of their existence. They pay their taxes. They worship their deities in orderly rites. Their deities are decidedly

not phallic. They live in populated areas with arable land and avoid out-of-the-way places and passageways. They do not live in the mountains.

Well-known ryōmin women don't drive men to distraction and frenzy with singing and dancing. They use well-known and suitable methods to attract their men.

Ryōmin are one of the things under heaven. They may not move anyone, but aren't you glad you're not a kugutsu?

By offering this text with tongue in cheek, I am suggesting that the original be read as fantasy, based only in part on perceptions of what itinerant performers, puppeteers, singers, and prostitutes may have been doing in the eleventh century. The *Kairaishi-ki* text serves to reinforce the status quo, and even create a reality, by carefully describing everything a literate person reading the text is not. As Keene has pointed out, there are no other texts from the period describing such nomadic groups in Japan. And we certainly do not have references to anything as exciting as peachwood puppets enacting the kinds of transformation presented by such Chinese artists as the *yulong manyan zhiyi*. Based upon this short text, however, all subsequent scholarship on itinerant puppetry in Japan has maintained the existence of these distinct performing groups as a single tradition, moving about the margins of Japanese society. Scholars have looked for confirmations of Ōe's description, and when the sources have not surfaced, have stuck by their text.

It would be going too far to say that Ōe no Masafusa imagined the very existence of these performers. Their existence is not a question of debate. Having confronted the dearth of medieval sources myself (and been tempted by the promising title of Ōe's text as well), however, it is clear to me that the really interesting area of inquiry regarding this text is how it has commanded such prestige as a document. The text came to have ideological clout in later Japanese discourses of alterity. The word *kugutsu*, rather than merely referring to a person who manipulated puppets, came to mean a person who fit the description in Ōe no Masafusa's text. Ritual puppeteers, who in fact performed a large number of different functions and who most likely lived a variety of lifestyles, came to be thought of as a distinct group. They had been named, and they had become a tribe. In short, in this text we see the beginnings of the invention of the Other—in this case itinerant performers—in Japanese history. What at first appears to be a clever word game mixing observation of prostitutes, descriptions from Chinese ethnohistories of wandering nomads and transformation artists, and references playing on word titles from current works in Japanese literature at the time, in the end becomes the launching of a discourse about marginality.

Kairaishi-ki *and the Bodies of Medieval Itinerant Women*

Another important aspect of this text is its reference to the bodies of women, which takes up more than two thirds of the piece. Women make up their eyebrows, wiggle their hips, flash their teeth, put rouge on their cheeks, and accept fancy clothes from men in exchange for sexual favors. All this is hardly unique: the text might as well be describing a prostitute from Colorado Boulevard in Denver or Sannomiya in Kōbe. The text offers little information about the women beyond these standard (and, it would seem, timeless) images of "bad girls." The text is grammatically divided into two parallel (though unequal) parts, one about men and one about women. Unlike the men, who weave their magic with puppet bodies, these women weave their magic with bodies that are their own—or perhaps created for them by Ōe no Masafusa.

This process of signification calls to mind an expression "signifying is worse than lying," used by Charles H. Long in the introduction to his *Significations: Signs, Symbols and Images in the Interpretation of Religion.* Long, an Afro-American who grew up in Little Rock, Arkansas, writes,

> From the colloquial and slang expressions of my youth I learned something about the forms of linguistic expression. Signifying is worse than lying because it obscures and obfuscates a discourse without taking responsibility for so doing. This verbal misdirection parallels the real argument but gains its power of meaning from the structure of the discourse itself without the signification being subjected to the rules of the discourse. As a matter of fact, the signifier may speak in agreement with a point of view, while the tone of voice creates doubt in the very act and words of agreement. Or the signifier may simply add comments that move the conversation in another direction. Or the signifier will simply say a word or make a comment that has nothing to do with the context of the discourse, but immediately the conversation must be formulated at another level because of that word or phrase. Signifying is a very clever language game, and one has to be adept in the verbal arts either to signify or to keep from being signified upon.[42]

Clearly, Ōe no Masafusa was adept in the verbal arts and was "signifying upon" kugutsu for reasons that probably had as much to do with poetry as a game as anything else. His introduction of Chinese phrases, his exaggeration of the itinerancy of these people, and even his plays on words and character compounds with references to Japanese poetry (such as *Ryōjin Hishō*), suggest he was creating a clever game. Most likely his contemporary readership knew and appreciated this. If we use a dialogical approach to the relationship between Ōe no Masafusa, aristocratic society in Japan (the audience for his text), and the actual people he may have encountered who manipulated puppets and sang and danced for audiences, we see a clear example of signification for all subsequent itinerant puppeteers and female performers. Who they are, what they do, and how they behave and relate to established authority has been writ in stone by a court poet, without any contribution from the people themselves. These performers now have a name, and the text clearly is written grammatically as a poetic *definition* (or, to use Long's expression, a signification) opening with the words, "The kugutsu are those who . . ." and closing with "The kugutsu are one of the things under heaven."

By looking at this text in this manner, we can account for a number of puzzling facts of the historical record. First of all, why do we not see more references to bands of kugutsu roaming the countryside? It would seem that such groups would have left more than the few passing references to puppeteers that occur in the historical record. Second, why do we begin to see a radical shift in the social status of itinerant puppeteers from the late Heian period on? The answers to these questions can be found, at least in part, not in gaps in the historical record but in the process of signification in which this celebrated text clearly participates. Ōe created a reality, and subsequent to this text, all itinerant puppeteers were regarded with a preset and defined conception: itinerant puppeteer = Ōe no Masafusa's definitive description in his text. We find no record of similar groups simply because they did not exist. Consciously or not, at the heart of his signifying process was a description of what it meant to belong to Ōe's class and to be Japanese. As these issues of national identity became more pronounced, so did the need to ostracize those who had already been labeled as being outside this circle of meaning.

At this point in Japanese history, if we admit that at best Ōe's account describes a partial reality (if not a fantasy) of the otherness of the kugutsu, we do not see evidence that these groups were regarded with disdain. On the contrary, the text seems to suggest that they were the object of fantastic curiosity and pleasure, at least to poets and scholars like Ōe no Masafusa. Read as a literary game, it is a fun and clever piece. As history, it is something else entirely. Every time we search through Japanese history asking for confirmations of this text, we have fallen prey to a slight of hand—not that of a puppeteer or a Chinese transformation artist, but that of a scholar who turns men and women into ink and paper, and ink and paper into gold coins.

Subsequent References to *Kugutsu*

After Ōe no Masafusa's text, we have a period of nearly two hundred years before another reference to kugutsu (as puppeteers) appears. The mid-thirteenth-century text *Chiribukuro* (Bag of Dust) merely confirms that kugutsu had ceased to be a source of fascination and were no longer doing performances. The text informs the reader that although once kugutsu-mawashi had done all kinds of entertainment, their women now were no more than prostitutes and the men were employed killing animals.[43]

In the fifteenth century, a reference to *tekugutsu* (written with the characters "hand *kugutsu*") in the diary of Sadafusa (emperor Go-Hanazono's father) mentions that *tekugutsu* came and presented Sarugaku, a popular performance style. The entry is dated the twenty-fifth day of the third month of 1416.[44] C. J. Dunn queries whether this can be taken as a reference to puppets at all, as it may have been a confused reference to *tesarugaku*, meaning Sarugaku by amateurs.

For nearly four hundred years after Ōe no Masafusa's text, we have negligible references to kugutsu. What happened to puppeteers during this time? Perhaps the *Chiribukuro* was right and their descendants were busy eking out other livings. Or perhaps they continued to manipulate puppets, but there were no records. We will never know. But we should not imagine their lives to be as fragmented as the evidence. Nor can we immediately assume that any reference to a kugutsu in the late medieval period implies a continuity of tradition with the late Heian phenomenon.

For studies of the early history of puppetry as dramatic entertainment, one of our best sources of information is the numerous period drawings of puppet performances, often showing detailed views of stages, methods of manipulation, audience responses, and general ambiance.[45] For itinerant puppetry, we have fewer drawings with less detail. But those we do have, scattered throughout various sources from the sixteenth through the eighteenth centuries, give us some information about how itinerant puppeteers worked, for whom and where they performed, what their puppets looked like, and how they manipulated them. Since these were low-ranking performers, we do not know where they came from. They are un-named in the pictures, but many, we can assume, came from the Nishinomiya shrine, a center for puppetry to be discussed in this chapter.

The earliest drawing of an itinerant performer is from a scroll called *Machida-ke kyūzō rakuchū rakugai*, depicting events in the outer parts of the Machida family estate from the first through fifth years of Daiei (1521–25).[46] The hazy picture shows a man holding a small box at waist level in which appear to be four or five small dolls. He wears a straw hat and trousers to his knees, as well as a *haori* of some sort. He appears to be standing on the street.

The next set of references we have is a series of four pictures in a scroll called *Uesugi-ke kyūzō rakugai*, probably drawn in Tenshō 2 (1574).[47] The first drawing shows four people near a gateway to a home. Since all are barefoot, we are to assume they are all performers, since going barefoot indicates low social rank. They appear to be passing through the gate onto a footbridge. The one in front has the lower half of his (her?)

These drawings from a scroll describing activities at the Uesugi estate (probably date 1574) show itinerant puppeteers. Note the location of the performances at a gate and outside a home.

face covered with a veil and bears on his head a box with a small doll protruding from it. The person in the rear in the drawing is possibly a member of the household showing the performers to the street. While we learn little about the puppets in this picture, the attention to the performance context is striking, as the entire picture is framed by the gate. The reader will recall the discussion of gates as performance spaces in the preceding chapter.

The second drawing from this collection underscores this description. It is a side view of two veiled persons with boxes on their heads, in which we see puppets. They are walking in single file on what appears to be a street. The third drawing, also from this collection and quite detailed, shows a crowd of people with children in tow and on their backs, standing outside the entryway of a home. A puppeteer with a box hung in front of him is standing just inside the door of a home in the part of the house that later came to be called a *genkan*. He is performing for two seated people up in the house; his face is not veiled, suggesting that he is from a different tradition of puppetry than those in the previous pictures. The box contains at least two small puppets.[48]

The style of puppet manipulation of this drawing was called *kubi-kake* (hanging from the neck), but the puppeteers were also sometimes called *hako-mawashi*.[49] A fourth drawing from the Uesugi manor scroll also shows veiled performers holding what appear to be puppets on stands in front of them. This drawing clearly indicates that they are performing at the gates of houses, and it appears to be the New Year period because potted pine trees are in front of the gates. Small children are watching on the streets.

The next drawing we have of puppeteers is from a scroll at the Mitsui-ji Enzokuin.[50] The scroll is thought to have been prepared to document a festival commemorating the completion of the rebuilding of the temple Enzokuin in Genna 5 (1619). Of all the drawings considered here, this one shows the most attention to detail and appears to be the work of a highly skilled illustrator. It shows two men holding elaborate stagelike boxes in front of them, clearly working together and manipulating puppets by putting their hands through the back of the box to hold their small dolls. Onlookers include a person carrying a tray of fish, a child, and two samurai. Because the design of the stages closely resemble Noh stages of that time, it is thought that these hako-mawashi were actually doing miniature Noh performances using puppets, suggesting that this may have been one of the many traditions of hako-mawashi that were to be found during the sixteenth and early seventeenth centuries. References in texts at this time referring to "Noh ayatsuri" ("manipulated Noh," *ayatsuri* being a word that came to denote puppet and puppeteer, almost replacing the term *kugutsu*) were probably to this practice.[51]

Another drawing, from an undated text called *Matabee furyūraku zu*, appears to be very similar to the previously discussed drawing, except that it shows puppeteers from the rear.[52] From this drawing we learn that these puppeteers worked as a team, and both have boxes hung around their necks. One box is more elaborate than the other, suggesting that if the Noh theory is correct, perhaps one performer manipulated the main character and the other the minor character. The two puppeteers in this drawing are performing before the window of what appears to be a *fusuma* (papered door) shop, as the materials for spreading the paste are in view. Women are leaning out of a window next door looking on at the performers in the street.

The next drawing from a scroll called *Yoshikawa-ke kyūzō rakuchū rakugai* is also from the early Genna era, and shows two performers (possibly even the same two from the previous drawing).[53] Again they are working as a team, each holding a box and inserting his hands to manipulate tiny puppets through the back. They are standing on the street at the entryway to a home, and women lean out of the house to watch. One of them holds a baby, and a small child also looks on.

One last drawing, from a text called *Konokoro-gusa*, dated Tenna 2 (1682), shows a close-up of a kugutsu-mawashi.[54] He holds a two-tiered box in front of him and is clearly presenting an intricate performance involving a fox. The puppets are at his eye level.

All of these drawings point to a widespread practice of itinerant puppetry, which was apparently becoming more and more popular by the sixteenth century. The pictures make it clear that the kadozuke context was common for the performance of puppetry. Although we get some idea of the kadozuke's appearance and the performance context, it is hard to tell from the pictures what kinds of performances they did and how they were understood. For this information, we have to rely on other kinds of sources. To learn more about these puppeteers, we may examine references to a type of puppetry that gained popularity at this time, Ebisu-kaki.

By the middle of the sixteenth century, we begin to have more reliable textual trickles of information indicating the rise of puppetry. Passing references in court diaries give us little information but confirm that puppetry rites for the deity Ebisu were becoming commonplace. A diary dated Tenbun 24 (1555), the twenty-fifth day of the second month simply states, "An *Ebisu-kaki* came."[55] Another diary from this time of ladies at court called *Oyudono no Ue no Nikki*[56] indicates that performers called *Ebisu-mawashi* or *Ebisu-kaki* would come from time to time to the palace. These brief entries begin in the second year of Kōji (1555) and continue through Tenshō 18 (1590), indicating the seasonal appearance of these Ebisu performers at court.[57] The diary notes that during the New Year

This drawing from Konokoro-gusa, dated 1682 (Tenna 2), shows the new level of intricacy in itinerant puppetry performance.

period of 1590, Ebisu-kaki were coming nearly everyday.[58] Sadly, we get little idea of their performance. Let us turn therefore to the center from which these performers came, the Nishinomiya shrine, and determine their relationship to the deity Ebisu. Examining the nature and development of Ebisu and other information relating to puppeteers from Nishinomiya should provide some idea of the intentions and content of these performances. Since it is from this center that Awaji puppetry eventually developed (and against this center that Awaji puppeteers define themselves), these Ebisu-kaki are an important source for understanding the rise of ritual puppetry on Awaji as well.

Affiliation as Nonecclesiastical Sacred Specialists: *Kugutsu* at the Nishinomiya Shrine

Nishinomiya, located in the present-day city of Nishinomiya in Hyōgo Prefecture between Osaka and Kōbe, has been the center of Ebisu worship from at least the Kamakura period. The original shrine on this site, Hiroda (or Hirota) was included in a list of shrines in *Montoku Jitsuroku* dated

Kashō 3 (850), indicating there has been a shrine on this site since the ninth century.[59]

The significance of the place-name *nishinomiya* (literally "western shrine") is puzzling. It may simply have referred to the fact that this shrine was situated on the road west of the capital. One hypothesis suggests that this shrine is the western counterpart of Ise (the "eastern shrine"), and just as Ise is the shrine of the sun maiden Amaterasu Ō-mikami (*hirume*, literally "sun maiden"), this shrine in Nishinomiya is the worship site for the Leech Child (*hiruko*, translatable also as "sun lad"). It has also been suggested that perhaps this shrine was originally a worship site for the rough spirit manifestation (*ara-mi-tama*) of Amaterasu, while her *nigi-mi-tama* (blessing spirit) is worshipped at Ise.[60] A further interpretation of the place name suggests that this was originally the site of an imperial tomb, and that female shamans capable of communicating with the dead were attached to the original shrine on this site, the Hiroda shrine (which later became a center for women of pleasure and their puppeteer consorts).[61] Speculation on the meaning of *nishinomiya* raises many interesting theories, none of which in the end can be proven.[62]

Sometime after the twelfth century (though no clear dates are available) a Sanjo district developed at the Nishinomiya site. In his definitive work on the early history of the Nishinomiya kugutsu, Yoshii Tarō (a hereditary priest from the Nishinomiya shrine) writes that this Sanjo district, a bit to the northwest of the main Nishinomiya Ebisu shrine precincts, was the abode of kugutsu from the early medieval period, and that the people who lived in this Sanjo district suffered from a lower status than others. The area was considered a polluted district, and women would go there to give birth. Nishinomiya shrine records from as late as the Genroku era (1688–1704) indicate there were thirty to forty households in the Nishinomiya Sanjo district which listed their sole occupations as puppeteers.[63] It was also in this district that we find the shrine dedicated to the patron deity of puppeteers, Hyakudayū.[64]

In the preceding chapter we discussed the symbolic significance of these Sanjo districts as liminal areas in the geography of meaning in medieval Japan. The people living in this Sanjo district were involved in the worship activities of the shrine and performed the appeasement rites of the deity Ebisu. They used puppets as goshintai, or spirit bodies, of the deity in their rites.[65]

These Ebisu-kaki of the court diaries were actually conscripted sacred specialists living in the Sanjo district attached to the Settsu Nishinomiya Shrine (usually called Nishinomiya Ebisu Jinja).[66] They were the precursors of the later dramatic tradition of ningyō jōruri, in which the art of ballad recitation, shamisen playing, and puppet manipulation were combined to create a new dramatic form in the early modern period. They were also the group from which the puppeteers who formed the Awaji puppetry tradition splintered. In the rest of this chapter, we will focus on the significance of the deity Ebisu as the liminal being par excellence in Japanese religions, and the relationship between this deity and the kugutsu of the Nishinomiya center. An obvious question opens our discussion. In Japanese religions, there are myriad kami. Why, then, do we not see puppeteers specializing in rites for every one of the other deities? Why not an *Amaterasu-kaki* or a *Susanō-kaki*? Why not a *Hachiman-kaki* or an *Inari-kaki*? To understand why there are special puppetry rituals for the deity Ebisu, it is necessary to appreciate something of this deity's liminal and dangerous nature. Since detailed sources in English for a study of Ebisu are not available, I present an overview of the important features of this deity before turning to a discussion of the Nishinomiya kugutsu.

Ebisu Worship: Possible Development

Why did Ebisu need to be handled by puppeteers? What was it about this deity that required this ritual treatment? What were ritual puppeteers trying to accomplish when they traveled the country presenting Ebisu rites?

In chapter 1, I noted that puppets are beings once removed from the human realm. They are objects capable of being possessed by sacred forces, but they remain separate from human beings. In the following discussion of Ebisu, we will see that Ebisu worship is fundamentally about the issue of containment. This dangerous deity, capable of causing any number of terrible problems in human society from disease to drought, needs to be localized, channeled, appeased, and entertained. A puppet in this case serves as a control for spiritual contagion. A disease metaphor is apt in this case, as we shall see. Rather than representing Ebisu's power with a human being, an intermediary body between the sacred specialist and the deity provides a protective ritual space for the resolution of Ebisu's problematic and amorphous nature. There is an intentionality in the representation of the unrepresentable—and unpredictable—deity Ebisu when a puppet is used that would not be present were a human actor to "impersonate" or become possessed by Ebisu. Puppets then are not merely aesthetic choices in this case; they are ritually necessary.

An important source of information for the study of some Japanese deities is the *shinzō* (shrine sculptures) and the *o-fuda* (iconographic depictions on placards) used in worship. These sculptures and pictures have served a number of ritual functions in Japanese worship. Often shinzō are spirit vessels (*mitamashiro* or goshintai) and lodging places for the kami who is summoned during rites. Sometimes, a picture of the shinzō is distributed as an amulet from the shrine in the form of an o-fuda. These placards were frequently distributed to worshippers so that they could put it on their own altar at home. They were understood to participate in the sacredness of the central image of the shrine, and they helped to distribute the power of that center.

A major role of the Ebisu-kaki setting out from Nishinomiya was to distribute these placards for worship purposes throughout the countryside. The puppet body became a sort of traveling goshintai, a physical object in which the deity was actually present. In this way, ritual puppeteers taking the sacred body of Ebisu from the ceremonial center into the periphery were literally spreading the presence of the deity around the countryside, and the o-fuda distributed were a source of revenue for the shrine, as were the performances of the puppeteers. There are no clear records indicating just how much revenue these puppeteers generated for the ceremonial center, but it is likely that in addition to augmenting the prestige of Nishinomiya as the center (which would have some monetary value), the itinerant puppeteers attached to this shrine did actually engage in fundraising of some sort.[67] As the o-fuda had depictions of Ebisu, we can use these placards as evidence for understanding how Ebisu was portrayed.

Depictions of Ebisu show remarkable variety. The earliest record of any depiction of Ebisu is a passing reference in a text dated the first year of Chōkan (1163) at the Iwashimizu Hachiman shrine. It is not an actual picture but merely a reference to the placard from this shrine: "As usual, Ebisu holds a fish,"[68] suggesting that by this date the association between Ebisu and fish was already well established. Perhaps this was always a central feature of Ebisu worship.

From the medieval period on, Ebisu has usually been depicted as a dark-faced, bearded, obese old man holding a sea bream under one arm and either a fishing pole or a sack of money in the other.[69] Almost invariably, the figure is smiling—a deity of the most docile and domesticated nature. In keeping with this image, Ebisu is usually described in encyclopedias and dictionaries of Japanese deities as "one of the seven gods of luck, who bestows blessing on fishing and business."

The history, iconography, and ritual invocation of this deity, however, point to a figure of much greater complexity. Frequently the depictions show Ebisu with a deformed leg or even a stump of a leg. He is often obese, and so appears almost amorphous. While iconographic standards vary widely for Ebisu, a common element in these depictions concerns the unformed and marginal, the ugly and the dangerous. Obesity, drunken stupor in his expression, a deformed leg—all these attributes point to the margins of everyday life.

According to Namihira Emiko, this quality of deformity is a key feature in understanding the significance of the deity Ebisu. Ebisu is often depicted as lame, deaf, one-eyed, hermaphroditic, or very ugly. All of these

This placard from the Nishinomiya shrine shows the standard iconographic depiction of Ebisu.

qualities, she rightly notes, are attributes of the unformed potential space of the margins of society, where categories such as beauty, gender, health, and order are as yet undetermined.[70] Furthermore, ugliness and deformity are considered polluting attributes in the Japanese ritual purity system, and so Ebisu becomes the deity presiding over this realm of chaos, pollution, and all the power and potential it contains. This liminal quality of Ebisu is evident in the many narratives describing the origins of Ebisu shrines, our next source of information for determining the emerging and conflicting nature of this deity.

The scholar Katō Genchi has suggested that there is even a sexual dimension to Ebisu's deformed leg. He argues that the stump of a leg suggests a huge stylized penis protruding from the lower extremities of the image, and that this subtle suggestion invokes the powerful world of sexuality.[71] More likely, the bad leg is meant to tie Ebisu to the Leech Child myth, to be discussed shortly. While there is no doubt Ebisu is often associated with excess avaricious desires, sometimes a bad leg may be just a bad leg.

Many of the images of Ebisu show him with a chin beard and dark skin. These qualities have been explained to me as proof that Ebisu works at sea, since fishermen working out in the sun and open air often have very dark skin. But it seems more likely that these depictions of Ebisu reinforce his foreignness. He appears as a dark outsider, absorbing some of the attributes given to threatening Mongols and other menacing continental types in standard Japanese iconography.

On the surface, iconographic standards for Ebisu may appear to be straightforward. In reality the simple, smiling fat man with a fish emerges out of a larger process of iconographic transformation. What does this beneficent façade obscure?

Engi *Narratives and Ebisu Worship*

Another important source we have for discerning the development and nature of a deity in Japanese religious history is a body of narratives describing the origins of sacred sites. Called *engi*, which means literally "origin accounts," these narratives usually describe some miraculous event which explains why a shrine or temple exists where it does, how it came to have the affiliations it does, and why certain kinds of worship practices take place at the site. For every shrine or temple in Japan that still has a record of its origin narrative, there are numerous sites for which such records have been lost. It is not unlikely that they were often redacted and updated throughout Japanese history and even developed anew at key points, providing definition for drifting traditions. (The Usa Hachiman materials cited earlier are a good example.)

Frequently engi are recorded in written texts, but not infrequently, these texts have been lost or destroyed, and only oral versions or fragments survive. Often, the texts or narratives are extremely old, and so are reliable documents for reconstructing early perceptions of deities and worship patterns. Sometimes, as we shall see in subsequent discussions of the Awaji myth tradition, the narratives appear to be the result of a process of carefully constructing a center and origin for a tradition. Here, we will look at a number of these narratives for Ebisu shrines throughout western

Japan, including the Nishinomiya center. All these narratives insist on the importance of ritually controlling the deity's potentially dangerous power and locating Ebisu in a set worship space.

Although worship shrines dedicated to Ebisu throughout western Japan differ greatly from one another, many share the common motif of "the drifting deity": the deity worshipped at a shrine arrived at its location by literally "floating in" from the sea. According to Ogura Manabu, a study of many of the tutelary deities in villages along the Noto Peninsula reveals that many of the deities are said to have floated ashore from the other world across the sea. In his fieldwork in the Noto Peninsula between 1947 and 1957, Ogura collected sixty-eight occurrences of the "drifted deity" tradition.[72] In each case, the shrine's goshintai, or receptacle of the sacred, was a stone or some other object that had somehow come ashore. In many cases it was said to have arrived unexpectedly. Ogura determined that there are generally two ways the deities are understood to have reached the shore: they are carried by the waves, or fishermen find them in their nets (often in the form of unusually shaped stones) and bring them ashore. In a number of the examples he studied, some of the deities arrive in boats, and some are carried ashore by an animal or fish (an octopus, shark, deer, tortoise). Ebisu figures prominently as a deity who arrives in the human realm in this way.

For example, the Ebisu shrine in Wakamatsu-shi in northeastern Kyushu has a large stone as its receptacle for the sacred. This stone, the origin myth claims, was tangled in the net of a fisherman and was later understood to be a manifestation of the deity Ebisu. A shrine was built for it, and Ebisu is worshipped there, with the stone as the *mitamashiro* (spirit vessel) or goshintai of the shrine.[73]

Another example, recorded by the folklorist Sakurada Katsunori, parallels this case:

> The Ebisu-gami at a small village named Seze-no-ura, on Koshiki Island, Kagoshima-ken, which I visited some years ago, is a mere stone. This rock is roughly pear-shaped and was said to have floated ashore. The rock is so enormous that not even two men could lift it and is definitely not a pumice stone, which is light. A certain villager who saw this rock drifting toward the beach made a shrine for it on top of a hill behind the village, deeming it an irreverent act to leave the stone in the water. Immediately, however, the stone began to roll back down the hill and halted at the spot where it is now enshrined. . . . It is further told that the stone had been very light before it was installed there, but that it has since become very heavy.[74]

In Shimane Prefecture, stones that are found in fish or fishing nets are called "Ebisu-san" and are worshipped on kamidana in private homes by fishermen. In Niigata Prefecture, on the island of Sadō, the goshintai of a local shrine is a stone shaped like a piece of Buddhist sculpture, which appeared out of the ocean. It is called "Ebisu." We could cite more examples of worship sites along the northern coast of Japan in which the spirit vessel is a stone said to have appeared or surfaced.[75]

In the Ōsumi Peninsula in Kyushu, the following practice is recorded: On the fifteenth day of the new year, young people from the community enter the sea, and bring out stones they randomly pick up from the bottom. These stones are worshipped as the goshintai for Ebisu in the shrine for the coming year. A similar practice on the nearby island of Koshiki-jima alters the practice slightly: if the fishing that year is bad, a new stone must be found and the previous stone is thrown back into the sea. A further case from Wakamatsu in northern Kyushu tells of a fisherman finding a glistening stone in the water, which was then worshipped as Ebisu.[76]

Or further still, consider the following practice: A fisherman comes across a corpse of an unidentified person floating in the sea. The corpse is pulled aboard the ship and taken back to shore, where it is worshipped as a manifestation of the deity Ebisu before being prepared for a proper funeral.[77] According to Namihira, this practice has a number of restrictions, namely that a drowned corpse from one's own group (i.e., a known person) is not considered to be Ebisu. Rather, Ebisu is the stranger, the outsider who comes ashore. The practice of picking up a corpse at sea seems to run counter to a strongly enforced taboo among fishermen never to be polluted by death when at sea, because the sea is a sacred space. But a corpse of unknown origin floating in the sea comes from the "other world" (*tokoyo*) and can thus be deified. Robert Smith mentions this custom in his work on Japanese ancestors:

> When corpses are found floating at sea, they are brought back to village for internment in a graveyard reserved for drowning victims. Called floating buddhas (*nagare botoke*), their spirits are thought to be the messengers or servants of some major god. This represents a contemporary version of the ancient concept of vengeful gods (*goryō-shin*, *tatari-gami*), that is, spirits of disaster victims that are thought to be dangerous if uncared for but beneficent if deified and properly treated. Indeed, these spirits are often appealed to in the expectation that they can increase the size of the catch. When the corpse is hauled out of the water, the fishermen speak to it, asking for assistance in return for having taken it up for burial.[78]

Further examples from Ebisu shrines reveal that the goshintai are frequently stones with odd shapes, often shaped like human beings, said to have appeared out of nowhere, floated onto the beach, or been caught in a net. This motif of the drifted deity appears to be central to Ebisu's manifestations to the human community. While this aspect of Ebisu worship shares something with the structure of marebito worship described in the previous chapter, there is one striking difference: unlike the marebito, who will probably make its appearance at a set time of the year (usually New Year), a floating deity may appear out of nowhere at any time. The human community has a significant lack of control over the visit of the deity, and its appearance (and disappearance) cannot be second-guessed. It therefore falls to ritual to contain these events.

The narrative device of the drifted deity appears in the origin myth of the Nishinomiya shrine. It is more complex than the above examples and shows a greater degree of ritual development surrounding the appearance of the deity on the waves. This complexity is probably due to Nishinomiya being the center of Ebisu worship and having absorbed other Ebisu narratives. Because this shrine has the status and prestige of the center, its own narrative has been carefully sculpted to be as inclusive and definitive as possible. And of course we cannot overlook the possibility that perhaps evidence from other shrines, which we assume to be intact, may in fact be fragmented, appearing less coherent than the Nishinomiya version because they have not been as well preserved.

Drifted Deity Motif and the Nishinomiya Shrine

As the center of Ebisu worship, Nishinomiya shrine's engi has a normative function in the Ebisu tradition; it can be seen as a paradigm of Ebisu worship and practice. The founding narrative of this shrine is a fascinating example of the drifted deity motif. It is easy to see how this legend of the center absorbs a number of related examples of the drifted deity motif. Here is Yoshii's synopsis:

> One day, a fisherman was out fishing about three kilometers to the east of present-day Nishinomiya when he caught something in his net that appeared to be an effigy of a deity [shinzō]. He thought nothing of it and threw it back into the ocean and continued fishing. Then, a bit further along the sea line, in the area called Wadahama[79] near Kōbe, he caught something else in his net. He thought it weird, and looked at it, and again it was this same effigy hanging in his net. Thinking this must mean something, he took it home and worshipped it. That night in a dream, he received an oracle from the deity. "I am the deity Ebisu. I have been traveling the country and have come to this place, but I would like to have a worship hall built for me a little to the west of here. I will show you the place." The fisherman was overcome with fear and spoke of his dream to other people in a village. Thereupon, they put the figure in a cart for transporting vessels containing sacred forces [o-mikoshi] and carried it to the

west until they arrived at the beach in front of where the fisherman had previously found the figure. There, they built a worship hall. It faces west [recall that the word Nishinomiya means "western shrine"] and to this day is the site of the Nishinomiya Ebisu shrine.[80]

The Nishinomiya narrative has a number of motifs that attract our attention. First, the deity presents itself to a fisherman, and he is slow to realize this object in his net means something. Are we to assume that fishermen catch shrine sculptures in their nets so often it is commonplace? This fisherman's catching the effigy twice enables the deity to make its intentions unmistakably clear: "If you don't pick me up in your net and keep me, I will keep appearing until you do so." Next, the fisherman decides to take the object home, and the oracle from the deity is delivered in a dream. The oracle reveals what the deity wants: a place to be worshipped. These motifs—fisherman, repeated appearance of an object until it is recognized, oracle delivered in a dream, and construction of a worship hall—form the major core of the Ebisu narratives.

What does this case have in common with all the other examples cited above? All of these appearances are in some way connected with the sea. The object worshipped as Ebisu has appeared out of nowhere and largely by chance. The person who finds the object has no control over its appearance. It either floats in, appears in the water, or continues to get caught in a net. In most of the cases, there is something unusual about its appearance. When it is a stone, it is a stone that floats, a paradox if ever there were one. When it is a corpse, that too is strange when found floating in the sea. These two features of the narratives, the strangeness of the object (be it stone, effigy, or corpse) and the unexpected and uncontrolled nature of the arrival seem to be the essential aspects of these divine manifestations. Also prominent in many of these narratives is the role of a dream or an oracle in which the identity of the object and the intentions of the deity are revealed. This device for introducing a new awareness of another order of reality is common in Japanese religions, both in Buddhist tales and in the larger realm of legends and myths not directly tied to the Buddhist tradition.[81]

Perhaps the most outstanding feature of Ebisu is its unexpected and spontaneous appearance. Inherent in the worship of these unusual objects that drift in from nowhere is the need to ritually control the unexpected and unknown. Enshrinement is not merely the first step in adoration, it is also the first step in containment. These unusual stones reveal the deity's radically different nature, and their enshrinement makes sure this quality is carefully localized so it can be controlled through worship and ritual action. This is the message of the floating deity (*hyōchakugami*) phenomenon: other beings can appear from across the waves at any time, on their own accord, and it is up to the human community to see that they are properly handled. How can this motif of the drifting deity help us understand other aspects of Ebisu worship?

Linguistic and Orthographic Evidence for the Development of Ebisu

A third, though highly problematic, source of information for studying Japanese deities is the characters used to write their names and the descriptive phrases that have been attached to them throughout Japanese history. Such an approach is problematic because characters were often attached to existing Japanese words with little concern for the original meaning of the character in Chinese. Characters used in this way are called *ateji*. When looking for meaning in the name through reference to the characters used, therefore, one runs the risk of being gravely misled. Characters attached to the name Ebisu, however, do not appear to be part of the ateji phenomenon. "Ebisu" was first a linguistically meaningful word with the meaning "foreigner" (or "barbarian"), and characters with that meaning in the original Chinese were later added to the word Ebisu.

There are a number of characters used to write the name Ebisu, all of which continue to be in use today, and these suggest early aspects and perceptions of this deity. The most common way to write the name is with a single character that means literally "barbarian," "foreigner," or "alien race." "Ebisu" in ancient Japanese texts refers to the tribal peoples subdued by the centralized government during the protohistorical period of state formation.[82] A second single character also often used for Ebisu also means "barbarian" but carries the added connotation of warrior. (In their Chinese readings, these two characters together, read *jūi*, mean simply "barbarian.") In the Heian dictionary *Iroha Jiruishō*, the word pronounced "ebisu," meaning "barbarian" or "foreigner" uses three other characters.[83] A single character is still often used to write the name of this deity, although the three-character compound, all ateji characters used for sound only, is more common. Inherent in all of these terms is the idea of a stranger. Namihira goes so far as to suggest that the derivation of the name Ebisu is from the word "Emishi," a name given to foreigners in ancient Japan.[84]

Because of this linguistic evidence, some scholars have suggested that the deity Ebisu is a remnant of a deity worshipped by a group of people who preceded the ethnic Japanese population that later populated and dominated the Japanese archipelago. This theory may in fact have some truth to it, but it is utterly impossible to prove. At any rate, discerning the historical origins of such a complex phenomenon as Ebisu worship and its transformation does not go far toward illuminating its significance.

Origuchi Shinobu, with much insight but little evidence suggests that the name Ebisu originally referred to a generic category of "visiting deities" who would arrive in the human realm at certain times of the year. These are marebito, discussed in more detail in the previous chapter. An important aspect of marebito is the ambiguous and undetermined nature of the deity's power. The stranger deity represents unknown power, which can be turned to benevolent or malevolent ends depending on how the deity's arrival and departure are ritually handled. Treated well, Ebisu bestows blessings. Slighted, he wreaks havoc in the form of storms, epidemics, droughts, and other disasters.

Although the double-edged nature of sacredness is most pronounced in the example of strangers, it is a common feature of all Japanese deities, who have four aspects to their sacredness. Each deity (and to a lesser extent each human being) has at once an *ara-mi-tama* (rough and vengeful spirit), a *nigi-mi-tama* (spirit of union and harmony), a *kushi-mi-tama* (spirit of mysterious transformation), and a *saki-mi-tama* (spirit of blessing).[85] Whether or not the deity bestows its benevolent nature on people is largely dependent on the power of the ritual system to carefully mediate and channel the potency of the deity's presence. Japanese ritual prayers indicate that people were well aware that one and the same deity could have different aspects, and so when a deity is addressed, it is invited to present a particular aspect suitable to the request. Furthermore, classical narratives refer to various aspects of deities, which are enshrined separately within the same shrine precincts.[86]

This discussion of aspects of deities helps us situate further evidence concerning Ebisu. Takeuchi notes that before the medieval period, the common name for this deity was "Ara-ebisu" (*ara* being the same word as in *ara-mitama*, meaning "rough") and was probably a deity of curses, *tatari-gami*.[87] This fear of a negative action against the human community by a deity has been proposed to explain why Ebisu has been made into a god of luck. Casting Ebisu in this light not only turns that which is negative into something positive, but also increases the ritual arena in which this deity's power can be controlled and channeled.

It is important to reiterate that Ebisu as a deity in Japanese religion is never mentioned by this name in the standard chronicles and mythic accounts of the *Nihongi* and *Kojiki*. Perhaps Ebisu worship by this name was not a strong enough tradition at the time these narratives were redacted to merit inclusion in the standard chronicles. Perhaps Ebisu worship was intentionally excluded. What is certain is that Ebisu is eventually tied into the main accounts through identification with deities who do figure in them, deities that have something in common with the liminal nature of Ebisu. These graftings not only underscore certain aspects of Ebisu in the deity's development in Japanese religion but also serve to expand the implications of Ebisu worship. The graftings also serve to create mainstream traditions for Ebisu worship, and the use of these *Kojiki* and *Nihongi* narratives suggests a certain type of mythological nostalgic discourse. Here, we turn our attention to the deities onto which the standard chronicles have grafted the worship of Ebisu.

Ebisu as the Adult Hiruko (Leech Child)

The reader will recall that in chapter 2, the myth of the failed creation attempt of Izanagi and Izanami was presented. The first of the two deities with whom Ebisu is usually identified is the offspring of Izanagi and Izanami, Hiruko, the Leech Child—a legless, amorphous blob that emerged from a failed creation attempt. This is the association most commonly used in tying Ebisu into the larger Izanagi and Izanami myth cycle. It certainly dates from at least the fifteenth century. Scholars have proposed a number of interpretations of this myth of failed creation, presented in *Kojiki* and *Nihongi*. Tsuda Sōkichi suggests that it reflects an early magical custom in which a body substitute of a first-born child is placed in a boat and floated downstream to magically protect the infant.[88] While such practices of body substitutes protecting infants are not uncommon in Japan, this interpretation seems unlikely because it fails to take into account the myth's insistence that this child was a failure. It also ignores the gender hierarchy that must be followed in male-female sexual relationships.

Another interpretation, somewhat far-fetched, maintains that although the word *hiruko* is written in the texts with the characters "leech" and "child," these are ateji, characters that should not be taken literally. Rather, the word *hiruko* should be understood as the male version of *hirume*, "sun maiden," and means "sun lad."[89] This interpretation has little to recommend it, save that it satisfies the desire to tie all myths in this redacted text into sun worship, and render unified that which is most likely more a case of mythological patchwork through redaction.

Both of these lines of interpretation, one using the myth as a veiled expression of history and the other assuming that the key to the myth's meaning lies in its phonetics, ignore the fundamental reality of how myths operate, survive, and are transformed in culture. Myths are created and survive precisely because they encode in a narrative structure existential meanings that cannot be expressed in other forms with the same results. Myths are dependent on a core story line, which can remain constant despite variation and that allows a range of possible interpretations of meaning.

The most credible interpretation of this myth addresses it on its own plane of reference as a story about creation. The birth of the Leech Child refers to the initial failure of creation.[90] The basic motif is that before the proper creation of the world can be accomplished, some false starts and failures are sure to happen. These failures are then abandoned (in boats at sea, in the woods, along rivers, in the wilderness or open fields, under bridges—in short, in any undetermined and uncharted space) so that the work of creation can go on. Lest we take the difficult work of creation for granted, we need to be reminded of the failures of first tries. Banishing the failure into the wilderness expresses the need to exclude things that did not turn out right from of the final order of a completed world. It also provides a narrative device for expounding on the structures and logic of the successful creation, the basic framework of a cosmogonic system.

Set adrift on the waves, Hiruko seems to have been successfully banished from the realm of creation. While nothing comes of the legless child again in the main narrative of the *Kojiki* and *Nihongi*, this deity is brought back into the mainstream of Japanese religious practice by means of another myth and ritual tradition: Hiruko grows up (or in some cases, merely comes ashore) and becomes Ebisu. The founding myths of various Ebisu shrines around Japan adapt this motif of the abandoned and floating child and claim it as the origin of the shrine. There is a direct connection between the account of Hiruko floating on the waves and the motif of the floating deity discussed above. Indeed, the Leech Child is the floating deity par excellence.

This identification of Ebisu as the adult Leech Child has become a standard aspect of Ebisu worship, and it plays a major part in the worship of Ebisu at the Nishinomiya shrine. A text called *Jingi Shōjū*, said to have been composed by Urabe Kanena from Chōroku 4 (1460), mentions the Ebisu shrine in Nishinomiya as follows: "Hirota Daimyōjin. *Chokushi* of the fifth rank. One worship at Hama-minami of Muko-gōri, province of Settsu, called Nishinomiya Ebisudono. Izanagi no Mikoto's third son, Hiruko."[91] Four deities are worshipped at this site: Amaterasu Ō-mikoto, Ōkuni-nushi no kami (who as we shall see is the father of the other deity onto whom Ebisu is grafted), Susanoo no Ō-mikoto, and Hiruko no Mikoto (the Leech Child, understood to be the child Ebisu). Not one of these is called by the name Ebisu. Ebisu is worshipped as Hiruko, the Leech Child. This pattern can be seen throughout Japan, as worship halls to Hiruko are often found within Ebisu shrines. It seems that this deity can exist simultaneously as both child and adult. Worship can be addressed to both stages, suggesting perhaps that the child's essence is always intrinsically present within the adult.

Nakayama Tarō presents the following story from Nishinomiya to show this continuity of ugliness. According to Nakayama, every year on the ninth day of the New Year period, the Leech Child of the Settsu Nishinomiya shrine pays a visit to the Hiroda shrine nearby, but the appearance of this deity is so strange and ugly that people hate to look at it. In contrast to other deity processions where people line the streets to view the passing portable shrine (*o-mikoshi*) carrying the divine presence, on this day, people close up their gates and doors and do not go out, for fear they may actually catch a glimpse of this ugly deity lumbering along.[92] Ebisu, as we know, is obese, hermaphroditic, deformed, and frequently intoxicated. As a child, too, Ebisu is so ugly that people refuse to look upon its passing form. What we have here is a worship practice which is in reality antiworship: people do the opposite of hailing the o-mikoshi—they avoid it. Ebisu, whether child or adult, is the ultimate *non*deity. One would wonder why there should be any bother with this ugly deity at all, since its presence evokes only aversion. But the fact that the practice exists points to the need to make this religious point: chaos, disorder, and liminality cannot be denied. These attributes must be allowed to exist; they must be ritually handled and periodically invoked, even if we have to avert our gaze in the process.

According to Namihira Emiko, there is yet another reason that people avert their gaze from the Leech Child. It is said that the Leech Child himself also hates to be seen and that anyone who looks upon this deity will be cursed (*tatarareru*).[93] The motif of a deity demanding that human beings not look upon it is common in world religions, with different reasons given for the prohibition in different traditions.

This example of the aversion caused by Ebisu suggests that the very power of Ebisu's sacredness is the ability to provide a focus for abhorrence and revulsion. How do you represent the unthinkable aspects of consciousness? Ebisu, whether child or adult, presides over and makes present the realm of the horrid. Ebisu has been grafted onto the main narratives of the *Kojiki* and *Nihongi* through the opportunistic segue of an ugly and abandoned failed creation, a miscarried and bloody blob best symbolized by a Leech.

Ebisu as Kotoshiro-nushi no kami

Some traditions of Ebisu worship attach the deity not to the Leech Child but to another fleeting character in the *Kojiki* narratives, Kotoshiro-nushi no kami. According to Yoshii, the identification of Ebisu with this deity appears to be relatively late, probably dating from the early Tokugawa period.[94] This deity Kotoshiro-nushi no kami, whose name means "the master of knowing things" (referring to divine oracles) is the son of Ōkuni nushi no mikoto and his second wife Kamu ya tate hime no mikoto.[95] (The reader will recall that Ōkuni nushi no kami is one of the four deities worshipped at the Nishinomiya shrine.) The significance of this deity Kotoshiro-nushi is considerable, in spite of the fact that he is mentioned in only a few lines in the *Kojiki*. Here is how the deity figures in these myths.

One of the central concerns in the first book of the *Kojiki* is the problem of hegemony. The Sun Goddess, having been granted the right to rule over the Plain of High Heaven, must also find a way to rule the land called Toyo Ashi Hara no Chi Aki no Naga Iho Aki no Mizu ho no Kuni, "The Land of the Plentiful Reed Plains, of the Thousand Autumns, and Long Five Hundred Autumns Fresh Rice Ears."[96] She dispatches various people in her entourage to subdue the land and grant permission to take it from Ōkuni nushi no kami. She sends Ame no ho hi no kami and then Ame no waka hiko, but neither is successful in their mission.[97] Finally, she sends two deities, Take mika tsuchi and Ame no tori-fune no kami. (Note how the deity with whom Ebisu is later identified conceals himself from the world.)

> We have been dispatched by the command of Amaterasu and Taka ki no kami to inquire: the Central Land of the Reed Plains, over which you hold sway, is a land entrusted to the rule of my offspring; what is your intention with regard to this?" Then he [Ōkuni nushi no Kami] replied, "I cannot say. My son Ya-pe Kotoshiro nushi no kami[98] will say. However, he has gone out to amuse himself hunting for birds and fishing at the Cape of Miho, and has not yet returned." Hereupon, Ame no Tori-fune no Kami was dispatched to summon Ya-pe Kotoshiro-nushi no kami, who, when inquiry was made of him, spoke to his father the great deity, saying, "With fearful reverence, let us present this land to the offspring of the heavenly deities." He then stamped his feet and overturned the boat; and by clapping his hands with a heavenly reverse clapping, he transformed it into a green twig fence, and concealed himself."[99]

The tale continues as attendants of the heavenly maiden inquire of the old man if he has other children who need to be consulted before he can hand over his land. He replies that indeed he has one other son, Take-mi na kata no kami. This son, when asked, also displays magical powers as he engages in a battle with the forces of the Sun Goddess, but in the end, they hunt him down and are about to kill him. Pleading for his life, he agrees to give up control of the land: "Pray do not kill me. I will go to no other place. Also, I will not disobey the commands of my father, Ōkuni nushi no kami, and will not disobey the words of Ya-pe Kotoshiro nushi no kami. I will yield the Central Land of the Reed plains in accordance with the commands of the offspring of the heavenly deities."[100] Following this, Ōkuni nushi no kami agrees to surrender his land, provided a worship hall is built for him. Further, he agrees to "conceal himself" and wait upon the new rulers.[101]

It is a matter of dispute just where Ōkuni nushi and his children are said to have concealed themselves. Motoori suggests he retired to the land of Yomi, the land of the dead, where Izanagi went to fetch Izanami after her death.[102] Philippi notes that other premodern commentators conclude that they withdrew to Izumo,[103] and he suggests that "Probably Opo Kuni nusi merely retires to the unseen world of the spirit."[104] Supporting this, book 9 of the *Nihongi* (the account of Jingū Kōgo) refers to this deity as "the deity who rules in Heaven, who rules in the Void, the gem-casket-entering prince, the awful Kotoshiro-nushi."[105] Given the evidence in the myths, if we read them as myths, Philippi's summation seems most plausible. The myth describes how one order of meaning supplants another, which withdraws into invisibility.

Why has Ebisu been identified with the figure Kotoshiro-nushi no kami in this myth? On an obvious level, we see in this brief passage a deity associated with hunting and fishing, and this identification is also mentioned in passing in the *Nihongi*. Kotoshiro-nushi no kami is also clearly capable of the mastery of ritual language. But more important is his final fate in the text: he disappears from creation and becomes invisible. Through his foot stamping, ritual clapping, and utterances, he brings about a magical transformation and withdraws from creation, supposedly so as not to get in the way of the new rule. It is this feature of the myth that most attracts our attention: here again, much as with Leech Child, a deity has been removed from creation, in this case through his own submission to the new rule (though one is always suspicious about these matters). Kotoshiro nushi has gone from being a visible deity to an invisible one,[106] and like his father, he has agreed to serve as "the rear and the vanguard" to the new ruling forces. The text states that if he "serves them respectfully, there will be no rebellious deities."[107]

The standard interpretation of this myth has been again decidedly euhemeristic:

> According to this reply, Opo Kuni nushi agreed to relinquish the political, external rule of the land to the emperors, while retaining a religious, ceremonial role. This is similar to the events of the Taika reform of 646, when the local rulers (*kuni no miyatuko*), who had formerly possessed hereditary powers in political and religious matters, were now deprived of political power and replaced by governors dispatched from the central government, although

allowed to retain their religious functions. No doubt the story of the abdication of Opo-kuni-nushi is a mythological reflection of some such process of historical development.[108]

While the similarity between this myth and the historical events leading up to the establishment of the early Japanese state are striking and highly recommend such an interpretation, accounting for a myth's origins in history does not exhaust the meanings it assumes as a religious idea. Our attention to this identification of the deity Ebisu with Kotoshiro-nushi can therefore not be satisfied with a euhemeristic interpretation. Rather, we must ask what is it about this figure from the mythical chronicles that invites identification with the deity Ebisu, in light of what we have already seen of Ebisu worship throughout Japanese history. Why does a deity of ambiguity and liminality become the deity from the invisible realm, the deity "who knows things?"

To answer this question, we have to read this myth as a myth and not as a veiled and symbolized history, although it may have worked as both. The myth seems to be about the power of the invisible (spiritual) world to insert itself into the visible (physical) realm of the new order. The myth suggests the workings of the unconscious or hidden aspects of human spirituality. One of its concerns is with the fear of reprisal of suppressed forces. What would happen if these forces, which have been commanded to relinquish their control over the affairs of the land, should try to resurface? Fear of reprisal may have been a real concern. Kotoshiro nushi's transformation from son of the ruler to "the rear and the vanguard" (to guarantee that there will not be any vengeful deities) suggests this.[109] Another example from early Japanese religious literature suggests this interpretation.

In 927 C.E., over two hundred years after the *Kojiki* myths were redacted and recorded, a number of ritual prayers used officially by the government were recorded as part of the *Engishiki*.[110] One prayer is entitled "Tataru Kami wo Utsushi-yaru" (To Drive Away a Vengeful Deity). The concern in this myth is with keeping vengeful deities from interfering with affairs of state. But strikingly, the handing of land over to the forces of Amaterasu by Ōkuni nushi forms the structure of the prayer. The prayer implores this deity and his forces with these words:

> May the Sovereign Deities[111] dwelling within the heavenly palace
> Not rage and ravage,
> Because as deities they are well acquainted
> With the matters begun in the Heavenly High Plain,
> May they rectify their hearts in the manner of the rectifying deities . . .
> And may they go from this place and move to another place of lovely mountains
>   and rivers

Where they can look out over the four quarters,
And may they reign over that as their place. . . .
I place these noble offerings in abundance upon tables
Like a long mountain range and present them
Praying that the Sovereign Deities
Will with a pure heart receive them tranquilly
As offerings of ease,
As offerings of abundance,
And will not seek vengeance and ravage,
But will move to a place of wide and lovely mountains and rivers,
And as deities dwell there pacified.
With this prayer, I fulfill your praises.
Thus I humbly speak.[112]

As this prayer makes clear, the mythical account of Ōkuni nushi surrendering the land, even two hundred and fifty years after the compilation of the *Kojiki*, was still the definitive narrative to express the fear of vengeance and reprisal of suppressed forces. From a religious perspective, these deities were more than previously defeated political forces. They represented the power of the invisible world to bring hardship, vengeance, rage, and havoc on the human realm. Ōkuni nushi and his sons are the power of the unseen world.

Why has Ebisu been identified with deities whose names appear in the mainstream mythical narratives? This identification is a Japanese example of syncretism, an appropriation of one religious system by another, in this case, the Shinto tradition absorbing a wider (and perhaps earlier) myth tradition.[113] What these two cases also reveal, however, is that Ebisu is connected to the repressed, the invisible, the deformed, and the abandoned. As the *Kojiki* narratives gained in power as representing standard religiosity, other religious systems sought ways to be identified with this powerful tradition.[114]

These two examples suggest that mainstream religions have a strong need to find a place for the unseen and unknown world. The fact that this abandoned deity finds its way back into mainstream Japanese worship suggests that those parts of creation that are half-formed, ambiguous, ugly, and even potentially dangerous have an essential place in the order of things. Banished, they reappear. Repressed, they force their way back into consciousness. Rendered invisible, they reclaim the visible realm. And how they resurface may be even uglier than before, when we first pushed them aside. Building a worship hall for Ebisu is, at a spiritual level, much safer and more comforting than the image of an unformed and misshapen child floating endlessly on the waves of the primordial ocean, waiting to come ashore from time to time to seek vengeance.

Absorbing and Handling Epidemic Deities

In Japanese religions, there is a category of deities referred to as *ekibyōgami,* or epidemic deity—a term created by scholars of Japanese religions. If properly worshipped, these deities can help prevent an epidemic; if neglected, they can cause one. Throughout Japanese history, there have been a large number of deities that have been connected with epidemic disease in some way, and the relationship between certain diseases and deities became very specific.[115]

For the most part, *ekibyōgami* in Japan are related to the most common—and most incomprehensible—epidemic disease that Japan has faced in its history: smallpox. In fact, deities associated with smallpox comprise their own class of epidemic deities, called *hōsōgami* (smallpox deities).[116] According to the historian Nakajima Yōichirō, smallpox reached epidemic proportions in Japan approximately one hundred times from the first major record of a widespread epidemic in 735–737 until the end of the nineteenth century. The physician and historian of medicine Fujikawa Yū is more conservative and lists only fifty-four occurrences of smallpox, with intervals between the outbreaks decreasing by the late twelfth century, suggesting that the disease had become endemic to the Japanese population.[117]

William McNeill, in his classic study of the impact of epidemics on human demographics, *Plagues and Peoples,* has argued that because of Japan's relatively isolated geographical location vis-à-vis the major population centers of Asia (primarily China), epidemic disease in Japan was quick to spread and devastate the population but slow to acquire endemic status and mimic the disease patterns of the Asian continent.[118] This meant that every time an epidemic spread throughout Japan, it would have disastrous results, sweeping from one end of the country to the other. The virus or bacteria would then die out completely, only to be followed by a new infection of the population half a generation or a generation later, with equally high mortality rates. Both Japan's isolation and relatively low population density prevented smallpox from becoming endemic in Japan until about the thirteenth century. After this period, we see the disease often referred to as a childhood disease.

Throughout East Asia, varieties of pestilence and disease—bubonic plague, smallpox, measles, influenza, cholera, typhus—were often understood to be the result of neglected deities, malevolent spirit forces, and epidemic demons. Consequently, major rituals of appeasement were undertaken to control the sickness by pacifying and expeling these forces from society. Japan was no exception to this description, and some of Japan's most elaborate ritual performances, including the Gion Matsuri in

Kyoto, began as spirit appeasement rites for epidemic deities. The connection between Ebisu worship, puppetry, and the appeasement of epidemic spirits is a difficult area of research, largely because so much of the practice of epidemic spirit appeasement was unwritten. While we do have sources documenting government-sponsored appeasement rites during times of pestilence in Japanese history, only a few sources, often made in passing, refer directly to the relationship between puppetry and epidemic spirit appeasement. The record suggests that the Usa Hachiman Hōjō-e began as the result of an epidemic and expressed a dual use of puppets, first in the military conquest of the Hayato and later in the ritual control of the epidemic said to have resulted from their defeated, malevolent spirits. This case is representative, and even with the paucity of sources is one of our better recorded cases. The other source of information for studying this connection comes from the fragments of evidence describing a small worship hall at the Nishinomiya Ebisu shrine, dedicated to the tutelary deity of puppeteers, Hyakudayū.

Hyakudayū, Women of Pleasure, Children, Puppets, and Smallpox

The worship hall dedicated to Hyakudayū is mentioned in an eleventh-century text by Ōe no Masafusa about the women who lived and worshipped near the what is now known as the Nishinomiya shrine. His *Yūjoki* (Chronicles of the Women of Pleasure) contains the following lines about the Hiroda shrine (and also gives us a date for situating kugutsu and performers at this site): "To the south is Sumiyoshi, and to the West is Hiroda. They [the women] made these the places where they pray for agreeable omens. In particular [they pray to] Hyakudayū. This is one name for *dōsojin*.[119] The number of these [character missing from text] they carve is in the hundreds and thousands. They can melt people's hearts. This also, is an old practice."[120]

Ōe no Masafusa's reference to the worship of Hyakudayū is intriguing, because it suggests that perhaps Hyakudayū was originally some sort of a carved object not unlike the effigies discussed in chapter 1. There is another story, this one from the Nishinomiya shrine itself, explaining the origins of this connection between Hyakudayū, the Ebisu shrine, and puppeteers. A text of the Kyōhō era (1716–1735) entitled *Meisho Nishinomiya Annai Sha* contains the following story, which we can read as a reflection of the founding myth of the worship site:

> North and a little bit separated from the main shrine precincts [of Nishinomiya] there is a small worship hall [*hokora*]. In the era of the deity Iwakusubuna, in this inlet, there was an old man named Dōkun. When he heard that the deity at this shrine at the age of three still could not walk,[121] he made a puppet to

entertain and raise the child deity. Even today, when a newborn child is one hundred days old, the parents bring the child to this worship hall, and here give the child a name. Objects worshipped at this site include five painted effigies. In this, we can see a practice which has been handed down from the age of the gods. Nishinomiya puppeteers, and also the practice of calling puppets "Dōkumbō [literally "the stick of Dōkun"] comes from this deity. Today, this place is where one comes to pray for the longevity of a newborn child.[122]

This text ties the practice of puppetry at the Nishinomiya shrine to the Hyakudayū worship hall. It also supplies what amounts to a founding myth of puppeteers at Nishinomiya: puppetry was invented for the purposes of entertaining and appeasing the Leech Child. The nature of Hyakudayū helps us understand more about ritual puppetry at the Nishinomiya center. Another Nishinomiya shrine document, *Nishinomiya Daijin Honki*, contains the following explanation—basically the same evidence—under the heading "Hyakudayū Worship Hall": "Once upon a time, in this inlet there was an old man named Dōkun, and to entertain and appease the deity Hiruko [Leech Child], he fashioned a small puppet and made it dance. This is the said origins of the Nishinomiya puppeteers. Moreover, people in this area carry their newborn babies to this shrine on the baby's hundredth day, and paint their baby's face with a powder from here. This is said to be good for the baby. Therefore, the name Hyakudayū comes from this practice."[123]

Why come to Hyakudayū to ask for the protection of a baby? A brief vignette from a text entitled *Setsuyō Ochiboshū* by Hamamatsu Utakuni (1776–1827), dated Bunka 5 (1808), adds a further dimension to the relationship between Hyakudayû, puppetry, Ebisu, and the protection of children. Under the heading "About the Nishinomiya Hyakudayū" there is the following:

> In Nishinomiya, to the north of the Ebisu shrine, there is a small shrine in which a statue of a child about three years of age is enshrined. The child is not a deity. Every year at New Year, there is the custom of taking about three or four cups of powder and painting the face of the statue with it, and then leaving it on. People in the area who have had children born that year rub the face of the statue and then rub the powder on their own children's faces. This is for the prevention of smallpox. It is also said here that this doll is the origin of Japanese puppetry. This doll is from the Kasai family of Nishinomiya, and the Naniwa puppet troupe came from that group. These people are called *tayū*, and this is why the statue is called Hyakudayū.

In Yamazaki Yoshinari's *Tanki Manroku*, volume 2, we find a section entitled "A Reduced-Size Copy of the Smallpox Protecting Deity in the Genuine Handwriting of the Venerable Kōtaku."[124] This piece of writing is almost identical to the same author's piece in his twenty volume work

Kairoku, written between 1820 and 1838, under the heading "Hyaku-dayū: Protective Deity of Smallpox." Here is what his heading in *Tanki Manroku* says:

> *Hyakudayūden in the Genuine Script by Kōtaku-Sensei: The origins of the Protective Talisman (O-mamori) during the Kyōhō Era at the time of a smallpox epidemic*

According to an oracle, before a person manifests smallpox, one should put up a protective talisman of (this) deity in various places. The mediator of the above-mentioned oracle noted that at the Settsu Nishinomiya shrine there is a hall called the Hyakudayūden, and this deity enshrined there is a protective deity for smallpox. The oracle says that in the event of smallpox, one should quickly call the priest of the Hyakudayû den to present the protective talismans. The priests say that the talisman is not effective unless the greatest calligrapher under heaven is summoned and, with the instructions of the priest, asked to write the four characters for Hyakudayūden upon it and hang it near oneself. If one has a devoted heart, there is no need to worry about the smallpox epidemic.

The calligrapher Hosoi Kōtaku was called, and according to the aforementioned priest's instructions, he wrote two sheets with the characters "Hyaku-dayūden" on them. The priest presented one of them to the Hyakudayū hall and gave the other one to Kōtaku himself. Kōtaku stores the piece in his home.

After this event, Kōtaku didn't contract smallpox, and was very pleased, but his son Bunzaburō got it anyway. Nevertheless, shortly hereafter, without much ado, the boy was healed. Then Kōtaku said that he should give the sheet with the characters on it to one of his disciples, Morooka Nanrin, who has many children. He then did so.

The Hyakudayū origins are written about in so much detail that I won't bother to do so here.[125] About the aforementioned Kōtaku Sensei, I heard this story from his disciple Nanrin-Sensei. This story was typeset on a board and written down in An'ei 7 [1778], in the fourth month.

This text refers to a practice that was common during the Tokugawa period of Japan, namely, using amulets for protection against small-pox, and refers to the efficacy of the Nishinomiya Hyakudayū to ward off smallpox.

Kugutsu attached to the Nishinomiya shrine considered Hyakudayū to be their tutelary deity (*ujigami*), and continued to do so until quite late. A source dated Bunka 13 (1817) indicates that when a group of Nishi-nomiya puppeteers presented a jōruri performance (against the wishes of the Nishinomiya shrine), they dedicated the performance at the Hyaku-dayū worship hall.[126] Sometime around the beginning of Meiji, this wor-ship hall dedicated to Hyakudayū was moved into the shrine precincts.

The Hyakudayū worship hall still stands today, although the Sanjo district is no longer distinct, and its environs have been reabsorbed into the larger Nishinomiya shrine. What can we make of these shreds of evidence—hints of ritual puppetry, glimpses into the nature of the enigmatic Hyakudayū, suggestions about Ebisu worship—and what was their relationship to the Ebisu shrine and the people whose primary occupation was the ritual handling of Ebisu?

The interesting feature of puppetry at this ceremonial center concerns the myth in which a human officiant, Dōkun, uses a puppet to entertain the deity child Hiruko, an event that is understood to be the origin of Nishinomiya puppetry. This use of puppetry has been generalized so that visits to this site are believed to prevent smallpox in children.[127] In local versions of these stories, there is a clearly implicit relationship among the following motifs: (1) a child deity is unable to walk and is abandoned on the sea (and floats ashore as a drifting deity), (2) a human shrine officiant creates a puppet to entertain and appease the child deity, (3) parents can then bring their child to this shrine on its hundredth day, (4) powder is rubbed on the child's face or on the effigies in this worship hall, (5) smallpox can be prevented by this practice, and (6) even the name of the Hyakudayū site in understood to be efficacious against the dreaded disease.

Fitted together, these fragments of evidence start to form a recognizable picture: puppetry was understood to be a practice capable of appeasing this dreaded deity Hiruko, later connected (even equated) with Ebisu. The effigies in the worship hall of Hyakudayū were understood to have been either body substitutes for children, or replicas of the puppets used in appeasement rites. Touching these effigies safeguarded one against the dangerous forces of the Leech Child.

It is interesting that evidence points to a connection between an effigy used to ward off disease and the origins of puppetry. The practice of using effigies to ward off disease has a long history in Japan. It was probably borrowed from China, although may also have developed independently. Felicia Bock writes this comment on a line in her translation of the *Engishiki* (compiled during the Engi era, 901–922): "Another custom borrowed from China to avert epidemic disease was that of fashioning in clay small images of cows (or bulls) and children and placing them at main thoroughfare gates around the palace."[128] Such effigies would serve as targets for an epidemic spirit's wrath, and real children (or animals) would be spared the illness. In all likelihood, ritual puppetry draws on this understanding of the power of the body substitute.

All the evidence relating to epidemics and the Nishinomiya center suggests a highly localized association of Hyakudayū, Ebisu, and *ekibyō-gami*—part of the Ebisu tradition that was absorbed into the Nishinomiya shrine complex and "cordoned off" into the single figure of Hyakudayū. All these pieces of evidence date from the Tokugawa period.

Regardless of the actual historical connection between these cases, the connection between Nishinomiya as a center for puppeteers and Nishinomiya Hyakudayū as an *ekibyōgami* was well known. This common perception may well have contributed to a fear of puppeteers as those who traffic with epidemic spirits.

The Gradual Breakup of the Nishinomiya *Kugutsu*

In spite of all we know, it remains to be seen what these Ebisu-kaki actually did. In chapters 4 and 5, I present a detailed description of the origins of the Awaji tradition and Awaji Ebisu rite, which grew out of the earlier Nishinomiya ritual and still retains some associations with this former interpretation of the deity. The Awaji case is probably the best source of evidence we have for understanding what these Nishinomiya Ebisu-kaki did when they presented ritual performances.

References to the Ebisu-kaki from Nishinomiya are numerous but disappointing. Their numbers indicate that the practice was widespread. The historical record is marred by the fact that by the end of the sixteen century ritual puppetry performances were so common enough that everyone knew what they were and they did not require description. By the early seventeenth century, for example, *Ebisu-kaki* already was a common term for puppeteer. Here is a text dated the ninth month of Keichō 19 (1616): "It was raining. Some performers came and presented a piece called *Amida no Munewari*. They were Ebisu-kaki types."[129] Although *Amida no Munewari* (Amida's Riven Breast) is a piece of early jōruri describing the deeds of Amida Buddha to save a young and pious girl, anyone presenting a play with puppets was "an Ebisu-kaki type."[130] We know that these puppeteers presented talismans for the Nishinomiya shrine and received some protection and a small salary for their services. As we shall see shortly, by the eighteenth century this center for puppetry began to shift, and performers living in the Sanjo district attached to the Nishinomiya shrine began to perform nonreligious ballads.

The accompanying drawing of an Ebisu-kaki is from *Jinrin Kummō zui*, a seven-scroll collection describing everyday life in the Genroku era, drawn in Genroku 3 (1690). The seventh scroll, dedicated to artists and women of pleasure, includes this picture, titled "Ebisu-mai" and bearing the caption, "They imitate Noh and do lots of things."[131]

Ritual puppeteers attached to the Nishinomiya shrine clearly performed duties, ranging from traveling around the country presenting Ebisu rites to working within the shrine precincts, and possibly even acting in some

A Nishinomiya *kugutsu-mawashi*, called here "Ebisu-mai."

capacity to help prevent the spread of smallpox through special rites involving their puppets at the Hyakudayū shrine. But by the early modern
period, a new trend was afoot. This trend, which as we shall see led to a
gradual decline of Nishinomiya as a center for puppetry rites, gave birth to
a new period in the history of puppetry. This was part of a larger development in Japanese performing arts, which later became the highly nuanced
ningyō jōruri tradition, a new context for puppetry as dramatic entertainment. This new development created a bit of consternation on the part of
Nishinomiya shrine authorities and led to an eventual split and the establishment of the new Awaji tradition.

This movement of puppeteers out of the shrine appears to have been
well underway by the early eighteenth century. A record from the twenty-
seventh day of the third month of Kyōhō 5 (1721) indicates that Nishinomiya puppeteers performed in a temple in Amagasaki; and on the nineteenth day of the tenth month of Kyōhō 8 (1724), a person from the
Nishinomiya Sanjo, in opposition to a shrine priest there presented a puppetry performance inside the shrine precincts. And again in Kyōhō 9
(1725) and Kyōhō 12 (1726), there were listings of performances by puppeteers from the Nishinomiya Sanjō district at temples in Amagasaki. So,
twelve or thirteen years later, in the Kanpō era (1741–1744), a line in
shrine records dated the fifth day of the eleventh month of Kanpō 1
(1741) reads, "In recent years, Sanjo mura distractions have been distress-

ing." This comment indicates that a lot of these new "puppet performances" were seen as distractions from their employment at the shrine. But
it appears that not just one group was absenting itself and conducting its
own affairs. In Bunka 13, Sanjo mura's Yoshi Fusaburō (second son) and
six others gave a puppetry performance and dedicated it at the Hyakudayū
shrine.[132] These references suggest that while puppeteers were still continuing their practice of situating their new performances in the context of
Hyakudayū worship, they were not merely acting as representatives of the
shrine; they were developing their own dramatic tradition, which was becoming an increasingly popular one.

It was in the context of Nishinomiya puppeteers breaking away from
their duties at the shrine that we see the rise of the Awaji puppetry tradition as a self-consciously constructed new center for spirit appeasement
using puppets.

4

A Dead Priest, an Angry Deity, a Fisherman, and a Puppet: The Narrative Origins of Awaji *Ningyō*

WARNING: This art is for the appeasement of *kami*.
People after this should not take this lightly. If
they do, it will weigh heavily upon them. Hereafter, people should be sorely afraid.
  —from the founding narrative of the Awaji
    tradition, *Dōkumbō Denki* (1638)

IN THE last chapter, we saw that puppeteers called Ebisu-kaki lived in the Sanjo district near the Nishinomiya shrine and were employed there as low ranking officials. They performed rituals to spread Ebisu worship and worshipped an epidemic deity called Hyakudayū. These Ebisu-kaki were extremely popular by the mid to late sixteenth century, judging by the numerous references to them at the time. By the middle of the sixteenth century, they began to expand their range of performances to include dramatic skits. The tradition of appeasing the deity Ebisu through ritual puppetry was said to have started when a priest named Dōkun made a puppet to entertain and raise the Leech Child.

In this chapter we turn to a discussion of the development of Awaji's Sanjo district in Ichi as the center of ritual puppetry in central Japan around the middle of the sixteenth century, a development coinciding with a splintering of the Nishinomiya kugutsu tradition. A major impetus for the rise of Awaji as a new center was the increasing amount of traveling and performing that puppeteers were doing outside the Nishinomiya area. They may have wanted to establish a new center of their own. A study of the development of ritual puppetry on Awaji provides hints as to how new performance traditions arose in late medieval Japan and how they sought to legitimate themselves as distinct traditions.

A central motivation of puppeteers on Awaji was establishing puppetry as a ritual practice free from the jurisdiction of the ceremonial authority of Nishinomiya while appropriating the religious authority of a priest from that shrine. This was accomplished in large part through the production of a unifying narrative. Basing their new tradition on a Kan'ei 15 (1638) document describing their origins, *Dōkumbō Denki*, Awaji puppeteers attempted to create a unique and legitimate identity for themselves as free-lance ritual specialists, traveling the country. The text emphasized the loosening of attachments to the Nishinomiya religious center. The rise of itinerant ritual puppetry on Awaji participates in a larger dynamic in Japanese religious history: when unordained and non-ecclesiastical religious specialists became highly popular, major religious centers (both Buddhist and amalgamated Buddhist-Shinto centers) sought ways to control their activities.

There are basically two lines of interpretation that account for the existence of the Awaji tradition. One argues that Awaji has been a center for puppetry from the late Heian period and that this center developed parallel to the Nishinomiya kugutsu groups. This interpretation provides the Awaji tradition with a longer history than historical documents can validate. The other line of interpretation, which I shall develop here, argues that Awaji puppetry developed in the mid-sixteenth century when Nishinomiya puppeteers left that center. From my reading of the fragmentary evidence, the latter interpretation is the only verifiable account of the origins of the Awaji tradition. I shall begin, however, with a discussion of the first interpretation, which represents a modern version of an older dynamic in the Awaji tradition—autonomy from the Nishinomiya center and the uniqueness of Awaji as a place.

The Cradle of Awaji Puppetry: A Sanjo District on the Mihara Plain

The ceremonial center of Awaji puppetry lies in the middle of the Mihara plain in the lower half of the island. The town is called Ichi (written with the character meaning "market") and the district is Sanjo. The center is a small shrine now called Ōmidō Hachiman Daibosatsu. Just how and when this site became a center for puppetry is a point of controversy, as historical records describing the early history of Awaji ritual puppetry are vague. A cluster of hypotheses, popular among folklorists, look for the roots of Awaji puppetry in the imagined religious universe of the early maritime people of the Inland Sea.

The Amazoku Hypothesis

According to archaeological studies conducted on Awaji, the central plain of Mihara-gun is among the oldest settled sites in the Inland Sea. For this reason, there have been attempts to tie the development of Awaji puppetry to the people who populated this island in the protohistorical pe-

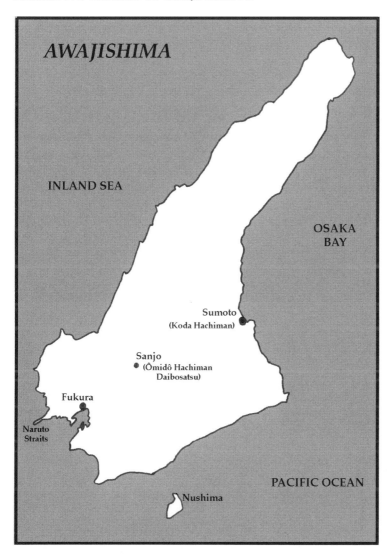

Map of Awaji showing the location of Sanjo and two of Awaji's larger towns.

riod, maritime people called by the general term *amazoku* or *ama* (sea people). How are we to understand the popularity of this kind of hypothesis, and what light can it shed on the dynamics of tradition formation in Awaji puppetry?

Wakamori Tarō, the folklorist who in the 1950s supervised a major investigation of Awaji's history, mythology, archaeology, and folklore, has argued that by the protohistorical, or late Kofun period (roughly the fifth to the seventh centuries C.E.), tribes of sea people were already organized into a sort of confederation in this region, so that the people living on the small island of Nushima and also at the western end of Shikoku could be brought to northern Awaji (across from present-day Akashi) to work as navigators of the Inland Sea and divers for pearls and seaweed. Wakamori suggests that perhaps the southern part of Awaji, called Ama, and the plain of Mihara may have been the center of power of the amazoku of the western Inland Sea.[1] Although Awaji is quite mountainous, this plain consists of a large stretch of relatively flat and arable land.

Miyamoto Tsuneichi writes that Awaji, Awa (on Shikoku), and the Settsu region (near present-day Nishinomiya) constituted a region dominated by amazoku. He cites a document dated the fifth month of 844 which says there were more than three thousand ama settled in groups along the beaches and bays of Awaji.[2] Perhaps the central plain of Mihara may have been the center of the "confederated tribes" of ama who controlled the western Inland Sea.

Little is known about the amazoku other than what can be gleaned about them from readings of *Kojiki* and *Nihongi*, interpretations of archaeological digs along the Inland Sea, references to the members of their tribes who, when subjugated, became performers for the imperial family, and speculation on their contributions to other religious traditions in Japan, particularly Hachiman worship.[3] From these sources, a hazy picture emerges of these people: Their leaders were female shamans who used oracles to organize their governance. They were involved in the practice of diving and fishing and were also adept at navigation from the sea using mountain peaks as points of reference, a skill that proved useful to the government of the emerging Yamato state as it sought to conquer western Japan.[4] Many of the myths found in *Kojiki* and *Nihongi* clearly have maritime themes and are considered to be traditional myths of these tribes, redacted to make a coherent narrative for the imperial line of Yamato rulers. It is widely speculated that Ebisu may have originally been a deity of the amazoku, a hypothesis that would partially explain why Ebisu worship is found all over Japan from an early time and why the deity is called only by the name meaning "foreigner" or "barbarian" and is not mentioned in the redacted myths.

One can postulate that perhaps an older tradition of divination, oracles, and appeasement of malevolent spirits is the common denominator between Awaji, Nishinomiya, and Usa. The coincidence of Sanjo districts where puppetry is practiced in lower Awaji, Nishinomiya, and Usa; the apparent relationship between Hachiman and Ebisu worship and *amazoku*; and the fact that small worship sites dedicated to Hyakudayū are present in all three sites are striking. The reader will recall that one interpretation of the origins of the word *kugutsu* proposed by Origuchi suggested that amazoku would actually carry puppets in their baskets (*kago* or *kugu*) used for gathering seaweed. This hypothesis has no evidence save the most far-fetched philological speculations to back it up, but it points to a strong tendency in some traditions of Japanese folklore studies to tie the mysterious amazoku to the development of Japanese puppetry.

There is not enough evidence to support the hypothesis, yet the very hypothesis itself is something of a datum in the study of Awaji puppetry. Like the debate over where the ancient ruler Pimiko was buried, the quest for the world of the amazoku constitutes something of a fad in Japanese folklore studies. Subjugated in the early period of the Japanese state, these maritime peoples represent a buried and forgotten past and have become icons for a lost part of the self in constructed identities in Japan today. The attempt to find the roots of Awaji ningyō in this ancient past seems to be nostalgia of a unique kind. The sea represents a fluid, mysterious, danger-ous, and powerful order of meaning. Reclaiming it as part of one's past is a powerful act.

The lure of this hypothesis was powerful enough to fuel the develop-ment of a short-lived theme park on Awaji, where one could "experience life the way that the ancient amazoku did" by living in huts, making salt out of sea water, and digging irrigation ditches for basic agriculture. Ar-chaeologists and historians on Awaji have been more circumspect about this theory, and though most of them find the hypothesis appealing, there is a tacit agreement that it is unprovable, to be left to energetic young scholars and archaeologists with a flare for the sensational.

The Usa Hypothesis

A parallel, and not totally unrelated hypothesis about the origins of Awaji puppetry concerns the relationship between the spread of Hachiman wor-ship from the Usa center, the use of ritual performance in deity appease-ment, and Awaji puppetry. In the late 1950s, Wakamori and Handa Yasuo (a folklorist from Oita University) proposed the hypothesis that the Awaji Sanjo site was actually a divination district controlled by *miko* (female sha-mans) who, under the jurisdiction of the Usa Hachiman shrine, main-tained a center of oracles and divination on Awaji. Wakamori and Handa argued that these shamans may have used puppets to appease deities, and they speculated that puppeteers from a different kugutsu group may have come later from Nishinomiya, joined forces with these shamans, and de-veloped puppetry from a strictly ritual performance into a more dramatic form of entertainment.[5] Such a hypothesis would suggest that Awaji puppetry arose as a parallel tradition to the Nishinomiya center, and al-though Awaji puppeteers were strongly connected to Nishinomiya, they may have had roots predating the breakup of the Nishinomiya kugutsu groups. The intention of this hypothesis was to formulate a history for Awaji puppetry that gave it a unique history not derived from the Nishinomiya kugutsu groups.[6]

Wakamori and Handa never developed their hypothesis beyond a number of basic questions, but these slowly assumed the form of an argument in the folklore studies movement. Like the amazoku hypothesis, and in some subsequent presentations on the subject, the Usa hypothesis was so often cited as fact that it assumed the status of data.[7]

Both the amazoku and Usa hypotheses render the history of Awaji puppetry exotic. They imply that this performance tradition holds the key to the hidden past of Japanese religious life. When seen as cultural productions, both of these hypotheses are fascinating; as historical reconstructions, they are less compelling. But if we can content ourselves with a more recent (and perhaps less scintillating) account of origins, the early development of Awaji puppetry reveals a great deal about the production of a tradition. What can we actually know about the development of ritual puppetry on Awaji?

Awaji Puppetry's Birthplace and Center: Ōmidō Hachiman Daibosatsu

The center of Awaji ningyō is a small shrine on a back street of the district called Sanjo in the township of Ichi. The shrine, Sanjo Ōmidō Hachiman Daibosatsu, is known simply as Ōmidō by people living nearby. One local legend I heard regarding this name maintained that the origin of the name Ōmidō came from *o-umi-dō* (birthing hall) and that this shrine had been a place where women would give birth.[8] This theory may arise from a need to make reference to the fact that the center is located in Sanjo. Most likely, the term is simply a double honorific referring to a place of worship. Throughout the Tokugawa period, the Sanjo district surrounding this shrine was written with the characters meaning "birth place," but it is possible that earlier the characters "place of divination" were used.[9]

To arrive at the shrine, one leaves the main road that runs from Fukura to Sumoto and heads straight west. A narrow side street passes directly through the Sanjo district where a hundred years ago numerous puppet theaters such as Uemura Gennojō and Ichimura Rokunojō stood side by side, and where ritual puppeteers made their homes. Now only the crumbling walls of these old theaters remain; but the shrine where they worshipped their tutelary kami still stands. One pulls off to the left of this small street into a tiny parking lot. There, outside the concrete *torii* (gate) demarcating the entrance to the shrine, there stands a large stone erected in the 1960s. Engraved on it are the characters "Awaji Ningyō Jōruri no Hasshōchi" (The Cradle of Awaji Puppet Drama).

One walks through the torii into an open area flanked on one side by a large wooden structure that once served as a stage and on the other by huge Cryptomeria trees, which keep the spot shady and cool on even the hottest of summer days. At the end of the open precincts stand the two structures that comprise the shrine: a *haiden* (worship hall) in the Irimoya style with a small stage for rituals, in which the deity Hachiman is enshrined and to the left, another smaller worship structure (*hokora*) dedicated to four figures, all of which are represented in clay effigies inside: Hyakudayū, Dōkumbō, Ebisu, and Akiba (the latter said by local people to be the wife of Hyakudayū, though few are sure of this).[10] The reader will recall that in the previous chapter I noted that Hyakudayū was an epidemic spirit worshipped at the Nishinomiya Ebisu shrine, and the tutelary deity of puppeteers who lived and worked there. On Awaji, Hyakudayū is the major figure in a very different kind of drama.

The date these effigies were made and put into the shrine is not known, but the sculpture said to be Hyakudayū has a marking on the back of it indicating that it was repaired in Bunka 2 (1805). Several scholars of art history on Awaji suggested that these effigies were probably made during the Genroku era (1688–1703).

This Hachiman shrine is in the Usa lineage.[11] In front of the Hachiman worship hall there are two lanterns and two guardian dogs (*koma inu*). Inscriptions on these offerings indicate that they were dedicated to the shrine in 1805 by puppeteers from the puppet theater known as Uemura Gennojō, considered the earliest and most powerful theater troupe on the island.

Niimi Kanji refers to Ōmidō as a subsidiary shrine (*keigaisha*) but does not provide the name of its parent shrine.[12] Throughout Japan, shrines are affiliated with major centers through a complex system of parent and child shrines. For example, the Nishinomiya shrine is the center (parent) of Ebisu worship in Japan, but has branch (child) shrines scattered throughout Japan. Near each of these branch shrines one will find still smaller local shrines, which maintain some sort of affiliation to the regional shrine as a means of participating in the power and authority of the large center. We see the same pattern with Hachiman worship as well. As studies of Hachiman *wakamiya* (child shrines) have shown, the original affiliations frequently become blurred or even forgotten in the case of very small local shrines.[13] This is certainly the case of Ebisu shrines throughout Japan. There are no written records describing the original affiliations of Ōmidō, and it is not mentioned in the records of any larger shrine on Awaji.[14]

The worship hall housing the sculptures of the mythical founders of Awaji puppetry.

From left to right: Akiba, Ebisu, Dōkumbō, Hyakudayū.

The center for puppetry appears at present to be affiliated with the Kōda Hachiman shrine about ten kilometers away, evidenced by the fact that most people in Sanjo consider themselves to be *ujiko* (literally, clan children) of Kōda Hachiman. Puppeteers from Sanjo were also instrumental in maintaining Kōda Hachiman in the early nineteenth century, for offerings at this site bear inscriptions indicating puppetry troupes were contributing to its upkeep.[15]

This affiliation between Ōmidō and Kōda has been largely implicit. Everyone understands that these two sites are connected, but since the affiliation is not mentioned in any records, it is impossible to prove. The pattern of affiliation of major shrine (*honsha*) to subsidiary shrines in Japan usually has them in closer proximity than the Kōda Hachiman shrine and Sanjo Ōmidō. Although evidence suggests the Sanjo Ōmidō center was affiliated with Kōda Hachiman, it is possible that this affiliation came about relatively recently, perhaps during the Genroku era. Perhaps the Sanjo shrine originally had other affiliations. What would a shift in shrine affiliations reveal about the formation of the Awaji tradition?

Ōmidō is actually quite near a larger Ebisu shrine. This shrine, the largest Ebisu shrine on the island, lies just at the edge of Sanjo and is the Awaji representative of the Nishinomiya center. The reader will recall that at the Nishinomiya center, just outside the main shrine precincts in a Sanjo district, there was a small worship hall dedicated to the deity Hyakudayū. I propose that the Sanjo Ōmidō site on Awaji was originally affiliated with the big Ebisu shrine, itself a child of the Nishinomiya center. The location of the Hyakudayū shrine in relationship to the Ebisu center was modeled on the Nishinomiya center. The Awaji center for puppetry was therefore originally something of a microcosmic version of the Nishinomiya center. As puppeteers entered into conflict with the Nishinomiya center, I suggest, they wanted to break out of this affiliation. So they sought another affiliation for their shrine, shifting their focus to the Kōda Hachiman shrine even though it was much further away.

Ōmidō has been the ceremonial center of Awaji puppetry for as long as there have been records. In fact, many of the written records discussed below situate the origins of puppetry in this place. As puppetry troupes became numerous on Awaji in the mid to late seventeenth century, they set up operations around this shrine in the Sanjo district, and Ōmidō became a local place of worship. Here, every New Year, any itinerant performer setting out from Awaji to perform appeasement rituals would present himself before the worship hall of Hyakudayū and pray for protection and success. Later, local jōruri troupes on the island would compete for the right to present Sanbasō before this worship hall on New Year's Day. (The honor was usually alternated from year to year between the two largest theaters on the island.) Today, the Ōmidō shrine is quiet but is still used as a local worship site. Its main attraction is as a gateball space, and every morning during the summer and fall months, elderly local people who work in the fields gather to play gateball at around ten o'clock in the morning. What kind of tradition was centered here? How did it become a tradition in its own right?

Onogorojima's Sanjo Dōkumbō: Early Records of Awaji Puppeteers

It is not clear when puppeteers became active on the island of Awaji. Using scattered evidence from the late sixteenth century through the early part of the twentieth century, it is possible to piece together a probable picture of the formative period of the tradition.

Our earliest record describing the activities of an Awaji puppeteer is dated 1570. It is a document a puppeteer carried with him as he traveled the country performing ritual puppetry. It reads: "Onogorojima's Sanjo Dōkumbō transmits Hikida Awaji's title. Now, he carries the seasonal ceremonies of the three shrines to the Imperial court. He was given the title of fourth rank. It is his Majesty's Imperial Will which decrees this case. Recorded in the second month of the first year of Genki."[16]

We learn from this piece of evidence that by 1570 there was a person named Hikida who had already been granted a name and a rank and given the right to perform and travel about the country presenting ritual performances, particularly those relating to seasonal rituals of the three shrines, Ise Jingū, Iwashimizu Hachiman, and either Kamo or Kasuga, all directly connected to the Imperial family. The type of performance to which this text refers is probably the Sanbasō ritual, to be discussed in detail in the following chapter.[17] The right of this puppeteer to perform was generalized to a category of performer, referred to in the text as "Sanjo Dōkumbō.[18]

In this document, Awaji is referred to by a mythical name, Onogorojima. The *Nihongi* and *Kojiki* creation accounts tell of an island called Onogorojima, the "self-curdling island" that congealed at the end of the heavenly jeweled spear lowered into the undifferentiated brine by Izanagi and Izanagi. The substance that dripped off the spear tip formed into land. The two deities then descended onto this spot, and from this small bit of land they proceeded to create the rest of the cosmos. What is the significance of this reference in this document and what does it tell us about the early Awaji tradition of puppetry?

In certain readings of the *Kojiki* and *Nihongi* myths, Awaji is regarded as the placenta of creation, and the myths say that Izanami and Izanagi "took no pleasure in it."[19] In symbolic terms, a placenta can be understood as a useless by-product of birth—necessary for the creation of life but of no value after life has been started. Throughout premodern and medieval Japanese history, Awaji was a liminal place, the island in between Honshu and Shikoku, a land where exiled emperors lived, where imperial princes went to kill game, where the defeated Heike warriors were said to have fled. This vision of Awaji presents it as a by-product of creation, a failed creation attempt.

But there is another, competing vision of Awaji to be presented, one that makes it not only the first island created but also the very navel of the universe: Onogorojima. According to Awaji legend, the actual Onogorojima exists within the island of Awaji. In an area near the border between Seidanchō and Nandanchō in southern Awaji, there is a small worship hall demarcated by torii. It is surrounded completely by water, creating a tiny island. The circumference of the moat is approximately twenty-five meters. A miniature footbridge connects it to the road and one can walk over to it and stand on the tiny bit of land. This site is considered to be the first piece of congealed land created by Izanami and Izanagi, and it is indicated by a sign explaining the mythological event. While the small shrine is not set in very triumphant surroundings, most people I spoke with were well aware of it and the story connected with it: It was Onogorojima.[20]

Wakamori noted this tendency to claim the primacy (and centrality) of Awaji in the local understanding of the world: "While there are different ways of narrating it, almost everyone claims that Awaji was one of the first islands created."[21] The Awaji ningyō tradition appropriated and in some ways contributed to this vision of Awaji's identity. The document from 1570 quoted above puts this vision of Awaji in the foreground: Awaji was the center of the cosmos, the location of Onogorojima, and using this name for a person from Awaji was a way of assigning primacy to both the island and its tradition of puppetry. The text reminds the person who reads it that this performer is from the very center of the universe, traveling throughout the land with the seal of approval from none other than the emperor himself. As will become apparent later (chapter 6), a major dynamic in the Awaji tradition has been insisting on the uniqueness and centrality of this performance tradition vis-à-vis others in Japan.

Ecclesiastical and Popular Religious Authority

Part of the tension that led to the development of the Awaji tradition as distinct from the Nishinomiya center is a common dynamic in Japanese religious history. Throughout the Muromachi period and the development of Tokugawa Japan, performers of all types were attached to various temples and shrines and were expected to perform at certain times of the year. These Sanjo hōshi, as they were often called, were allowed to engage in work outside the shrines at other times of year, and this usually meant "freelance" ritual and theater work. As we have seen, puppeteers living in the Sanjo district of the Nishinomiya shrine were clearly conscripted performers with duties related to the shrine, but they also gave occasional performances elsewhere.

Various references in Japanese history and theater narratives describe the problems that arose when performers with responsibilities at shrines and temples found that working on their own was more lucrative (and possibly more fun) than being attached to ecclesiastical centers. For example, Zeami wrote of this problem and admonished his performers to stick to their obligations: "Under the pretext of making tours, some actors neglect the Religious Services; some arrive late, others stay away from the religious service at Kasuga shrine. Therefore, they will come to a bad end. Even if they are prosperous for a while, at the end they will be punished. The religious services are our basic duty, while tours are just to secure our livelihood in the spare moments in between."[22]

We know that while puppeteers were affiliated with and lived in the precincts of the Nishinomiya shrine, their status within the shrine was decidedly low. For the most part, they were subcontractors with the shrine, operating under the jurisdiction of the shrine as they spread the worship of Ebisu around the countryside by performing rites dedicated to the deity and distributing Ebisu amulets for a fee. They were required to remain attached to the Nishinomiya center in some way and needed permission from that center to perform Ebisu rites regardless of where they went. In this way, the shrine maintained control over not only the puppeteers' lives but local access to Ebisu rituals, understood to be helpful in securing a good fishing catch for the year.[23] The real problem came up when they became popular in their own right and discovered that working on their own was highly lucrative. (It is also possible to discern a new concern with artistic freedom. In performances outside the shrine, there was greater possibility for artistic and dramatic development.) As we saw at the end of the last chapter, many puppeteers started to operate without securing proper permission from shrine authorities, and their status at the shrine became more tenuous. From this movement arose Awaji puppetry. A key problem in inventing a new tradition concerns finding the structures and histories to legitimate it, which often entails borrowing and appropriating existing devices from competing (and frequently parent) traditions.

All of the texts we consider below trace the origins of the Awaji tradition to the teachings of a non-ecclesiastical sacred specialist. An examination of these texts reveals that while puppeteers were concerned with liberating themselves from the Nishinamiya ceremonial center, their chief concern on Awaji seems to have been to establish a parallel sphere of religious authority and practice with Awaji as its center, elevating the puppeteers to the level of sacred specialists even though they were no longer part of a recognized center. "Awaji puppetry" meant more than just another place for puppeteers. It constituted a new tradition, constructed against the authority of the center in Nishinomiya. Rather than viewing themselves as merely the "little" version of the "greater" traditions of those centers, these itinerant artists produced their own notions of religious authority and legitimation, founded on their ability to enact magical transformations of matter and spirit and bring about spirit pacification through the medium of puppetry. On the strength of what was presented as a sacred and secret document describing the origins of Awaji puppetry, they maintained their autonomous and even imperially sanctioned right to present Ebisu appeasement and purification rites throughout the country. The case of itinerant performance gives us some evidence to suggest that for many Japanese people, the activities of major religious centers were sometimes largely irrelevant to their lives, and meaningful and significant religious action was made available by unordained, "non-ecclesiastical" sacred specialists.

Records throughout the Tokugawa period indicate that ritual puppetry (using the term Dōkumbō mawashi) was a common occupation on Awaji. Census records from the middle of the Bunka era (1804–1818), currently stored in the Mihara municipal office, indicate that in Sanjo alone, 92 out of 144 households listed Dōkumbō mawashi as their occupation. Similar records for (then) neighboring Ichi indicated that 22 out of 173 households were those of Dōkumbō mawashi, and other villages in Mihara-gun had approximately 20 percent of their families listed as puppeteers.[24] They traveled widely in Japan and yet maintained a common identity as Awaji puppeteers.

Just how far from Awaji they traveled is answered in part by a recent discovery. In 1987, a woman named Ai Suzue living in Morioka in northeastern Japan was cleaning out her family storehouse when she found puppets and documents relating to Awaji puppetry (including a copy of *Dōkumbō Denki*, to be discussed below). Research subsequently done by scholars from the Iwate Prefecture historical museum revealed that these had been brought to Morioka in 1641 by Suzue Shirobe, one of Mrs. Suzue's ancestors and an Awaji puppeteer. This discovery indicated that by the mid-seventeenth century, Awaji puppeteers were already traveling throughout the country, presenting themselves as members of a distinct puppetry tradition and performing before lords and even the emperor.[25]

What was the relationship of these puppeteers to the Nishinomiya center? How did they understand the nature of their work? To answer these questions, we have two types of written sources, each following a different line of interpretation: One emphasizes the origins of Awaji puppetry in a conflict between a Nishinomiya shrine priest and a puppeteer employed there. The other downplays the Nishinomiya origins, and carefully appropriates this earlier tradition while legitimating Awaji puppetry as a tradition in its own right. Throughout the years, these two types of narratives have been interwoven, and oral versions on Awaji reflect a synthesis of the two. All versions, however, reflect the tensions between a Shinto priest attached to a shrine (the Nishinomiya shrine) and a puppeteer without a formal shrine affiliation. Our earliest record, from the middle of the seventeenth century, is the formal origin myth of the Awaji tradition, considered to be a sacred document. This document provides a fluid central narrative that unites puppeteers on Awaji into one tradition and places the practice of spirit appeasement at the center of their art. This carefully fashioned narrative absorbs the mythical tradition of the Nishinomiya center, blunts issues of difference, and all the while insists on the Awaji tradition's legitimacy.

Here, I present a translation and discussion of this document following a presentation of our second kind of evidence, nineteenth-century historical references to the early history of Awaji puppetry. I have chosen to present these sources out of chronological order because the apparent intentions of the earlier document are best appreciated when seen in context of the other narratives dating nearly a hundred and fifty years later.

A Remembered Past: Arguing Priests, Litigation, and a New Tradition

The reader will recall that puppeteers on Awaji were involved in both ritual activity and the presentation of dramatic entertainment in the jōruri tradition. While ritual puppetry tended to dominate the early development of the tradition, the theatrical tradition of ningyō jōruri was the main activity of Awaji puppet theaters by the early nineteenth century. Records from Bunka 7 (1811) indicate that there were over twenty full-time performing troupes on Awaji, half of them located in Sanjo. Several of them had multiple repertoire companies, which traveled independently from one another all over Japan. Uemura Gennojō, for example, was divided into five separate groups. One or two always stayed home and presented theater on Awaji, while the others kept a heavily booked traveling schedule.

Many ritual puppeteers found seasonal employment in the large theaters, the recorded histories of which contain passing references to the early history of ritual puppeteery. During the Bunka period, as the popularity of ningyō jōruri peaked in Japan, there was a flurry of activity among puppetry troupes on Awaji, each seeking to document its unique puppetry styles and prove that it had been the first and the best. Many of these documents, which describe the relations among different *jōruri* troupes on the island, make passing references to the origins of Awaji puppetry as a whole. An examination of these documents provides some of the information we have for an early history of ritual puppetry, even though it is fragmented and sometimes unreliable. Because a Dōkumbō mawashi was of lower social status than a puppeteer who manipulated puppets in jōruri performances, these histories often tend to downplay or even omit references to ritual puppetry.

One of the most elaborate descriptions of origins comes from a text published in 1825 called *Awaji-gusa*, authored by a father and son, Fujii Yōshin and Fujii Shōmin. It is clearly based on an interview with someone in Sanjo describing the early history of Awaji puppetry.

> First, said a village elder, at the time that Hyakudayū came to Awaji, he stayed for several days in the house of a puppet-head carver named Kikudayū.[26] After that, he [Hyakudayū] made love with Kikudayū's daughter, and she became pregnant.[27] After more than a hundred days, Hyakudayū suddenly died from an illness. Because of this, the imperial order of Hyakudayū[28] has remained here, and in later years, there were arguments and litigation between the Nishinomiya puppeteers and the Awaji Dōkumbō. But Kikudayū was in possession of the imperial order of Hyakudayū, and therefore it was determined that he was the very best in all the land.

A very similar version of events is recorded twenty-six years later in 1851 in a text by Gyōshō Sei called *Awaji no Kuni Meisho Zue* (A picture book of Awaji famous places).[29] This book also contains a drawing of an itinerant Awaji puppeteer.

Meisho zue (picture books of famous places or name places) constituted a genre of popular travel guide books during the Edo period. *Awaji no Kuni Meisho Zue* is the Awaji example of this genre.[30] This document seems to have relied on two sources, Dōkumbō Denki (discussed below) and *Awaji-gusa*, so it gives us little new information. The picture it contains may well have been based on verbal descriptions of puppeteers, for it closely resembles the picture of an Ebisu-kaki presented in the previous chapter. The text states that "Nishinomiya's Hyakudayū came to Awaji and brought along a puppet, and for a long time he stayed in this village [i.e., Sanjo] at Ōmidō while he was sick. At some point in time, a puppet-

Drawing of an Awaji puppeteer from an 1851 travel text describing Awaji.

head carver of this village by the name of Kikudayū accompanied Hyakudayū, and when he brought Hyakudayū home with him, Hyakudayū
made love with Kikudayū's daughter."

These two versions (which I will consider together, since the latter
seems to have relied on the former) have a number of important points.
First, they suggest that Hyakudayū was the founder of Awaji puppetry and
that he originally came from Nishinomiya. Second, they note that he
stayed at the home of a puppet-head carver, which implies that there was
already some sort of puppetry activity on Awaji prior to the arrival of the
Nishinomiya puppeteers. Third, they mention the marriage of an outsider
to a local girl, a narrative device that allows for the localization of an im-

ported practice.[31] Fourth, they both refer to the litigation between the Nishinomiya center and Awaji puppeteers.

This last point, the controversy over the rights of Awaji puppeteers to perform independently from the permission of the Nishinomiya center, is the focus of this source.[32] Apparently, there was a problem with Hyakudayū (or whoever this person was) bringing ritual puppetry to Awaji and performing. His imperial order served as his license to perform, similar to the 1570 document quoted earlier.

The next version does not even mention Hyakudayū but rather begins immediately with the issue of litigation. The puppeteer loses and has to leave Nishinomiya. In an Ansei 4 (1857) text by a father and son named Konishi Tomonao and Konishi Kinkō, *Ongyoku Michi Shirube*, we find the following:

In the Settsu Nishinomiya Ebisu Shrine, a priest [*kannushi*] by the name of Mori Tango had an argument over the authority of the shrine with a priest [of lower rank][33] employed in the same shrine named Mori Kanedayū. In the decision from the administrative office, Kanedayū was defeated, and so he entrusted his young son with Mori Tango and went to a temple called Shōnenji in Amagasaki, where he stayed.[34] As a means of making a living, he made small puppets, and using an old sutra box, he walked around the streets of the town, doing puppet performances based on stories he made up himself, which he sang the way one sings the *Tales of the Heike*.[35] The spectators really praised him. He then went up to Kyoto and lived the life of a wandering puppeteer [*ningyō mawashi*]. At about the time that there was a fire in the imperial court, and from the land left by the fire, through a crack in the hedge, a young prince saw the performance.[36] So these performances were seen by people high and low in society.[37] Then, from this prince he received many gifts. The prince also proclaimed a title: "Of the various and assorted arts, the greatest puppeteer in Japan; the name Uemura (or Yamamoto) Kanetayū is bestowed upon him." Later in the fifth year of Tenshō [1578], it was delivered orally by the prince. Later, Uemura Kanedayū went to Awaji Mihara-gun Sanjo mura, and there he taught the art of puppetry to the poor farmers. He then received permission from the Lord of the Castle [probably a reference to the Hachisuga family in Awa, discussed below] and began to give puppetry performances. This was the beginning of *jōruri shibai*.

This document suggests that it was a former Nishinomiya puppeteer, kicked out after a dispute with another person from that shrine, who was given the name Uemura and who came to Awaji to start puppetry, although it makes no mention of ritual puppetry and uses the neutral term *ningyō mawashi*. During the Tokugawa period, family names were granted to peasants or artists to give special recognition for merit, and possibly the puppeteer was given this name to honor his performance.

What attracts our attention is the detail that this puppeteer entered into a conflict with the Nishinomiya center, became a wandering puppeteer with no affiliations, stayed for a while in a nunnery in Amagasaki, and eventually ended up on Awaji.

The next version appears in an anthology edited by the scholar of Edo history, Mitamura Engyō, entitled *Awaji Awa Ningyō Za Kyūki Zassan* (Assorted old documents for the Awaji and Awa puppetry troupes).[38] One document from the anthology is *Ningyō Ganso Honke Uemura Gennojō Jireki* (The original puppeteer family Uemura Gennojō's history). The text does not have a date but is thought to have been written in the Bunka period (1804–1817). It states:

> Dōkumbō was from the Sanjo district of Kyoto, and so he was called Sanjo Dōkumbō. Manipulating puppets, he served the Leech Child of the Nishinomiya shrine. After his death, a priest [*kannushi*] named Mori Kanedayū succeeded Dōkumbō. And then, after that, Hyakudayū of Nishinomiya, the founder of puppetry, starting with the Leech Child of Nishinomiya, traveled all over the country serving in village shrines, both along the coast and inland. Eventually, he came to Awaji, and there he stayed a long time at the home of Hikida. There, he married Hikida's eldest daughter, and she gave birth to a baby son. This child was called Shigedayū, and after Hyakudayū's death, he took the name "Gennojō" (The Original). This Hikida Awaji name became the originator of manipulated puppets, and he taught the art and techniques of Hyakudayū to the farmers and established the Awaji troupe [*za*]. At the time of Emperor Goyōzei, he performed before the emperor. And then in 1570, in the second month, an imperial name was bestowed on him. After this, Hikida took the stage name of Uemura.

This document has three noteworthy features: First, it gives us a source for Dōkumbō, asserting that he was from a Sanjo district, a twist we do not see in any other source, even the Nishinomiya sources for Dōkumbō. Second, it traces the origins of Awaji puppetry from its mythical beginning with a priest named Dōkumbō to a priest named Mori Kanetayū, who somehow hands the rights over to a person named Hyakudayū; the latter comes to Awaji and marries into the Hikida family, which finally changes its name to Uemura. Third, it indicates that this person was given his name by an emperor, establishing the oldest puppetry troupe on Awaji.

In another nineteenth century text, *Zōho Jōruri Taikeizu* (The new and revised jōruri lineage chart), we learn the following:

> A man named Hikida, who hailed from Awaji, had from birth a great deal of talent in all sorts of performing arts of the *fūryū* style, and he was able to make different faces for young and old, men and women, and he devised clever ways to express a wide range of emotions,[39] and was able to manipulate puppets

so that they were just like human beings. This was seen by many lords, and he was praised as "hallmark and founder of Japan's many performing arts." On one of those occasions Hideyoshi heard about him, saw his performance, and was deeply moved. Hideyoshi granted him performance space in the Shijō Kawaramachi district in Kyoto, and there his performances were seen by many people. After this, Shigedayū was summoned to the imperial court, and the emperor saw the performance and gave him the title Hikida Awaji Tayū.[40]

Although the text makes no mention of the Nishinomiya origins, it indicates that this important Awaji puppeteer was granted a title by the emperor before whom he performed.

It is not possible to maintain that all of these versions were based on the same source. Our intention was to determine how they represent tensions concerning the right to perform.

Two ideas stand out in these sources when they are read together. First, it is clear that Awaji puppeteers originally came from Nishinomiya and struggled to find an identity for themselves in relation to this center. Second, these early puppeteers wanted to have their own tradition. These origin accounts suggest that having a history and being a tradition was a form of legitimation in its own right.[41]

Now we turn back in time from these sources to a discussion of the earliest version of a "history" of the Awaji tradition, a text that, I would argue, was carefully produced to create a unified tradition.

A Dead Priest and an Angry Deity: *Dōkumbō Denki,* Kan'ei 15 (1638)

Puppeteers who were centered on Awaji in the Sanjo district were not merely a scattered group of freelance ritual artists: they were a tradition, created not through consensus about performance style but through the production of a unifying narrative. To be an Awaji puppeteer meant one shared the same story with other puppeteers about who you were, where you came from, and why you did what you did. Other aspects of tradition were secondary to this central story. Part of the work of tradition is to ensure its continuity and survival, to provide a vision of consensus and center, and to be, in the most basic of terms, hegemonic about discourse.[42]

The founding myth of the Awaji tradition, *Dōkumbō Denki,* is a fascinating document in Awaji puppetry's history. Because it is clearly a mythic narrative, it has been left aside by scholars studying the origins of the Awaji tradition. For example, in his essay "Genroku ki Awaji Ayatsurishibai no Chihō Kōki," Sakaguchi Bunnō discusses the history of Uemura Gennojō troupe but dismisses this text with one sentence: "Concerning the origins of Awaji puppetry, beginning with the anonymous *Dōkumbō Denki*, sources narrate something about a connection between puppeteers attached to Nishinomiya and Awaji Sanjo-mura."[43] But the structure of this mythical document, particularly when it is read nonchronologically, reveals its purpose.

Clearly both mythical and historical, the text narrates the founding event of the tradition and creates and legitimates Awaji puppetry as a tradition in its own right. Every Awaji puppeteer carried a copy of this document as he traveled throughout Japan. Having a copy of the scroll meant you were part of the Awaji tradition.

My hypothesis is that this text represents a creative fusion of a large number of elements already present on Awaji at the time it was written; it serves as a confederative document for various factions; and it reveals how a performance-based cultural practice creates a mythical tradition. We are able to see the considerations that create and give form to a tradition. The basic narrative mutes the historical issues while absorbing the myth tradition of Nishinomiya and even the larger issues of Ebisu worship. It also blunts the conflicts between different claims to origins on Awaji (Uemura, Kanedayū, etc.) and creates a new identity for the enigmatic Hyakudayū. Hyakudayū, I argue, is the name given to the first puppeteer in this narrative because he is the paradigmatic puppeteer of the tradition, capable of being at once every one and no one (not unlike the puppets he is said to manipulate).

Even though it is our earliest written narrative, I argue that this text is a late creation in the phenomenon of puppetry on Awaji. Recorded sixty-eight years after our document identifying Awaji puppeteers (the 1570 "license"), it was designed to meld a number of competing claims to origins on the island, thereby enabling Awaji puppetry to possess a myth of origins legitimating it as a distinct tradition against the pressures from Nishinomiya shrine authorities seeking to reassert their control. The Awaji tradition developed from competing factions each claiming to be the first. *Dōkumbō Denki* reflects what became the canonical version of events, free to be nonhistorical and even fanciful.

As I have discussed elsewhere in my studies of Japanese ritual and its relationship to myths, myth as a narrative structure makes it possible to include a number of diverse elements and synthesize them in a unique way.[44] It is not merely that myth allows one to be loose with the facts. Rather, myth makes facts secondary to religious and ideological sentiments and concerns, which become powerful and at times quite dangerous. Mythical time is not just about "realities lived and stories told." It can be about realities rewritten and stories retold or left out as well.

The text of *Dōkumbō Denki* is solely in Chinese characters.[45] The narrator claims that the contents are based upon a previous written document lost at the time of its compilation, another rhetorical device that allows the text to transcend history while at the same time claiming to narrate it definitively.[46] The tone of the text gives the impression that it is narrating an old oral tradition, and it uses a standard genre for origin texts in Japanese religions, known as *engi*, in which the beginnings of the text frequently reiterate lines from the Japanese mythical narratives of the *Nihongi* and *Kojiki* (two heavily constructed narratives in their own right).[47] The text is divided into two rather distinct sections. The total number of characters in the text is 1079, and an additional sixty-eight characters appear at the end of the text in the postscript (*okugaki*), indicating the date and conditions under which it was recorded and the name and rank of the scribe and reciter.

Scrolls of *Dōkumbō Denki* were regarded as sacred objects by puppeteers and were treated with special care and devotion clearly because this document provided a center for the tradition. The scroll was kept on a kamidana in theaters on Awaji and was carried in the box containing ritual implements for the puppet Sanbasō when a puppeteer traveled. All the puppet troupes originating from Awajishima during the Tokugawa period took a copy of this document with them. The document has been found in the locations to which Awaji puppetry spread: Yamanashi, Nagano, and Morioka. In each discovery, the text had been carefully stored, frequently in the same box with the sacred puppets of Sanbasō, Okina, and Ebisu. These puppets, unlike those depicting jōruri characters, are afforded a special status, since they are used in the performance of sacred rites. Warnings in the theater lore often state that in the event of fire, the Sanbasō puppets and the *Dōkumbō Denki* must be saved, or else terrible things will ensue.

To date, the existence of eight copies of this text have been ascertained: one in the Kuroda Ningyō Za in Nagano Prefecture, a theater started by an Awaji puppeteer in the eighteenth century; three in the Awaji Ningyō Jōruri Kan (Awaji Puppet Theater) in Fukura; three in the home of the Toyota Hisae family in Sanjo mura on Awaji, descendants of the Uemura Gennojō troupe;[48] and one in Morioka in 1987 in the home of Suzue Ai, the descendant of an Awaji puppeteer who performed in Morioka in 1648. A further copy, discovered in Yamanashi Prefecture and mentioned by Nagata Kōkichi in his book *Ikite Iru Ningyō Shibai*, has been subsequently lost.[49]

The calligraphy styles of the eight scrolls differ considerably. The date of all eight is Kan'ei 18, although some are dated in the summer and some in the twelfth month of that year. According to the *okugaki* of all the texts, the person who narrated the content of the text is a certain Sakagami Nyūdo, whose name indicates that he was a member of the Buddhist clergy but about whom nothing is known.

That each subsequent branch of the Awaji tradition had as its founding narrative the *Dōkumbō Denki* accounts for the tradition's perceived cohesion over several centuries, despite the itinerant status of many puppeteers. The text provided a vision of the center for the tradition. Geographically, the center is Awaji. In narrative terms, the center is the story of Hyakudayū. Religiously, the tradition centers on appeasement rituals.

The narrative can be divided into two parts.[50] The reader will recall that in the previous chapter, the deity Ebisu was grafted onto the mythical failed creation attempt of Izanagi and Izanami. This small child deity, the Leech Child, was abandoned on the waves by its parents. The first part of the narrative (not translated here) is an abridged but verbatim account of the *Nihongi* creation account. The text presents that myth up to the point where the Leech Child is set afloat. This is usually where the Leech Child is left in standard mythologies in Japan. This is where the Awaji tradition of puppetry begins.

Dōkumbō Denki
[second part]

The Leech Child drifted on the waves for many years and months. Before that, he arrived at Wakokuzaki and had the shape of a wheel. There he became a kami of light. At that time, there was a fisherman by the name of Murogimi. (From this time, the leader of the fishermen began to be called Murogimi. Later his surname became Fujiwara, and his first name was Hyakudayū Masakiyo.) At a certain time, he was riding in a fishing boat when suddenly the sky became dark, clouds gathered and darkened the sun, and lightning flashed all around. Noting the strangeness of this occurrence, Hyakudayū drew near to a small child he saw floating in the water. The child had the shape of a kami and was only about twelve or so. The child turned to face him and delivered the following oracle: "I am the Leech Child of long ago. Until now, I have had no worship hall. Build me a temporary worship hall on the seashore." The hall built as a result of this oracle was the Nishinomiya Daimyōjin (Ebisu Saburō Den) in Nishinomiya.

In this shrine, a person by the name of Dōkumbō was capable of mediating for this kami and receiving his messages. But after the death of Dōkumbō, there was no one to appease the deity, and so the Leech Child caused heavy rains and winds, fishing disasters, and mishaps on land. Hyakudayū reported this to the head of the Fujiwara family [in Konoeden], who was in the capital, and an imperial order came down. It said that he should make a puppet with the same face and posture as Dōkumbō. Following this order, he manipulated the puppet before the worship hall of the Leech Child, and the deity's spirit calmed down. After this, puppets of this type in the likeness of Dōkumbō were unusually effective in appeasing the Leech Child. After this, Hyakudayū went around to many provinces, worshipping many gods. After this, Hyakudayū-Dōkumbō[51] stopped at Awaji and transmitted this art. It was at this place that the gods created the great country of Japan, and here is the island of Toyoakizushima.[52] After that, he was titled *ayatsurimono* [a puppeteer]. Hyakudayū lived at Awaji Mihara, Sanjo, and there he transmitted this art. It is said that here the people of old worshipped the myriad (eight million) kami. After his death, he was worshipped somewhere in Nishinomiya. He was given the imperial edict from the capital to appease divine spirits, and as an appeaser of kami Hyakudayū was later given the following proclamation: "The great country of Japan is a divine country. Therefore, this person who appeases divine will is the ultimate person of many talents."

WARNING: This art is for the appeasement of *kami*. Hereafter, people should not take this lightly. If they do, it will weigh heavily upon them. People after this should be sorely afraid.

POSTSCRIPT: There was a record of this story before, but it has been lost, and the previous was based upon a secret letter from the house of Yoshida, but since the old document has not been well checked, I have believed only the oral version.

Sakagami Nyūdo
Midsummer, Kan'ei 15

It is apparent from looking at this text, even in translation, that it assumes a certain amount of knowledge of the characters and events involved. The transcriber claims he was attempting to recreate a written document (the secret letter) by listening to someone narrate its contents. This "secret letter" was itself probably based upon an oral tradition. It is impossible to determine whether the original document ever in fact existed. Regardless, this device in the text allows for the creation of a new version of events, while nodding to the authority of another, older record.

Here, I would like to focus on five strategies of tradition formation in this document: the appropriation of myths and motifs from a larger and stable religious center; the formulation of a religious problem and a ritual solution; the expression of legitimation from outside the tradition; the establishment of a new geographical center; and the expression of the new tradition's power and importance. These five strategies indicate that this document was concerned not merely with recording what had happened before, but also with launching a new tradition of ritual puppetry, distinct from the tradition out of which it developed.

This text absorbed two myths from the Nishinomiya tradition and framed them to highlight the Awaji puppetry tradition. First, the text refers to the arrival of the Leech Child at the beach at Wakokuzaki. The reader will recall that the engi text of the Nishinomiya shrine narrates the strange occurrence of a floating effigy being repeatedly caught in a fisherman's net until finally in a dream it is revealed that this object is none other than the deity Ebisu. The Nishinomiya version specifically mentions a place-name—Wadahama. The Awaji narrative has absorbed this part of the Nishinomiya engi and has altered the name slightly to read Wakokuzaki.[53]

The second myth that this Awaji document takes from Nishinomiya concerns the puppeteer Dōkun, here called Dōkumbō. According to the Nishinomiya myth of puppetry, recounted in chapter 3, "In the era of the deity Iwakusubuna, in this inlet, there was an old man named Dōkun. When he heard that the deity at this shrine at the age of three still could not walk, he made a puppet to entertain and raise the child deity." In *Dōkumbō Denki*, this mythical tradition is continued but altered slightly. The Nishinomiya text specifically says that a person named Dōkun used a doll to appease the Leech Child. The Awaji tradition states that this person named Dōkumbō (a name which already meant "puppeteer") merely entertained the Leech Child. But the Awaji version then adds a new dimension to the account, and this in turn creates a new ritual development.

According to the Awaji tradition, a crisis arises when the priest Dōkumbō from the Nishinomiya shrine dies. This Leech Child, a malformed and failed creation abandoned by its parents who comes floating in off the waves, is suddenly without a human officiant. Who will see that his potentially malevolent nature is appeased, now that Dōkumbō is dead? With no one to take Dōkumbō's place, disasters of all sorts occur. The point could not be more clear: Awaji puppetry was started by the person who literally stepped in and took the place of the original priest, making this new tradition the rightful heir to Dōkumbō's ritual authority. The text then uses this narrative moment to launch a new beginning (that is to say, a retelling of "history") for ritual puppetry. Whereas in the Nishinomiya myths it was Dōkun who first used a doll (or puppet), in the Awaji version of events the first puppet is used by a person named Hyakudayū. *Dōkumbō Denki* narrates that Hyakudayū received his orders from the imperial family indicating what should be done: make a puppet in the likeness of Dōkumbō to appease this angry deity. The text relates that not only was this particular puppet effective, but thereafter all puppets in this likeness were effective in appeasing the Leech Child. This fact, noted in the text, allows for the tradition to expand to include more than one puppeteer by making the potency of the puppet generalizable to many puppets. It is not enough for Hyakudayū to have such authority. His authority must be extendable to subsequent performers. The puppet has become the priest, a device which allows the Awaji tradition to absorb the ritual authority of the Nishinomiya center while deflecting the challenge this entailed.

At this point, it is important to note what seems to be a veritable confusion of names and places in *Dōkumbō Denki*. Why does the place-name Wadahama get changed in the Awaji text? Why does a priest called Dōkun here get called Dōkumbō? Why does a deity named Hyakudayū in Nishinomiya become a person in the Awaji account? On the one hand, the text could be read as a garbled account of the Nishinomiya records, somehow confused in the process of transmission. Such an interpretation, however, is based on the assumption that oral traditions have no safeguards for accuracy at the level of detail and can maintain only the most general of plot lines. This is clearly not the case. I would argue that the confusion of names and places in this text is intentional. What would such a shifting of names accomplish for the process of tradition creation?

Dōkumbō Denki, as a document unifying Awaji puppeteers into one self-conscious tradition, sought to present a narrative that could be *any* puppeteer's narrative but that remained distinct from the Nishinomiya center. By relying on the figure of Hyakudayū as its central character, the tradition allowed for a mythical hero. Just as Hyakudayū's authority gets generalized in the text, so too does his prestige in the tradition. Hyakudayū could be any Awaji puppeteer.

Another feature of this text stands out: its insistence that the decision to make a puppet "in the likeness" of Dōkumbō was the result of an imperial order. When combined with the title that Hyakudayū is said to have received, the result is a legitimacy for the new tradition that the Nishinomiya authorities could not challenge. The latter part of the text focuses on the transmission of the art of puppetry to the center on Awaji, referring to it by yet another mythical name underscoring its primacy, Toyoakezushima, "the world-opening island."

This mid-seventeenth century document served to unify the Awaji tradition early in its development. Later texts revealed different textures within this tradition, but *Dōkumbō Denki* gave it a narrative center.

Control of Awaji Puppetry by the Hachisuga Family

Although puppeteers were able to break away from Nishinomiya and establish their own tradition on Awaji, it would be inaccurate to assume that they enjoyed a world free from the constraints of status codes. Awaji puppeteers, as we noted in chapter 2, were regarded as outcasts in Tokugawa Japan, and although there were other outcast groups with lower status, ritual puppeteers suffered from restricted mobility and discrimination. Ritual puppeteers in particular had a low status both because they were itinerant performers and because they performed sacred rites in which they were polluted by contact with beings from another realm. While most outcasts in Japan were under the control of the leader of the outcasts, Danzaemon, Awaji puppeteers were not; they were controlled by the same family that controlled the rest of the Awaji-Awa region, the Hachisuga family, whose main castle was on Shikoku in Awa, near Tokushima. It is widely thought that this exception to the rule of Danzaemon's leadership explains why Awaji troupes (which numbered over forty during the nineteenth century) became such a dominant puppetry tradition and enjoyed so much freedom to travel and perform.

How Awaji puppeteers came to be under the control of the Hachisuga family is the subject of an interesting legend, the veracity of which cannot be ascertained. According to the legend, because this family supported the Tokugawa family, when the head of the Hachisuga family wanted to send letters to Edo to discuss the war, he had a difficult time enabling his retainers to travel there from Shikoku. The fastest and safest route was overland across Awaji, but this area was controlled by the opposing army. Samurai working for the Hachisuga family from Awa, so the legend maintains, would disguise themselves as puppeteers from the Uemura puppetry troupe. They then could travel back and forth across Awaji and even over onto Honshu, and in this way were able to carry out their duties unnoticed.

There is an old document discovered in Nishinomiya in the home of the Taida family that narrates this story. According to this document, a man named Taidai Genzaemon received an order from his lord, the head of the Hachisuga family, saying that he was to go to the battle camp of Tokugawa Ieyasu, and so he set off from the domain of Hachisuga in Tokushima. Genzaemon went overland through Awaji, and in order to break through the network of the opposing forces, he made an arrangement with the head of the Uemura puppet troupe and disguised himself as a puppeteer. While they were doing puppetry performances, he slipped away and managed to get to Ieyasu. When he arrived at Ieyasu's camp, he was wearing the damask coat of the Uemura puppeteers over his armor. Genzaemon sang the praises of Uemura to Ieyasu, and from his own name he took one character and gave it to Uemura, and after that Uemura was called Uemura Gennojō. Therefore, the legend maintains, the Hachisuga family protected the puppeteers because they had allowed their samurai to pass as puppeteers in the decisive final days of the war.

Under the protection of the Hachisuga family, Awaji puppetry was able to flourish. In addition to the numerous ritual puppeteers who lived on Awaji in Sanjo, many puppet theaters developed and were able to maintain rigorous touring schedules all over Japan. A standard phrase on Awaji referred to the "Awaji forty," although this large number probably counted the repertory companies within large troupes as individual theaters. According to records dated 1811, there were twenty troupes on

Awaji, half in Sanjo and the other half in Aibara. *Awaji-gusa* (1825) lists eighteen troupes. The Uemura Gennojō troupe divided into five repertory companies. The number of these troupes remained constant until the beginning of the Meiji period (1868), when they slowly declined. By the middle of the Shōwa period (1925–1989), only four theaters remained, and shortly after the war, they existed in name only.

The history of these puppetry troupes is beyond the scope of this study of ritual puppetry, but it should be noted that many of the rituals we examine in the next chapter were maintained by puppeteers who worked most of the year for these larger troupes. We turn next to a discussion of what ritual puppeteers on Awaji did when they "made Dōkumbō dance."

5

Puppets of the Road, Puppets of the Field: *Shiki Sanbasō, Ebisu-mai,* and Puppetry Festivals on Awaji

Kadozuke Ningyō: **Puppets of the Road**

When these Dōkumbō-mawashi from Awaji visited homes and performed on fishing docks and near shrines, what did their rites and puppets look like? How were these puppeteers organized among themselves? How were their performances received? What happened to their puppets when they were broken and could no longer be used? How do people living on Awaji today remember these performances? These are some of the questions addressed in this chapter.

As I have pointed out, evidence for a study of ritual puppetry is fragmented, due to the low status of puppeteers and the popular, oral, and highly localized nature of their traditions. By the time we get to the development of the Awaji tradition, there is more evidence. Puppet kashira and implements, descriptions of performances by people who remember seeing them as children in the prewar period, transcriptions of the words recited in the performances, old photographs, and even films of some of the last performances of the early postwar period provide enough information to piece together a fairly accurate picture of ritual puppetry. Through studying and comparing the puppets, records and rituals that developed out of the Awaji tradition, including revived performances on Awaji, it is possible to get a clearer idea of what Awaji Dōkumbō-mawashi did in puppetry's heyday during the Tokugawa period.

In this chapter, the discussion focuses on the sacred rituals of the itinerant puppeteers who hailed from the center of ritual puppetry, Sanjo, on the island of Awaji. These puppeteers, the tradition maintains, are the professional descendants of the fisherman-turned-deity-appeaser Hyakudayū. They performed appeasement and purification rites from door to door at set seasons of the year, before audiences ranging from the poorest peasants to the imperial family. While many of them also worked at the major theaters on the island throughout the year as puppeteers for ningyō jōruri, they drew sharp distinctions between these performances and their ritual duties, referred to as *shinji* or *kamigoto* (sacred matters). Many also farmed small plots of land.

Their ritual performances were of two types. On the one hand, there were Sanbasō performances, solemn and graceful rites of magical purification and revitalization entreating three deities to visit the human realm to bestow felicity and blessing through the apotheosis of a puppet into a visiting deity. On the other hand, there were humorous deity plays depicting and honoring the deity Ebisu, his love of sake, and his control of the fishing catch.

Puppetry as a Profession: Nomenclature, Status, and Territories

The reader will recall that puppeteers on Awaji took their name from the mythical priest at the Nishinomiya shrine, Dōkun (Dōkumbō according to the Awaji texts), who entertained and appeased the Leech Child. Upon Dōkun's death, the puppeteer Hyakudayū is said to have made a puppet to appease this angry (and perhaps grieving) Leech Child. This mythical narrative, and its religious ideas of deity appeasement and containment through ritual performance, formed the core of the Awaji puppetry tradition with the Dōkumbō-mawashi as its sacred specialist. To be a Dōkumbō-mawashi meant that one presented one or both of these rites, Sanbasō and Ebisu.[1]

Shiki-Sanbasō and Ebisu-mai rituals should be considered a pair in the Awaji tradition. These two performance forms have distinct lines of development in the history of Japanese performing arts, but by the time the Awaji tradition emerges, they are interrelated, mainly through the story presented in *Dōkumbō Denki*.[2] The two rituals are opposed to one another in their intentions. Ebisu is regarded as a polluted deity, whereas the deities invoked in the Sanbasō ritual are those of purity and vitalization. When seen as part of the same tradition, the two rites suggest the awareness that both pollution and purity are powerful and necessary.

By the early nineteenth century, Dōkumbō-mawashi began to specialize in either Sanbasō or Ebisu performance. It is tempting to argue for this development on religious or even aesthetic grounds, but it should be noted that this specialization also coincides with the development of larger puppets. Whereas throughout the sixteenth and early seventeenth centuries the puppets were small enough to be presented from a box hung around the neck, by the end of the seventeenth century, as the practice of ningyō jōruri became popular and Awaji kashira became larger, the size and weight of the puppets made it difficult to carry so many at one time. A specialist in Ebisu might carry only one puppet, whereas a Sanbasō-mawashi might carry one, two, or even three puppets along with ritual implements.

Another reason this specialization occurred is likely due to the higher status afforded to Sanbasō performers, as we shall see shortly. The Ebisu rite, because it has a simpler series of performance demands, was easier to master, and those who were skilled in the Sanbasō performance, which included music, percussion and elaborate puppet manipulation, were likely regarded as more skillful artists.

Performance Territories and Patronage

Clearly it was not possible to support a family through ritual puppetry alone. Consequently, most Dōkumbō-mawashi had other forms of employment to augment their incomes. Even though ritual puppetry may have occupied some of these performers for only several weeks a year, it is noteworthy that those census records kept during the Tokugawa period that mentioned puppeteers at all listed people on Awaji who did puppetry as Dōkumbō-mawashi, regardless of how much of their income this represented. Being an itinerant puppeteer was a quality of being, something that gave one a fixed (albeit low) status in society.

Itinerant puppeteers were organized in two ways. A large number of them worked for the major puppet theaters on the island. During the periods of the year when they were not touring with these theaters, they were free to perform as Dōkumbō-mawashi. They were essentially subcontractors in these theaters.

Other itinerant puppeteers had no affiliations with proper theaters but depended on alternate forms of livelihood. Many of these freelance puppeteers had small plots of land, given to them in the early seventeenth century when land was given to outcasts by the government to improve the yield of villages and open up new land.[3] These people were regarded as *kawata hyakushō* (unclean farmers), and their presence was often resented by people living near them. But this meant that as itinerant puppeteers, they were free for a greater part of the year than those employed at the major theaters.

These itinerant performers, regardless of their patronage and affiliations, presented their rites throughout the island of Awaji. Niimi notes that while many of them stayed close to the center of Awaji, some traveled to its northern tip and across to the Hanshin area (Kobe and Osaka). Some toured Shikoku and went to Kyushu. There are also reports of Awaji Dōkumbō-mawashi performing in Kyoto, and of course the case of Suzue Shirobē in Morioka, discussed in the previous chapter, shows that some ventured far from Awaji and never came back.

As noted earlier, puppeteers, agreed upon territories in order not to overlap with one another and cause unnecessary hardship. Niimi relates an interview with an elderly puppeteer in 1970, in which they discuss these territorial restrictions, called *nawabari*. The puppeteer, Mr. Saitō, was in his eighties at the time of the interview, which meant he was performing as a Dōkumbō-mawashi in the 1920s and 1930s. We learn from this interview that individual puppeteers agreed upon territories through the main performance theaters with which they were connected. So, for example, if one were affiliated in some way with the Hisadayū troupe, a puppet theater on the island, one was free to perform in the Ama region of southern Awaji, but not in Seidanchō. Some areas were very strict about their territorial agreements, but the area surrounding Fukura (where the Awaji Ningyō Jōruri Kan is today) was an open territory, and anyone was allowed to perform there. But if a puppeteer from Hisadayū was asked to perform in Seidanchō, for example, they would have to refuse the offer and turn the request over to the Dōkumbō-mawashi who controlled that territory.[4]

Mr. Saitō notes, however, that some people had their own patrons outside the established theaters, and these puppeteers would ignore the territories and perform where they wished. He was probably referring to puppeteers who did not rely on established theaters for their seasonal employment. These puppeteers were referred to as *furifuri Sanbasō* (casual, "by chance" Sanbasō). I asked a number of people about this category, but few recognized it. One man told me that puppeteers with no theater affiliations were seen as being of lower social status than those from the theaters. They were considered less skilled and artistic.

These territories served a number of purposes. They ensured that a single given area would not be flooded by ritual performers and thus made it more likely that puppeteers could make some sort of a profit. They also ensured that their whereabouts were known to the authorities, and that they would report their earnings to the Hachisuga family in Awa through their base theaters. Puppeteers kept a record of what they were paid when they performed in the kadozuke context. I recall being shown such a document in 1984 when I was invited to the home of an elderly man whose father had been a Dōkumbō-mawashi. The document recorded earnings of money, rice, lodgings, and sake received during several New Year periods.

Recollections of Prewar Performances

During my studies on Awaji, I interviewed many people who remembered the seasonal visits of Dōkumbō-mawashi from the period before the war.[5] Many of them were children at the time, and their recollections were often hazy. But there was a clear pattern in their responses, for children tended to notice the same things about the performances. Frequently, answers to questions would develop over several meetings, and people would even phone back to say they had remembered something else they had failed to tell me the first time. Interviews, from the most formal to the passing conversation, consisted of a series of questions. I began each inquiry by asking people what, if anything, they remembered about the visits of puppeteers to their homes. Was the performer someone the family knew in some way? Where did they recall the performance taking place? What did family members do before, during, and after the performance, and how did they relate to the performer? What particular features of the experience remained in the person's mind after all these years?

A marked pattern emerged in response to my questions, namely, a sharp distinction between the perceived status of Ebisu and Sanbasō performers. For the most part, Sanbasō-mawashi were more frequent in communities not directly bordering on the sea, and they were of course more popular at the New Year, weddings, and boat launchings. Most people connected Sanbasō with agriculture, which many people noted was a "clean" occupation, as opposed to fishing. But Sanbasō-mawashi were also regarded with greater respect than those puppeteers who only presented Ebisu rites. I was repeatedly told by people involved in farming that an Ebisu performer would never be allowed into the house but would be kept at the gate (or maybe the kitchen), whereas a Sanbasō puppeteer could be allowed up into the zashiki. The explanation given for this difference was that an Ebisu-mawashi was of lower social status than a Sanbasō-mawashi.[6] Two people commented that they considered the Sanbasō-mawashi to be "cleaner" and better dressed, an attitude that probably reflects the ambivalence about Ebisu at some level.[7]

Others told me families engaged in business had more respect for an Ebisu-mawashi. Most people were not sure why they still remembered this distinction, but it came up often enough to constitute a pattern in the interviews. Many remembered Ebisu performances taking place in the kitchen. In most old farm houses, the kitchen was a part of the house where one did not have to remove one's shoes, since it had a dirt floor. Performing there indicated that the performer was not being allowed further into the house. The reader will recall the drawing from a scroll included in chapter 3, showing a puppeteer standing on the dirt inside a doorway, beneath the householders sitting inside. Most people remembered that Ebisu always caught a fish and that the performance had to do with good luck for the coming fishing season. Many people remembered the moving eyes of the Sanbasō puppet, which has symbolic significance in the rite but also appeals to children and has great entertainment value.

When people would hear the Sanbasō-mawashi was coming near their neighborhood, they would return home if they were out, prepare for the performance, put on nice clothes, and wait for the performer to arrive. Responses to whether or not the performers were known depended on where the person answering the questions lived. Most people said they were not aware that their family knew the performer. If they were were children at the time, they remembered being called in by the parents and grandparents to watch the performances, and many of them remembered seeing an exchange of food, money, or rice for the performances. Quite a few people told me that neighborhood children would sometimes follow the puppeteers from house to house while they made their rounds. Many people said that the puppeteers often gave the children sweets and trinkets. This appeal to children is a feature that comes across clearly in the early drawings of the itinerant puppeteers presented in chapter 3. While these performances were not intended as entertainment for children, a puppeteer knew that if his performance was appealing to children, his popularity at a home was likely to increase. Both of the ritual performances we shall consider below include elements that make them appealing to people of all ages.

It was also clear that a few people on Awaji had not liked the itinerant performers. On numerous occasions people had vivid recollections of the prewar puppetry festivals where jōruri had dominated the day and were pleased to consider these festivals as part of their Awaji identity. But when asked about their recollections of Sanbasō-mawashi and Ebisu-mawashi, they gave vague and noncommittal answers. Pushed further, a number of people suggested that these performers were beggars and should not be considered part of the Awaji tradition. I was occasionally directed away from this line of research with the admonition that a study of the religious aspects of Awaji puppetry was either off the mark, unimportant, or worth leaving out of the record altogether. One man I interviewed told me it was a real shame I was only interested in such "embarrassing" parts of the tradition.

It will be remembered that throughout the Tokugawa period, laws were enacted that made it impossible for one to escape from outcast status and that maximized the distinction between peasants and outcasts, so that the military government and local lords could exert maximum control over society and suppress peasant unrest. This carefully crafted social ideology, which made certain groups of people defiled outsiders, meant that social discrimination against outcasts, ritual puppeteers included, was not only rampant but also legally enforced. Discrimination was seen not as an evil to be overcome but as a system the violation of which would upset the order of society. Many major studies of Japanese puppetry have neglected a study of itinerant puppeteers altogether, and that this attitude clouds the recollections of the tradition even by people on Awaji.

Playing with the Color of the Morning Sun:
Sanbasō Ritual

Puppeteers who performer Sanbasō ritual were called Sanbasō-mawashi, and their rite had a number of different names, depending on its context: Hōnō Sanbasō (Consecrated Sanbasō), Shiki-Sanbasō (Ceremonial Sanbasō), Okina-mai (Dance of Okina), Okina-watari (Okina Crossing Over), Kuro-Okina (Black Okina). Like the Ebisu rite, this one has also undergone a gradual transition to being performed on the stage, with a very established set of rules for its presentation. But it is also possible to preserve the basic structure while abbreviating it considerably, as a comparative examination of Sanbasō rites clearly indicates.

The Sanbasō rite is common to all Japanese performing arts. Although its origins are debatable,[8] a number of things are clear: It was originally intended for divine audiences, and is understood to be a ritual with the magical power to bring about a spiritual revitalization. The text is of unknown authorship, but it probably reflects a ritual chant used in the past. It closely resembles the descriptions of Senzu manzai, adding felicitous words and incorporating *Saibara* into the chant. Clearly the two are related. The basic performance we see here appears to have been adopted into Noh, where the ritual chant was written down and the choreography and iconography of the rite were largely determined. Although the Noh versions of Sanbasō and those found in Kabuki, Bunraku, and ritual puppetry all differ, they share significant aspects of the performance such as chants, costumes, and music. What is interesting about the puppet case, however, is how the itinerant context of this performance kept the magical intentionalities of the ritual alive. These ritual performances have the overriding theme of the creation of the cosmos and the establishment of the cosmic order. All the characters in the performance—Okina (an old man), Senzai (a youth of one thousand years), and Sanbasō (a third old man)— are visiting deities from across the sea (*marebito*) who bring special blessings (and, potentially, curses) in their seasonal visits.[9]

In Noh, the Sanbasō dance is presented as the dance of Okina.[10] The puppetry rite uses the same text as that used in Noh, with some variation. Because large parts of the Sanbasō rite were forgotten in the last fifty years, in the process of reconstructing it, gaps have been filled in by using the Noh piece and standard *yōkyoku* (Noh text), making it appear almost entirely derivative of the Noh Okina dance.[11] Most likely, the puppetry version was originally distinct, but it also was more vulnerable to the vicissitudes of time because it was presented at a popular level. Surviving Sanbasō performances from the Awaji lineage in Nagano Prefecture show a performance structure which is quite long, has little or no chanting, and focuses on dance almost exclusively, with many repetitive gestures. It is quite clear that this performance structure, akin to Kagura, was clearly not meant to entertain a human audience, since it can be quite boring (lasting for hours). It was presented, like Kagura, at festivals in shrines in front of the worship hall to entertain the deities while human beings went about their business of eating, gossiping, and playing games, occasionally glancing over at the performance. Watching a four-hour Sanbasō performance with rapt attention is behavior that could be expected only from a supernatural being.

Occasions for the Sanbasō Rite

On Awaji, the Sanbasō rite was used for a number of dramatically different purposes. I review them here according to the typology most people on Awaji intuitively use when they classify performance occasions.[12] Within this typology, there were basically two styles of performance. One, Shiki Sanbasō, consisted of music, dance and poetry and was both interesting to watch and relatively short (lasting from five to fifteen minutes, making it suitable for a kadozuke performance), and appealing to human audiences. The other, Hōnō Sanbasō, was long and consisted almost exclusively of dance and movement; it was used in shrines as a form of Kagura with puppets. It does not survive on Awaji but does in Nagano Prefecture at Waseda Jinja near Iida City and resembles the Sanbasō dance found in Kagura. The performances discussed below are Shiki Sanbasō rites, unless otherwise indicated.

Kotobuki Sanbasō. Most commonly, Shiki Sanbasō was performed at the beginning of something: when the main pillar of a house went up (*mune-age no sai*), at a wedding party, when a boat was first put into the water (*umi-ire*), or on the morning of the third day of the New Year. All of these events have two things in common: they are ritually pure moments, and they are characterized by *kotobuki* (felicity), symbols of which are painted, sewn, and carved into the Sanbasō puppet or sung in the chant. Because everything in this rite points toward to newness, vitality, and longevity, the ritual invocation of these powers in the cosmos served as a felicitous blessing of the event.

Hōnō Sanbasō. Situations where the audience was clearly and exclusively divine required the Hōnō Sanbasō (*hōnō* meaning consecration or worship). For example, rites were performed at water sources in the mountains, in rice seedling nurseries, and before shrines at New Year. Unlike the Shiki-Sanbasō rite's limited use of the flute and drum followed by chanting of poetry and dancing, in this rite the flute and drum are played throughout the performance to attract and soothe the kami, and

Umazume Masaru holds a small Sanbasō puppet, of the variety used by itinerant performers in the eighteenth and nineteenth centuries.

the repeated dance movements of the puppet purify the four directions using the sleeves. Although a human audience was sometimes present at these rites, they were not the fundamental recipients of the performance.

Kami-okuri Sanbasō. The Sanbasō rite was also used in the process of purification of a home or village from evil, pollution, and noxious forces. This appears to be part of a wider context of ritual puppetry called by the general name *kami-okuri ningyō* (sending the kami puppet) or *tamayori ningyō* (spirit possession of a puppet). In this rite, worshippers would first gather and watch a puppet performance of Sanbasō and then proceed through the streets of the community to a fixed point outside the boundaries of the village carrying the puppet on a palanquin. The puppet was understood to be a spirit vessel, and epidemic and other spirits on the

This photograph, taken before the war, shows a Sanbasō performance at a small worship site in the middle of a rice field. Courtesy of Fudō Satoshi.

road, attracted by the performance, would possess the puppet as it passed through the community, and so be carried away.[13]

Particularly important was the attraction, capture, and expulsion of the spirits of insect pests, which could ruin an entire harvest. This rite has not been performed on Awaji since before the war. I was curious about the efficacy of this rite and how people had understood it. Was this all people did to prevent the infestation of insects? "Of course not!" was always the reply. "People weren't stupid!" I was told that farmers hand picked insects off crops, used rotational planting, and smoked fields to rid them of insects. The purpose of the puppetry rite was to address the spiritual aspect of insects. When expelling them from a village, it was necessary to consider their feelings, lest they come back the next year and

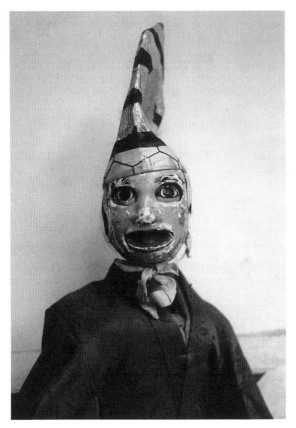

This puppet from the Waseda shrine in Nagano was used in annual rituals to purify the village. The puppet was understood to attract noxious forces and the spirits of harmful insects and carry them beyond the village boundaries.

create even more problems. This required the ritual use of puppets. Puppets were beings for dealing with problems in the spiritual, not the material, realm.

We do not know what this kind of rite looked like on Awaji, but we can study extant examples of the ritual use of Sanbasō at other centers to which Awaji puppetry spread. In the Shinshū region (Nagano Prefecture), where an Awaji puppeteer established the practice of ritual puppetry in the early nineteenth century, the practice of the Sanbasō puppet being used as a *tamayori ningyō* has recently been revived, based on descriptions of the practice from the early 1950s, when it died out. The ritual begins at the local shrine, called Waseda Jinja, where the puppet is consecrated before the worship hall. This performance uses the Hōnō (consecratory) Sanbasō, as opposed to the Shiki (ceremonial) Sanbasō. The sweeping movement of sleeves in purification is performed repeatedly; so too is the chant "Oosai ya Oosai ya, yorokobi ariya" as the puppet purifies the four directions. After the dance, the puppet is carried out of the shrine, through the streets of the small town, and out to a designated spot at the edge of town, where another rite is conducted to divest the puppet of the pollution and spiritual forces it has absorbed. The puppet is said to attract spirits of insects and also epidemics.[14]

Sanbasō Rite as Ritual Purification of the Home. As discussed in previous chapters, the Sanbasō rite was used to ritually purify a home or community. This process was accomplished by two interrelated principles. One was the understanding that through the power of the performance, any dangerous spirits or noxious forces in the homes would be attracted to the puppet and possess it, following the same logic as the tamayori ningyō discussed above. But there was also the understanding that through the ritual of revitalization expressed in the Shiki-Sanbasō chant—and actualized as the body of the puppet literally "comes alive" when it is picked up and moved—the dominant form of ritual pollution, namely, the degeneration of the year, could be driven away. Vitality replaced exhaustion, and purity replaced pollution. The rite affirmed the reality of the new, the vital, the pure, and the felicitous.

Amagoi Sanbasō (Okina watari)

Sanbasō puppets were also used in rites requesting rain, called *amagoi* (petitioning for rain). Lack of rain was and still is a serious concern in rural Japan. Rice depends on an abundant water supply, and major famines have resulted from droughts like that of 1732, when one third of the peasant population of Japan is said to have died.[15]

The rite performed in the amagoi context is the Shiki-Sanbasō, but it is frequently referred to as Okina-watari . Lines taken from the chant—"The sound of the waterfall, the sound of the waterfall, even if the sun is shining, will not cease"—refer to the blessing of abundant water even if there are many sunny days. The rite is thought to be efficacious in petitioning for rain. Puppetry appeases angry deities who are withholding their beneficence from the human community out of revenge and chastisement.

Amagoi rites were not uncommon on Awaji. Frequently, the Sanbasō performance would be followed by a longer festival in which other jōruri pieces were presented, a pattern of ritual activity we consider the end of this chapter. In Kyōhō 9 (1724), dry weather threatened to destroy the planted crops. The Uemura Gen no Jō troupe performed a rain rite using Sanbasō puppets in the Hachiman shrine in Sumoto, followed by the five-act jōruri piece "Sugawara Denju Tenarai Kagami." As a result, it rained nonstop for twelve days. This is mentioned in shrine records at the Sumoto Hachiman shrine. Seventy years later, during another major drought in Kansei 6 (1794), puppeteers from this same troupe performed a rain-requesting rite, but it did not rain as a result. They then decided to follow the exact pattern they had followed at the Hachiman shrine in Sumoto seventy years before. They again performed the amagoi rite and then the five-act jōruri piece, the same one presented before. Rain soon fell, and it continued for ten days. It is said that the Okina mask used in both the Kyōhō and Kansei performances was magical. A black Okina mask, it reflected the color of clouds full of rain.

During a drought in early Shōwa (the late 1920s), Uemura troupe puppeteers again performed an amagoi rite in the Hiyoshi Shrine in Matsubara in Seidanchō. Following the presentation of Okina-watari, a dragon appeared on stage, the symbol of a stormy sky, and a long prayer for rain was recited. The next part of the performance was a presentation of jōruri pieces, and as the tayū was finishing chanting, it suddenly started to pour. The puppets, their costumes, and all the performers and audience got entirely soaked. It was reported that the kami from this shrine really hated puppets, and so he soaked them before the puppeteers had a chance to put them away.[16]

Shiki Sanbasō

The basic ritual used in these performances consisted of a set use of musical instruments, chant, and puppets. What follows is an analysis and annotated translation of the Shiki Sanbasō rite. I have relied on a series of sources: old films of the last performances of this rite in the kadozuke context, photographs, firsthand recollections from people on Awaji who both saw and performed the rites, the performances at the theater today, and interviews with Umazume Masaru, who in the late 1940s was taught the performance by elderly puppeteers in Sanjo.

Ritual Symbolism

Three puppets are used in the rite: Okina , Senzai, and Sanbasō. At the beginning of the puppetry rite, before the puppets are picked up, a flute and drum are played. This attracts the spirit—in most cases understood to be the deity of the rice fields—and invites it to enter the puppet. Each puppet, preparing to be possessed, in turn covers its face with the sleeves of its elaborate costume, indicating its submission to the greater spirit which has been summoned.

The initial movements of the first puppet are intended to purify the surrounding space prior to the possession, which will take place when the deity enters the puppet's body. First, the arms of the puppet move in the four directions, creating a dramatic effect as the long sleeves of the costume snap with each gesture. The puppet shakes a rattle, to further purify the space and bless the audience. This gesture is also understood as a *tamafuri* (spirit shaking), which invigorates the performance (although many farmers with whom I spoke said it was an imitation of sowing seed). One puppet, Sanbasō, slowly begins to dance and eventually goes into a frenzied and ecstatic trance,[17] made apparent by a change in the shape of his eyes: they go from normal human eyes to round eyes that look into the other world—eyes of fear, pain, wonderment, intense rage, frenzy. As the preparation for the possession goes on, the movements of the puppet become erratic: he stamps his feet, rolls his eyes, and waves his arms. This foot stamping (*ashibyōshi*) is also understood as an act of driving out evil and summoning up powers from the earth. All this is to but a preparatory stage to the powerful transformation about to take place, the actual possession. In this way, the puppet becomes a body substitute on yet another level: he takes the place of the shaman, who also may undergo an ecstatic transformation in preparation for possession. It is understood in this rite that the deities summoned are too powerful to be contained within the body of a human mediator, so the puppet stands as a bridge between the human and divine communities.

The actual possession in full form is made apparent by putting masks on the puppets (or sometimes just on the puppet Sanbasō) in the middle of the rite. If we consider that puppets are once removed from the realm of human performers, we have now a second level of removal from the ordinary, profane world of meaning when a puppet has a mask on its face. Even though puppets are substitutes for actual human beings in the rites, they too must be must be symbolically insulated from the sacred. This is accomplished by wearing a mask, after which, the puppet's movements become more controlled, although more forceful.[18] Another level of power has settled into the puppet, and the deity is now in full control.

The purpose of the puppet's possession—which originates in a tradition wherein a dead person returns in the form of a puppet, Dōkumbō, and which continually harks back to this origin—is to bring fecundity and new life to the people in the audience, their homes, their rice seedlings, and the community in general. Just as the puppet made of lifeless matter is brought to life during the first stage, when it is made to move and then is, so to speak, ontologically upgraded to a being possessed by the divine, so too is the community's vital energy restored and strengthened. These two aspects of the puppet's movement suggest vitality: the initial movement out of inertia and the secondary possession by a divine force.

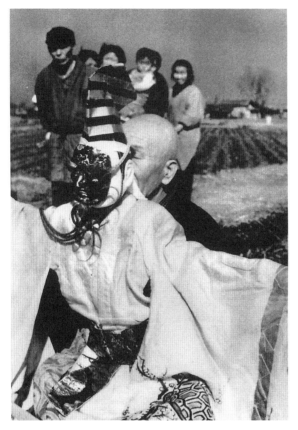

This prewar photograph of a Sanbasō performance shows the puppet wearing a mask. Courtesy of Fudō Satoshi.

The Puppet Costume

Further evidence that the puppet embodies a hope for vitalization—or revitalization, as the case may be—can be seen most clearly by examining the puppet's costume.

The costumes consist of a series of superimposed images referring to longevity and eternity. The most identifying aspect of Sanbasō, so much so that it has become his trademark, is the hat. On it, we see thirteen stripes of dark and bright, indicating the waxing and waning moons, images of both the passage of time and a cyclical renewal.[19] On one side of the hat is a full moon, and on the other, a crescent moon, further reinforcing the temporal, cyclical, lunar aspect of the hat. At the base of the

Sanbasō *kashira*

hat, the stitching connecting the hat to the kashira is a series of six-sided shapes, considered to represent the shell of a turtle (symbol of ten thousand years). (This six-sided pattern also appears on the costume of Senzai.)

Next, there is the clothing worn by the puppet. The turtle appears again on the back of the small kimono, as does the crane, which signifies a thousand-year longevity. Sanbasō's two companions, Okina and Senzai, both embody the dimension of age, since Okina is old and Senzai (a mere thousand years of age) is youth. These images are often beautifully drawn on the costumes or sometimes crudely embroidered. As the puppets perform and move their sleeves about, these visions of temporality flash in and out of view. One sees a turtle, then a crane, and now and again a waxing or waning moon.

This rare puppet, discovered in Morioka in 1987, shows the symbolism on the costumes of puppets in the Sanbasō performance.

The Chant

Perhaps the most problematic aspect of this rite is the ritual chant (*to-naegoto* or *jiuta*) used in it. It seems to defy any logical translation, and at times appears to be a medley of symbols and a salad of words. The problem with the text, however, lies perhaps in our expectation that it should behave like a more conventional text—have a narrative structure, be translatable, etc. On one level, the text can be seen as the "speaking parts" for the human officiant (the puppeteer as shaman) and the deities who enter the puppets during the rite. The use of poetic imagery, literary references, and ritual utterances of untranslatable meaning suggest, however, that another level of language is at work here. Let us examine the special nature of the language in this rite before turning to a translation of the chant itself.

As Maurice Bloch has correctly noted concerning the unique nature of language in ritual contexts, "Ritual is . . . a place where, because the ordinary forms of linguistic communication are changed, we cannot assume the semantic processes of more ordinary communication."[20] Ritual language, and ritual poetry in particular, is understood to have the magical capacity to create the realities it describes. This understanding is not an uncommon feature of ritual language in the history of Japanese religions. Two celebrated cases from the history of Japanese religions eloquently underscore this point:

An early reference to the power of language to create realities can be found in the *Kojiki*. In the myth, the god Susanō, brother of the sun goddess Amaterasu, declares he has won a match for power with his sister, and he "rages with victory" by destroying the order that his sister had created in the form of dikes between rice paddies, and defecates in "the hall where first fruits are tasted," then spreading his excrement about the hall. His sister's response is incomprehensible, unless we consider the power of language. She says, "That which appears to be feces must be what my brother has vomited and strewn about while drunk.[21] Also, his breaking down the ridges of the paddies and covering up the ditches—my brother must have done this because he thought it was wasteful to use the land thus." The text continues: "*Even though she spoke thus with good intentions, his misdeeds did not cease*, but became even more flagrant."[22] As Philippi notes concerning this passage, her attempt to "speak good words correctively" (*nori-naoshi*) most probably reflects the belief that "one could turn evil into good by speaking well of it."[23]

Second, the Japanese preface by Ki no Tsurayuki to the early-tenth-century text *Kokinshū* (or *Kokinwakashū*) directly refers to this capacity of the Japanese language, properly used:

> The seeds of Japanese poetry lie in the human heart and grow into leaves of ten thousand words. Many things happen to people of this world, and all that they think and feel is given expression in descriptions of things they see and hear. When we hear the warbling of the mountain thrush in the blossoms or the voice of the frog in the water, we know every living thing has its song. It is poetry which, without effort, moves heaven and earth, stirs the feelings of the invisible gods and spirits, smoothes relations with men and women, and calms the hearts of the fierce warriors. Such songs came into being when heaven and earth first appeared.[24]

A further reflection of an ancient Japanese conviction of the magical efficacy of ritual language, absorbed into many later Japanese ritual contexts, can be seen in what is referred to as *kotodama shinkō*, or the belief (*shinkō*) in the spirit (*tama*) of words (*koto*). According to Konishi Jin'ichi, this archaic and ancient view of the power of ritualized speech—phrases uttered in the proper context and with the proper tone and pronunciation—survived in Japan well into the Middle Ages, at the time the rite under discussion here was being formed. Konishi specifically notes a feature we will see shortly in the Sanbasō chant. He writes that "priests composed [poems] in the belief that speaking a great many longevity-related phrases would propel the *kotodama* in their utterances toward their sovereign and grant him long life. . . . The priests were aware that their [poem], a virtual list of auspicious things, was recited in anticipation that the *kotodama* would function."[25]

Finally, we can not overlook how the power of language can express religious and political power relationships. As Gary Ebersole observes in his book *Ritual Poetry and the Politics of Death in Early Japan* "Song was frequently used and experienced as a form of the exercise of power. It was a linguistic means of manipulating religio-political power in the human sphere as well as of manipulating the spiritual powers, including the *kami* and the spirits of the dead. Song was sung and poetry recited not only for aesthetic pleasure but as a means of ordering and controlling potentially dangerous aspects of the world. This sense of the efficacy of poetic language survived until much later in Japanese history and was prominent in the Heian and medieval periods. Indeed, it is still found in the present in attenuated form in certain rural areas and ritual practices."[26]

The text for the Sanbasō rite, which I translate below, has often been neglected by translators and commentators precisely because it relies so heavily on notions of language extremely foreign to most people living in Japan and the West today.[27] Part of the difficulty in understanding this text, it seems, comes from the expectations modern readers have brought to it as text alone, divorced from its ritual context. When seen as an expression of ritual speech, the incomprehensible opening lines, lack of narrative, and layering of symbol upon symbol and literary reference upon literary reference, as we shall note below, all make sense. The realities of vitality, longevity, and harmony are invoked through the use of potent language in a ritual setting.

The following performance description is based upon that of the Awaji puppet theater today. I have carefully compared it to a film made in the late 1940s of two elderly Sanbasō-mawashi from Awaji, and the text and movements of the puppets are nearly identical. The slight variations in ritual action between the present-day Awaji puppeteers and the elderly men from the 1940s need not concern us. After translating the performance text, I offer a discussion of the motifs and ritual speech elements in it.[28]

SANBASŌ

The performers begin by creating a sacred space for the performance. They cut white strips of paper (gohei) *to indicate the site is "marked off" from the profane. Next, they offer white uncooked rice and sacred sake to the deities invited. While one of the performers plays a small flute to summon sacred forces, a second performer beats a small drum and recites.*

Part One: Invocation of Deity

OKINA: *Tō tō tarari tarari ra*
          Tarari agari rarari tō
CHORUS: *Chiriya tarari tarari ra*
          Tarari agari rarari tō.[29]
OKINA: Live a long, long time
CHORUS: We will also live a thousand autumns—
OKINA: The ages of the crane and the turtle[30]
CHORUS: Let us enjoy good fortune in our hearts
OKINA: *Tō tō tarari tarari ra*
CHORUS: *Chiriya tarari tarari ra*
          Tarari agari rarari tō
OKINA: The sound of the waterfall
          The sound of the waterfall[31]
          Even if the sun is shining
CHORUS: Will not cease
          Tō tari ari u dō dō dō[32]
SENZAI: It will not cease
          Tō tari ari
          It will continue as usual

[*Senzai performs a slow dance, waving his sleeves from side to side to purify the space*]

SENZAI: May you will live a thousand years
          A heavenly maiden's robe of feathers
          Even if the sun is shining
          The sound of the waterfall will not cease
CHORUS: It will not cease
          Tōtari ari utō tō tō

[*Senzai is put down, and Okina is picked up*]

OKINA: *Agemakiya ton dō ya*
CHORUS: *Hiro bakari ya ton dō ya*

[*These two previous lines are from a Saibara and refer to a sexual moment between two lovers. During the following chanting, once again shared by the two performers, the drumming continues, and the Okina puppet bows, spreads its arms, and then makes points sharply into the sky and flips both sleeves behind its head in dance movement.*]

OKINA: Although we're seated
CHORUS: Let's begin!
OKINA: We have been celebrating since a long time ago
           Since the age of the gods
CHORUS: *Soyo yari chiya ton dō ya*
OKINA: The thousand-year crane
           Sings the Manzairaku song of longevity
           And the turtle who has lived in the pond for ten thousand
              generations
           Carries on his shell the three songs[33]
           The sand rustles and spreads out on the seashore
           And plays with the color of the morning sun
           The water cascades cool and pure
           Clearly floats the evening moon
           Peace under heaven!
           Tranquillity throughout the land
           This is today's prayer

[*The invocation ends. Okina pauses briefly, as if to listen to these following lines.*]

CHORUS: Who are those old men?[34] Who are they? Where are they from?
OKINA: Since this is the dance of a thousand autumns and ten thousand
              ages, let's do one dance of longevity, the Manzairaku.[35]
CHORUS: Manzairaku!
OKINA: Manzairaku!
CHORUS: Manzairaku!

Part Two: The Trance Dance of Sanbasō

The puppeteer puts Okina down to his left and picks up Sanbasō. This puppet has feet, as opposed to the other two, with only trousers. Sanbasō is holding a rattle made of small bells with streamers attached. It is inserted into a small hole in the puppet's right hand. Shaking the rattle serves to purify the space, and the rattle itself serves as a torimono, *an object into which a sacred force will descend. When the puppet's arm moves, the rattle sounds. He does a brief dance to drum accompaniment, which includes the stamping of feet—to drive out evil—and rapid movements of the eyes—to indicate he is undergoing a transformation into sacred status.*

Part Three: The Apotheosis, Sanbasō as Sacred Presence

When Sanbasō's dance is finished, the puppeteer puts the doll down and puts a black mask over his face. The drummer puts aside his drum, puts a white

mask on Okina, and both puppets are manipulated without accompani-
ment.[36] *Note that in the following discussion, Okina serves as the "straight*
man" for Sanbasō. In the Noh versions, this part is played by Senzai or a
minor actor (omote). The conversation is carried out with both puppets
being held with their faces covered by their sleeves.

SANBASŌ: Oh! Such joy, such joy, such joy! I won't let it slip out of here!

OKINA: How felicitous! I will talk to the lead dancer who dances in the later part.

SANBASŌ: Aha! That's me!

OKINA: You are to dance the felicitous thousand autumns and ten thousand ages for today's blessing. You, the black Okina.

SANBASŌ: For today's blessing, this black Okina is to felicitously dance the Senzu manzai. There is nothing I would like more to do! But first, sir, you must return to your seat.

OKINA: I will not return to my seat. First you dance, sir, and then I will return to my seat.

SANBASŌ: First, you return to your seat.

OKINA: First, I am going to enjoy the dance, and then I will return to my seat.

SANBASŌ: First, you return to your seat!

OKINA: No! First you dance!

SANBASŌ: No! Return to your seat!

OKINA: How felicitous. Begin with the bell!

SANBASŌ: What a great deal of trouble this is!

The conversation is thus concluded, and Okina is put down. The performer
who manipulated Okina now picks up his drum for the masked dance of
Sanbasō, called in the Noh versions, the "bell scene." Both the mask and bell
indicate that Sanbasō is now fully possessed by sacred forces.

Part Four: The Words of Blessing

Sanbasō dances frenetically to the following chant. His rattle cuts through
space and shakes wildly from side to side. He leaps about in the air. The
energy intensifies as the performers chant the text, beat the drum, and voice
cadence calls.

CHORUS: Oh how grateful we are for this manifestation of the deity,
How blissful to give thanks to the deity with this *kami asobi.*[37]
Indeed, there are so many dancing girls
At Suminoe we will hear their clear, lovely voices.
There the blue waves are said to reflect the shadow of the waves.
You and the road of the kami should lead straight to the lively capital in springtime.

This is the dance of *Genjōraku*,[38]
And for Manzairaku, you use Omi robes.
With a striking arm, we purify you of all evil, and in our hands
  we gather longevity and good luck.
The dance of a thousand autumns caresses the people and
  lengthens their lives.
Together, the pine trees and the wind enjoy making their voices
  whisper.[39]
We depend on the wind in the pines.

As the chant concludes, the puppet ceases his dance, shakes his rattle from side to side as if to bless the space, and then is placed in the sleeping position in the carrying box. The performers clap their hands together and bow and the end of the rite.

This use of highly poetic and felicitous language presented in a ritual context unleashes the power of the words themselves to create the realities they so beautifully describe. Here, let us direct our attention to three uses of language in this ritual text: the magical use of language as sound, the use of language to invoke nostalgia and tradition, and the phenomenological use of language to create imaginary and visual experience.

The first stanza of the text opens and closes with the untranslatable syllables *tō tō tarari tarari* and closes with a similar *chiriya tarari tarari ra*. While these syllables have no readily available meaning, they serve a number of purposes in the text: First, they sensitize the listener to the onomatopoetic qualities that occur later in the text, and hence to the magical use of language. Second, they set the stage for some audial puns in the text, when the same verb ending *rari* and the syllables *dō dō dō* come to have meaning. This allows the listener to move between two levels of language, the level of meaning and that of sound. We see a subtle shift from the use of language as sound to the incorporation of these syllables into meaningful phrases. But then we see them used once again onomatopoetically. By prefacing the entire piece with this sort of ritual utterance, therefore, the participant or audience is immediately forced to open to various levels of comprehending ritual sound. This ritual use of language I call a "magical use of language as sound."[40] The text then plays with this openness of the participants in at least two further ways.

The next element in the text to which I would draw our attention is what I have chosen to call a "medley effect." A medley, a song or piece which borrows and places in seemingly random order readily recognizable bits and pieces of popular songs of the day, is capable of quickly creating a mood or ambiance. It becomes unnecessary to reinvent the wheel for each new ritual event. One has only to think of the intentions behind and mood created by a brief medley of "The Star Spangled Banner," "America the Beautiful," "You're a Grand Old Flag," and "My Country 'Tis of Thee" (with maybe Bruce Springsteen's "Born in the U.S.A." at the end to draw in a younger crowd), or of the frequent use of medleys in Memorial Day parades and Fourth of July celebrations. Indeed, when a medley is effectively used, it is often preferable to new pieces of music with the same theme, as new pieces lack the power of nostalgia and the authority of tradition. Another important aspect of the medley effect is its economy. The briefer the reference to another work, the better. A good medley uses only enough of a piece to capture the mood before moving on to another.

This Sanbasō chant employs such an apparatus to condense a number of meanings into one ritual moment. A series of famous one-liners from classical Japanese poetry, names of other performances (from Kagura and Gagaku, two other performing acts with strong ritual origins), references to myths, legends, and felicitous symbols are all thrown into the text. For example, "the sound of the waterfall" is a line from the *Ryōjin hishō*, and Agemaki and Hiro bakari refer to Kagura performances with similar motifs of longevity, peace, and felicity. "The three songs" on the turtle's back are felicitous songs from the Noh theater. The simple line "A heavenly maiden's robe of feathers" calls forth an entire myth and a profound notion of eternity, the Vedic idea of a *kalpa* as a measurement of time. A maiden descends to earth once every one hundred years and brushes a rock (forty *li* in breadth) with her robe of feathers. As long as it takes to wear down this rock is one kalpa.[41] The result of this "medley effect" is a high degree of ritual condensation and efficiency. The ritual is literally packed with each of these references.

A well-educated listener in medieval Japan might have been familiar with a number of these references. Today most people attending this rite will be largely unaware of them. They must rely on the power of the images and poetic utterances without recourse to their contextual origins. It is still possible, however, for a person witnessing it to have a profound experience of it at the level of language, because the ritual chant includes a third use of language, an appeal to a phenomenology of the senses. References to waterfalls, the sun, turtles, and cranes, and poetic lines like "The sand rustles and spreads out on the seashore, and plays with the color of the morning sun," have an evocative power. One is able to visualize the realities described, and through visualization in the ritual, these peaceful and vibrant images become reality at the level of the spirit. When reinforced by the other simultaneous events in the rite—the movement and transformation of the puppet, the flute and drum music, the designs on the costumes, and the incessant ringing of tiny bells—the full meanings of these linguistic images can be felt. I have often interviewed people who have come to watch the Sanbasō performance, and many often remark that the lovely visual images, understandable even today, create a soothing and pleasant mood.

If, therefore, we look for a narrative in this text, we will find a thin one: a few old men show up from the land of the gods and perform a dance after a bit of humorous negotiation. If, on the other hand, we direct our attention to the ritual use of language, we will see that this text is not about narrative but about the creation of mood, image, and effect. Language is in the service of a greater analogical realization taking place in the rite: death is being turned into life. And for the mood to be fully felt, the text cannot be separated from the other ritual elements—myths, symbols, timing, perceptions of the performers.

An Endless Era of Felicity: *Ebisu-mawashi*

In chapter 3 we discussed how Ebisu is a liminal deity—ambiguous, potentially dangerous, and in continual need of ritual appeasement and containment. While we do not know precisely what the Nishinomiya Ebisu-kaki did, we have a good idea of what Ebisu performance on Awaji looked like. Ebisu-mawashi performed at private homes, along fishing docks, and at the gates to small Ebisu worship sites. Each performance space entailed a different idea of host-performer relations and gave the performer a different amount of control over the space. Let us look first at what is known about the kadozuke context at private homes (also sometimes referred to as *montsuke* on Awaji, an alternate reading for the character meaning "gate").

Performance Context: Kadozuke Ebisu-mai

Ebisu-mawashi traveled on foot to homes where they would present their short performance in exchange for some sort of remuneration. It was common to see Ebisu performers during the New Year period, to inaugurate the fishing season, or to bring in good business. Old photographs of these performers show them holding puppets that were about half as tall as they were. Frequently they had carrying bags hung on their backs. Their heads were uncovered, and often they were wearing dark-colored pants bound up around the calves and straw sandals. Ebisu as well was dressed in the clothes of an itinerant person, with straw sandals on the feet and pants tied up at the calf. The puppet wore an *eboshi*, a type of hat that flopped down to one side, and often the puppet had a bell in one hand (tied through a hole in the wooden hand) and in the other frequently held a fishing pole from which an artificial fish was hanging, as if caught on a hook (this was to be a featured part of the performance). Invariably, the puppet had a simple kashira with no internal moving parts, and a painted, smiling face and a small beard.[42] The puppet was manipulated by one person. The puppeteer held the rod onto which the kashira was attached by inserting his left hand through a hole in the back of the puppet's costume. The puppeteer manipulated the right hand of the puppet by inserting his right hand into the sleeve of the puppet's costume. He could then move the arm and sometimes the jointed wrist of the puppet with some grace.

Almost all itinerant Ebisu-kaki worked alone. One person carried the puppet and recited a simple story, which appears to have varied among performers. According to Gunji Masakiyo, a standard version included three scenes. In the first, the puppeteer would sing a lament describing the plight of fisherman unable to catch fish. This song may have served as the performer's call announcing his arrival. In the next scene, known as "calling the deity" (kami yobai), the puppeteer would then beseech Ebisu to appear and catch the first fish of the season, so the year's catch could be released. In the third scene, the puppet, understood to be the shintai for Ebisu, would appear and catch a live sea bream, the king of fish (whose name, tai, is felicitous, since this syllable occurs in the word medetai, "felicity"). Thereupon the puppet deity Ebisu would perform songs and dances for the spirit of the fish, coaxing it to release the year's catch. It was not possible to use a live fish if the performer was presenting his piece from door to door, so this part of the dramatic effect was reserved for Ebisu performances presented at fishing festivals. The piece would end with the recitation of felicitous words.[43] I have not seen this version of the performance, but a few fishermen on Awaji remembered it. It is possible that this three-part version is an older example of Ebisu ritual and may resemble the performances done by Ebisu-kaki from Nishinomiya.

In some versions, Ebisu would ask the householder or people assembled to share a drink as a toast to a good fishing season. In all performances, Ebisu would "row out to sea" and catch a fish, the symbolic first catch of the year. The actual fish in most of the itinerant pieces was made of *papier-mâché* or carved out of light wood and hidden in the puppeteer's sleeve until it was time for it to appear. This performance was usually referred to as "Ebisu no tai-tsuri" (Ebisu catches a sea bream). Puppeteers would recite the chant describing Ebisu's miraculous birth and then have the deity perform a dance. These dances were understood to be for the spirit of the fish in the sea, made present through the caught fish (real or artificial). Of note here is that the piece involves the invocation of two Others: Ebisu and the king of the fish (who was never referred to by name). Ebisu was in essence the "keeper of the catch," the deity who embodied the "luck of the sea" (umi no sachi).

Ebisu *o-fuda* distributed by Awaji itinerant puppeteers.

There were many places in the chant where the performance could be elaborated to include current events, make specific blessings, and in general assure its relevance. Common to all these performances was the utterance of the felicitous words at the end: "Oki wa tairyō, oka wa manzaku, shōbai hanjō, tsukisenu godai koso medetakere!" (In the offing is a big catch, in the hills, an abundant harvest! Business booms! This is an endless era of felicity!)

After the performance, the puppeteer would leave the householder with an o-fuda on which was drawn a picture of Ebisu, usually depicting the deity smiling with a fish under its arm. Many of these o-fuda bore the name of the Nishinomiya shrine. This could be placed in one's own kamidana in the home or at a place of business. Often, it was carried on a boat. It served as proof that the person had the rite performed and also embodied some of the sacredness of the performance. At the end of each year, the o-fuda was thrown away in a special receptacle in a shrine,[44] and a new one was received, either from an Ebisu-mawashi or directly from an Ebisu shrine.

Most of the chants and plot lines used by itinerant Ebisu-kaki are lost, and we can form only a vague idea of what their performances were like. As puppetry festivals lasting several days became more popular during the late eighteenth century, people wanted to see these rituals incorporated into the festivals as stage performances, and this entailed a transformation of the itinerant version of Ebisu performance. These performances are still presented and have been carefully preserved. I have read the several versions of Ebisu performance texts that have been written down and there are slight variations among them. The performance piece translated below, now the standard Ebisu-mai piece in the Awaji theater, seems to be representative.[45] The lines recited by the puppeteer in performance (*serifu*) that I translate here reflect a late period in this process of transformation from ritual to stage.[46]

Performance Context: Ebisu-mai *at Shrines and on Docks*

Ebisu performance was also presented at festivals held in Ebisu shrines throughout the country, usually observed on the twentieth of the month, the festival day (*ennichi*) for the deity.[47] The most common setting for this rite in the Inland Sea area was on fishing docks or small Ebisu worship sites near docks, where fishermen would pray each morning on their way out to sea. This meant that unlike the door-to-door kadozuke context, which required a great deal of spontaneity and adaptability on the part of the performer, some attention could be given to the preparation of the performance space. Rituals in these locations would have sponsors, perhaps the head of a fishing collective or the local attendant at a small worship site. The sponsors would clean the Ebisu shrine worship hall, where the goshintai, or spirit vessels, of the deity were kept, and offer sake and newly cut branches of the *sakaki* tree (considered to be sacred) to the deity. Fresh o-fuda could be prepared in advance to distribute to everyone who came. The Ebisu-mai performance was frequently part of a longer series of festivities, which included decorating boats and cleaning them out so that Ebisu could be invited aboard for the year.

In 1960, as part of a larger wave of nostalgia in Japan, people on Awaji sponsored a number of fish festivals (*gyosai*) based on those of the prewar era. Fortunately, one of these festivals was documented by the photographer Mune Torasuke.[48] Having cross-checked his photographic record with the recollections of numerous people on Awaji, I am convinced that this record is a reliable description of an Ebisu ritual in a fish festival.

The 1960 ritual was sponsored by the Fukura Fishing Collective.[49] Several days before the festival on April 3, 1960, signs were posted around the docks which read:

> This coming April 3, we have arranged to have a fish festival, and therefore ask that you observe this day as a no-fishing day. Sanban [(Sanbasō)] and Ebisu-mai will be performed. The Fishing Collective[50]

Refraining from fishing on this festival day was important because it ensured an audience. More important, fishing on that day would be a sign of disrespect, since the purpose of the festival was to ask Ebisu to ensure a good catch.

People involved with the fishing collective began to build a stage several days before the event. Rolls of matting to be used as a floor for the audience and as a roof are visible in the background of the photograph. The stage consisted of a platform about three meters square, around which was wrapped a *shimenawa* (sacred rope) and sakaki branches, demarcating the space as sacred.[51]

The morning of the festival began when a puppeteer manipulated Sanbasō before the local Hachiman shrine. The puppets and puppeteers faced the worship hall, and an audience looked on from behind. A shinto priest sat nearby, presiding over the ritual.[52] Next, the proceedings moved to the building which housed the offices of the fishing collective. The puppeteer manipulated the Ebisu puppet before the kamidana set up in a *tokonoma*[53] on the second floor. The tokonoma contained bottles of sake and rice, and in it hung a scroll on which was depicted Ebisu holding a fish under his arm. These two rituals, clearly intended for a divine audience with human beings as "uninvited guests," invoked the deities in whose honor the festival was being presented.

The morning of the festival, each member of the sponsoring group presented himself before the worship hall at the local Ebisu shrine, poured some sake over the sacred image, or set a cup on the offering stand. Prayers for safety at sea and possibly abundant harvests were then offered. The sake was poured over the deity to "get him ready" and "loosen him up" before the performance. Sponsors then joined the spectators for the performance.[54]

In midmorning the festival began in front of the fishing collective, and people began to congregate. Because the collective was adjacent to the docks, the very attentive audience was able to sit on their boats, which had been decorated with banners and sakaki branches for the occasion. Farmers also came in their flatbed trucks and sat in them to watch the performance of Ebisu-mai and Sanbasō, this time for human audiences.[55]

During the Ebisu rite, the puppet deity drank a round of sake for each kind of fish caught by members of the collective, allowing everyone to get merry for the rest of the festival.[56] Crowds of people gathered round the small platform laughing as the performance took place, all clearly having a good time.

After the performance, o-fuda depicting the Ebisu were distributed, and fishermen then put these on the small kamidana in their fishing boats so they could "take Ebisu to sea with them."[57] For the rest of the day, there was a party and a feast, with various local groups providing entertainment of all kinds. The party was understood to be for both human beings and the divine guest.

What was the content of the actual Ebisu rite used in this fish festival? I describe here the Ebisu rite as enacted by a group of ten performers (the usual procedure today on Awaji). It can also be presented by a single performer, who enlists the aid of a sponsor in offering sake to the deity in the place of the landowner indicated in the script. I present the more elaborate version of the rite here, referring to all stage directions from that version as "*jōruri*" and the variations for a single-performer version in the kadozuke context as "kadozuke." The performance combines details about the deity Ebisu—his birth, likes and dislikes, and powers—with descriptions of how to worship him properly, as well as humorous expressions of his liminal and drunken nature.

Ebisu-mai[58]

Jōruri: *On a flat space prepared in advance, a small chanting stand is erected to the right of center. Here sit a chanter who will recite the performance and a musician who will provide flute and drumming. A small screen is erected between the performers and the sponsors to demarcate the stage and hide the activities of the puppeteers from view. Altogether, five or six puppeteers are necessary. Each puppet—there are three in this elaborate version—is manipulated by puppeteers wearing* kuroko *(black hoods).*

Puppets: Ebisu (manipulated by three puppeteers), a landowner (also three puppeteers), a fisherman (one or two only)

Chanting: one chanter and one shamisen accompanist

Kadozuke: *When two performers present this rite, one serves as the musician and chanter and one manipulates Ebisu. Because these puppeteers were itinerant, they were not allowed to wear head covering. When there is only one performer, as was usually the case, the performance has no music; the puppeteer performs and recites the story while manipulating Ebisu.*

Puppets: Ebisu

Chanting: by puppeteer

From the northwest[59] enters Ebisu. A fishing pole slung over his shoulder, he
    enters noisely.

EBISU: The best god of luck in the entire cosmos[60] has arrived!
LANDOWNER: Well, well! Welcome and do come in! Right this way!
                [*Speaking to his servant, a fisherman*]
                Clean up the house and get out some sacred sake.[61]
FISHERMAN: Yes, yes, yes. I understand!
LANDOWNER: [*To fisherman*]
                Hurry up about it!
CHORUS: If this Ebisu is offered three cups[62] of sake, then he will perform
                    a dance.

Jōruri: *Ebisu is offered a cup of sake and drinks it with great relish, much
to the amusement of the sponsors. He then slowly begins a dance interlude.*

                If you are asked about the date of birth of this felicitous Ebisu,
                tell them he was born in the first year of Fukutoku, on the third
                day of the new year, just before sunrise, in Shinshū Shinano, in
                a shrine called Takeigamiya! So easily he was born, he was born,
                he was born, he was born![63]
                [*Ebisu dances throughout this description of his felicitous birth.*]
                Take hot water from the storeroom and lukewarm water from
                the warm spring, and mix the hot water and the lukewarm
                water for the baby's first bath water.[64] This beneficent old man,
                Ebisu Saburōzaemon from Nishinomiya, will bestow luck on
                people who have faith in him. With the other protective gods,
                he will bestow luck. Carefully wrap a sacred rope around the
                storehouse, gather together the people of the village and play
                a flute and drum. The child of the turtle will mix with the voices
                and bells of the maidens, and Ebisu will get carried away, car-
                ried away, carried away!
                [*Ebisu dances, becoming more and more intoxicated*]
                Wearing a folded black hat[65] and a hunting robe, sharply
                creased, and four-eyed straw sandals, he comes flying into the
                storehouse with a shuffle, shuffle, shuffle! He looks sharply in
                all four directions!
EBISU: The luck of the sea! The luck of the mountain!
                I heap them both up and pull both lucks to me.
                Shall we drink another round?

Jōruri: *Sake is poured into a cup and is offered to the puppet. He drinks
it with great relish. Each of the sponsors for the rite also take a drink.*
Kadozuke: *At this point, a kadozuke performer may have shared a felicitous drink with his host. The piece may also have been chanted with no
accompanying actions.*[66]

> Let's drink a round so we can catch lots of fish!
> Let's drink a round so we can catch lots of plaice.
> Let's drink a round so we can catch lots of whatever!

Jōruri: *At this point, each fisherman calls out the name of his special fish, and a round is imbibed for each fish usually caught. This part of the rite, which can take up to half an hour becomes more and more humorous as people become totally drunk and try to think of every name of every fish they possibly can to prolong the sharing of sake.*[67]

CHORUS: And then, this Ebisu, feeling so drunk, reels to the right—
          Stagger, stagger, stagger—
          And then he reels to the left—
          Stagger, stagger, stagger, stagger!

Jōruri: *The puppet reels to the right and left, a clever imitation of a drunkard. Since the sponsors at this point are also quite drunk, this part of the festivity can go on for quite a bit of time.*

> To this place, he transfers his luck, he transfers his luck! In a flash, he flies out to the ridge. He rows out to the offing.

Jōruri: *The fisherman who was the servant of the landowner assists Ebisu in rowing. As he pushes the boat off with a long pole, however, he gets left behind and is stranded holding the pole. He precariously balances but then falls into the water, and Ebisu has to rescue him from the waves. Once back in the boat, they continue on.*

> He is already in the offing! Suma and Susaki[68] are visible beyond the cresting and falling waves. The voices of the sand plovers on the beach can be heard calling to their friends, "*chiriya*! *chiriri*!" Just as they scatter and fly away, Ebisu successfully catches and lands a fish.

Jōruri: *At this point, a real sea bream, understood to be the most felicitous fish and king of all fish, which has been kept in a tub of water below the performance area, is pulled from the tub and caught by the deity Ebisu.* Kadozuke: *An artificial fish is used.*

> Then he dances and dances!
> [*Holding onto the fishing pole, Ebisu performs a dance of luck*][69]
> In the offing is a big catch, In the hills, an abundant harvest!
> Business booms! This is an endless era of felicity!"[70]

Jōruri and kadozuke: *This final line is recited in a slow and sonorous voice, for it is the magical chant of felicity and good luck. Before the performance concludes, the fish is presented to the sponsor who has done the most to make the ritual possible. In some cases, it is prepared as sashimi and distributed to all present as part of a ritual meal following the performance.*

Ebisu catches a fish as a finale to the performance.

Nogake Butai: Puppets of the Field and Shrine

Thus far in this book we have examined the practice of ritual puppetry by looking primarily at the itinerant context for these performances. Ritual puppetry within the kadozuke context continued in the Awaji tradition until the end of World War II, even though the basis of the tradition shifted from ritual to dramatic theater. Kadozuke ningyō performances were not the only expression of puppetry in a ritual context on Awaji, however. While Awaji puppet theaters were popular throughout Japan and maintained busy touring schedules all year, their greatest popularity was at home on Awaji, and here they combined ritual puppetry, jōruri contests, and displays of costumes, stage settings, and implements to cre- ate the magical world of Awaji ningyō. Puppetry festivals (combining performances from both the shinji and jōruri dimensions of the tradition) were a major cultural performance for Awaji people and an important source of their identity. People on Awaji, I was repeatedly told, were different, more *nonbiri* (laid back) than other Japanese, and this was evident during these elaborate events. I turn now to this other aspect of the Awaji tradition, the several-day puppet festivals (*ningyō matsuri*) presented on temporary stages built on harvested rice or onion fields (*nogake butai*, "stages set up on farmland") in the spring or fall.

Shibai wa asa kara, bento ga yoi kara

The first time I interviewed someone on Awaji about their recollections of puppetry, the discussion was dominated by a detailed description of the contents of a picnic box (*bentō bako*). The woman with whom I spoke was in her late seventies. She described how she made one container of *chirashi zushi*, another of assorted dried fish, another of various fresh vegetables including *eda mame*,[71] a container of various pickles (*o-tsukemono*), and an entire box of rice balls (*o-nigiri*) for the children. She also said that she made a big jug of cold tea and always remembered to tuck her husband's pipe and smoking tobacco into the sleeve of his kimono as they headed out. She also brought along a flask of sake for him to share with his friends. As I copiously copied all this information into my field notebook, I thought perhaps I had been misunderstood. Why all this discussion of mixed sushi, boiled soybeans, and cold tea when I had asked about puppets?

After doing research on Awaji for several months, it became apparent that I had not been misunderstood at all. Food was a major part of what people remembered when they thought about puppets. The Awaji expression "shibai wa asa kara, bento ga yoi kara,"[72] (the plays are from the morning because the picnic is good) reveals how people sustained themselves through marathon three- or four-day festivals of puppetry performances.

These performances, usually hosted by one or several of the puppetry troupes on the island, were the main social event of the year on Awaji. Many people told me that either they, their parents, or someone they knew had first fallen in love or met their spouse at a puppetry festival. As one man told me, "a ningyō matsuri was a great place to meet the girls." Young couples could meet freely at these events and go for strolls. A group of elderly men I spoke with played with the pun of going to a ningyō matsuri to "look over the dolls." Clearly a lot more went on at these events than sacred puppet rituals. Business got conducted, people caught up on gossip, and children had a chance to play freely with their friends.

The timing of these festivals was significant and reveals their underlying ritual structure. They were usually held immediately after the harvest or, if in shrines, perhaps right after planting in the spring. These two times, called in Japanese *nokanki* and meaning "free time from agriculture," became occasions to offer rituals of thanks to the deities who made planting and harvesting possible.[73] The presentation of dramatic entertainment from the jōruri tradition was a secondary entertainment following the dignified rites of Sanbasō. The *nogake* event was a form of harvest ritual.[74]

The atmosphere was festive and casual, and everyone would bring tatami mats to sit on, elaborate box lunches, and gourds of cool sake to share. In the middle of the day, there was about a two-hour break, and everyone would break open the bentō and socialize. The performers would sometimes join the audience for the feast, creating a social event where the distinction between "performers" and "audience" became nonexistent and all were participants. Furthermore, the kami invited to the festival were also present. This picnic to end all picnics is a reflection of the Japanese religious practice of the *kyōen*, or *naorai*, a banquet prepared in honor of the visiting kami. Concerning this aspect of a performance event, Raz writes: "The *kyōen* indicates one basic facet of the Japanese theatre and its audience—the party spirit, pleasure-seeking banquet, in which distinctions between performers and spectators, though existing, are blurred by the nature of the event."[75]

The nogake event began with the construction of a temporary stage, either in fallow rice fields right after harvest or in the open areas in front of the haiden of major shrines (usually Hachiman shrines). The construction of the stage took a few days, and the lumber and labor were provided by the people of the village, whose responsibilities in the fields were temporarily over now that the planting or harvest was over. The building of the nogake butai involved a series of brief purification rituals, understood to be preparing the site for the invited kami guests.

The day of the performance, people would arrive around eight or nine in the morning and find their places. Each day would begin invariably with a performance of Shiki Sanbasō. This performance served to purify the space and the village, bless the audience, and invite the kami of the village to come to the festival and enjoy the performances, for it was largely in their honor that the entire event was taking place. It has been suggested that the elaborate series of jōruri performances lasting several days were secondary to the main purpose of inviting and blessing the deity.[76]

The next part of the festival, namely the day's entertainment, took a variety of forms, but was understood to be entertainment for both the human audience and the deity.[77] After the performance of Sanbasō, one of the major jōruri pieces would be presented. In a usual day, the theaters would present one piece in its entirety and perhaps two or three famous scenes (*dan*) or soliloquies (*sawari*) with which nearly everyone present would be well familiar. Some people in the audience frequently were amateur reciters of jōruri and would know the pieces by heart, listening intently to the performance to improve their technique.

The presentation of scenes rather than entire pieces raises an interesting issue for our understanding of these puppetry festivals. Since a scene is by definition only a part of a larger play, presenting only this segment means that the audience had to fill in the rest. Before and after the performance of a single scene, I was told, nearly everyone present would reconstruct the rest of the play, arguing occasionally over nuances or details. This arrangement provided a built-in opportunity for meanings in the puppet theater to be reinterpreted and experienced. These conversations before and after the presentation of *sawari* should therefore be understood as an integral part of the performance.

Much like the Noroma ningyō discussed in chapter 1, or the use of kyōgen in Noh, short light entertainment during intermissions made it possible for people to absorb the heavy tragedies of the day's jōruri performances. There were two common forms of short performance, both of which dealt with the theme of rapid transformation and impermanence. The first was called *hayagawari*, (rapid changes). It involved a series of seven transformations (*nana-bake*) of dolls and costumes and was considered to be very amusing. One puppeteer (not a puppet) would come onto the stage, and in a short period of time he would strip away his outer costumes and reveal a different identity under each layer. The standard seven transformations were a fox, a princess who becomes a demon, a *zatō* (masseuse), a *hanagusa* (flower vendor), *kaminari* (a thunder and lightening demon), a fox again, and two dolls, a *jorō* (prostitute) and her *yakko* (customer), sometimes played by the puppeteer and a doll he would manipulate and often involving a gender switch on the part of the puppeteer.[78]

We have noted that the annual ningyō matsuri took place on temporary stages, constructed each year for the event. These stages were by no means simple; they had several levels, enabling backdrops to be changed and the area of the stage to be brought closer toward or further away from the audience. The result was a stage with several depths. During the intermission, this device was put to another purpose—that of *dōgugaeshi*, a distinct genre of performance is still presented in an abbreviated form at the Awaji Ningyō Jōruri Kan.[79] The inner stage was illuminated with a row of candles, and while the shamisen performer played a lively piece with a percussion accompaniment of wooden clappers, as many as eighty-eight scenes would change on the stage in very rapid succession. The images varied depending on the number of screens, but they usually depicted either a journey or motifs associated with longevity, felicity, the seasons, and purity, as well as animals and mythical beasts. These were usually presented during the evening intermission, when the fading light would create a dreamlike impression.

Umazume Masaru, the director of the theater and my chief source of information, suggests that the dōgugaeshi's significance can be understood as an expression both of the status of the particular theater group staging the performance and of the more general sense of illusion and fantasy that the world of the puppet stage seeks to create. Concerning the former, he notes that the number of scenes that a particular theater stages (from fifteen or twenty to as many as eighty-eight) reflects its prosperity. The screens are heavy and are carefully painted (traditionally on mulberry paper). Consequently, having a large number of screens is a vivid and staged display of having the means to have them painted and hauled around from performance to performance. Furthermore, various theaters would advertise their dōgugaeshi as one of the marvels of their performance. Umazume recalls that as a child, he and his friends would go to the day-long performances mainly to see the changing screens, for this was the part of the performance that most appealed to children.

Umazume also suggests that the changing screens express what is called "yūgen no sekai." While this phrase has a more precise meaning in the world of Noh aesthetics, in general usage it connotes the world of profundity and mystery always present at the edges of everyday consciousness. The rapid change of screens took place behind a wall of candles, which flickered when the stage props were moved, creating the illusion of another world, growing deeper and deeper as one image was superimposed upon another, not unlike the world of dreams or half-consciousness. The images formed a series of free associations between visual, mythic, and poetic motifs in Japanese culture—the plum or cherry tree, Mount Fuji, various temples, the seven gods of luck, tornadoes, dragons, the phoenix—all presented one right after another accompanied by shamisen and wooden clappers in a most dramatic ambiance.

Like the hayagawari, the theme of dōgugaeshi is transformation, the motif of the ningyō matsuri. On Awaji, it was understood that the world of puppetry was one of inner transformations, whether the performances were rituals or dramatic pieces. The puppets, as being once removed from the human realm, prompted one to explore the life of the spirit, an exploration reflected in the plays and rituals and underscored by the rapidly changing scenes of the dōgugaeshi and the quick identity changes in the hayagawari.

The Last Puppet Show: Broken Puppets and Sacred Parts

In 1960 the last major puppetry festival took place on Awaji. It was organized by the fledgling Awaji Ningyō Za, a reconstituted puppet troupe put together in response to a request for a foreign tour. Major pieces were presented by people formerly associated with Uemura Gen no Jō, once the largest and most prosperous theater on the island. There had not been a major ningyō matsuri on Awaji for nearly two decades, and this was a charged and nostalgic event. It was photographed by the Sumoto photographer Mune Torasuke, and so a record of the entire process has been preserved.[80] Many people I spoke with remembered this festival. One man told me that he had a great time there, much as one has a good time at a funeral banquet, remembering a past life even while acknowledging that it is dead and gone.

The discussion of ningyō matsuri as a cultural performance showed that puppets formed a nexus around which other significant actions turned. Rituals surrounding the treatment of puppets themselves—how they were handled, respected, and repaired—can also tell us something about the meanings of Awaji ningyō in people's lives.

The puppets used in the Sanbasō rites were accorded a different status in the Awaji tradition than other puppets. They were regarded as shinsei (sacred) and had to be stored in a designated location. A ningyō mawashi would keep them in a high place in his home, often even on the kamidana itself. Many people recalled seeing these puppets up on kamidana in theaters with offerings of rice and sake before them. Even today at the Ningyō Jōruri Kan in Fukura, the Sanbasō puppets are kept in a special case with offerings in front of them. Unlike jōruri puppets, which could be taken apart after each performance, Sanbasō puppets remained assembled at all times, except when they were being repaired.

What happened to puppet kashira which could no longer be used for some reason and were beyond repair? Until the late nineteenth century, they could not simply be thrown away or recycled. And it was not sufficient to put them in art collectors' cases as examples of folk art. Puppet heads and body parts of the Sanbasō puppets received preferential treatment: they were buried, and a *kuyō* service was performed for them.

Kuyō, technically a Buddhist term, refers to a ritual practice that is at once a worship service, a formal apology and an expression of gratitude, an appeasement rite, and a funeral. Often recipients of the rites are inanimate objects such as needles, calligraphy brushes, household cleaning instruments, and even underwear. A kuyō is conducted when these objects are brought to a temple or shrine; the people who brought them make a series of invocations and statements of apology or gratitude; the objects are then ritually disposed of in a way that concretizes the feelings of the people who used them.[81]

Broken puppets routinely had kuyō rites performed for them, and after the rite was concluded, they were buried in a cemetery. Near the Sanjo Omidō on Awaji, there is an area which was once the puppet cemetery, called *dekozamma*. The practice of burying these images carved "in the shape of the human" suggests an awareness that while matter and spirit may appear to be separate orders, once spirit has encountered a material form, the latter cannot return to mere matter but becomes matter set apart. A dilapidated puppet—a head, arms, perhaps a costume, rattles, flutes and masks—will never again be merely the sum of its parts. Today, they are put in museums or glass cases, a practice that worries many older puppeteers.[82]

Ritual Puppetry and the Power of Symbolic Action

The rituals described above raise a fundamental issue that occupied us in chapter 1: Why use puppets and not human actors? On the one hand, this could be considered a matter of aesthetics and even fashion, as in both Ebisu and Sanbasō rituals around Japan, there are examples of these rituals being presented with human actors. Even within a relatively circumscribed tradition such as Awaji ningyō, there is not a single answer to this question, since the decision to use puppets has several ramifications for the semiotics of the rituals themselves. There are a number of shifting, overlapping, interpenetrating, and interdependent understandings of the puppets in these rituals: (1) the puppet as a spirit vessel (*torimono*) for sacred beings; (2) the puppet as a body substitute (*bunshin*) for an absent (deceased) ritual specialist; (3) the puppet as a protective shield (*tate*) for the puppeteer; and (4) the puppet as a concrete metaphorical self (*daiyaku*) for the puppeteer.[83]

The most significant use of the puppet in both of the above rituals was as a torimono, a physical object that served to draw and contain spirits summoned to the human community in the ritual context. Using a physical object as a receptacle for sacred forces is a common practice in Japanese shamanism. Inherent in it are the dual ideas of containment and protection. The physical object allows the sacred forces to be contained in a single location, and it allows the religious specialist who has summoned the force to be protected from the danger that a supermundane force entails. To the extent that the puppets in these rituals were torimono, they are typical of a wider pattern in Japanese religious practice. But this was not the only meaning of the puppet.

The myth which founds the Awaji tradition makes it very clear that the puppet is actually a ritual substitute for a deceased priest. If we take this myth and generalize the meaning of this single motif, we can see that the puppet is a surrogate sacred specialist. When puppeteers challenged the authority of the Nishinomiya shrine by setting out on their own and establishing their own center, the puppet, not the puppeteer, became the new locus of authority. The ritual device of using a puppet allowed for the direct challenge to the Nishinomiya center while deflecting the power through a substitute object.

A third understanding of the puppet was its role as a protective barrier between the puppeteer and the liminal beings and noxious forces he summoned. Because part of the role of the puppeteer was to remove pollution from villages, the puppet stood between the puppeteer and the forces his performances attracted, serving as a sort of a shield and protecting the puppeteer from these forces.

Finally, we notice that as the ritual tradition developed, the puppets gradually became larger and larger, until by the end of the nineteenth century they stood nearly half as tall as the puppeteers themselves. It is possible to argue that at some level, the puppeteers understood these puppets to be metaphors for themselves. Just as puppets were the target of powerful and dangerous forces in society, so too were the puppeteers as members of Japan's marginalized outcast group, a target for the projection of negativity in society. Puppeteers manipulated puppets to control dangerous spiritual forces just as the ruling powers manipulated outcasts to control the danger of peasant unrest.

Perhaps the most important feature of puppets as ritual media is their imitative quality. Puppets can never be equated with or reduced to that which it imitates. They are once removed from the human realm and express the awareness that although the spiritual world can be metaphorically described through reference to the material world, it can never be reduced to it. As Umazume Masaru put it, "Awaji puppets aren't second-class human beings. They are first-class ningyō."

6

Puppets and Whirlpools: Icons, Nostalgia, Regionalism, and Identity in the Revival of Awaji *Ningyō*

The Man with the Bicycle

In September of 1957, at the invitation of the All Japan Regional Performing Arts Convention (Zenkoku kyōdo geinō taikai),[1] a puppeteer from Awaji presented a brief demonstration of puppet manipulation at the annual meeting held in a Tokyo hotel. The audience was predominantly foreign, and the entire demonstration took only about a half an hour. Attending the event was the director of the National Museum of Moscow in the Soviet Union. He was fascinated with the large puppets, wanted to offer an invitation for Awaji ningyō to perform in the Soviet Union, and asked to which theater on the island he should direct his invitation.

At the time, only three theaters on Awaji still existed. The war had been over for only twelve years, and the economic situation in rural Japan was still strained. Prewar puppeteers had either boxed up their puppets and stuck them in storehouses, sold them to collectors and foreigners, or used them as firewood to heat their baths. Most puppeteers had not picked up a puppet since the late 1930s. Although three theaters still remained, they existed in name only, and none of them had any puppeteers. There were not enough people interested in Awaji puppets on the island to scrape together a troupe. It would be necessary, then, to combine all the extant resources on the island to get together enough people for a proper performance, crossing lines of prewar troupe formations.

The following year, a full troupe of Awaji performers went to the Soviet Union and performed in Moscow and Leningrad. The performers, ranging in age from sixteen to seventy-five, were widely acclaimed. To the audiences who saw them perform, they appeared to be a unified group who had worked together for many years. The story of this troupe's formation, however, is more complex and reveals the dynamics of tradition reformulation and invention, the showcasing of "traditional culture" to foreigners, and the realities of the postwar fascination with a return to roots through what has come to be called *minzoku geinō* (folk performing arts).

At the time of the Soviet invitation, Umazume Masaru (the director of the successful Awaji Ningyō Jōruri Kan until the end of 1994) was in his late twenties. He had grown up in the village of Sanjo, near the Omidō Hachiman Daibosatsu, the ceremonial center of Awaji puppetry. His father, a farmer by profession, had played the shamisen for local puppet troupes. He remembered walking down the street in Sanjo-mura as a boy to the Yoshida Troupe, the prominent theater on the island, and watching preparations for rehearsals and performances. He had spent much of his childhood hanging around the theaters listening to the puppeteers, chanters, and musicians discuss and practice the various jōruri pieces. He looked forward to the annual ningyō matsuri from one year to the next. Umazume himself had learned how to participate in the sacred performance of Shiki Sanbasō as a reciter.

But in 1957, Awaji performances no longer took place. Seasonal dōkumbō mawashi did not come door to door at New Year to offer rites of blessing and purification. The puppet Sanbasō was not made to dance in front of household altars or small shrines in rice fields, near water sources, or in the worship halls of Hachiman and Ebisu shrines. People no longer congregated in one another's homes in the evenings after a day's work to practice jōruri recitation. Ebisu-mawashi no longer performed on fishing boats or Susaki Island in Fukura Bay to ensure a good catch and a safe year at sea. Twenty years before, these events were commonplace. It seems that the tradition of Awaji puppetry, with both its ritual and jōruri components, once such an everyday part of the life on the island, had died a rather sudden death because of the poverty of the post war period, the censorship of the occupying forces, the advent of cinema (and later television) and the neglect and even hostility of Awaji people themselves. Like many performance traditions throughout rural Japan, Awaji puppetry was defunct.

When he heard of the invitation to go to the Soviet Union, Umazume recognized an opportunity to reorganize the older puppeteers on the island into one group, which would ensure that Awaji puppetry would survive in at least some form. There was a lot of talk about the invitation, but no one seemed to do anything about it, so he took it upon himself to get everyone together. He got on his bicycle, rode around Awaji, and took the ferry over to Shikoku. He visited all the old puppeteers and chanters and tried to convince them to put together a troupe just one more time. He tracked down farmers, fishermen, and workers in prefectural offices who had once been puppeteers, frequently interrupting them at work. In the end, two other performers agreed to come together to practice. Along with the puppeteer who gave the performance in Tokyo, that made four, including Umazume. A few others slowly joined up.

In the meantime, the National Theater of Japan had invited the group to Tokyo for a warm-up performance and had given them a small loan, but it was not enough to support their practices. They needed stage props, new costumes for the puppets, and some small remuneration for the performers to make all the effort worthwhile. They began to ask people on Awaji for contributions. When a small troupe was finally assembled, one of the recruits, Naniwa Kunie, sewed the costumes for the puppets, and Umazume helped paint and decorate them. A practice hall was set up on Awaji, and they made it to Tokyo for the performance at the National Theater. Soon thereafter, the troupe made its successful trip to the Soviet Union.

Back on Awaji after the tour, the newly formed troupe managed to raise enough money to pay off some previous loans. It moved first to a small building owned by a savings and loan firm and later to a small theater in Fukura above a tourist gift shop near the waterfront. There they gave brief performances to tourists several times a day. In 1987 they moved to a new location on the cape overlooking the Naruto Straits, the narrow passage connecting Japan's Inland Sea and the Pacific Ocean.

This new center is a modern building housing a theater specially built for puppetry, with green rooms, showcases for artifacts, an elaborate stage with a custom-made curtain, and a business office. The complex, a miniature mall, also has a gift shop, restaurant, and movie hall attached to a scientific exhibit hall explaining the natural forces that create the Naruto whirlpools. Outside, a large parking lot can accommodate dozens of tourist buses. The building of this new theater and tourism center was made possible in part when in 1976 the Awaji puppet troupe was granted the status of an important intangible folk-cultural property (*jūyō mukei minzoku bunkazai*), a formal designation from the Agency for Cultural Affairs (Bunkachō), which provides formal preservation status and funds for the preservation of this performance tradition.

When I first encountered Awaji puppetry in its former location in the fall of 1977, all the performers were essentially volunteers, and the small theater doubled as a museum, displaying objects and old manuscripts relating to Japanese ritual and jōruri puppetry. Now, more than thirty five years after the successful Soviet Union foreign tour, Umazume, who had ridden his bicycle around the island and over to Shikoku to find enough performers, continues as the director of the new theater in Fukura. He told me why he went to such effort back in 1957 and over the years since then to establish Awaji ningyō performances as a viable theater: "At that time, I had a terrible sense of loss. I felt like something of Awaji was slipping away. My childhood. The sounds. The banners announcing the ningyō matsuri. The rehearsals. The fancy dōgugaeshi. I can't really make light of my reasons. They felt very serious to me then. I still feel that way now. It was painful to feel something so meaningful sliding through your fingers, and yet do nothing but talk about the good old days."

His bicycle ride around Awaji over thirty years ago set in motion a process which must in some sense be called a revival of the tradition. Today, the Awaji Ningyō Jōruri Kan operates with a troupe numbering over thirty full-time paid performers, an office staff, and a full-time director. During holidays and the summer months, there may be as many as eight performances daily, presenting works from the large repertoire of jōruri. The performers are all paid by the prefectural government as civil servants, an irony not lost on the members of the troupe, given the "nonhuman" status puppeteers suffered in the past. The troupe makes numerous overseas tours and is frequently featured in the Japanese media and even international films as proof that performing arts can be rescued from extinction and made viable again.[2] Everything about this revival indicates that Awaji puppets have made a comeback, that the damage of time has been undone. Umazume Masaru (who now drives a car) is a frequent guest on national talk shows. He still lives in Sanjo, where his family has lived for generations and where his father once played the shamisen for the local puppet troupes. All this success and activity raises a fundamental question: What does this revival reveal—and conceal—about people's experiences of their own puppetry tradition?

Clearly for Umazume Masaru and other people on Awaji involved in this hard work, something about Awaji puppets was part of their identity—an identity held with mixed emotions, since many of them have suffered from the stigma of being the descendant of a puppeteer. But this ambivalent relationship to the past is absent from discussions about reviving the tradition. Most of the people involved speak of the deep pain they felt when they remembered the prewar period and realized that this past was disappearing. A common response has been to devote oneself to preserving the tradition. The Japanese terms most often used to denote this process are *fukkatsu* (revival, even resurrection), *fukkō* (restoration), and *saikai* (reopening). Regardless of the term used (and most people use them interchangeably), inherent in this process is an orientation toward the past as a time of value and meaning. What is authentic, in other words, is what is past.

This charged orientation toward the past, as the engine that drives the revival, suggests a number of things about this interesting cultural process. On the one hand, such revival movements suggest that people cannot live without a past, even though restructuring it involves inventing large segments of it, reworking others to adapt to the contemporary situation, and marketing it in ways and contexts that would previously have been out of the question. The revival of a ritual tradition decades after its demise is therefore an excellent place to study how people develop narratives for their identities through orientation to both ritual and the past. On the other hand, a revival movement becomes an opportunity for revision of the past as well. In this case, revisionist revival may well have an anesthetic effect. As a defunct tradition is brought back, new dimensions of the tradition can be invented and extant aspects of the past can be enhanced and enlarged; meanwhile old and painful realities can be blurred or omitted and ironies of sponsorship ignored. Our discussion, then, must allow for both the ideological and therapeutic aspects of revival. Awaji puppetry reveals the relationship between the past and the present, nostalgia and identity, reality and fiction, creative remembrance and selective forgetting.

What was an Awaji puppeteer doing in Tokyo giving a lecture-demonstration about "a living theater tradition" when in fact the tradition was already defunct? Why was the audience primarily non-Japanese? What idea of cultural display was at work in this event, and how did it influence the next stage of this process, assembling a reconstituted theater group uniting traditionally distinct troupes each insisting on its own style and aesthetics?

Further questions arise. What is the significance of this major comeback of a performance tradition using puppets when supported by heavy government subsidies? What role did nostalgia play in this process? How did this process appropriate *and* become appropriated by other discourses of identity and nativism in Japan? How does the invocation of foreignness operate in this process of retrieval? Most important, what has happened to the ritual structure of the kadozuke puppetry performances in this revival?

This plethora of questions requires discussion of the following aspects of the revival movement: (1) the participation of Awaji revivalism in the larger discourse of folk studies and folk society preservation; (2) the discourse of nostalgia in contemporary Japan; (3) regionalism and the process of icon creation in the production of Awaji as a regional identity, and the role of puppetry as a focal icon; (4) the shift to a new "exoticism" in the retrieval of the ritual tradition of Awaji puppetry (performances of Sanbasō and Ebisu); (5) the significance of moving these itinerant rituals into the theatrical semiotics of stage performance; (6) the appearance of new splinter groups of revival activity on Awaji; and (7) the role of the foreign scholar in this process of revival.

Stages in the Process of Revival

In the last several decades, the move to "reclaim Japan's past" has focused largely on the revival of folk performing arts (*minzoku geinō*). The use of general terms to group together disparate ritual, aesthetic, and performance genres was necessitated through the growth of the *minzokugaku* (folk studies) movement, which gained momentum in Japan at the end of the Taishō period, largely under the charismatic leadership of Yanagita

Kunio. This new movement needed to delineate its focus of inquiry, and consequently it devoted much discussion not only to what constitutes "the folk" but also to where and when they existed and to what kind of value should be attached to the products of "folk culture." [3]

Before World War II, the term *minzoku geijutsu* (folk arts) was fashionable, but as the term applies also to nonperforming arts, it proved too inclusive a category to be useful. The term *kyōdo buyō* (regional dances) also missed the other dramatic aspects of the performance traditions, many of which did not privilege dance as the center of performance. The term *kyōdo geinō* was the norm during much of the 1950s, although *kyōdo* implies a regionalism and rural quaintness that made the term difficult to apply to urban traditions. Nevertheless, the overtones of what I will call "regionalism" remain in the folk studies movement in Japan. Inherent in the idea of regionalism is the view that although there is a common world that unites all phenomena of the folk, each region has its own unique version of this larger reality. Recreating these regional identities, frequently as tourist destinations, has been a major part of contemporary nostalgic discourse in Japan. It can be argued that Japanese nostalgia now constitutes something of a space time-continuum: nostalgia is felt not only for the past but for a past tied to a geography, and both are produced through discourse and through regional development campaigns. Often, folk performing arts make good icons for such regionalism, and this was certainly the case with Awaji.

It was Honda Yasuji who developed the criteria for determining what would be considered minzoku geinō. His schema has become normative and is to a large extent uncritically accepted by scholars in Japan.[4] For Honda and others, the problem has been one of delineating the lines between theater and ritual. Are minzoku geinō merely theater traditions of the countryside? Honda and others of the minzoku geinō school make the distinction that these performances, unlike the formal theater traditions of Noh, Kabuki, and Bunraku, are tied to the seasonal religious life of the people and must be interpreted in that context. He insists that these rituals must be seen as part of the larger phenomenon of what is termed minkan shinkō ("folk shinkō"). The key term here is *shinkō*, which is frequently mistranslated into English as simply "belief" but conveys the nuances of world view, praxis, and faith as well as belief.[5] Honda would argue that Awaji puppetry must be understood as part of the everyday lives of people on Awaji if it is to be understood at all. The categorical schema of minzoku geinō, based on belief and insistent on a limited understanding of context, becomes problematic when revival implies an "intervention" (to use Richard Schechner's term) that reshapes ritual according to the sensibilities and constraints of stage performance. In what way is revival a kind of cultural performance? Honda's agenda insists on a traditionalism that claims that only the past is authentic.

In 1950, influenced both by the sense of loss of traditional culture that the postwar era fostered and also by the growing popularity of the minzokugaku movement, the Japanese Diet passed legislation designed to protect its cultural heritage. The Bunkazai Hogohō (Cultural Properties Protection Law) raised the important issue of what constitutes cultural property.[6] Who and what is worth preserving and who and what can be allowed to become extinct? What constitutes art and performance? In the same year, as part of this larger agenda and through support from the Ministry of Education, the All Japan Regional Performing Arts Convention was formed as an annual convention where regional performing arts could be presented. Renamed the All Japan Folk Performing Arts Meeting (Zenkoku Minzoku Geinō Kai) in 1958, these annual meetings not only showcased "traditional Japan" for foreign scholars and even tourists, they also provided incentive for regional groups to get together and practice. Performance forms that had been defunct for decades were reinvented, based on recollections of elders, scholarly inquiry, and imaginative regional comparison. Ritual performance traditions still barely alive were given the chance to gather strength in the face of modernity and find a new audience at a national level. Being a participant in these large public events was highly prestigious and had a cachet of authenticity.

Each convention served as a sort of academic conference where ethnographers, folklorists, and anthropologists could present their research on the various traditions being showcased. Since these events became important moments in the building of academic careers, it was in the best interests of the academics that these performances be as "authentic" as possible.

Each of these performance events represented an incredible amount of logistical planning, research, and retrieval activity. Some claimed that only the version of the past that they presented, threatened by the current situation, could be considered truly Japanese. Scholars in the minzoku geinō school claimed that various ritual performances around Japan represented at once the true and the vanishing. Efforts to preserve these rituals often had a decidedly religious zeal: the authentic Japan was being rescued from the onslaught of modernity. At stake was a definition of authenticity and nativism. What does it mean to be truly and authentically Japanese? Veracity concerned more than merely determining what had happened before; it became an exercise in the staging of value. The presentations by scholars, often from the same stages where the performances were to take place, became as much a part of these events as the "ritual performances" themselves.

Throughout the 1950s, the Ministry of Education asked regional and prefectural boards of education to identify local performance traditions. In numerous villages throughout Japan, committees were formed to iden-

The priest from the Kohyō shrine near Usa in Oita Prefecture demonstrates
the manipulation of a puppet.

tify the folk performances of local shrines or temples and carefully reconstruct their histories, often filling in details and borrowing dance, music,
and costuming from other areas to lend an air of authenticity. Claiming
historical accuracy was of ultimate importance, even if the performance
tradition had been interrupted by as much as eighty years.

A stunning example comes right out of the history of ritual puppetry.
In chapter 3 I noted the involvement of ritual puppeteers in the Hōjō-e
of the Usa Hachiman shrine. Texts from that shrine claim puppeteers
played a role in the defeat of the Hayato by the centralized government in
720 C.E. Until the late Meiji period, puppeteers from two subsidiary
shrines of the Usa complex, the Kohyō and Koyō shrines, presented a
sumo match with puppets as part of this larger Usa rite. In spite of this
tradition being defunct for over eighty years (long enough for firsthand
informants to have died), today these rites have been revived, and the
performances are incredibly detailed. The Kohyō shrine has received large
subsidies to rebuild its main structures, including a new fireproof struc-

Musician puppets from the Koyō shrine.

ture to house the ancient puppets. Basing their reconstruction of performances on written texts, the physical capabilities of the extant puppets
they possess, and on the most general ideas of Shinto performance, puppets again perform the ritual appeasement ceremony every four years as
part of the Usa Hōjō-e, although its resemblance to the earlier tradition
is dubious.[7] The new puppet ritual is presented as an example of an ancient Japanese folk performing art. It appears, however, that only one
part of this ancient rivalry between these two shrines is now represented:
the other shrine that had been involved in this rite in the past, Koyō,
received no subsidies and has not been able to do more than maintain its
very old puppets.

In the early postwar period, the Ministry of Education (Mombu Daijin)
and Ministry of Cultural Affairs (Bunkachō) also encouraged the formation of *hozonkai* ("preservation societies") for folk arts, especially those
that were primarily performance based. People in Cultural Affairs offered
guidance and consultation to municipalities on how to organize a hozonkai and how to enable it to function most effectively. These societies

worked to ensure the continual transmission of tradition, to safeguard the stages, props, texts, and other physical artifacts of the tradition, to record the histories of their development, and to see that opportunities were created to keep those who were central to the tradition involved in it. Frequently, however, the financial burden of these activities was borne not by the government but by wealthy private patrons. This allowed for a certain freedom at the local level, but it also meant that personal bias and favor could be manipulated. What got preserved, in many cases, and how it got presented in a larger context was frequently left up to the personal tastes of the patron. The revival of Awaji puppetry is no exception.

In 1976 the Cultural Protection Law was revised to provide tangible support for such theater traditions. Beginning in this year, awards were made recognizing certain traditions as important intangible folk cultural property. Recognition was granted based on recommendation by a board of scholars, most of whom were folklorists from the minzoku geinō school. As a result, to receive such a prize, ritual traditions had to conform to the aesthetics of rusticity, regionalism, and rurality. As already noted, Awaji ningyō shibai was among the recipients of this funding.

For Awaji, efforts at preservation were started locally even before such organizations became fashionable and government subsidy was possible. As early as 1935, an organization calling itself the Awaji Puppetry Arts Revival Society (Awaji Ningyō Geijutsu Fukkō Kyōkai) was organized with Nakano Toraichi as its head. This organization was interrupted by the war, and in 1949 Fudō Saiichi (the father of Fudō Satoshi, the old man with the photographs mentioned in the opening pages of this book) founded the Awaji Ningyō Hozonkai.[8] An employee at the local city hall, Fudō Saiichi wrote the small but extremely useful *Awaji Ningyō Shibai no Yurai* (Origins of Awaji puppetry), which marked the founding of the new *Awaji Ningyō Hozonkai* organization. This book was followed by local efforts to collect documents and preserve artifacts, but the fact remained that out of the eighteen fully functioning troupes at the beginning of the nineteenth century and the more than several hundred itinerant puppeteers living in Sanjo, hardly any troupes and no itinerant puppeteers were performing at the time. In 1907 the number of troupes was twelve; in 1936, seven; and in 1951, only four, none of which was really managing to survive. The revival movement had an obvious task, but in spite of its efforts immediately before and after the war, the trajectory toward extinction did not really slow down.

It seems clear that nostalgia, for all its clout in the folklore studies movement, needs a constellation of other factors to enable any movement to get off the ground. Nostalgia demands a focal point, an icon around which the currents of feeling can flow.

Nostalgia as Experience, Nostalgia as Ideology

Most people in Japan commonly use the adjective *natsukashii*, the verb *natsukashimu*, or the noun forms *natsukashisa* or *natsukashimi* to describe this vague sense that "things just aren't what they used to be." These are everyday words in Japanese, used to refer to events and sensations that evoke connections with the past and feelings of home. For example, a person when eating a good bowl of *soba* after eating only those from machines for months may remark, "Aah! Natsukashii!"

This term *natsukashii* has a variety of referents, including "feeling," "yearning for or missing someone," "becoming attached to someone." Alone as a noun, the written character means "bosom, heart, breast, pocket," implying something close to one's heart and seat of emotional attachment. Sometimes the character is translated simply as "nostalgia."

In Japanese these days, people familiar with contemporary discourse in literary critical studies may use the word *nostarujii* is used to refer to the general cultural phenomenon of romanticizing the past. This imported word (and example of *gairaigo*, or "word coming from outside") conveys this general sense of recollection and desire to return to a romanticized past. But because the word *nostarujii* has entered Japanese largely through the channels of literary criticism, it is usually invoked only by scholars, current affairs commentators, and others familiar with metadiscourses of contemporary society. People on Awaji don't use the word *nostarujii* to discuss what they are feeling and what motivates them to try to revive their puppetry tradition. They refer to the power of natsukashisa. To use the term *nostarujii* is to make an imposition on the data, for the act of "longing for the past" is understood within contemporary critical studies to mean participation in a hegemonic discourse: people using *nostarujii* in Japanese are likely to be referring to a cultural and political trend in which a fictionalized past is invoked to further a particular political agenda (usually a conservative one). This interpretation of nostarujii lacks subtlety and does not do justice to the complexity of "nostalgic activities" in Japan. In short, nostarujii and natsukashimu are not simply synonymous. While the nostalgic overtones of the folklore movement may veil a history of violence and are undoubtedly great money makers, for many people, connecting with their past through the process of longing constitutes a healing process. In the case of itinerant puppetry, remembrance means finding a way to situate a painful past within a present context. The manipulation of nostalgic currents (whether conscious or unconscious) can be a way to redress a painful past without simple revisionism.

A strong tone of natsukashimi runs throughout the motivations for reviving the Awaji puppetry tradition. The power of the past is a potent force in contemporary Japan, and the surface fashion of what one Japanese called "indigo and unpolished wood" conceals a more fundamental process of identity and hegemony. The government, for its part, would prefer to cultivate and manipulate a previously marginalized and oppressed people's return to an idealized past than deal with tendencies toward social revolution. Such a return posits a shared experience, whereas in fact there was a system based on differences. At stake in the nostalgic journey for people on Awaji is a re-forming of their identity. When government ministries take over and appropriate this discourse, it has a decidedly different face, making it necessary to ask, "Whose nostalgic discourse is this, anyway?"

From Medicalization to Politicization

Our term *nostalgia* is derived from the Greek gerund *nostos*, which means simply "returning home." But added to this word is the ending with which most of us are all too familiar, "algia," which refers to any painful condition (for example, a neuralgia). So nostalgia refers not just to a sense of pleasantly remembering the past but also to the charge of pain which goes with it. The term was first used by the Swiss physician Johannes Hofer in the late seventeenth century to describe what he considered to be a clinical condition: Swiss soldiers fighting away from home became very homesick, and suffered from "despondency, melancholia, lability of emotion, including profound bouts of weeping, anorexia, a generalized 'wasting away,' and, not infrequently, attempts at suicide." [9] Other clinicians and scientists of the seventeenth and early eighteenth centuries concerned themselves with finding the root and cure for what they understood to be a physiological condition. Originally created to label what was thought to be a medical condition, this term was later taken up by psychologists who, though not convinced of its physiological roots, were nevertheless given to regarding nostalgia as an ailment. A common thread ran through understandings of this condition, the experience of interruption. As Fred Davis points out, "nearly all theories of nostalgia, from the most mechanistic and physiological to the most existential and psychological, draw on some notion of sudden alteration, sharp transition, or marked discontinuity in life experience to explain the phenomenon." [10]

Davis has rightly pointed out that the history of this term has undergone transitions from a medical term to a term used largely in psychology and finally to an everyday word for both simple homesickness and the tendency to regard the past with special affection and to desire to return to it in some way or another.[11] Davis argues that a shift in meaning of the term nostalgia has occurred as the notion of home as a physical place has eroded in contemporary society. This insight is particularly relevant in contemporary Japan, where a huge exodus from rural areas into the cities in the past forty years has left some villages empty of all but the most elderly occupants. These villages have become symbols for a dying way of life in Japan. "Homesickness" no longer evokes a place but a time. In essence, home has been temporalized; it now refers to a time in a person's life, the past, rather than to a particular place. As Davis writes, "because . . . home as such can for so many no longer evoke the 'remembrance of things past' it once did, it has fallen to other words, 'nostalgia' among them, to comprehend the sometimes pedestrian, sometimes disjunctive, and sometimes eerie sense we carry of our own past and of its meaning for present and future."[12]

In Japan, nostalgia now has a new dimension. It has become powerful political capital, capable of being spent but never exhausted. The term used today refers to a general desire to "return to the good old days," a pronounced aspect of popular culture. Tourism, media, and advertising have waged a war on the urban present with destinations, dramas, and images of a bucolic and thatch-roofed past. This spatial bias of folklore studies and the nostalgic discourse of which it is a part have been summarized by Stephen Nussbaum: "This concerns the interchangeability of geography and history, the notion that one may travel back in time by moving spatially toward the hinterland. According to this way of thought the city is an important locus of cultural change and the entire country becomes a living museum."[13]

One of the watershed academic works to directly address the dynamics of nostalgia is Raymond Williams's *The Country and the City*.[14] His work is an exploration of the strong tendency in English literature and historiography to posit a longing for a golden age in which the city (and the forms of complex social organization it both produces and comes to represent symbolically) was not the dominant venue of human life. His study reveals that this bias toward the rural as the authentic can be seen as a dynamic throughout English history. Nostalgia for the rural he argues, is an ever present trope in English conceptions of time and space. We can see a similar tendency in Japanese nostalgic ideologies as well.

Recent scholarship in anthropology and sociology has begun to look at the role of nostalgia as a means of temporal (rather than spatial) orientation in ideologies of value. Usually, nostalgic discourse is identified with the undercurrents of fascism, because it creates a false sense of a shared past that is better than the present, and therefore is able to draw current social problems into dramatic relief against a carefully constructed and filtered past. What are the implications of the aesthetic appropriation of the past, and how is the past of an oppressed people appropriated by their oppressors in nostalgic discourse?

Fredric Jameson in his article "Postmodernism, or the Cultural Logic of Late Capitalism,"[15] an often cited work in the deconstruction of nostalgic discourse, points to numerous examples in modern art, film, and architecture in which various "signs" from the past are appropriated, with no concerted effort to find a complete context for such appropriations. The aesthetic result he calls a pastiche, a patchwork of unrelated objects, set side by side as if to call attention to (and, I would add, even fetishize) themselves. For Jameson, this is the aesthetic mode of postmodernism. It is not merely a question of a particular aesthetic decision, one choice among many, but rather, an expression of the time itself: "I cannot stress too greatly the radical distinction between a view for which the postmodern is one (optional) style among many others available, and one which seeks to grasp it as the cultural dominant of the logic of late capitalism: the two approaches in fact generate two very different ways of conceptualizing the phenomenon as a whole, on the one hand moral judgments (about which it is indifferent whether they are positive or negative), and on the other a genuinely dialectical attempt to think our present time in History."[16] This tendency to appropriate the past into a collage of images is what Jameson calls "the nostalgic mode."

We need to ask a question that Jameson only begins to address: Is nostalgia as we see it today (in, for example, the revival of the Awaji tradition) a unique feature of this particular moment in history? If so, does it reveal something about the late twentieth century in Japan? If not, what can it tell us? If we read Jameson correctly, it appears he would argue yes to the first question. The "nostalgic mode" is "a desperate attempt to appropriate a missing past." Since this has been projected onto a larger social movement (as in the current conservative nostalgia for the 1950s in America, for example, or in Japan's nostalgia for the late Edo period and the rural), it "is refracted through the iron law of fashion."[17] Nostalgic modes of discourse are attempts to reclaim that which never really was. For Jameson, and perhaps on this point he can be said to speak for postmodernists as a whole, a nostalgic enterprise ultimately reveals a crisis in our relationship to the entire issue of temporality. We have come to realize that the past as a knowable unit does not exist, but is forever subject to the hermeneutics of suspicion. We are, simply, unable to rely on a logical temporal construction as a means of orientation. The subject, Jameson writes, "has lost its capacity actively to extend its pro-tensions and re-tensions across the temporal manifold, and to organize its past and future into coherent experience, it becomes difficult enough to see how the cultural productions of such a subject could result in anything but 'heaps of fragments' and in a practice of the randomly heterogeneous and fragmentary and the aleatory."[18]

Fred Davis said basically the same thing a number of years earlier, without the "pastiche" of semiotics and psychoanalysis:

> If, as I have maintained, nostalgia is a distinctive way, though only one among several ways we have, of relating our past to our present and future, it follows that nostalgia (like long term memory, like reminiscence, like daydreaming) is deeply implicated in the sense of who we are, what we care about, and (though possibly with much less inner clarity) whither we go. In short, nostalgia is one of the means—or, better, one of the more readily accessible psychological lenses—we employ in the never ending work of constructing, maintaining, and reconstructing our identities. To carry the optical metaphor a step further, it can be thought of as a kind of telephoto lens on life, which, while it magnifies and prettifies some segments of our past, simultaneously blurs and grays other segments, typically those closer to us in time.[19]

Jameson sees pastiche in its nostalgic mode as something of a schizophrenic endeavor. Basing his discussion of schizophrenia on Lacan's account, he writes that when Lacan's category is taken descriptively (rather than clinically), it is useful for understanding the postmodern moment. While not including all postmodern artists under the label of schizophrenic, he considers schizophrenia an illuminating aesthetic category.

> Very briefly, Lacan describes schizophrenia as a breakdown in the signifying chain, that is, the interlocking syntagmatic series of signifiers which constitutes an utterance or a meaning. . . . The connection between this kind of linguistic malfunction and the psyche of the schizophrenic may then be grasped by way of a two-fold proposition: first the personal identity is itself the effect of a certain temporal unification of past and future with the present before me; and second, that such active temporal unification is itself a function of language, or better still of the sentence, as it moves along its hermeneutical circle through time. If we are unable to unify the past, present and future in the sentence, then we are similarly unable to unify the past, present and future of our own biographical experience or psychic life.[20]

Jameson argues that the prevalence of nostalgic discourse is due to the crisis in the experience of time and history as a way of organizing meaning, a crisis that he refers to as "the breakdown of temporality."[21] While a person experiencing this sense of crisis would probably find that expression alien to his or her experience, it suggests a moment when the past seems alien in the present, creating a crisis concerning the significance of both the present and the future. If I cannot identify or even locate the substance of my "remembrance of things past," how can I have an identity in the present? If I have no identity, what can guarantee that the future will not be even more chaotic? What, then, can be extracted and even serve as icons from my past, icons that can come to stand for my entire lost self?

Our case provides a field in which to explore the complexity of what Jameson refers to as "the nostalgic mode," for unlike his cases in which pastiche is the dominant cultural element, we are looking at a case in which the revival of a tradition grows out of itself. The "heaps of fragments" of the Awaji tradition are being carefully rebuilt into a new picture of the tradition, and this construction can claim to be "retrieving" its own past. On Awaji—unlike postmodern examples, drawn from middle America where French bistro ads are placed side by side with Greek sculpture, American beer signs, and English china—puppets are retrieved from an Awaji past and placed into an Awaji present, and frequently returned to the spatial contexts where they once were common. Puppet performances of Shiki Sanbasō and Ebisu-mai in the 1990s on docks and in rice paddies are good examples. The pastiche, then, is not comprised of promiscuous cultural borrowing; it is a retrieval of the past into a different context—the here and now. To place the past back into its "authentic" context implies that time must remain static in order to be authentic.

The revival of Awaji puppets is not without a serious dose of kitsch. Elements of the tradition have been singled out and decontextualized as icons for the entire past. In the theater gift shop, one can buy sake in a bottle shaped like a puppet head. Fans in the shape of famous characters from the jōruri pieces are also on sale, and Awaji puppet telephone cards are big sellers. Tea towels depicting scenes from *Keisei Awa no Naruto* are popular gifts, and sweets stamped with the raging head of Hachiman Tarō are the fastest moving items on the culinary side. But the entirety of this revival is not simply about market forces and making tourism viable as a base for regional economy. Rather, I suggest that the semiotics are infinitely more multivalent. Who owns this nostalgia? Can the nostalgic experience of the young man on the bicycle be described in the same way as that of the ethnographer from Kanagawa who studies Awaji, or the middle-aged man from Tokyo who travels to Awaji to see the theater to reclaim his identity as a Japanese? When Umazume Masaru reinvents Awaji ningyō as the director of the new theater, he is not randomly borrowing the past in a collage of unrelated images. He is consciously selecting elements of his tradition that he considers viable in a late-twentieth-century context, and which he sees can become icons for the entirety of a lost tradition and focal points for its future.

The reader will recall an important distinction within the Awaji tradition between the jōruri performances, intended for human audiences and having a "secular" agenda, and the kadozuke performances, presented on ritual occasions. In the process of revival, a decision, at times only half-conscious, was made to present the whole of the tradition as the jōruri tradition. Umazume explained that was done largely because this part of the tradition was most likely to be viable. This decision seems rational. Just as no one would claim that staging Shakespeare today constitutes a simple and naive "return to the past," so too the jōruri ballads contain motifs, issues, and ideas which, though wrapped in the history of their times, can speak to people of any generation and even different cultures. Themes of love, divided loyalties, betrayal, jealousy, murder, and incest are the stuff of timeless pieces of drama. That this tradition is being revitalized should not be a cause for puzzlement, since the jōruri tradition has maintained a continuing appeal, although at a more urban and formal level. The presentation of jōruri pieces on the Kabuki and Bunraku stages has continued with little interruption. Reviving these performances on Awaji affects the content of the plays less than who performs them, where they are performed, and with what aesthetic and theatrical sensibilities. The key issue is this: the jōruri tradition initially was limited to one piece, and this single piece became an icon for a vanishing past.

The decision to make the performance tradition (jōruri) of Awaji puppets stand for the entire "lost tradition" in the early stages (1950s through 1970s) and then to shift to the kadozuke aspect of the tradition in the latter stages (late 1980s to the present) reflects the shifting hierarchy of symbolization, responding to subtle changes in the nativist discourse in contemporary Japan. The element of "postmodern schizophrenia" in this retrieval activity becomes most apparent when we explore how the Awaji puppet tradition is being placed within a larger context of tourism on the island. Let us look closely at just which parts of the tradition bore this burden of representing the entire tradition and how those aspects of tradition get wedded to other regional features to represent "Awaji as a state of mind."

Puppets and Whirlpools: Icons of the Vanishing

In the process of revival, Awaji puppets have been the wedded to a larger process of regionalism. In the 1970s and 1980s, the tourist industry in Japan launched two very successful campaigns to promote rural Japan as exotic and yet a place where people could discover something authentic in their identity as a Japanese.[22] *Jisukabaa Japan* (Discover Japan) and *Ekusochikku Japan* (Exotic Japan), both products of the Japan Tourist Bureau, cast the return to a mythical past in rural Japan—an escape to the roots, as it were—in foreign words, a linguistic decision designed to underscore the possibility of an experience of the exotic and even the ethnic right here at home. Posters show, for example, a young lady standing in a dense forest near a mountain temple; she watches while an ascetic walks away into the hill. Images of masked performances and traditional arts made room in the posters for the solitary (usually female) traveler in time and space. One could "get real" and never leave Japan. While it is clear these campaigns have created a discourse of their own about exoticism, I argue that they reflect a deeper cultural process at work, a regionalism which has its roots in the folklore movement of Yanagita Kunio.

The success or failure of any project to promote regionalism depends on the production of a visible icon that can symbolize a region's past by standing for its vanishing, endangered, or lost realities and values, and that advertises the region and its complex system of meanings. By icon, I refer to a single image serving this multiple capacity—flashy, eye catching, readily remembered, and easily reproduced. Here, I examine the creation of the "iconography" of Awaji regionalism and the role of puppetry in that process.

In the early stages of the revival of Awaji puppets (and later as well), the pilgrimage scene from *Keisei Awa no Naruto*, a mere twenty-eight minutes long, was presented as the only surviving piece of the Awaji repertoire. This play combined with elements of the Awaji landscape to assume the role of an icon in the process of revival. During the 1960s the struggling theater above the gift shop did not even have a regular chanter, so sometimes the piece was presented accompanied by a recording of a *tayū* chanting this tragic jōruri tale of a mother and daughter encountering one another after a separation of several years. This single scene has been presented several times every day for decades, and until quite recently this was all that Awaji puppetry as a revived theater consisted of. I suggest that this piece is best understood as an icon not only for the revival movement but for the larger movement to create Awaji as a new Mediterranean in Japan, that is, as a carefree place far from the madding crowd of the city, the new vacation spot for urban Japan. But why is this piece such a powerful icon linking Awaji puppets with Awaji regionalism?

In the scene, a woman is sitting in her home when she hears a pilgrim arrive at her door. From the hat the young pilgrim is carrying, we know she is on the Saikoku Pilgrimage.[23] The pilgrim, it turns out, is a mere child. The woman, surprised to see such a young child alone on a pilgrimage, asks her where her parents are. The child replies, "I am going in search of my parents. I am from the province of Awa, from Tokushima, and was separated from my parents at the age of three when I was left to be raised by my grandmother. Now, I have come looking for my parents. I want to meet them. I want to see them." (In Tokugawa Japan, when mobility was highly restricted, people frequently used pilgrimage as the pretext to conduct business—family or otherwise—which required traveling.)

The mother in *Keisei Awa no Naruto* looks longingly for her child after she has sent her away. Courtesy of Fujimoto Yasurō.

The mother realizes that this is her own daughter, whom she and her husband had to abandon several years before when they learned of the danger they were in due to her husband's political affiliations. Now, her own child has come begging at her door. The mother struggles over whether or not she should reveal her identity to the child, but, realizing that to do so would endanger the girl, she decides against it. Nevertheless, she pulls her inside the door to get a closer look at her. She looks for, and finds, a telltale mark on the child's forehead identifying her as her daughter. The remainder of the play is a tragic enactment of this mother's agony as she holds her vulnerable child close to her and hears how the child is being abused on her travels. It ends when she tries to give the child money and sends her away. The mother is left alone on stage and laments the separation and the painful realities that have made this necessary. The scene closes as the mother decides to go looking for the child.

In the next act (which is rarely performed, and is never presented at the Awaji theater in everyday performances) after leaving the person who is her mother, the child encounters her father on the road. Unaware that this is his daughter, he tries to rob her. She tries to get away from his grasp, and in the ensuing struggle he accidentally kills her. Not recognizing his own child, he brings the body to his home and lays it out on the tatami. His wife arrives home and tells him that their child has come. She describes a young pilgrim, the person he has just robbed and killed. When he realizes what he has done, he tries to convince his wife that this dead form to his right is actually only sleeping and begs her not to wake the child. When the wife discovers her child is dead, she goes crazy. Her husband delivers a famous soliloquy in jōruri lamenting his fate as the murderer of his own child and the strange twists of fate that have led him to this tragic moment.

This act gives the play its real power as theater. Since the entire piece is so deeply affecting, why has this latter part of the play been left out of the revival process?[24] Quite simply, the sheer weight of this tragic scene makes it too heavy to bear the burden of the iconographic process. The new image of Awaji regionalism is of a carefree, rural place, lighthearted and perfect for a vacation. Awaji regionalism is decidedly not about myths and epics of Oedipal proportions. The gravity of Awaji puppetry as drama is thus made subordinate to the revival process, a fact not lost on many elderly people on Awaji who feel that the tradition is not being retrieved but merely fetishized into one short piece.

A number of logistical reasons justify the decision to use the pilgrimage scene from *Keisei Awa no Naruto* as the sole performance. First, the piece requires only two puppets, one of whom is a child, which means that it can be manipulated by two people (even one in a pinch) rather than three. In all, that means that five puppeteers can present the piece. Second, the scene can stand as a playlet in its own right, and people not familiar with the longer play can be deeply moved by the pathos of the tragedy of a mother and child. Third, it is famous, and people have often heard something about it, even if they know little about the classical jōruri tradition. And fourth, since there are only two voices and both of them are female, it does not require a chanter with an extensive range to prepare the piece and therefore serves as a starter piece for chanters to learn the art of recitation.

But a deeper logic was at work in selecting *Keisei Awa no Naruto* as the lifeline rescuing the tradition from extinction. The piece participates in the Japanese nostalgic discourse of regionalism. In spite of the fact that

regional variation in language, food, ritual performance styles, and custom have been eroded dramatically through rapid urbanization and mass
media, the nostalgic discourse insists that if one retreats from the cities to
the rural areas, one will find these regional distinctions still intact. But the
regionalism must be made so apparent that it will jump out at you from a
rapidly moving tour bus.

Keisei Awa no Naruto works as an icon for the Awaji tradition because
it is a regional piece. People will recognize the place-name in the title and
associate it with Awaji. The title refers to the Naruto Straits, a location
literally within a stone's throw of the theater. But the title also suggests
that human life (in Tokugawa Japan at least) is not unlike the geological
squeeze created by the proximity of Shikoku and Awaji. After watching
The Tragic Straits of Naruto, one could board a boat and go out to see the
whirlpools of Naruto firsthand. The play, then, was one part of a packaged
deal. Awaji regionalism meant puppets and whirlpools, and when the two
could be superimposed upon one another, all the better. The theater over
the gift shop at Fukura Bay was just across a narrow street from the harbor
where one boarded the boat to go and see the whirlpools. In fact, one
could buy a ticket for both the boat and the theater from the same little
booth. While the whirlpools captured the imagination because they appear so dangerous (and actually are), the puppets also appeal to the hun-
ger for the rustic (and implicitly, the wildness that rusticity implies). Awaji
puppets were seen as the rustic but real origins of the more refined Osaka
Bunraku puppets. Both the puppets and the whirlpools, the analogical
construction seems to suggest, have a natural innate wildness. The two
icons reinforce one another.

When I went back to Awaji in 1984, I was surprised to discover that the
pilgrimage scene of *Keisei Awa no Naruto*, was the only piece being performed. Still in its location over the gift shop, the troupe was starting to
attract young members from around Awaji who were trained in high
school clubs. The troupe had just returned from a trip to Holland and
Belgium. Awaji puppets were starting to make a comeback, but even in
their local setting their performances were limited to this one scene.

In 1987 when I returned to Awaji to conduct extensive field work over
a two-year period, the troupe had moved to its present location on the
cape overlooking the Naruto Straits, and even though it now had government subsidy and a fancy theater, the pilgrimage scene of *Keisei Awa no
Naruto* was still the troupe's only offering. The new theater is in a larger
building called the Naruto Kaikan (Naruto Hall), in which the icons of
Awaji regionalism are carefully displayed. A small movie and natural science display hall explains the whirlpools of the Naruto straits. After looking at the natural science exhibit, one enters a movie hall, where one can
watch (with 3-D glasses) a film of the whirlpools and get the feeling of

actually being in them. Fish pulled from the whirlpools seem to jump right into your face. Other seasonal events from the Awaji ritual calendar pop off the screen at you in three-dimensional clarity. The Naruto Kaikan also has a gift shop selling sweets with the motifs of whirlpools and puppets as well as regional delicacies such as Naruto *wakame* (seaweed). In the puppet theater, a fancy brocade curtain decorates the stage. On it are depicted (it should come as no surprise) the mother and daughter from *Keisei Awa no Naruto* against a backdrop of whirlpools. The semiotics had not changed, but the packaging had become more slick. Instead of whirlpools accessible by boat, they are visually accessible. One can climb up to the viewing deck and look over the Naruto Straits through binoculars (for 100 yen). The iconography is the same: puppets and whirlpools, both standing for Awaji as a whole, as a rural place, a part of Japan's vanishing past.

In 1987, I asked members of the troupe how they felt about performing the pilgrimage scene from *Keisei Awa no Naruto* several times a day, day in and day out. Every one of them expressed feelings ranging from boredom to rage at the redundancy. No one denied it was a powerful piece, but they resented the fact that the theater had to stick to this one piece for public performances. The troupe was actively involved in practicing other pieces, and even presented them occasionally at local events around Awaji, but for the most part the daily fare at the Awaji Ningyō Jōruri Kan was *Keisei Awa no Naruto*. I asked Umazume-san why they did not expand the performance repertoire. His answer was telling: "When we first started to present the plays at the previous location, we wanted something people liked. Although many people were familiar with both the larger piece from which this scene is taken and also the larger repertoire of jōruri pieces, this was a favorite, and a regional piece referring to lower Awaji and Tokushima. But eventually, it got to the point where people would only come to see that piece. It is the only piece of theater they associate with Awaji ningyō. Awaji ningyō means *Keisei Awa no Naruto* these days. If a tour bus calls to book a showing, they request that piece. Whenever I suggest that perhaps the performance might change, the tourist industry becomes uncomfortable."[25]

The decision to make *Keisei Awa no Naruto* the iconographic centerpiece of the revival movement was an act of inclusion. Meanwhile there was a parallel act of exclusion. During my fieldwork, I was interested in the kadozuke aspect of the Awaji tradition, decidedly absent from the new, "iconographically correct" situation. I was interested in how the religious past of the tradition would be understood, ignored, or appropriated as the tradition of Awaji ningyō was being revived. The puppets for the Sanbasō performance were kept in a small case to the left of the stage, on display, but the performance was rarely presented and hardly ever discussed. It was clear this ritual piece could not be used as an icon for the Awaji tradition (even though it is a highly distinctive aspect of it, in fact more typical of Awaji ningyō's past than the jōruri tradition), so it was relegated to a glass case. Even within the revived theater, some aspects of the tradition are acknowledged as part of the past, while others (puppets and whirlpools in Keisei Awa no Naruto) are part of its present and future. As of the early 1980s, ritual puppetry had quite simply lost its context as performance and become a museum object. The glass case, it can be suggested, was the symbolic space in which kadozuke puppets still made sense—as relics of the past.

Perhaps another dynamic was at work in this tendency to de-emphasize the kadozuke tradition and showcase the jōruri aspects of the tradition. Renato Rosaldo suggests that our assumption that nostalgia is something common to human beings at all times is highly suspect. Using Davis as his sole source for the history of the term, he argues that because the term itself has undergone such variation since its invention, nostalgia cannot be seen as a constant: "the changing meanings of 'nostalgia' in Western Europe (not to mention that some cultures have no such concept at all) indicate that 'our' feelings of tender yearning are neither as natural nor as pan-human, and therefore not necessarily as innocent, as one might imagine."[26] Rosaldo notes the role of nostalgia in the writing of ethnographies (and as it appears in contemporary films about the colonial period), and claims many ethnographic enterprises are the result of the yearning by certain people (ethnographers, missionaries) for the "traditional" cultures they have destroyed. He calls this "imperialist nostalgia," and describes it as follows:

> Curiously enough, agents of colonialism—officials, constabulary officers, missionaries, and other figures from whom anthropologists ritually dissociate themselves—often display nostalgia for the colonized culture as it was "traditionally" (that is, when they first encountered it). The peculiarity of their yearning, of course, is that agents of colonialism long for the very forms they intentionally altered or destroyed. Therefore, my concern resides with a particular kind of nostalgia, often found under imperialism, where *people mourn the passing of what they themselves have transformed*. Imperialist nostalgia revolves around a paradox: A person kills somebody, then mourns the victim. In any of its versions, imperialist nostalgia uses a pose of "innocent yearning" both to capture people's imaginations and to conceal its complicity with often brutal domination.[27]

Few ethnographers in Japan would step forward and confess to having murdered folk performing arts in Japan, and arguing such would be perhaps taking Rosaldo further than he would want to go. Nevertheless, this insight into the use of nostalgia to veil violence and domination applies to our case in an interesting way. The nostalgic enterprise on Awaji, which is rapidly creating a modern context for ritual puppetry as a showcased cultural performance, has almost completely co-opted the participation of children of ritual puppeteers in the *burakumin* civil rights movement.

As I have suggested, a decision seems to have been made in the early stages of the revival movement of Awaji puppets that the jōruri aspect of the Awaji tradition should be maintained and resurrected, while the kadozuke origins should be noted but not fostered. In the 1970s and early 80s, kadozuke materials were showcased in such a way that they appeared to be a part of Awaji ningyō's very distant past, but the more recent examples of ritual activity were neglected altogether. For evidence of this, we can cite but a few examples. First, jōruri material only was presented on all foreign tours. Sanbasō ritual was not presented even within Japan, where the ritual tradition stood some chance of being recognizable to audiences. Second, in spite of the fact that Sanbasō puppet heads were the most common of kashira (because there were so many itinerant performers), more of these kashira than jōruri heads were actually lost or destroyed. Third, while younger puppeteers were trained in the recitation of jōruri pieces, it was not until the late 1980s that these puppeteers even took an interest in learning the Sanbasō pieces. As late as 1987, none of the younger puppeteers in the Awaji theater knew the story of Hyakudayū, the "founder" of ritual puppetry, although they were well versed in the histories of the various dramatic troupes on the island. I frequently was in the embarrassing situation of knowing more about the ritual history of Awaji ningyō than the young performers in the theater, who were often amazed to learn that itinerant performers did more than present "skits" for entertainment. The irony of this de-emphasis on the ritual tradition is that while the jōruri tradition is based on written texts and is relatively easy to transmit from one generation to the next, the kadozuke tradition is most vulnerable in the transmission process because so much of it is based on oral transmission. Many of the variations in kadozuke performance were simply never recorded and have been lost forever just in the past few years, when they could have been preserved. This fact led me to conclude that something beyond a task of retrieval was at work in this revival movement. If preservation and retrieval were the task, why not immediately focus on that which is most vulnerable to time?

These simple points suggest that in the early stages of revival, the kadozuke tradition with its ritual performances was deemed wanting as an appropriate icon for a lost past. And as a result, an important thread in the history of this tradition was eclipsed. This decision to ignore the kadozuke tradition was largely based on the perception that this itinerant performance was somehow an embarrassment to a modern Japan. It looked like begging and was inextricably linked to popular religion. Furthermore, it was the very itinerancy of the performance that had contributed to the outcast status of the performers.

As we have seen in past chapters, ritual puppeteers were regarded as both polluted and outcast in society before the twentieth century. Today the struggle continues against this hereditary stigma. Puppet theaters which presented jōruri also suffered from this social stigma because they were in the performing arts and were itinerant. In the postwar period, and particularly during the occupation, as theaters began to reopen around Japan, puppetry troupes were often the last to receive funds and permission to reopen their doors. Discrimination against these groups continued, and people were encouraged to discard the practices of ritual performances, because they were an embarrassment to Japan that was trying to put on a modern face and distance itself from any overt signs of "superstition" and "folk religiosity." In the postwar period, moreover, the context for popular "folk" performance forms, puppetry included, was dramatically eroded by three factors: the censorship of the occupation forces over the presentation of plays with feudal themes (a category into which many of the jōruri ballad pieces fell), the widespread appearance of movie theaters around Japan, and a rapid urbanization of the population. By the end of the 1950s television was added to this list of factors which had a severe effect on the survival of popular performance forms.

This ban on "the traditional" was not unilateral. Tea ceremony, for example, a highly elite art form practiced only by a select group of people with significant access to wealth, was held up to the world (and the occupying forces) in postwar Japan as proof of the cultivation of the Japanese people. A carefully calculated decision was made about just who and what could represent Japanese cultural arts, and outcast arts were deemed an embarrassment. Both fashion and funding underscored this attitude, and as a result, ritual puppetry quickly came to an end.

The reader will recall that at the end of our discussion of kadozuke performance in chapter 2 we noted that many of the postwar campaigns to wipe out itinerant performance actually came from the people within those performance traditions. Their reasons implicated them in the cycle of oppression and were probably in part the result of some kind of internalized oppression. Because the practice of puppetry had made it impossible for people to escape from hereditary pariah status during the Tokugawa period, any indications that this practice might continue into the postwar period needed to be wiped out, lest they compromise the hope for a viable liberation movement.

By showcasing the jōruri tradition on Awaji, it was possible for Awaji puppets to participate in a "geography of value" in Japan that suggested that the rural is the authentic, the "folk" is the real. This authenticism is best captured by the claim (possibly true) on Awaji that Bunraku in Osaka was started by an Awaji puppeteer named Uemura Bunrakuken. Awaji puppets, then, are to Bunraku puppets what ancestors are to those of us in the modern period—our true selves, less sophisticated, dead, but participating in a reality that we moderns can only approximate.

Regionalism for Awaji has meant a careful assessment of Awaji's history as a center of ritual puppetry. Outcast puppeteers presenting ritual purification rites and performances for a tempestuous and even dangerous deity who sometimes causes epidemics do not make good icons. Mother-daughter tragedies do (while father-daughter murder stories do not). But if this set of priorities were to be turned on its head, as it has been in the past five years, what would that mean and what would it say about the local Awaji appropriation of nostalgic discourse and regionalism for its own ends?

Reviving *Kadozuke:* From Ritual to Stage

Around 1990, there was a shift in the revival movement to highlight the ritual tradition of the Ebisu and Sanbasō performances as the distinctive features of the Awaji tradition. Perhaps this shift was due to the fact that the revived tradition of Awaji puppetry was now stable enough to begin enlarging its repertoire and retrieving larger aspects of its past. But I argue that the sudden interest in the kadozuke tradition was in part a response to a new thread in nativist and nostalgic discourse in Japan, and had a redressive function in the social drama of extinction, intervention, revival and renewal of Awaji puppetry. According to this subtle shift in nativist discourse, real capital for revival was now found in those traditions that could in some way lay claim to exoticism. The more esoteric and enigmatic a tradition was, the greater its value as a cultural commodity. Rituals, by virtue of their heavy use of multivalent (and frequently unintelligible) symbols, are almost by definition exotic and enigmatic.

Marilyn Ivy, in her study of nostalgic discourse in contemporary Japan, rightly points out that a part of this process of a "return" to traditional Japan lies in making Japan seem other to itself.[28] This insight raises the question of how the exotic and strange can be manipulated as both a symbol and a commodity in the process of revitalization. How can Awaji puppets be made to appear other while still remaining Japanese? Otherness, as we have seen, is something ritual puppeteers know a lot about. But in this new discourse of exoticism, otherness does not place ritual puppetry outside of Japanese mainstream society. Otherness is what makes it truly Japanese! The Sanbasō rite (to a larger degree than the Ebisu rite) was suddenly made the central concern of people in the theater. While the daily performances continued to present a slightly wider repertoire of jōruri pieces, scholars and members of the theater were suddenly obsessed with retrieving the Sanbasō performance.

My research on this subject was suddenly of great interest. The irony is that if retrieval alone had been the actual goal of this revival movement, the attempt came about ten to fifteen years too late, even though in the 1970s people had been well aware of how vulnerable this part of the tradition was to the vicissitudes of time. At that time, it simply had not seemed that important or valuable.

Basically, the kadozuke tradition became the focus of "reenactment" activities, and was also the centerpiece of a series of summit meetings for the revival of Japanese puppetry, organized by Umazume Masaru and designed to further the revival movements of puppet theaters all over Japan.

"A Past of Things Present:" Reenacting Ritual Puppetry in its Traditional Contexts

In July of 1990, two self-consciously "historic" performances took place on Awaji, about two days apart.[29] The puppeteers from the Awaji Ningyō Jōruri Kan did something that had not been done in over forty years: they performed the rite of Ebisu on the small island called Susaki in Fukura, and the Sanbasō rite in the precincts of the Omidō Hachiman shrine, the ceremonial center of the Awaji puppet tradition. Now, members of the new and revived theater on the island, the Awaji Ningyō Jōruri Kan, were attempting to recreate these rituals by returning to the sites where they had often been presented in the prewar period. These performances marked the beginning of a new dimension in the revitalization movement. Ritual performances, and not just jōruri pieces, were now being considered as objects of retrieval.

The central activity of these performances is "reenactment." Examples of reenacted rituals, frequently doctored up and greatly transformed to respond to the demands of new media (film or video, stage, television), new audiences (anthropologists, foreign tourists), and new aesthetic sensibilities are common in the history of anthropological discourse. Many of the documents we have for the study of other cultures are based on the careful staging and scripting by scholars concerned to make a certain point. The portraits of native Americans in ceremonial garb (and the women frequently half nude) by Edward Curtiss are among our earliest examples. Curtiss's case reveals how the camera lens constructs an image of the other that reinforces and legitimates the violence of domination, particularly when a dominant (and in the case of the conquest of America, genocidal) power holds the camera. This creation of noble savages is part and parcel of reenactment as a trope of the anthropological enterprise.

The transformation in reenactment responding to the new presence of the camera lens is not always inaugurated by foreigners. Gregory Bateson and Margaret Mead's 1938 film *Trance and Dance in Bali* underscores how people within a tradition can feel the need to transform a ritual for the sake of a new audience, even while rejecting what could be considered authentic within their own tradition for the purposes of the new context. The Ballet Folklorico in Mexico with its stage presentation of the deer dance is another example of rituals being made into stage performances, and eventually coming to have lives of their own as pieces of theater divorced from a ritual context.

Richard Schechner, in *Between Theater and Anthropology*, explores the process of retrieval, reconstruction, and staging of rituals, often wrenched from their traditional context and performed for tourists mainly for money. Some of the cases he cites are quite tragic, as is the case of the "mudmen" dancers from Papua New Guinea, who invented dances for tourist buses, but saw only 10 percent of the money they generated.[30] When Schechner views such cases from the standpoint of a theater director (which he is as well as a scholar), he is inclined to accept this transformation of rituals into theater as part of the modernization process, implying that a shift from ritual to theater is the natural progression of all performance events. The dual impact of intervention (by the camera lens, the anthropologist, or the postmodern situation itself) and invention (of tradition) is simply an event in the world of performance:

> I see nothing amiss in restorations of behavior [like Bharatanatyam and Purulia Chhau]. Arts and rituals . . . are always developing, and restoration is one means of change. What happened [in Bharatanatyam and Chhau] is analogous to what the French dramatists of the seventeenth century did when they conformed to what they thought were ancient rules of Greek tragedy. The dramatists had at hand Aristotle, Horace, the Greek and Latin playtexts, architectural ruins, pottery, but they did not have the actual behaviors of the ancient Athenians. The restorers [of Bharatanatyam and Chhau] had living arts they had presumed were vestiges of older, more classical arts. They also had ancient texts, sculptings, and their own deep knowledge of Hindu traditions."[31]

The decision to enact ritual puppetry as stage performance could be seen as an example of what Schechner calls "restored behavior." Transforming a ritual onto the confines of a stage by definition implies an audience, a new feature of performance from the perspective of itinerant ritual. Though Schechner claims that there may be "nothing amiss" in this phenomenon, this does not lessen our need to analyze the retrieval and staging process and determine how important issues in a critical history of ritual puppetry are addressed, ignored, or even enhanced.

In the case of Awaji puppets, we can explore the semantics of reenactment by examining what happens to the following aspects of the ritual: (1) the marking of the performer as an outsider, an issue of central meaning in these rites; (2) the creation of ritual space and the relationship of that performance space to the unknown space of the road, to which the puppeteer must by definition return after his performance; (3) the relationship of the audience to the performers and vice versa; and (4) the important commitment of the audience to the "outcome" of the performance. How does the idea of the "agent" of a performance shift? What is the new nexus of the performance?

For a number of reasons, reenacted rituals are obviously transformed rituals. A reenacted ritual presents us with a major semantic shift. The contents of the semiotic process may appear to be unchanged: the same masks, puppets, and cranes, the same chants, possibly even the same performers. Elsewhere, I have noted that all rituals have what I call a nexus, a central feature around which all other disparate elements in the rite must orient themselves. In the traditional context, this nexus was invariably the puppet body and the process by which it "comes alive."[32] What has become the nexus in the performance reenactment is not the content of the original ritual, but *time* itself. Reenactment has made *temporality*, and the existentially disturbing experience of a rupture of its continuous nature, the nexus of the rite. Reenactments are our new rituals to symbolically confront this rupture, to try to undo time. Reenactments are ritual celebrations of nostalgia. To explore these issues, let us examine two cases of reenacted ritual performances and see how they came about.

Reenactment 1: Ebisu-mai *on Susaki Island*

Susaki Island in Fukura Bay, which measures only a few hundred meters in length, forms a natural barrier between the quiet waters of Fukura harbor and the Pacific Ocean, and is now owned by the Fukura fishing collective. The place-name Susaki is often used along the coasts of Japan, as the term refers to small islands or stretches of land created by alluvial action or slow movements of tides in and out of bays. On Susaki in Fukura Bay, there is a small shrine dedicated to Ebisu, and it was before this worship site that the puppeteers presented their performance in 1990.[33] Before the early postwar period, itinerant Ebisu-kaki would be requested to present their rituals on this island, for it literally marked the gate between the fishing harbor (a safe space) and the unknown ocean (a dangerous, uncharted space where anything could happen to a fisherman in a small boat). Fishermen would often stop at this shrine on their way out to sea if they had some important request or wished to ensure their safety. This

The small worship hall on Susaki serves as the backdrop for a reenactment of a ritual Ebisu performance in July 1990.

small shrine was thus an important location for worship, mediating safety and danger, the known and the unknown. Ebisu was the deity who resided at this important passage. The shrine, which still exists, has a *haiden* (worship space) with a small stagelike structure, a *honden* (inner sanctum) with a stone effigy of Ebisu, and a concrete torii demarcating the space. Other than that, the island is mostly empty, except for a few warehouses where fishing equipment is kept. The island is artificially stayed by webs of enormous entangled concrete shoreline reinforcements.

The decision to perform Ebisu on this site (and Sanbasō at the Sanjo site a few days later) appears to have been in part the result of the "observer effect" of my own fieldwork. On this particular research trip, I had brought along a student from the United States and video equipment to document some of the performances. My permission to film these performances coincided with repeated requests from scholars on Awaji interested in the history of Awaji ningyō to record the performances in their traditional settings. There was a real sense that having video footage of these "reenactments" was of great value, and there was quite a bit of competition and behind-the-scenes jockeying for position to get tripod locations at these performances. While these performances were not staged solely for my benefit, it was clear that my presence (and that of my assistant) was a catalyst, and that the possibility of foreign students viewing Awaji ritual puppetry held a great deal of appeal to the people involved. These performances were also intended as something of a gift to me. Although I had worked for several years studying the past of Awaji puppetry, I had not yet had the pleasure of experiencing the performances in their historical contexts.

Prior to the performance on Susaki in 1990—the first on the island in nearly forty years—permission had to be obtained from the proper authorities and from the fishing collective to land on the island and stage the event. Local people were invited along as an audience.

On the afternoon of the performance, members of the theater made their way to the docks right after the theater closed. The day was cool and clear, and a slight wind was picking up. Theater members began to unload their equipment from mini-vans and onto boats: all the makings of a complete stage, a box of puppets, and musical instruments. My assistant and I went over by boat, carrying our video equipment. The fishermen took their own boats, and several trips were necessary to get everyone from the theater across. By the time we arrived, a number of local ethnographers had already set up their video and recording equipment. They did not turn their cameras on until the actual performance began, whereas my research assistant and I were interested in recording the entire framing of the event as a reenactment.

Once on the island, while the theater members were setting up their performance space, each person, film crew, theater member, and local person from the audience presented himself or herself before the Ebisu shrine *honden*. Inside this honden, which was opened up for the performance, there is a small stone-shaped shintai, the spirit vessel for the deity Ebisu, in the typical shape of a fat old smiling man holding a sea bream under his arm. Taking a bottle of sake and pouring it over the head of Ebisu, each person then closed hands in prayer. At this point in the proceedings, it became clear that while people were viewing the ritual as a "reenactment," they also realized that proper behavior was necessary for those who worshipped at the Ebisu site. This part of the day seemed unscripted and not a reenactment. People were not acting, not pretending to be a traditional audience. They were just being themselves.

With the prayers completed, the performance began. Fishermen sat around under the stone torii, many with their grandchildren sitting in their laps or by their sides, and two other camera crews set up under the torii recorded the event.

The content of the performance was the same as that translated in the previous chapter: a humorous play, in which Ebisu appears at the door of a wealthy homeowner, announces his arrival, and asks for sake. As he be-

The audience at this Ebisu performance on Susaki sat under the *torii* demarcating the shrine.

comes intoxicated and dances, he tells of his miraculous birth, how he is to be worshipped, and what blessings he bestows on those who pay attention to him. At the end, he catches a live fish, a sea bream. At the close of the performance, this fish was presented to the head of the fishing collective, who was in the audience. It was a gift for having allowed the performance to take place.

    After the performance, I was able to interview members of the audience and the theater. To the last person, the overriding emotion was one of a strange sadness, which can only remind us of the original sense of nostalgia as "a pain to return home." Everyone remarked that seeing the ritual was "natsukashii," and many of the men recalled coming with their parents and grandparents as children over to the island once a year to watch the performance. Many wondered why this performance was not pre-

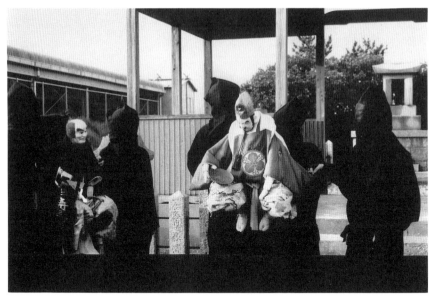

A scene from the Ebisu performance.

sented at this site more often. A few of them directed their questions to Umazume-san, who jokingly responded that "you couldn't afford us!" He then reiterated his claim that the puppeteers at the Awaji Ningyō Jōruri Kan are professionals (for which he used the gairaigo term *purofu-eshona-ru*). Although said in jest, the comment had an air of truth about it because for the theater to survive, it had to continue to present jōruri pieces to tourists. Awaji puppetry could no longer afford to be an example of a local cultural performance.

When we consider this performance in light of the four aspects of ritual reenactment listed above, the semantic shift in this new performance is dramatically apparent. First, the marking of performers as outsiders appears to be almost entirely subsumed under the activity of theatrical costume. Both performers and audience arrived at Susaki together, and both live in the same area in Fukura. In their everyday lives, they all shop at the same Daiei supermarket, send their children to the same schools, and even have their family graves in the same temples. The difference between them here, then, was the temporary difference of the conventional, modern idea of theater, in which actors and audience are delineated through the creation of a stage. The performers and audience were both outsiders to the island of Susaki, and it was only when the performers donned their costumes that there was any distinction. The marking of the performer as an outsider was no longer an issue in this reenactment in the way it had been. Now accomplished through costume, the marking served to delineate actors from audience, rather than the sacred realm of the specialist (and the otherness of the road) from the public, domestic world of the householder.

The issue of the creation of ritual space was more complex. At three levels, this performance was in a space removed from everyday life: it was on an island where people never spent any time, it was within the precincts of a shrine, and it was within a temporarily constructed stage. Regardless of the modernity and even artificiality of this performance, this layering of differentiated space was an important feature. Although different from the ritual space of itinerant performances in the past, it was ritual space nonetheless.

The highly mixed audience for this event consisted of ethnographers, fishermen, their grandchildren, and the staff from the theater. My assistant and I, along with the other ethnographers, may have had the greatest investment in the performance. Much as past patrons depended on the efficacy of these performances for their prosperity, we needed a complete and accurate record of the performance for the substance of our academic careers.

The other audience members' stake in the performance was one of distant attachment. The older fishermen and senior members of the theater were participating in a remembrance, but neither had any special stake in the outcome of the performance. For the audience, it was a reenactment of the past evoking times before the war. For the theater, it was an experiment in reenactment and, as well, a potential addition to its repertoire and a source of prestige. And at a very basic level, we were all playing with nostalgia and having a good time.

Reenactment 2: Sanbasō *Performance at the Omidō Hachiman Daibosatsu in Sanjo*

A few days later the performers from the Awaji Ningyō Jōruri Kan staged a similar event. This time, the Sanbasō rite was presented at Omidō Hachiman Daibosatsu, the worship hall of the ceremonial center of Awaji puppetry in Sanjo. The location of frequent puppet festivals for hundreds of years, this shrine has a large open and flat space where audiences used to sit. Flanked by huge Cryptomeria tress, the area is shaded and cool, even on a hot, July morning. Inside the precincts, the regular worship hall consists of a stagelike haiden and behind it a smaller inner sanctum (*honden*) dedicated to Hachiman. To the left of this worship hall is a smaller subsidiary worship site (*hokora*), where the legendary figures of the founding of Awaji puppetry are enshrined in shrine statuary: Dōkumbō, Hyakudayū, Ebisu, and a woman said to be Hyakudayū's wife but most probably the vestige of a shamanic figure.[34]

Traditionally, itinerant Dōkumbō mawashi setting out from Sanjo during the New Year period would stop at this shrine and present a performance before this worship hall. On the first day of the year, all the local puppetry troupes living in Sanjo would take turns performing Sanbasō before this shrine. Even today, this rough and humble site is the ceremonial center of Awaji puppetry.

On the morning of the performance in July of 1990, two performers from the Awaji theater arrived at the shrine dressed in blue jeans and shirts and shoes. They had driven directly from home in the theater's van, which one of them had driven home the night before. They brought their costumes with them in a case, and all the puppets, paraphernalia, and equipment in boxes. The shrine, located on a country road near Sanjo, was quiet and deserted as usual. The worship hall of the Hachiman shrine next to the small hokora for puppetry served as a dressing room where they changed into the ritual performer's costume. After dressing, they spread a small straw mat on the ground before the worship hall and arranged the box of puppets and instruments in front of them. Other ritual items were brought in and placed before their performing space.

As they were setting up, the camera crews (including my research assistant) proceeded to set up their tripods on the actual worship hall itself, so that they could film the performance from the perspective of the "original" intended audience: the sacred patrons of puppetry inside the hokora.[35] When both puppeteers and camera people were ready, the puppeteers sat down on their performance space and reenacted the type of performance that would have taken place in front of the small worship hall in years gone by. But this time, the eye of the kami was replaced by the lens of a camera, which would relay this performance to students of anthropology, theater, and religion around Japan and the United States.

The Sanbasō performance was the one outlined in the previous chapter, which approximates those of itinerant performers before the postwar period. At the end of the performance, the puppeteers repeated the performance again, so that it could be viewed from a different angle. The repetition also allowed the editing out of an error in the first performance, when the mask of one of the puppets slipped off its face. While dealing with such unexpected things is always part of the challenge of a ritual event, in this case, it could simply be edited out of existence. Repeat the ritual until it happens correctly.

In the process of this reenactment, other interesting and unexpected things happened.[36] First, when the puppeteers were preparing by warming up on the flute and small hand drum used in the Sanbasō performance, some children riding by on bicycles stopped and looked into the shrine from the torii. Umazume-san called out to them, "Come watch the puppets," and with great reluctance, they slowly approached the performance space. As soon as they arrived, Naniwa-san and her daughter dragged

A Sanbasō performance at Ōmidō Hachiman before the war.

A Sanbasō performance at Ōmidō Hachiman in 1990.

benches over from along the edge of the gateball court so the children could sit down. The children, slightly nervous, sat there and chatted with Umazume-san and among themselves. We treated them to sodas that we had brought along. A few minutes later (the event was a bit behind schedule) the elderly gateball brigade arrived for their midmorning game and discovered, much to their delight (for many of them remembered puppetry performances from their youth) that a Sanbasō performance was about to begin. Usually, their gateball game begins as each of them pray before the shrine, but this morning, they went straight for the area where we were performing. The old folks joined the children on the benches, and the "ritual" began.

After the performance, the performers from the theater, Umazume-san in particular, stayed in the shrine precincts for about forty-five minutes playing gateball with the elderly neighbors. Umazume-san was quite familiar with them, since he lives nearby and grew up in this small village. In the past rituals were frequently followed by performers and members of the audience playing together or having a meal. We stayed at the shrine until it got too warm when we loaded everything into the van and headed back to the theater.

Unlike the Susaki case, which required an intentional trip to see the performance, this reenactment was very easily reabsorbed into daily events. Everyone living near Sanjo knows that this site is the center of ritual puppetry, and it seemed natural to see the puppet group performing there. A revival, it became clear, must be examined both as it is understood by people outside the tradition (who are reclaiming it as something their own, but who in fact have no relationship to it) and as it is seen by people with a living relationship to it—in this case the seniors who play gateball or the children who play hide-and-seek and ride their bikes on the grounds of this ceremonial center

Let us return to our four categories for analyzing the semantic shift of reenactment: the marking of performer as outsider, creation of ritual space, relationship between audience and performers, and the commitment of the audience to the performance. Here, the marking of the performer as outsider is enacted through costuming rather than a highly marked arrival and departure from the world out there, that is, the road. The ritual space in this case would come to include the haiden of the Hachiman worship hall, for it is here that this transformation of an actor into a ritual specialist takes place.

The status of the audience in this performance is complex. Again, we have several groups: staff from the theater, ethnographers, the cameras (which alone faced the performance directly while spectators viewed it from the side), and an accidental audience of young children and elderly gateball enthusiasts. Origuchi Shinobu's category of the uninvited guest (that is, human beings at a ritual event) seems to have been reinvented, although in this case the primary audience consisted of cameras, and not a kami.

These events in the summer of 1990 were early stages in the process of reviving the kadozuke aspects of the Awaji tradition. Although these performances were presented from time to time on other occasions, the 1990 reenactments marked a new moment in the revival process. After this point, not only did kadozuke performances become objects of retrieval, they became a central concern of scholars attached to the Awaji tradition and to the members of the theater, for they represented the legitimacy of Awaji puppetry's history. Itinerant performance was how Awaji ningyō spread, and it is what gives Awaji the right to proclaim itself the "cradle of ningyō shibai." The embracing of the kadozuke tradition was a strategic step in ensuring that Awaji puppetry remained the premier example of rural puppetry in the face of many impostors entering the scene and riding the waves of the *dentō geinō būmu* (traditional folk performing arts boom).

While Awaji puppets have certainly been the most celebrated case of a rural puppetry tradition being made viable and even lucrative as a theater, there have been other efforts around Japan to follow in the footsteps of the Awaji tradition, even when this meant fabricating a history of puppetry. In this climate of "reclaiming the vanishing," ritual puppetry and puppet troupes presenting ballad dramas have been revived and even "discovered" throughout Japan. In a few cases, which will here remain nameless, villages with no history whatsoever of puppetry, or those where one puppeteer may have lived briefly, have decided that puppetry is good business—jōruri performances in the countryside make pleasant tourist outings, and hence are good for the tourist trade. These *ningyō no furusato* (hometowns of puppetry) have sprung up around Japan as a result of this veritable boom.

We turn now to the next stage in this revival process, which put kadozuke front and center: the summit meetings of 1991, 1992, and 1993.

The Politics of the Center: Awaji and the Zenkoku Ningyō Shibai Samitto

In the summer of 1991, I was privileged to witness the next stage in this revival process, the development of the Zenkoku Ningyō Shibai Samitto (All Japan Puppetry Summit), a forum for enhancing the revival of puppetry all over Japan, designed and organized by Umazume Masaru.

By this time, Awaji puppetry could safely be considered stable in its process of revival. Umazume, who genuinely loves Awaji ningyō and wants it to remain viable as a theater form, developed an arena wherein the experiences, struggles, and successes of the Awaji troupe could be used to strengthen the revival movements of puppetry around Japan. The Awaji tradition had already confronted the issues of funding, recruiting new members to the theater, preserving the related arts such as puppet-head carving and costume creation, and advertising and going mainstream with the tourist industry. It is clear that while the All Japan Regional Performing Arts Convention, the activities of preservation societies, and the new Minzoku Geinō Taikai (Folk Performing Arts Convention) have been a popular success in the media, they have not dealt effectively with the context and complexity of the revival of rituals and the performing arts. A different kind of forum, one less geared toward the public with little knowledge of theater, was in order. The summit is a new model of meeting for the retrieval and preservation of folk performances. Prior to the early 1990s most public settings for scattered folk performances were annual meetings at which diverse performances would be presented. The summit focuses on one genre of performance (puppetry, in this case, or regional Kabuki, Kagura, Dengaku) and brings together specialists and people directly involved in the nuts and bolts of reviving theater. This model recognizes the need for a more critical look at the current state of "traditional" theater in Japan.

Umazume's idea was straightforward: bring all fledgling puppetry preservation societies (*ningyō hozonkai*) to Awaji for several days to meet, discuss the problems they are facing with the logistics of revival, and see how they can help one another. Following a trend in other folk performance groups of using the "summit" model, he decided to convene such a summit for puppetry.[37] The summits, to continue for several years, would begin that fall and would take place on Awaji. Inherent in this move was a modern version of an older reality: Awaji would still be the center of puppetry. Because of Awaji's unique status in the history of Japanese puppetry, coupled with its recent success in the process of revival, it was the natural setting for such a summit.

Preparations for these summits consisted largely of inviting the heads of puppet groups around Japan to attend. To this end, Umazume decided that it would be a good idea to travel to those groups in western Japan and meet with them individually. That summer, I traveled with Umazume and a scholar of the Awaji tradition, Nakanishi Hideo (a high school teacher and the director of the high school puppetry club), throughout Shikoku and Kyushu for several days while we visited various puppetry groups and invited them to the summit that fall.[38]

During this trip, we visited a number of small puppetry groups, some no longer active, some being revived through school clubs and student groups, and others attempting to emulate the Awaji model by building modern theaters. At each theater, Umazume-san was involved in inviting the troupes to attend the Awaji summit. Although I learned a great deal about ritual puppetry and the histories of a number of small troupes around Japan, it rapidly became clear to me that the interesting anthropological event was not history or even the puppetry groups but the process of tradition building in the postmodern era. The Awaji scholars and directors were constructing a revival, and the language and action of this process were heavily coded with created meanings and the staging of identities, power, hierarchy, money, and politics of a very real kind. In short, the performance here was not the one that had taken place in the past; it was the interaction between the directors of the various theater groups; the "actors" were no longer puppets but those who manipulated their manipulators—troupe managers and the financiers of the many hozonkai throughout Japan.

There can be no doubt that Umazume Masaru is genuinely interested in seeing puppetry performance, particularly jōruri, become a living performing art in Japan again, and not solely in the expensive national theaters in Osaka and Tokyo. For several hundred years in the history of Japanese performing arts, as the classical traditions of Bunraku and Kabuki were solidifying their aesthetics, highly inventive and talented performance artists were maintaining theaters throughout Japan. These theaters thrived without the patronage of the urban centers, and they developed important performance styles that urban theaters often copied. Umazume was concerned to preserve these traditions not merely because they were populist, nor was he motivated solely by economic impulses. He felt that the themes and aesthetics of Awaji ningyō shibai are deeply significant, and he genuinely wanted this theater form to be handed down to future generations. He often talked about how the range of emotions and senses brought about by working in the theater touched him at a deep and existential level, and provided a narrative for his own life. Something about the puppets, the plays, and the tradition was, to borrow Tennessee Williams' expression, emotionally autobiographical for him.

I was interested to watch on this trip how the directors of the theaters in Johnny-come-lately hometowns of puppetry tried to curry favor with the Awaji tradition, and how at the same time Umazume controlled access to these summits in such a way as to assure the role of Awaji as the center of this new movement in nostalgia and the invention of tradition. He decided which theaters would be considered actual historical theaters and which would be allowed to participate as "modern inventions." Unlike other festivals, such as the popular Folk Performing Arts Convention and the older All Japan Regional Performing Arts Convention, where authenticity and an air of the ancient were important, in this new forum it was meaningful and even desirable to have new puppetry clubs participate.[39]

From Umazume's perspective, reviving puppetry as a theatrical medium around Japan can only be good for the Awaji tradition. But the very success of these summits created problems in the local setting. After the third summit, covered widely in the national media, tensions arose among people on Awaji concerning what was perceived to be a dilution of Awaji's uniqueness as other puppet theaters around Japan became viable again. As the summit drew to a close and the Awaji Ningyō Jōruri Kan staff collapsed in exhaustion, one of the major financial backers of Awaji puppetry came to the theater to complain that this new format threatened the momentum that had been built on Awaji. Umazume was severely chastised for taking a national (zenkoku) perspective in his attempts to revitalize puppetry. Though the summit has been a great success, Umazume admitted that he had created a difficult political problem for himself at the local level. He was unable to conceal his frustration and disappointment that his intentions were not being fully recognized by local people.

From Ritual to Stage: The Problems of Context in the Preservation Movement

The Zenkoku Ningyō Shibai All Japan Puppetry Summits represented a new era in the revival movement of Awaji ningyō. Since then, there has been a self-conscious attempt to retrieve the ritual tradition and transpose it onto the stage. As demonstrated in previous chapters, ritual puppetry is dependent on a highly constructed context to be experienced as effective. The ritual depends on a shared commitment to the performance on the part of performer and ritual sponsor in whose house (or on whose boat or dock) the rite is being presented. What happens when the ritual context and the relationship between the performer and the sponsor shift dramatically? What happens when ritual hits the stage?

In this chapter I am suggesting that part of the dynamic involved in reviving the ritual dimension of puppetry has been a response to a constructed discourse of nostalgia, in which the quest for the truly Japanese becomes the quest to reclaim the vanishing and the exotic. The outward expression of this shifting discourse, I maintain, has been the initial neglect of the kadozuke rituals of the Awaji tradition followed by the sudden and intense interest in retrieving these rituals and casting them as stage performances.

There are scholars in Japan and the United States who claim that this tendency to retrieve rituals by making them stage entertainment makes it impossible for the theater in Japan to develop, since these icons of the past inhibit the dynamism of the theater as a reflection of and response to the present.[40] Sasahara, one of the more outspoken critics of this

"stage movement," observes that the time and space of the stage are artificial, so that at folk performings arts conventions, a summer *bon-odori,*
a cherry blossom viewing dance, and a fall dew Kagura are stacked one
on top of another, all deracinated on the stage. He decries the implicit
ideology of "origins," "the ancient," and the constructed aesthetics of
"loveliness" and "beauty," and he denounces these new "staged rituals"
as sham rituals.[41]

The problem with the critique of Sasahara and others is that they have
restricted their definition of the cultural performance to merely what is
presented on stage. They are primarily concerned with identifying what
these performances may mean for outside audiences. From my research, it
is clear that the actual staging of the rituals is but one moment in a larger
series of cultural performances which intersect on the stage. People on
Awaji have one cultural performance in mind when they see these revived
rituals. People from Tokyo have another. And scholars from abroad have
yet another. While Sasahara and others correctly identify the manipulation
of nostalgia in this process, they have focused only on the nostalgia of the
outside consumers of these rituals. For people on Awaji, attempts to stage
these rituals are not simply statements about the past. They are open-
ended questions about it, ways of exploring what these rituals meant and
what they might still mean. People are actively posing the question, Do
these rituals still mean anything at all? And they are decidely open to the
answer that perhaps the rituals will be only remnants from the past, remembered onstage.

In the latter stages of my fieldwork, I noticed a marked attitude of
experimentation and play at work in the theater. People were genuinely
engaged in exploring the question of what these rituals might mean again
in the modern context. Once, while we were sitting in a back room discussing the meanings of reviving Sanbasō, I noticed that the Sanbasō puppets were simply hanging on stands, a practice which would have been
considered disrespectful fifty years ago. I noted this, and Umazume responded with a laugh, "I think Sanbasō is getting used to all these
changes, and can tolerate just about anything these days."

Perhaps for people from elsewhere, retrieving kadozuke rituals was part
of a discourse of nostalgia and exoticism. For people on Awaji, it was
about exploring a eclipsed part of their historical experience. Suddenly it
was okay to talk about itinerant performance and to explore its semiotics,
its textures, and its constraints and freedoms.

The decision to transform *kadozuke* performances into stage pieces
proper is an ideal case study for studying what happens when ritual becomes theater. The decisions here have been made consciously, with the
intention of retrieving and showcasing the past, while fully aware that the
context has been lost.

I have already indicated that the first step in this process was the unsuccessful return of puppet rituals to original contexts—on Susaki and in the historical center of ritual puppetry in Sanjo. These performances failed to bring back these rituals, for they merely served to confirm what people already knew: at best the audiences for these reenactments would be fabrications, people brought onto the scene artificially to play the role of audience. At a deeper level, these reenactments were haunted by the sense that perhaps the rituals in these contexts were meaningful only for ghosts of times now past.

Next, the pieces were cast as stage performances. How this dramatic shift in context affected the ritual process is best seen the staging of the Sanbasō rite. The four versions of the Sanbasō ritual most commonly performed as stage entertainment reveal the recognition and acceptance of the constraints and liberties of this new medium, particularly for the anonymous, disinterested, and frequently ignorant audience. Ironically, the new context constrains the audience. While it would be perfectly acceptable to drink sake or beer, or to belch, smoke cigarettes, and stretch out, or even to talk, get up, and walk around during a Sanbasō ritual in a shrine, anything short of complete quiet and feigned rapt attention while in the audience at a staged performance is unacceptable. Consequently, such performances are exhausting, as they were usually not designed to be watched with such an attention to detail. A Japanese man I know who was a student in the United States in the early days of television said that watching a Sanbasō ritual on the stage was like staring at the picture of the Indian that decorated the TV screen when the station had gone off the air.

I will review each of these four Sanbasō versions with attention to (1) the nature of the puppeteer's role as performer, (2) the significance of the box of ritual implements carried by itinerant performers in the ritual context, (3) the meaning of the performance space, and (4) the relationship of the audience to the performance. These four components reveal the creative response to the loss of the ritual context as a new semiotics comes into play. Each component of the Sanbasō rite assumes a new level of signification as it is introduced into the performance space of an indoor theater stage. The Russian folklorist Petr Bogatyrev has argued that "the stage radically transforms all objects and bodies defined within it, bestowing upon them an overriding signifying power which they lack."[42] This "manifesto" (as Elam calls it) of the Prague school maintains that "All that is on the stage is a sign."[43]

As shown in previous chapters, the role of the puppeteer as outsider to the community was a key element in the efficacy of the ritual. The puppeteer and his puppets embodied many opposites: puppet vs. human, puppet vs. sacred, human vs. sacred, and itinerant puppeteer (*hinin*) vs. agrarian settled person (*ryōmin*). Much of the performance was about the manipulation and resolution of these relationships of alterity. The puppeteer was marked as an outsider by being dressed in special ritual attire and carrying a box slung over his shoulder. Special footgear, usually straw sandals, indicated the puppeteer's low social status, as did the fact that his head was always uncovered. Prior to the performance, a call on the flute served to announce the arrival of an outsider. But when the ritual piece is transposed to the stage, how will these signs be carried over? Because the puppeteer is now someone employed at the theater, the real outsiders are members of the audience. It is they who arrive at a theater and then leave, unlike the previous context where a puppeteer arrived at a home and then left. Is a theater puppeteer who presents itinerant ritual as stage entertainment a new kind of actor? Arrival and departure are still essential to the event, but the roles are shifted.

Version 1: Low-Level Contextual Shifting Sanbasō as Stage Performance

The earliest attempts to present Sanbasō as a stage performance began in about 1987. I first saw this version of Sanbasō on stage at the Fukura theater on New Year's Day in 1988. What struck me about the performance was that attempts to adapt the performance of a ritual to the constraints of the stage were minimal.

The performance took place on a small raised platform outside the regular theater at the Naruto Kaikan. It was about eleven o'clock in the morning, and as the event had been announced in the local paper, a few people from the town had come up to the theater with children and grandchildren. A crowd of about thirty or forty people gathered. The performance itself was brief, with little attention to arrival and departure. The performers simply came out from the back of the theater carrying their puppets onto the platform (which had been prepared in advance with a mat), set them in place, and then began the performance with the musical instruments. When the performance was over, they picked everything up, went back inside and left the stage for an impromptu appearance by another outsider: the mayor of Seidanchō announced that a foreign scholar was visiting and asked me to ascend the platform and comment on the performance. Tempted as I was to comment on "mysterious visitors at New Year," I refrained from irony and discussed the ritual significance of this performance of Sanbasō at New Year again after a hiatus of several decades.

This performance of Sanbasō, unself-consciously and presented on the spur of the moment in a rather matter-of-fact way, was the first step in the revival of the Sanbasō rite as part of the New Year's events at the theater.

After the performance, I spoke with people in the theater and asked them how they felt about it. No one seemed very moved one way or another, but there was a concern that the performance had been flat. Something had not clicked. This performance, I surmise, initiated a consciousness that Sanbasō ritual was worth the efforts of preservation but that the process would be tricky. The subsequent performances on stage (combined with the attempts discussed above to return the ritual to its original context) were levels of discovery in this process. People at the theater and elsewhere were actively asking the question, Can we bring this back, and if so, how?

Version 2: Kadozuke on Stage

Until very recently, when Shiki Sanbasō was presented on stage, it was always an exact replica of the kadozuke performance, following early postwar filmings of the rites in that context. The two puppeteers walked onto the stage and all their instruments and puppets were set out for them. There was little concern or reflection about effecting a shift from ritual to theater. In the performance, the theater used a curtain with a pine tree painted on it, the same backdrop used in Noh for the dance of Okina. The most significant aspect of the performance was that the offerings made to the deities in the beginning of the rite were omitted completely, suggesting that for a ritual to become theater, it must be divested of its overtly religious content.

This was the standard version of Shiki Sanbasō on stage that I saw repeatedly during my fieldwork. For people familiar with the piece, the dance, music, and chanting make it an evocative presentation. But the consensus at the theater was that somehow this piece lacked the depth that would have given it a transformative power.

Version 3: New Actors in the Shiki-Sanbasō Performance

At the third puppet summit, the Awaji Ningyō Jōruri Kan premiered its latest version of the Shiki Sanbasō rite. It represents a new stage in the shift from ritual to theater. In it, the puppeteers are actors, who play the role of itinerant puppeteers. While the greater part of the performance is copied from the performances of postwar kadozuke performers and is identical to the previous performance, this subtle shift in the performance changes its meaning entirely. Here is how it is accomplished:

At the beginning of the performance, the curtain rises to reveal a stage decorated with the masks used in the performance. They are placed on an offering stand in full view of the audience. After a few moments, from stage left, two men dressed in black *haori hakama* enter. One puppeteer carries on his back a box wrapped in a black *furoshiki* (cloth) and the other person carries a bag. They stop, face the masks (and the audience), and then set up their performance space, carefully spreading a cloth on the ground and unpacking all their ritual instruments and puppets. This part of the performance takes about three or four minutes. The performance then proceeds exactly as the other Sanbasō rites described above, except that when it is over, the puppeteers stop and pack up their puppets and instruments in full view of the audience, and then get up and walk offstage. Only then does the curtain come down.

It was interesting to watch the audience reaction to this statement that the puppeteers are now actors playing the part of itinerant performers. When the last puppet was put down, some people in the audience felt free to get up, move around, and talk to one another. Others in the audience politely asked them to sit down, as the actors were still on stage and the performance was not over. No curtain had come down yet. One man, who by the end of the summit had earned himself the nickname of "Gekijō no Fudō" (ferocious guardian of the theater), was quite upset and began calling out to people to sit down until the curtain fell.

Since several Sanbasō performances from around Japan were being presented at this summit, I asked a number of people what they thought of this idea that the transition from ritual to stage meant that the puppeteers were now actors playing the role of itinerant puppeteers and the puppets props for the performance, rather than media for ritual. Most people initially found this to be a very disturbing idea, but after some thought noted that indeed this notion of acting was apparent.

Version 4: Noh Aesthetics on a Puppet Stage

The fourth version of Sanbasō I have seen on stage was also premiered at the 1993 puppetry summit. The piece combined two features not seen in any of the other versions. First, rather than having the puppeteers recite the chant, it was chanted by a chorus seated to the right of the stage in the chanter's box. Members of the chorus held small drums, and their postures and style were clearly an imitation of the Noh theater. Second, it devoted much more attention to dance and movement on the stage, showing much more of a family relationship with the extant Awaji lineage Sanbasō performances found in other parts of Japan. It is clear that this piece reflects a synthesis of two different strategies for bridging the worlds of ritual and theater. On the one hand, it retrieves a part of the performance from another location and reintroduces it on Awaji, a move that

argues for a simple return to the past. On the other hand, the piece completely avoids the dilemma by appropriating Noh aesthetics, a move suggesting that the project of bringing ritual onto the stage *as ritual* had been
abandoned.

These four versions of Sanbasō performance reflect the dynamics involved in crossing over from ritual to theater. People at the theater expressed some frustration with the process, but everyone concurred that
the symbolism in Shiki Sanbasō was coherent and powerful enough to
communicate something to people regardless of its framing, and for this
reason, they are continuing to play with the piece to see how to best present it in the new context.

Other Voices of Revival: Amateur Puppetry on Awaji

Thus far, our attention to the revival of Awaji puppetry has focused on the
activities of the only professional theater on the island, the Awaji Ningyō
Jōruri Kan, under the direction of Umazume Masaru. We have seen how
this theater has had to work with the demands of a nativist discourse requiring that it be part of a packaging of Awaji as the rural and exotic.

The professional theater on the cape overlooking the Great Naruto
Bridge is not the only future for Awaji puppetry. Awaji was considered
"the island of the puppets" for several centuries not simply because there
were numerous professional theaters and ritual performers on the island,
but because people living on Awaji took an avid interest in jōruri recitation, puppet manipulation, and even puppet kashira creation. A story I
was often told while I was on Awaji (though no one remembered exactly
when or where the events occurred) reflects the pride people had in their
identity as "the island of the puppets." A chanter from the Osaka Bunra-
kuza (the major puppet theater in Osaka at one time) came to Awaji as a
"guest" reciter. Apparently he underestimated his rural audience and was
tired and bored as he chanted the jōruri. People in the audience were
outraged that his performance was so poor, and they began to yell and
demand that he stop. Finally he got down off the stage, and a farmer from
the audience jumped up and finished the performance.

Did this really happen? Who knows? But I was told this story many
times to underscore the conviction of people on Awaji that at one time,
nonprofessional reciters from the island were better than a chanter from
Osaka on an off day.

This amateur tradition on Awaji, which suffered the same fate as professional theater in the postwar period, has also been revived in recent
years. In Mihara in particular, another revival movement is in process,

one that self-consciously presents itself as "the real thing, done by real people and not professionals." A number of times during my fieldwork, I was contacted by people from this rival preservation society and encouraged to give up my studies of the "artificial stage puppets of the theater" and come "back to the hometown of puppetry," where real people were working to keep this tradition alive. This split between the amateur and the professional has been a dynamic as old as Awaji ningyō, it seems, and it should come as no surprise that it appears again in this stage of the revival movement.

Although they do not have the formal theater or the professional staff, this group of people in Mihara is nonetheless reviving puppetry. They get together to chant jōruri, an activity which has always been a part of life on Awaji,[44] learn to carve and create kashira, prepare puppet costumes, and practice puppet manipulation. This group does not perceive itself as professional but rather as a local group interested in their local art form. They meet in the civic hall and at senior centers and attend lectures on the history of Awaji puppetry given by local scholars. Many of them are studying the arts of their parents and grandparents. Most are over sixty-five and many recall puppetry from before and immediately after the war.

This group also has made a concerted effort to revive the related art of carving and painting kashira. Making a kashira that can easily be manipulated is quite difficult to master. Ōe Minosuke, advanced in years, has a studio in his house across the bridge on Shikoku in the town of Naruto, where he carves kashira for the Bunraku stage. On Awaji, the grandson of the famous puppet-head carver Urakame has taken his grandfather's arts name and learned the art of making kashira. He hopes to revive this essential aspect of puppetry on Awaji.

On Awaji in Sanjo, a number of people have taken up this problem in earnest and produce beautiful (though perhaps not very practical) kashira. I have interviewed a number of them, and they all stress their concern that this important part of puppetry is dying out. Many indicated that the kashira they were carving could never actually be used as real puppet heads, because they could not ever expect to master the construction of the complex karakuri (inner workings) of the kashira.

At the 1993 summit, in the lobby of the theater while performances were going on, Urakame sat on a small platform demonstrating the art of making a puppet head. He was there for both days the summit met at the theater, working from morning until evening. The purpose of "staging" this aspect of the tradition as an ongoing performance in the lobby was to draw attention to the plight of puppetry as an art form and to make a very important point: If no one knows how to carve puppet heads, how can ningyō jōruri continue?[45]

Ōe Minosuke, the master puppet-head carver, in his workshop in Naruto-shi.

This group also has its own scholar, a Mr. Fujino, who is an energetic retired schoolteacher and an avid camera and video enthusiast. He is also very interested in learning to carve kashira and writes and self-publishes detailed and exhaustively researched articles on the history of various aspects of Awaji ningyō.

Self-publishing has become an important means of expression for people connected with this amateur revival group. This expresses the lack of access they have to mainstream academic publishing houses, but to an even greater extent, it is a function of their intended audience. Writing chiefly for themselves, they produce enough copies of their books and articles to share with other people involved in this process. Mr. Fudō Satoshi, the old man with the photographs I mentioned at the start of this book, has followed in his father's footsteps and has written his version of the revival of Awaji puppetry. The book contains copies of primary source documents for studying Awaji along with recollections about the revival process. These self-published articles and books should not be assessed only on an academic level, needless to say; they should be seen as part of a larger cultural performance of identity construction and presentation on Awaji today.

There is some tension between this loosely affiliated group and the formal theater, since the amateurs often point out anything that appears to be new or invented in the professional theater. In spite of the tensions, when national events have focused on Awaji, these two groups—the professional puppeteers of the Ningyō Jōruri Kan and the informal Mihara group—have chosen to present a united front. The first day of the third Zenkoku Ningyō Shibai summit in October 1993 was convened at the local city hall near Sanjo in Mihara-chō, and while performers from the professional theater in Fukura represented Awaji on the stage, display halls were set up throughout the building showing the history of Awaji puppetry and displaying the new kashira and costumes being made by local people from the local group.

Homegrown Ebisu-mai: *Amateur Revival*

On Awaji in the summer of 1990, I had an opportunity to see how this amateur process compared with other revival activities of ritual puppetry at the professional theater. One elderly man by the name of Inai Haruichi has revived the practice of itinerant Ebisu performing, and travels about Awaji in his car giving Ebisu performances in local schools, senior citizens centers, and local festivals and shrines. He only uses puppets he has made completely himself, with the help of his wife who sews the costumes. The

Inai Haruichi with his homemade puppet of Ebisu.

kashira of the puppet he uses is decidedly rustic, and the paint job on the face is not in the tradition of adding ground seashell to the paint to give a special patina to the "skin." His kashira and costume are quite bright, and the puppet body has hands and feet, like all Ebisu puppets. Although Mr. Inai admits that his puppet is soboku (rough-hewn), he works hard at manipulating it well. He performs for free, and seems to have a great time doing so. He carries his stage materials in a box in the back of his car. A native of Sanjo, he has recently become a wealthy man, the owner of a large house surrounded by farmland on the site of his childhood home. Now nearly eighty, he says he hasn't had so much fun in years. Most interesting about his activities is the fact that he seems to be naturally recreating a niche for Ebisu-mai as a relevant performance, and not merely a "reenactment."

When he discovered that I was studying ningyō, Mr. Inai came to Fukura and presented a performance in the zashiki of my host family's house. It took him a few moments to set up his temporary stage, and because it was the first time he had performed for a foreigner, he was quite nervous. Into the basic story of the Ebisu performance he wove elements intended to appeal to me, and he added comments and blessings for my research, my marriage, my future as a mother, and even hopes that I would write good books about Awaji puppetry. His performance took full advantage of the flexibility built into the Ebisu performance to make it relevant to the situation. Because the house where I lived was open to the narrow street, people passing by stopped in while the performance was in progress, and a few children from the neighborhood made a lot of noise and tried to run up behind the screen while he was performing. Mr. Inai dealt with these unexpected events by weaving them into the performance. Ebisu, quite drunk, chastised the children in local dialect, and everyone laughed.

Later that week, he performed Ebisu-mai on stage at the local Ebisu festival in Sanjo. It was evening, and everyone from the village had assembled for the festivities. Stalls sold sweets and grilled corn and toys for children. Everyone present made a trip to the main worship hall of the Ebisu shrine to pray and drink a small glass of sake with the deity before crossing the street to where most of the festivities were taking place. A stage had been set up with chairs scattered about, and members of the community were taking turn at karaoke, singing words to famous songs backed up by an "empty orchestra." Because I was at the festival that evening, I was asked to introduce Mr. Inai. He presented his performance on the stage rather than in front of the shrine and in his recitation of the chant made several humorous references to the festival.

The style of Mr. Inai differs greatly from that of the theater. When performers from the theater present the Ebisu performance, they are concerned with the "reconstruction" of an authentic past and maintaining the performance as a period piece. The Ebisu performance is now a standard part of the repertoire of Awaji ningyō when they perform abroad, and the universally recognizable situation of someone intoxicated being acted out by a puppet is always very popular. Their style and chanting are beautiful, and the puppet manipulation is highly skillful. By contrast, when Mr. Inai presents Ebisu, he also makes the performance humorous by enhancing the drunken aspects of Ebisu, but his concern is with making the performance as relevant as possible. For example, Ebisu now asks for sake by brand name, which draws much laughter, and references to blessings are specific to the audience.[46]

Friendships, Play, and Blue Eyes: The Role of a Foreigner in the Process of Revival

It remains to be asked what most anthropologists until recently asked and answered only within the private spaces of their own journals: How did my presence influence the process which took place before me? How did my own experience influence what happened? Why did I ask the questions I did? In the course of doing this research, I became very attached to the people working on Awaji to revive puppetry. Their motivations and dedication to their tradition, to trying to work out what Awaji puppetry meant to their own identities, moved me, deeply at times. For people like Umazume Masaru, Fudō Satoshi, Naniwa Kunie, Inai Haruichi, Nakanishi Hideo, and many others, reviving Awaji puppetry was a major part of the stories they are constructing and telling about their lives. As I worked and traveled with them, and helped sort through the fragmented evidence of Awaji ningyō's past, I became a small part of the story, and their stories became a part of my story. Here, I am interested in how these stories start to interconnect.

It is not possible for me to discuss the revival of the Awaji tradition and the meanings of nostalgia without implicating myself in this process. My awareness that I had already been implicated came one afternoon in the summer of 1988 while I was reading in the Awaji Historical Archives in Sumoto. In a volume on Awaji puppet heads, I read an article written by Umazume Masaru. In this article, Umazume writes that the relationship between puppetry and religion is an important one, and "even a blue-eyed girl from the University of Chicago is investigating this."[47] The next day at the theater, I asked Umazume-san about the comment. (I was particularly concerned that he had gotten my eye color wrong.) His response was interesting: "Saying someone has blue eyes is simply a way of saying the person is a foreigner. The relationship between religion and Awaji puppetry is one area that has been a problem to study.[48] When I mention that a scholar from abroad is interested in this subject, it makes it okay for us to talk about it." In the process of writing this chapter, this comment has come to have a new significance to my study, for it implicates me in the revival of Awaji puppetry and its growing inclusion of religious dimensions in the constructed narrative about what Awaji puppetry means.

Umazume himself has had a deep interest in the kadozuke tradition of Awaji puppetry. The first time I met him in 1984, he drove me around Awaji to show me the geography of Awaji ningyō. We went to the shrine in Sanjo, walked along country roads, and visited sites where Sanbasō performances had been common. He was especially animated when he discussed the ritual dimensions of puppetry, and he described the Sanbasō performances with great attention to detail. It became clear, however, that as a theater director he was finding it difficult to develop his keen interest in kadozuke.

Over the years since 1984, Umazume and I have worked closely, and many of the viewpoints I have taken in my research have been suggested by him. In many ways, I have been something of a foil for him. Because I am a foreigner, it is possible for him to use my presence to ask a lot of questions that would otherwise remain unasked. Manipulation of this foreignness has been an important part of my participation in the revival of this tradition.

There was also a certain playful quality that was possible during my fieldwork. Much of the work I did with Umazume-san had an academic purpose but was also just plain fun. Driving around in the countryside looking at inscriptions in deserted shrines, going on walking tours of Sanjo and talking to elderly people about their recollections, taking boats out to deserted islands to look at amazoku tombs and telling stories of retributions from malevolent spirits to scare each other, traveling around Kyushu meeting people and looking at their puppetry collections while we invited them to the ningyō summit meetings, opening the inner sanctum of a childhood shrine—all these experiences afforded Umazume-san a certain freedom his job as director of the theater would not have made possible had he not had the responsibility of taking care of a foreign scholar. For many historians of religions and anthropologists, this aspect of play in the fieldwork experience and deep relationships that develop from it become an important part of our hidden interpretive schema and the motivation in our work. Our nostalgia for the "good old days" when we did fieldwork often inspires us in our teaching and writing, and in how we design our future research. Being a participant observer may be less about trying to live other people's lives than about the natural human activity of play as a means of self-discovery and of understanding others.

My presence as a foreign scholar studying puppets was also manipulated consciously and unconsciously in more formal ways. Most of the formal research trips I conducted on Awaji were directed toward studying the past of this tradition, tracking down elderly people, old photographs, puppet heads, costumes and paraphernalia, and old documents. Initially, as an historian of religions, my interest lay in discerning the structures and intentions of the ritual tradition of puppetry as an example of widespread religious practices and beliefs at various points in Japanese history. During each of these periods of research, I was often taken to other parts of Japan, from Kyushu to Nagano. But three events, one in 1988, another in 1991, and a third during my most recent trip in 1993, stand apart from the rest of my research experiences. On these trips off Awaji, or whenever Awaji's place in a larger Japanese context was central (as in the summit meetings), what I was doing on Awaji was always an important issue. A whole new arena for performance was opened up, and the focus of my study underwent a dramatic shift. This enabled me to ask a different series of questions about the meaning of tradition in contemporary Japan, and to explore the power of an age-old malaise, nostalgia, to motivate, manipulate, and maneuver activity in remarkable ways.

Event 1

In August 1988, I accompanied the two leading scholars of the Awaji puppet tradition, Nakanishi Hideo and Takeda Shin'ichi, to Nagano Prefecture. Both of these men are high school teachers on Awaji and were born and raised on the island. Mr. Nakanishi is in his midforties and is the director of the Mihara-gun High School Puppetry Club, an organization which trains young people in the art of jōruri recitation, puppetry, kashira carving and costume creation, and shamisen, and which supplies artists for the professional theater on the island. Mr. Takeda is in his early sixties, and before retirement he taught early Japanese history. Both publish extensively in Japanese journals and are great aficionados of the ningyō jōruri tradition.[49]

The purpose of our trip to Nagano was ostensibly to attend the International Puppetry Festival staged each year in Iida-shi. This event, sponsored by UNIMA,[50] attracts puppetry groups from Australia, Europe, Vietnam, Japan, and even the Americas. We went by car, leaving Awaji at midnight and catching the first ferry to Kobe so that we could arrive in Nagano by midmorning. The real purpose of this trip, I soon discovered, was to track down the graves and remnants of a Tokugawa puppeteer from Awaji who had settled in Nagano and started a puppetry group there. The man had died in the 1700s, and my colleagues wanted to find out about his life and the influence he had on the puppetry traditions in Nagano. We knew the name of the temple where his mortuary tablets were kept and the cemetery where his bones are said to have been buried. In the heat of an August afternoon, we spent several hours in a mountain cemetery trying to find the actual gravestone of this Awaji puppeteer. On the surface, finding his grave was a way of proving the connection between Awaji puppetry and Nagano puppetry. Situating Awaji puppets as the center of ritual puppetry in Japan is an important dynamic of the process of revival.

At another level, it became clear that for these scholars, this was a visit to the past, and the effort to find this grave was motivated by more than academic or "political" reasons. Finding this grave was an attempt to make some sort of contact with this dead puppeteer. When they actually found the grave, both of the men solemnly cleaned off the stone and made offerings. Worshipping and visiting a grave in Japan entails more than paying one's respects. It says something about the relationship of the worshipper to the deceased; it implies a tie. The visit to the grave was about forging a bond between the dead and the living, between the past and the present. And this involved no small amount of sweat and inconvenience. Searching for and worshipping at a remote mountain grave became the central drama of the trip to Nagano, rather than the UNIMA festival. For Nakanishi and Takeda, the visit to the grave brought the story of this puppeteer into their lives.

When we went to Nagano in 1988, I was in the midst of my doctoral field research, and I was presented in all meetings and gatherings simply as "a Ph.D. student from the University of Chicago" writing a dissertation on the Awaji tradition. Meetings with leading performers and scholars of ritual puppetry around Japan were enhanced by having a foreign scholar studying the Awaji tradition. My presence gave Awaji ningyō an extra prestige within the world of ritual traditions. During research trips off the island of Awaji, however, I quickly learned that different replies were required of me when asked why I was doing a doctoral research on Awaji ningyō. The proper answer depended on the audience. If I were asked this question by people from established theaters in urban areas (of which the National Theater is the best example) or by a member of the Ministry of Education, I remarked how this tradition was an excellent example of "true Japanese ritual tradition," how the plays were most poignant, and how the rural versions of the theaters had a rough and authentic feel to them. I was to respond with the formulaic expression that a return to the rural and the marginal was in fact a return to the authentic. It was also acceptable to mention that marginalized groups which had been ignored should now be seen for what they are—true Japanese performance. This interpretation seemed to have been agreed upon as the reason a great deal of money was being channeled into revival efforts by various organizations and government agencies.

If, however, my audience consisted of other ritual puppeteers or people directly connected with the various traditions around Japan, this previous answer merely drew smiles and knowing winks. The answer required by this audience was to point out the centrality of the Awaji tradition as a unique nexus and source tradition for most ritual puppetry traditions around Japan (which is in fact correct). Both of these responses rely on the hidden prestige of Awaji ningyō being perceived as important by an outsider. The only difference in the answers is what that foreigner is perceiving.

Event 2

Another case from my field notes indicates the prestige of outsider appreciation. A few years later, Ph.D. in hand and hired at an American university, I had a different status vis-à-vis the tradition I studied. I was traveling around Kyushu during the preparations for the ningyō summit. Although I was essentially extraneous to the discussions (since they largely centered around money, funding for travel, timing), at each theater I was introduced as the American scholar with a recent Ph.D. (now a professor at an Ivy League school) who had done a dissertation on the Awaji theater. Although the introduction was usually followed with such humility markers as "They give Ph.D.'s for things like that in America, odd, I know, but anyway she did her Ph.D. on us," it was clear that I was an important stage prop in this performance. Since a major component of these trips was to solidify Awaji as the center of puppetry in Japan (aside from the classical Bunraku stage), my presence (and the extra clout of my status as an academic) was important political capital.

Event 3

At the most recent trip to Japan, I was keynote speaker at the third annual ningyō summit. This event, unlike the previous two, was to draw significant media attention. This three-day event focused on the "revival" of the Sanbasō performance, and several puppetry groups from around Japan presented their performances of Sanbasō side by side for comparison. The media billed it as "a battle of the Sanbasōs," and the theater was packed. The ratio of photographers to regular theatergoers was unusually high, and film crews rivaled one another for the best angles in the theater. It was difficult to see and even more difficult to hear the performances, and it was clear this was a "media event" and a rare photo opportunity for the puppetry groups to be on national news. A foreign professor as the keynote speaker lent a further air of gravity to the event. Again, it became clear that my foreignness was an important component in this three-day media event. This was most apparent when I looked at the media coverage of the summit on national news. In spite of the fact that there had been a number of rare performances (in the model of the Minzoku Geinō Taikai that Sasahara laments), most snippets on the national news gave as much coverage to my keynote address as they did to the remarkable performances, a regrettable reflection of what makes news in Japan even in these days of *kokusaika* ("internationalization," the recent buzzword of the Ministry of Education).

Unlike the previous events where I had a heavily scripted role to play, at this summit I was given free rein to speak on whatever topic I chose. (I spoke on the meanings of revival and the significance of nostalgia as a motivating force.) While on one level my comments could be seen as "deconstructing" the very event itself, the atmosphere was open, and the implicit message was that Awaji was now so clearly the center of this revival movement that it could risk the unscripted and even critical comments of a foreign scholar.

Throughout these three experiences, people in Awaji used my foreigner status to further their own revitalization movement. This experience could not point out more directly how the presence of the observer affects the outcome of events. While it would be grandiose and arrogant to claim any credit for the revival of this tradition as a viable theater, it is clear my presence—as an invisible and constituted Other—gave strength to participants in this process.

Fragments to the Light

It would seem simple enough to reveal how hidden meanings in the Awaji puppetry revival are constructed and manipulated. Once we have understood these deeper ideological functions, we can be content that we have understood the process itself. The problem with such an approach is that it ignores a very important part of this entire process: the sense of identity of the people involved. For Umazume-san, as well as many of my other informants, the larger social and political context of the dentō geinō būmu—the boom in folk arts in Japan—cannot exhaust the deeper meanings of their actions.

Revival, it seems obvious enough, encodes ideologies about value, taste, aesthetics, and class, and it appeals to an easily manipulated aspect of us all—the desire to undo time and return to the past. Deciding just what will be retrieved, what will be left on the dust heap of history, and how this past shall be presented constitutes a hierarchy of meaning. Revival also appeals to people at the level at which we are least inclined to be suspicious—the past.

In reflecting on how the Awaji tradition has been revived, I have tried to identify how certain aspects of the tradition have been required to become symbols for the entirety of the "vanishing past." For different groups of people, criteria for those decisions differ, at times dramatically. The process of symbolizing the past is always in motion, responding to subtle changes in larger discourses of identity in Japan.

The uses of nostalgia in the revival of Awaji puppets cannot be understood simply as a uniform ideological appropriation of the past, for the puppetry tradition has had different pasts for different people, depending on their relationships to both the tradition and one another in various power structures. This revival is a vibrant example of an ever developing discourse on what "being Japanese" means to different people, appropriated in any number of ways. This river of nostalgic discourse has had three currents, at times confluent: (1) people living on Awaji who as children or young adults witnessed (and even helped to bring about) the end of the "island of the puppets," and for whom the associations with puppetry have been simultaneously a source of regional pride and social stigma; (2) "outsiders" in Japanese media, arts, and academia, for whom this revival provides a "living museum" from which they can draw materials for the business of marketing the past or furthering their academic careers; and (3) people in government, most specifically the Ministry of Education and Bureau of Cultural Affairs, for whom the celebration of Awaji puppetry as a folk performing art makes it possible both to posit a mythology of a common past shared by all Japanese people through an appeal to the idea of *kokumin* (national folk) and to camouflage a history of oppression of Japanese outcast groups.

In this chapter, I have discussed how the Awaji tradition both participates in and moves beyond the significance of this larger movement in Japanese society in the latter part of the twentieth century. For the revival movement of Awaji ningyō to succeed, a delicate balance has to be struck. On one level, the revival is about going "mainstream" with a tradition which has in the past been the root of marginalization. On another level, reviving Awaji puppetry helps create a local tourist trade and a new identity for Awaji as Japan's "Mediterranean." Revitalization encompasses a larger ideological construct of finally becoming part of mainstream Japanese folk art culture, albeit under the rubric of a somewhat fictitious category. Revitalization encompasses such issues as identity, liberation, autonomy, and, of course, economics. It is also about finally claiming an identity and a relationship with one's ancestors.

I have tried to show how the nostalgic discourse in Japan in the last several decades has played an important (and at times even dominant) role in the revival of Awaji puppetry. But another, sometimes ironic and partly unconscious movement has been afoot. To dismiss the entire complex process of recasting ritual performances as stage pieces solely as a part of a nostalgic enterprise misses an important point. Mr. Umazume and other people on Awaji are cognizant of the fact that the contexts and intentions of kadozuke ningyō are no longer extant in Japan. Ostensibly, according to the larger nativist discourse promoted by the Bureau of Culture and the Ministry of Education, the rituals are to be kept alive for two reasons: they open a window to the past and they serve as a source for creative new performances.

Umazume is fully aware of the limitations of keeping these ritual performances alive by casting them in an artificial context, and he realizes that they are no longer rituals but are now in fact theater. But this, he says, is preferable to letting the art forms be lost altogether. Mr. Umazume, like many others on Awaji, feels that the actual symbolic content of these rituals—even when removed from their contexts—may be potent enough to transform people. Though the distance created by the formality of the stage may dilute the potential for a transformative experience, the rites' power to affect people persists.

At a deeper level, the fact that outcast arts are suddenly being heralded as "authentically Japanese" has a healing effect. Many people on Awaji were deeply attached to their puppetry tradition, and when in the twentieth century it was regarded as something no longer useful or necessary but merely a source of embarrassment and stigma, people felt great conflict about letting it die (or even actively killing it). This new era, for all its problems, has allowed many people to claim what their parents, grandparents, and even great- and great-great-grandparents did as something meaningful, beautiful, and even Japanese. In the short period of time I have had contact with people on Awaji (from 1977 until now—a little under twenty years), people have gone from denying that they had any connection with Dōkumbō mawashi in the past to showing me with great pride the remnants of their family puppet collections or paraphernalia. People who in the early 1980s told me their ancestors had been farmers have since come to me and said, "Did I say my grandfather was a farmer? Well, he was, but he also manipulated puppets. I guess I forgot to mention that." Perhaps a larger discourse of exoticism and nativism created the context for the revival of kadozuke ningyō. Perhaps the revival is an awkward and hopeless false start which will never overcome the limitations of casting ritual onto the stage. Maybe a lot of it is about Awaji regionalism and the tourist industry. And perhaps the larger nativist discourse will once again reabsorb this newfound affirmation of the history of ritual puppeteers and turn it into something else, something divisive. But for the time being, a lot of people on Awaji are able to situate themselves in relationship to the lives and livelihood of their parents, grandparents, and great-grandparents. They have been able to pick up the fragments of evidence from these nearly invisible puppeteers' difficult and often painful yet talented lives, hold them up to the light, and ask, "How is this part of my story?"

Umazume Masaru at Ōmidō Hachiman in 1990.

Epilogue

SINCE the research for and writing of this book were completed, a major earthquake hit Hyōgo prefecture in Japan. Awaji was the epicenter of the quake. While none of the people connected with the theater lost their lives or homes, the damage on Awaji was considerable. The main highway which traverses the island was repaired only in March 1996, a full fourteen months after the quake.

As a result, the business at the theater has been very bad, and people are again worried that Awaji puppetry will be nothing more than a passing tourist attraction. When I spoke with Umazume-san in May 1995, he was pessimistic about the revival being anything other than a short-lived dream. With the reconstruction of the highway and the soon-to-be completed bridge between Honshu and Awaji, people are hopeful that Awaji puppets will draw larger Japanese audiences than before. Others entertain serious doubts that the theater will survive the setback caused by the earthquake.

In 1995, Umazume-san retired as director of the theater, and his successor was chosen from among the younger puppeteers. Bandō Sentarō was thirty-one years old when he assumed leadership of the theater, the same age as Umazume-san when he began trying to revive the tradition. This is considered to be a lucky coincidence by people in the theater.

I wish him well.

Notes

Introduction: Of Stories and Fragments

1. It is common in Japanese to use the term *jōruri* to refer to puppet theater, although the term literally means "pure lapis lazuli." The connection between puppetry and this name comes from the famous love story of Lady Jōruri and Ushiwaka (the boyhood name of Yoshitsune), which made this genre of ballad recitation famous. See C. J. Dunn, *The Early Japanese Puppet Drama* (London: Luzac, 1966), pp. 7–13. In Japanese, see the exhaustive study by Wakatsuki Yasuji, "Jōruri hime monogatari," chap. 2 in *Jōruri-shi no kenkyū* (Tokyo, 1943).

2. Jane Marie Swanberg-Law, "Puppets of the Road: Ritual Performance in Japanese Folk Religion" (Ph.D. diss., University of Chicago, 1990).

3. From 1987 through 1989, I was a researcher at Tsukuba University in the Institute of Philosophy, funded by a research scholarship from the Japanese Ministry of Education. During these two years I spent large segments of time on Awaji doing research.

4. For a discussion of narrative knowledge, see Jean Françoise Lyotard, *The Postmodern Condition: A Report on Knowledge*, trans. Geoff Bennington and Brian Massumi (Minneapolis: University of Minnesota Press, 1983), pp. 18–23.

5. Hori Ichirō, *Folk Religion in Japan: Continuity and Change*, ed. Joseph M. Kitagawa and Alan M. Miller (Chicago: University of Chicago Press, 1968), p. 10.

6. Ibid., pp. 10–11.

7. Joseph M. Kitagawa, "'A Past of Things Present': Major Motifs of Early Japanese Religions," in *On Understanding Japanese Religion* (Princeton: Princeton University Press, 1987), p. 48.

8. Ibid., pp. 43–58.

9. Ibid., p. 70.

10. During the years that I studied with Professor Kitagawa, he often made the point that the future of Japanese scholarship lay in finding ways to bring the issue of "others" to the foreground. It was Professor Kitagawa who, in numerous conversations we had near the end of his life, encouraged me in my study of Japanese outcasts and ritual puppeteers, precisely because he saw the value of what he considered to be a "corrective" to the unitary meaning structure approach to Japanese religions.

11. H. D. Harootunian, *Things Seen and Unseen: Discourse and Ideology in Tokugawa Nativism* (Chicago: University of Chicago Press, 1988), pp. 419–420.

12. Lyotard, *The Postmodern Condition*, pp. 81–82.

Chapter 1: In the Shape of a Person

1. Most studies of Japanese puppetry focus almost exclusively on methods of manipulation, to the neglect of other aspects of puppetry. An excellent and informative example of this approach is Dunn, *Early Japanese Puppet Drama*, which

explores the early jōruri tradition. He mentions ritual puppetry and religion only in passing on pp. 21–26.

2. This comment was made to me on December 23, 1988, when I interviewed Professor Nagata at the nursing home in Yudawara where he was living. He was then ninety-nine years old.

3. E. Gordon Craig, "The Actor and the Übermarionette," in E. T. Kirby, *Total Theater* (New York: Dutton, 1969), pp. 54–56. This essay was originally printed in *The Mask* 1, no. 1 (April 1908). It also appears in Michael J. Walton, *Craig on Theater* (London: Methuen, 1983). I have relied on the latter transcription of this famous essay.

4. Bil Baird, *The Art of the Puppet Theater* (New York: MacMillan, 1965), p. 13.

5. In Margareta Niculescu, ed., *The Puppet Theater of the Modern World*, trans. Ewald Osers and Elisabeth Strick (Boston: Plays, Inc., 1967), p. 58.

6. This is a contentious topic in Japan. It seems most likely that the use of puppets arose out of a need to dissimulate artistic responsibility and risk.

7. Ibid., p. 35.

8. With minor variations, this story is recounted in most of the major works on Chinese shadow theater. See Rene Simmen, *The World of Puppets* (New York: Thomas Y. Crowell, 1972), p. 79; also Genevieve Wimsatt, *Chinese Shadow Shows* (Cambridge: Harvard University Press, 1936), pp. ix–x.

9. Craig, "Actor and Übermarionette," pp. 38–50.

10. Niculescu, *Puppet Theater,* pp. 18–19.

11. Paraphrased from Lotte Reiniger, *Shadow Theatre and Shadow Films* (London: B. T. Batsford, 1970), pp. 20–21.

12. Nagata Kōkichi, *Nihon no ningyō shibai* (Tokyo: Kinseisha, 1974), p. 2.

13. Carmen Blacker, among others, has suggested that the female clay effigies found in these tombs are actually the representations of *miko* (ancient female shaman). To support this quite probable hypothesis, she points to the headgear, posture, and ornamentation of the figures. One such haniwa, discovered in Okawamura in Gumma Prefecture wears a perfectly flat headboard, and is sitting in a most unusually upright position with a focused and peaceful expression, suggesting the posture of one in an intent trance. Around her neck, she wears beads, and from her waist hangs a mirror. Another figure, similarly adorned and in the same posture, wears *magatama*, the comma-shaped jewels believed to have spiritual power in ancient Japan. The beads, similar to those found in tombs throughout Japan, surely had a powerful magical role as spirit lures, inviting the kami to dwell in the body of the shaman. These magatama ornaments were originally made out of either bone or animal teeth and eventually were carved out of stone and semi-precious stones. It is possible that the origins of their shapes stems from a belief in the power of animal spirit helpers, whose teeth gave shamans special powers in their rituals. Blacker and others have compared this ritual attire to that of the Siberian shaman. Carmen Blacker, *The Catalpa Bow: A Study of Shamanic Practices in Japan* (London: George Allen and Unwin, 1975), pp. 106–109. Tungusic shamans in northern Mongolia used copper mirrors as a de-

vice to see the soul a dead person. Concerning this, Eliade writes that such copper mirrors are clearly Sino-Manchurian in origin, and while their meanings differ from tribe to tribe, "the mirror is said to help the shaman 'see the world' (that is, to concentrate), or to 'place the spirits,' or to reflect the needs of mankind, and so on." Mircea Eliade, *Shamanism: Archaic Techniques of Ecstasy*, trans. Willard R. Trask, Bollingen Series, no. 76 (Princeton: Princeton University Press, 1964), pp. 153–155. Ryūzō Torii also maintains that northeast Asian shamans suspend mirrors from their waists, which give off light and jangle as they dance, giving the mystical, synesthetic effect of dance, light, and sound. In the case of the mikos, the female shaman, this sound and light may have served to invite the kami to enter her body. The history of Japanese performing arts and the Japanese religious conception of possession (*kami-gakari* or *tsukimono*) certainly support this hypothesis. Mirrors also have a wider meaning in Japanese religious practice. Often it is a mirror that serves as the vessel (*shintai*, *yorishiro*, or *mitamashiro*) for the kami during a rite.

14. A standard interpretation of this term has been that there were seven rivers, but since the character used refers to shallows within a river, it appears more likely that there were seven parts of a particular river in which these rites could take place, places where the current slowed enough to create a safe ritual site. These places along the river were also understood to be sacred sites. It is not known which river was the actual site for these rites, although Yamagami Izumo suggests that it may have originally been the Kamo River. See "Nanase harai no genryū," *Kodai bunka* 22, no. 5 (August 1970): 126–127.

15. For a discussion of this practice, and a transcription of the kambun text describing it, see Kitamura Tetsurō, "Ningyō," *Nihon no bijutsu*, no. 11 (March 1967): 1–29; also Nagata, *Nihon no ningyō Shibai*, pp. 19–25. Tsunoda Ichirō also mentions the relationship between puppets and the removal of pollution. See his *Ningyō geki no seiritsu ni kansuru kenkyū* (Osaka: Kuroya Shuppan, 1964), p. 248.

16. Yamagami, "Nanase no harai no genryū," p. 130.

17. Yamagami Izumo, *Miko no rekishi* (Tokyo: Yūzankaku, 1984), p. 26.

18. Kitamura, "Ningyō," p. 30.

19. Nagata Kōkichi, "Ningyō shibai no kigen shiryō," in *Geinō ronshū* ed. Honda Yasuji (Tokyo: Kinseisha, 1976), pp. 635–637. This article by Nagata also presents some clear photographs of extant hitogatas from various archaeological museums around Japan.

20. A photograph of this figure appears in ibid., p. 30.

21. See Nagata, *Nihon no ningyō shibai*, pp. 25–28.

22. Murasaki Shikibu, *The Tale of Genji*, trans. Arthur Waley (London: George Allen and Unwin, 1935), p. 366. Waley writes, "The Heavenly Children were dolls which were intended to attract evil influences and so save the child from harm" (p. 366n).

23. "Ise ke hisho tanjō no ki" is cited by Kitamura, who argues that it was believed that if during pregnancy the doll grows hair, the child will be a girl and if not, a boy. I have found no sources to support this claim. Kitamura, "Ningyō," pp. 30–31.

24. Effigies at the Nishinomiya Ebisu shrine, discussed in detail in chapter 3, were venerated as capable of protecting tiny infants from smallpox.

25. The ten types take their names from villages or resorts in the Tōhoku region: Tsuchiyu, Tōgatta, Naguro, Yajirō, Yamagata-Sakunami, Zaō-Takayu, Hijiori, Nambu (Hanamaki), Kijiyama, and Tsugaru. For a clear and well-illustrated description of the ten, see Chizuko Takeuchi and Roberta Stephens, *An Invitation to Kokeshi Dolls* (Sendai: Tsugaru Shōbo, 1982).

26. William LaFleur, *Liquid Life: Abortion and Buddhism in Contemporary Japan* (Princeton: Princeton University Press, 1992), pp. 99–107. LaFleur's discussion of abortion and infanticide in Japan is the most extensive study available in English.

27. This comment was by the Tokugawa Confucianist Sato Nobuhiro (1769–1850). Ibid., p. 107.

28. One way that these "erased children" were allowed a presence in the lives of people in Tōhoku was in the form of the *zashikiwarashi* (child of the zashiki), also called *zashiki bōko* or *zashiki bokko*, a small and mischievous spirit about which stories would be told, and which was said to be always present in a house, playfully haunting its inhabitants.

29. See LaFleur, *Liquid Life*, pp. 97–102.

30. The leading authority on Sado puppetry is the elderly Yamamoto Shūnosuke. His authoritative book is the only work in Japanese devoted wholly to puppetry on this island. See Yamamoto Shūnosuke *Sado no ningyō shibai* (Niigata-ken, Sado-gun, Mano-cho, Shinmachi: Sado Kyōdō Kenkyūkai, 1976). In the summer of 1991, with a faculty research grant from the Cornell University East Asia Program, I conducted research on the island of Sado and interviewed Mr. Yamamoto. In his home he has one of the finest collections of Sado puppets, including rare puppets not found in museums.

31. Because Sado puppetry was not central to my research, I only spent a short period of time on Sado in the summer of 1991. Since I did not know anyone well, it is likely that the dearth of information I received about these sex puppets reflected the embarrassment many people felt in talking about these puppets with a stranger, let alone a foreign woman.

32. Yamamoto, *Sado no ningyō shibai*, p. 126.

33. Donald L. Philippi, trans., *Kojiki* (Tokyo: University of Tokyo Press, 1968), pp. 81–86.

34. Ibid., p. 84f.

35. Ibid.

36. Yamamoto goes on to say that a puppet exactly like this Kinosuke, who urinates on the audience, can be found in Korea.

37. This comment was made to me by the master *ningyō-shi*, Ōe Minosuke. I interviewed Ōe Minosuke at his home in Naruto-shi, Tokushima-ken, in August 1988. Masks in the Noh theater were also said to be "well born" if they held spirits.

38. In the jōruri tradition, a puppeteer is responsible for getting and assembling his own puppet. This process is referred to as "helping the puppet find its body."

Chapter 2: *Kadozuke*

1. This description is based on interviews, ethnographic films and descriptions, and old photographs I collected during my fieldwork. For the purposes of this discussion, I have composed a general description of a puppeteer presenting a Sanbasō performance, the most common type of ritual performance using puppets during the New Year. I discuss the actual content of this type of performance in detail in chapter 5.

2. To a certain extent, these names referred to different styles of puppetry.

3. Bernard Harrison in his *Form and Content* (New York: Harper and Row, 1973) discusses what he calls the "discrimination thesis," namely, "the most fundamental level of discourse about experience is the level at which we state facts, so far as they are known to us, about our own and others' ability to discriminate between particular types of present stimuli. If we ask whether there is not some more fundamental level at which we can describe the phenomenal character of experiences between which we discriminate, the reply must be that there is not. Experience talk boils down ultimately to discrimination talk" (p. 4).

4. Michael Theunissen, *The Other: Studies in the Social Ontology of Husserl, Heidegger, Sartre and Buber*, trans. C. Macann (Cambridge: MIT Press, 1984), p. 1.

5. For this reason, it seems that the standpoint of history of religions is not incompatible with contemporary critiques of ideological systems.

6. Early in the history of contemporary anthropology, studies of non-Western peoples as "primitive" often isolated the category of the stranger and the fear of strangers as a unique feature of "the primitive, savage mind." Consider the following quote from the *Encyclopedia of Religion and Ethics* (New York: Charles Scribner's Sons, 1934), s. v. "strangers": "We have seen that, to the savage, the world which lies beyond the community to which he belongs—i.e. beyond his group and the groups associated with it on terms which are friendly rather than hostile—is a world strange and mysterious, peopled with beings whom he hates or fears as his deadly foes. He thinks of them as belonging to an order other than his own, as less or, it may be, as more than human; and he looks upon them as absolutely rightless; for the sphere of rights is codeterminous with the sphere within which he himself lives. As regards himself, life is possible for him only within the little circle of his community."

7. For a thorough analysis of this phenomenon, see Edward W. Said, *Orientalism* (New York: Pantheon Books, 1978).

8. See Harootunian, *Things Seen and Unseen*.

9. See Ernst van Alphen, "The Other Within," in *Alterity, Identity, Image: Selves and Others in Society and Scholarship*, ed. Raymond Corbey and Joep Leersen (Amsterdam: Rodopi, 1991), pp. 1–16.

10. Michel Foucault, *Madness and Civilization: A History of Insanity in the Age of Reason* (New York: Pantheon Books, 1965), pp. 8–9. One doubts whether being mentally ill and homeless could have been "easy," regardless of the freedom this provided.

11. Here, Douglas is in line with Turner in his discussion of liminal states in ritual processes. See Victor Turner, *The Ritual Process: Structure and Anti-Structure* (Ithaca: Cornell University Press, 1969), pp. 94–130.

12. Mary Douglas, *Purity and Danger: An Analysis of the Concepts of Pollution and Taboo* (London: Routledge and Kegan Paul, 1966), pp. 114–115.

13. Ibid., p. 122.

14. Comprised of elaborate rules and ritual behaviors for dealing with the natural functions and processes of the human body and its products, ritual purity systems are a dominant feature in many religious systems throughout the world. Important studies responsible for setting out the general categories of interpretation are Louis Dumont's study of the Hindu caste system, *Homo Hierarchicus: An Essay on the Caste System* (Chicago, University of Chicago Press, 1966), especially chapter 2, and Douglas, *Purity and Danger.* Other recent studies include Emiko Ohnuki-Tierney, *Illness and Culture in Contemporary Japan* (Cambridge: Cambridge University Press, 1984), Robert Parker, *Miasma: Pollution and Purification in Early Greek Religion* (Oxford: Oxford University Press, 1983), and Howard Eilberg Schwartz, *The Savage in Judaism: An Anthropology of Israelite Religion and Ancient Judaism* (Bloomington: Indiana University Press, 1990).

15. Yokoi Kiyoshi, *Chūsei minshū to seikatsu bunka* (Tokyo: Tokyo Daigaku Shuppan Kai, 1975), p. 267. Ohnuki-Tierney (*Illness and Culture*, pp. 21–74) explores how notions of purity and pollution, insider and outsider, and above and below continue to operate as essential distinctions in Japanese society.

16. A recent explanation for the rebuilding of the shrine concerns the need for builders to be trained in the correct techniques of construction. Since rebuilding must be done every twenty years, there will always be persons alive who know how to rebuild the shrine.

17. Ohnuki-Tierney, *Illness and Culture*, p. 37.

18. Ibid., p. 269.

19. See Namihira Emiko, *Kegare no kōzō* (Tokyo: Seidōsha, 1992), particularly chapters 4 and 5. See also Yokoi, *Chūsei minshū to seikatsu bunka*, pp. 267–294.

20. Ibid., p. 267.

21. Yokoi, *Chūsei minshū to seikatsu bunka*, p. 269.

22. Quoted in Yamagami Izumo, *Miko no rekishi*, p. 27.

23. Yokoi, *Chūsei minshū to seikatsu bunka*, p. 280.

24. Philippi, *Kojiki* 1:1. The literal sentence "they hid their bodies" is translated as "their forms were not visible" by Philippi.

25. Awaji is considered to be the location of Onogorojima, and even today there is a sacred spot on the island where it is said the heavenly jeweled spear first created the self-curdling island. I discuss this in more detail in chapter 4. The nearby island of Nushima (off the southern coast of Awaji, also has a shrine said to be the site of Onogorojima.

26. It has been suggested that this is also a reference to the island of Awaji.

27. This deity is also called Hi no Kagu Tsuchi no Kami.

28. *Kojiki* 1:7, 18–22.

29. For a summary of these interpretations, see *Kojiki*, additional note 5. See also Daniel C. Holtom, *The National Faith of Japan: A Study in Modern Shintō* (1938; reprint, New York: Paragon Books, 1965), pp. 93–121. Holtom

argues against a euhemeristic interpretation and prefers to see these myths as expressions of a "socialization of experience with nature," particularly the weather (p. 121).

30. *Kojiki* 1:7, 26–28.

31. Ibid. 1:8, 1–5.

32. Ibid. 1:8, 6–14.

33. The obvious parallel with the Orpheus and Eurydice myth is striking.

34. *Kojiki* 1:9, 6–15. It is interesting that the corpse of the mother is divided into the same body parts as those of her son, the fire deity, after he is murdered by the father.

35. Ibid. 1:11, 1.

36. Ibid. 1:11, 1–25.

37. Dumont, *Homo Hierarchicus*, p. 47. Douglas has also pointed out this common misunderstanding of ritual purity systems. Douglas, *Purity and Danger*, pp. 29–40, 73.

38. Yokoi, *Chūsei Minshū no Seikatsu Bunka*, pp. 283–287.

39. Louis Dumont, *Homo Hierarchicus*.

40. Several surveys of the transformations of the meanings associated with these specialists of impurity are available in English. One is the 1933 study by Ninomiya Shigeaki "An Inquiry Concerning the Origins, Development, and Present Situation of the Eta in Relation to the History of Social Classes in Japan," *Transactions of the Asiatic Society of Japan*, 2d ser., 10 (December 1933): 47–152. In this early and often cited work, Ninomiya presents an overview of the major theories put forth to account for the existence of an outcast group in Japan (called in 1933 by the derogatory word *eta*, written with the characters "much *kegare*"), and his discussion evaluates the various theories, from the ridiculous to the credible. He proposes that hereditary occupation led to the institutionalization of the pariah status in Japanese society. Another is a brief discussion (summarizing Japanese sources and drawing on Ninomiya) in Emiko Ohnuki-Tierney, *Monkey as Mirror: Symbolic Transformation in Japanese History and Ritual* (Princeton: Princeton University Press, 1987). Ohnuki-Tierney has outlined the transformations in status of these "specialists in impurity" in Japanese history, whom she refers to as "special status people." She shows not only how different groups of people fall into this category for a variety of reasons but also how the meanings attached to outcast people as a whole change dramatically throughout Japanese history. The general group of people she calls special status people is actually comprised of a wide variety of people, including those involved in imperial funerals, ritual purifiers, itinerant performers, monkey trainers, puppeteers, prostitutes, midwives, latrine cleaners, street sweepers, mausoleum guards, tatami makers, leather tanners, falconers, sandal weavers, ink makers, and indigo dyers among others. What all of these people have in common is that their professions were understood to be polluting according to the ritual purity system outlined above. The transformations in their status throughout Japanese history are due to transformations in the importance and meanings associated with ritual purity itself, a point that is tied directly to nativism and nationalism. A new work, Michele Marra's excellent study *Representations of Power: The Literary Politics of Medieval Japan* (Honolulu: University of Hawaii Press, 1994), also discusses the issues of

exclusion in ritual efficacy and provides valuable sources concerning the history of Japanese outcasts. None of these excellent studies, however, focuses directly on the importance of the imagination of the human body as a symbolic language of society and the cosmos although the data clearly point to the human body—its physiology, its representation, and its handling, as the central component of the ritual purity system.

Recent studies by Japanese scholars have been critical of the view that outcasts arose out of an anonymous historical process. They argue that the Tokugawa government intentionally created and manipulated the statuses of outcasts. Outcasts were maintained in their liminal state through carefully designed laws so that they could serve as guards, executioners, and policemen to suppress peasant riots during the dictatorial Tokugawa shogunate. For an overview of this approach to Japan's outcasts, see Nagahara Keiji, *Nihon no Chūsei Shakai* (Tokyo: Iwanami Shoten, 1973). In English see Nagahara, "The Medieval Origins of the *Eta-Hinin*," *Journal of Japanese Studies* 5, no. 2 (1979); Ian Neary, *Political Protest and Social Control in Pre-War Japan: The Origins of Buraku Liberation* (Atlantic Highlands, N.J.: Humanities Press International, 1989), pp. 12–30.

41. These people have at certain times in Japanese history had a very high status. I choose to call them outcasts, however. I am fully aware that this general term cannot cover the wide range of historical transformations that Japan's pariah groups have undergone. I do so for several reasons: First Ohnuki-Tierney's term "special status people" is too euphemistic; it softens the hard truth. Second "outcast" draws attention to the important dynamics of this case.

42. For a 1935 map with populations of *burakumin* per thousand by prefecture, see Neary, *Political Protest*, p. 6.

43. See Mihara Rekishi Kenkyūkai, *Mihara gun shi*, pp. 480–488.

44. Yoshida Teigo, "The Stranger as God: The Place of the Outsider in Folk Religion," *Ethnology* 20, no. 2 (1964): 88.

45. The term *waza* originally carried the connotation of "unrevealed divine will" and came to include the idea that divine will could be responsible for scourges, bad omens, and disasters.

46. Combs were traditionally made of tortoise shell, so persons in this occupation were involved in the killing of animals. Killing turtles was also a symbolic violation (although the products of dead turtles were highly prized): a turtle was the symbol of ten thousand years.

47. Yokoi, *Chūsei minshū no seikatsu bunka*, p. 335. *Kawara no mono* literally means "people who live along riverbeds."

48. See Jonathan Z. Smith, "The Influence of Symbols upon Social Change: A Place on Which to Stand," in *Map is Not Territory: Studies in the History of Religions* (Leiden: E. J. Brill, 1978), pp. 129–146.

49. Yokoi, *Chūsei minshū to seikatsu bunka*, pp. 337–339.

50. Nagahara, *Nihon no chūsei shakai*, p. 217.

51. Hayashiya Tatsusaburō, *Chūsei geinō shi no kenkyū: Kodai kara no keishō to sōzō* (Tokyo: Iwanami Shōten, 1975), pp. 269–280. The *Chūyūki* text fragment is presented on p. 271.

52. Kita Teikichi, "Sanjo hōshi kō: Kodai shakai sōshiki no kenkyū," *Minzoku to rekishi* 1, no. 3 (1921): 125.

53. Ibid., pp. 128–130.

54. "Belief in *marebito*" is how most folklorists in Japan have referred to the events and symbols surrounding the visiting stranger. Although I use the term below, following other scholars writing on Japanese popular religion, it seems unfortunate to lump this important constellation of ritual and highly imaginary symbolic action under the rubric of "belief." The use of this word greatly limits our appreciation of how these rituals worked in Japanese society. If people did not "believe" in these visitors, does that mean their ritual appearance could not have some sort of symbolic affect on the community? It seems to me that these nomenclature born in the Protestant Reformation and absorbed by the Japanese folklore movement confuses the data and veils the significance of these customs as ritual and symbolic expressions of a more subtle ideology of the cosmos. It reduces our understanding of why ritual actions are experienced as powerful and transformative by people.

55. Origuchi's discussion of marebito is scattered throughout his large collected works. His work on this subject has recently been called into question by scholars in the field of Japanese religions, for they claim that he based his definitive discussions of marebito on scant evidence and flights of fancy with the data. His tendency to base assumptions about the "essence of the Japanese mind" on ancient sources, an approach to Japanese folklore studies he championed, undeniably places him in the nativist tradition of the *kokugaku* scholars, and consequently the nationalist agenda of his work cannot go unexamined. Nevertheless, many scholars have also recognized that while Origuchi's evidence was at times scant and his method highly poetic at best, his insights were remarkable, and his discussion of marebito reflects a shared meaning and structure in a large number of disparate sources in Japanese religious history. With this in mind, we will briefly review the basic pattern of marebito belief, as set forth by Origuchi, Hori, and others from the Japanese folklore studies movement.

56. Origuchi Shinobu, *Origuchi Shinobu zenshu*, ed. Origuchi Hakase Kinen Kodai Kenkyūjō (Tokyo: n.p.), 2:33–37.

57. Yoshiko Yamamoto, *The Namahage: A Festival in the Northeast of Japan* (Philadelphia: Institute for the Study of Human Issues, 1978).

58. The map on p. 17 in Yamamoto, *Namahage*, shows the distribution of these "New Year's visitors" practices throughout Japan.

59. This term also includes a number of performances that do not use puppets. An exhaustive study of this interesting class of performances is Park Jon Yul, *Kadozuke no kōzō* (Tokyo: Kōbundō, 1989).

60. See Chie Nakane, *Japanese Society* (Harmondsworth: Penguin Books, 1973). See also Emiko Ohnuki-Tierney, *Illness and Culture*.

61. Michele Marra, *Representations of Power*, p. 68.

62. For this reading of the term, I am following the suggestion of Morita Yoshinori. See his *Chūsei senmin zō geinō no kenkyū* (Tokyo: Yusankaku, 1981), p. 117.

63. The name is written with those four characters but is also seen written with the characters "a thousand good things (*kotobuki*) ten thousand years."

64. We will see vestiges of this performance form in the discussion of the Shiki Sanbasō rite in chapter 5, which borrows much of the language. One character even asks the other to "dance to Senzu Manzai."

65. In some parts of Japan, these performers were simply called *manzai*.

66. Quoted in Morita, *Chūsei senmin zō geinō no kenkyū*, p. 125. This passage is also mentioned by Hayashiya Tatsuburō in his *Chūsei geinō shi no kenkyū*, pp. 320–321.

67. This practice is widely described. Comparative studies from other parts of the world indicate that strangers often carry a marker to indicate that they come in peace or to identify them as coming from outside the village they are entering. By marking themselves as such, they minimize the fear that they are trying to cause trouble, since they are openly admitting that they are outsiders.

68. Misumi Haruo, *Nihon minzoku geinō gairon* (Tokyo: Tōkyōdō Shuppan, 1974), p. 151.

69. Written with the characters "hail (the precipitation) running."

70. W. G. Aston, trans. *Nihongi: Chronicles of Japan from the Earliest Times to A.D. 697* (Rutland, Vt.: Charles E. Tuttle, 1972), p. 411. See also references on pp. 414, 421. Aston points out that the other name for *ararebashiri* performances was *manzairaku*. From this series of references, it is possible to discern that tōka performances of some sort were popular at court from this early period and were understood to be ritual performances for the longevity of the sovereign.

71. Morita, *Chūsei senmin to zō geinō no kenkyū*, p. 123.

72. It is not possible to determine whether or not the Senzu Manzai is directly derived from the practice of reciting tōka, but the commonalities between these two performance traditions are striking enough to give the theory some weight.

73. Morita, *Chūsei senmin to zō geinō no kenkyū*, p. 125. Morita also points out that the practice of Namahage in the Akita region of Japan is also an example of this belief.

74. Misumi, *Nihon minzoku geinō gairon*, pp. 170–180.

75. Erika Gerlinde de Poorter, trans., *Motoyoshi's Sarugaku Dangi: A Description and Assessment with Annotated Translation* (Leiden, 1983), p. 156. In her note on this section, the translator defines matsu-bayashi as follows: "Special sort of music with dancing which was performed at New Year and was very popular in the first half of the 15th century. It was presented by singing monks or ordinary people. They visited the residences of noblemen and performed this music, for which they were then rewarded" (p. 277). De Poorter's annotated translation of *Sarugaku Dangi* contains excellent source material in the notes.

76. My discussion of these aspects of kadozuke is informed in part by Origuchi Shinobu's analysis, cited in Jacob Raz, *Audience and Actors: A Study of Their Interaction in the Japanese Theatre* (Leiden: E. J. Brill, 1984), pp. 36–41.

77. See Ninomiya, "Inquiry Concerning Eta," p. 118.

78. Gerd Baumann, "Ritual Implicates 'Others': Rereading Durkheim in a Plural Society," in *Understanding Rituals*, ed. Daniel de Coppet (London: Routledge, 1992), p. 98. Baumann argues out the problems with this series of assumptions by looking at rituals in what can clearly be considered pluralistic societies. The multi-ethnic London suburb of Southall is his chief example.

79. Edmund Leach, *Culture and Communication: The Logic By Which Symbols Are Connected* (Cambridge: Cambridge University Press, 1976), p. 45, cited in Baumann, "Ritual Implicates 'Others,' " p. 97.

80. The jōruri tradition, though under the threat of total demise, was not yet completely defunct.

81. This was said to me by an old man living in the village of Fukura on Awaji in 1988, as he remembered the childhood visits of the puppeteers from the early part of this century.

82. Hajime Nakamura, *Ways of Thinking of Eastern Peoples* (Honolulu: University of Hawaii Press, 1971), p. 587.

83. Robert J. Smith, forward to Yamamoto, *Namahage*, pp. 1–2.

Chapter 3: A Crippled Deity, a Priest, and a Puppet

1. J. Z. Smith, "Influence of Symbols," p. 131.

2. This case is significant because it has been argued that later kugutsu groups developed out of the puppetry groups affiliated with the Usa shrine.

3. All translations of and emphases in this text are mine. I translate the entire text and discuss this rite in detail in "Violence, Ritual Reenactment, and Ideology: The Hōjō-e (Rite for Release of Sentient Beings) of the Usa Hachiman Shrine in Japan," *History of Religions* 3, no. 4 (May 1994): 325–357.

4. This twist on the story clearly reveals the role of Hachiman belief in the spread of belief in *goryō* (malevolent spirits of the deceased). A discussion of the Gion festival as a *goryō-e* can be found in Neil McMullin, "On Placating the Gods and Pacifying the Populace: The Case of the Gion *Goryō* Cult," *History of Religions* 27, no. 3 (February 1988): 246–269. See also Ichirō Hori, *Folk Religion in Japan: Continuity and Change* (Chicago: University of Chicago Press, 1968), 115.

5. Corresponding to 724 C.E. The note is in the text and was probably added to make the various accounts of the rite agree.

6. This is also a common theme in early Chinese martial treatises and tales. The recent film *To Live* by the Chinese filmmaker Zhang Yimou casts this issue of puppeteers in battle in a modern light when two shadow puppeteers are taken prisoner and manage to survive by performing for the Red Army during the fight against the Kuomintang.

7. See Gina L. Barnes, *Protohistoric Yamato: Archaeology of the First Japanese State* (Ann Arbor: University of Michigan Press, 1988), pp. 269–277.

8. Yamagami Izumo, *Miko no rekishi*, chapter 1.

9. See Nakano Hatayoshi, *Hachiman shinkō-shi no kenkyū* (Tokyo: Yoshikawa Kōbunkan, 1976), 1:92–93.

10. While on one level this problem seems arcane, the issue of the "uniqueness of Japan" is a central ideological point in much Japanese scholarship relating to ritual performance.

11. Cited in Misumi Haruo, *Sasuraibito no geinō shi* (Tokyo: NHK Books, 1974), p. 35.

12. See Dunn, *Early Japanese Puppet Drama*, pp. 64–65.

13. Tsunoda, *Ningyō geki no seiritsu ni kan suru kenkyū*, pp. 198–204. We assume that Tsunoda's "gypsies" are Eastern European Greek puppeteers.

14. Donald Keene, *Bunraku : The Art of the Japanese Puppet Theatre* (Tokyo: Kodansha International, 1973), p. 19.

15. Ibid., p. 20.

16. Tsunoda, *Ningyō geki no seiritsu ni kan suru kenkyū*, p. 352.

17. The standard version of this text used by scholars is found in *Gunsho ruijū* (Collection of texts), vol. 9 (1928), pp. 324–325. I have used this text in my translation, though many reliable versions are available scattered throughout Japanese secondary sources on performance and puppetry. For a discussion and partial translation of the text in English, see Donald Keene, *Bunraku*, p. 20. In German, a translation appears in Hagen Blau's *Sarugaku und Shushi: Beiträge zur Ausbildung dramatischer Elemente im weltlichen und religiösen Volkstheatre der Heian-Zeit under besonderer Berücksichtigung Seiner Sozialen Grundlagen* (Wiesbaden: Otto Harrassowitz, 1966), p. 235. Kawajiri Taiji presents a version of the text in modern Japanese in his *Nihon Ningyō Geki Hattatsu Shi, Kō* (Tokyo: Bansei Shōbo, 1986), pp. 100–101. For further discussion in Japanese, see Yamaji Kōzō "Kugutsu," in *Chūsei no minshū to Geinō*, ed. Yamaji Kōzō, Mori Fumiko, and Kyoto Buraku Shi Kenkyūjo (Kyoto: Aunsha, 1986), 54–59. Hayashiya Tatsusaburō discusses the text in his *Chūsei geinō shi no kenkyū*, 8th ed. (Tokyo: Iwanami Shōten, 1987), pp. 323–326. These are but a few examples of discussions of this text. To facilitate reading the text in translation, I have added stanzas, divisions following the topic divisions used by most Japanese scholars when discussing the text.

18. Here, Ōe no Masafusa uses the proper name for a group of Chinese performers very popular in Han China, the *yulong manyan zhixi* (literally "transmutations of fish and dragons"). This direct reference in the text indicates Ōe Masafusa's familiarity with Chinese performance. These performers are discussed by Wu Hung in "A Sanpan Chariot Ornament and the Xiangrui Design in Western Art," *Archives of Asian Art* 37 (1984): 38–59. See discussion below.

19. There is a character missing from the text. The word "dazzle" is suggested by Tsunoda.

20. This would indicate that they do not even raise silkworms, since mulberry leaves are food for these insects.

21. The text uses the characters "hyaku shin" (hundred gods). For a complete discussion of the issues raised by this reference in this text, see my article "Of Plagues and Puppets: On the Significance of the Name Hyakudayū in Japanese Religions," in *Transactions of the Asiatic Society of Japan*, 4th ser., 8 (1993): 107–131.

22. The term in the text is *fukusuke*, a ritual object representing a person, decidedly phallic in shape.

23. The women were singers and dancers. A number of the names mentioned here appear elsewhere in texts from the period. It is difficult to know just how the author intended these names to be read, and most scholars tolerate a variety of guesses.

24. The next two lines of the text list types of songs sung by the women. *Imayō* and *Furukawayō* refer to two styles of short poems of an entertaining nature put to music.

25. *ta-uta*

26. *kami-uta*

27. *tōka* The reader will recall the discussion of this performance form in chapter 2.

28. *tsuji-uta*

29. *fuzoku*

30. *hōshi*

31. Yoshinobu Inoura and Toshio Kawatake, *The Traditional Theater of Japan* (New York: Weatherhill, 1981), p. 173.

32. Hayashiya, *Chūsei geinō shi no kenkyū*, p. 323; emphasis mine.

33. Wu Hung "Sanpan Chariot Ornament," p. 53.

34. Tsunoda, *Ningyō geki no seiritsu ni kan suru kenkyū*, pp. 332–335. Also see Keene, *Bunraku*, p. 20.

35. Yamaji "Kugutsu," p. 55.

36. Keene, *Bunraku*, p. 20.

37. Yamaji, "Kugutsu," p. 55.

38. Ibid., pp. 54–59.

39. See Felicia Bock, *Classical Learning and Taoist Practices in Early Japan with a Translation of Books XVI and XX of the Engi-shiki* (Tempe: Center for Asian Studies, Arizona State University, 1985), p. 45.

40. Ibid., p. 83 n. 35. The wood and bark of the peach tree are also medicinal.

41. The ethnobotanist Christine Franquemont suggested to me that "peach-wood" could have been applied to a tree in Japan that did not necessarily correspond to the tree designated by the same characters in China. This, she noted, is a common pattern in the history of early Japanese botany.

42. Charles H. Long, *Significations: Signs, Symbols and Images in the Interpretation of Religion* (Philadelphia: Fortress Press, 1986), p. 1.

43. Cited in Tsunoda, *Ningyō geki no seiritsu ni kan suru kenkyū*, p. 468.

44. Sadafusa, *Kammon gyōki*, vol. 1 (1944), p. 12.

45. The most exhaustive study of drawings of puppeteers in source books is Shinoda Jun'ichi and Ningyō Butai-shi Kenkyūkai, eds. *Ningyō jōruri butai-shi* (Tokyo: Yagi Shōten, 1992). The work includes a detailed discussion of every pictographic reference to puppeteers in Japan that exists. The concern of the book is to trace the development of the jōruri stage, but it includes interesting discussions of the various performances. Pictures were also used to great effect in the reconstruction of the early history of old jōruri by Dunn, *Early Japanese Puppet Drama*. His book includes many drawings of theaters and stages but only one picture of a kugutsu-mawashi (the same one that I include).

46. As reprinted in Shinoda and Ningyō Butai-shi Kenkyūkai, *Ningyō jōruri butai-shi*, p. 191.

47. Ibid., pp. 191–192.

48. The interesting thing about this performance context is that it is identical to one that I have seen on Awaji in recent years (the work of an elderly gentleman who is reviving Ebisu performance), down to the detail of children gathered in the street. I discuss his performance in chapter 6.

49. The box is considered to be the first "stage" of the puppet theater in Japan.

50. Ibid., p. 192.

51. Ibid., p. 194.

52. Ibid., p. 196.

53. Ibid.

54. Ibid.

55. Cited in Morita, *Chūsei senmin to zō geinō no kenkyū*, p. 191.

56. The diary itself spans the period from Bunmei (1469–87) through the end of Edo.

57. See Kotaka Kyō, comp. *Chūsei geinō shi nenpyō* (Tokyo: Meicho Shuppen, 1987), pp. 350–440 (sporadic references in assorted listings).

58. Ibid., p. 438.

59. For an exhausting, if not exhaustive, study of the textual references to changes in this shrine, see Richard Ponsonby-Fane, *The Vicissitudes of Shinto* (Kyoto: The Ponsonby Memorial Society, 1963), pp. 34–80. The reference to *Montoku jitsuroku* is on p. 68. Ponsonby-Fane's detailed and garbled discussion of this shrine confuses the matter in that he insists on referring to it as Hiroda, although by the Kamakura period this was no longer the name used to refer to this shrine.

60. This hypothesis was argued most vehemently by Ponsonby-Fane to support his own theory of spirit aspects. He may not have been wrong, but his evidence is far from convincing.

61. The Hiroda shrine appears to have been divided from the earliest times into two parts, the main shrine (called Hiroda) and the shrine on the southern beach (Hama-minami). Perhaps this is the meaning of the reference to directions in Ōe no Masafusa's snippet. In 1132, there appears to have been a struggle to separate the two shrines into autonomous units. Ponsonby-Fane has suggested that the Hiroda shrine was originally the place for the worship of the rough spirit of Amaterasu, and that "an extraordinary metamorphosis . . . befell Hirota," and this single deity site was transformed into a site where five deities were worshipped, and the identity of Amaterasu Omikami was entirely lost. He notes that this change took place in Jishō 1 (1177). By the mid-Kamakura period, it was again united; and when it was subsequently divided, it became two shrine units, the Hiroda shrine (referred to as the northern *hokora*, or worship site) and the Ebisu shrine. Both were referred to as Nishinomiya after this time, leading to a great deal of confusion that no one (including shrine priests at Nishinomiya) has been able to sort out.

62. For a list of theories ranging from the plausible to the ridiculous explaining the meaning of the name "western shrine," see Yoshii, *Ebisu shinkō to sono fudō*, pp. 380–387. Concerning the Ise theory suggested by Ponsonby-Fane, Yoshii notes that no one in Ise believes it.

63. Yoshii Tarō, "Nishinomiya no kugutsu," in *Minzoku to rekishi* 1, no. 1 (Taisho 8): 29.

64. I discuss the various associations of this name in my article "Of Plagues and Puppets."

65. Morita, *Chūsei senmin to zō geinō*, pp. 196–197. See also Yoshii, "Nishinomiya no kugutsu," p. 30.

66. A hand-drawn plan of the shrine from 1978 can be found in Yoshii Sadatoshi, *Ebisu shinkō to sono fudō* (Tokyo: Kokushō Rikkōkai, 1989), pp. 328–329.

67. Janet Goodwin has written about the role of itinerant sacred specialists in the voluntary donations campaigns of medieval Japanese Buddhist centers. She suggests that this strategy used by Buddhist centers probably "inspired a rash of imitators." For thorough discussions of these methods of securing funds, see her "Alms for Kasagi Temple," in *The Journal of Asian Studies*, 46, no. 4 (November 1987): 827–841.

68. Yoshii, *Ebisu shinkō to sono fudō*, p. 10.

69. Ibid., pp. 15–38, presents twenty-four Ebisu shrine placards depicting Ebisu. Those on pp. 21, 22, 26, 27, 28, 32, and 33 show the standard image of Ebisu as a cheerful old man.

70. Namihira Emiko, "Suishintai o Ebisu to shite matsuru shinkō: Sono imi to kaishaku," *Minzokugaku Kenkyū* 42, no. 4 (March 1978): 334–355.

71. Katō Genchi, "A Study of the Development of Religious Ideas among the Japanese People as Illustrated by Japanese Phallicism," *Transactions of the Asiatic Society of Japan*, 2d ser., supp. to vol. 1 (December 1924): 13, 53–54.

72. Ogura Manabu, "Noto no kuni hyōchakugami no kō," *Kokugakuin zasshi* 55, no. 3 (1954): 30–43. See also Sakurada Katsunori's in-depth study, "Noto no hyōchakugami no kenkyū," *Nihon minzokugaku* 1, no. 4 (1954): 91–94.

73. Sakurada Katsunori, "The Ebisu-gami in Fishing Villages," in *Studies in Japanese Folklore*, ed. Edward Dorson (Bloomington, Indiana University Press, 1963) p. 124.

74. Sakurada, "The Ebisu-gami in Fishing Villages," p. 125.

75. See Yoshii, *Ebisu Shinkō to sono fūdo*, pp. 189–191, for a list of examples.

76. Ibid., p. 3.

77. Namihira, "Suishintai o Ebisu to shite matsuru shinkō."

78. Robert J. Smith, *Ancestor Worship in Contemporary Japan* (Stanford: Stanford University Press, 1974), p. 45.

79. Until the twentieth century, the major event of the Ebisu shrine was a festival in the ninth month on the twenty-sixth day, when the *o-mikoshi* of the Nishinomiya shrine was carried from the shrine precincts along the shore line to the area called Wadahama.

80. Yoshii, *Ebisu shinkō to sono fūdo*, p. 2.

81. In early medieval Japan, the idea that conversations in dreams could be taken literally as instructions to the dreamer was not uncommon. This idea of "conversations while dreaming" (*muchū mondo*) has been introduced by William LaFleur in his *The Karma of Words: Buddhism and the Literary Arts in Medieval Japan* (Berkeley: University of California Press, 1983), pp. 4–8. See also George J. Tanabe, *Myōe the Dreamkeeper: Fantasy and Knowledge in Early Kamakura Buddhism* (Cambridge: Council on East Asian Studies, Harvard University, 1992). While both of these studies argue for a Buddhist interpretation of dreaming, the idea of dreaming as a mode of direct revelation was common in medieval Japan.

82. See for example, the textual references in Richard Ponsonby-Fane, *Visiting Famous Shrines in Japan* (Tokyo: Ponsonby-Fane Memorial Society, 1964), 6:341–342.

83. *Nihon Rekishi Daijiten*, vol. 2, s.v. "Ebisu."

84. Namihira, "Suishin o Ebisu to shite matsuru shinkō" p. 340.

85. Kitagawa, *Religion in Japanese History*, p. 14. For an extensive study of this four-aspect phenomenon, see the tangled discussion by Ponsonby-Fane in his *Vicissitudes of Shinto*, pp. 41–56. It has been argued, based on references to the divine aspects in early texts, that the latter two are actually just aspects of nigi-mi-tama.

86. For example the "rough" spirit of the sun goddess Amaterasu is enshrined in the Ara Matsuri no Miya (literally, shrine for worshipping the rough aspect) at Ise. References to this location are made in prayers number 18, 19, and 22 of the *Norito*. See Philippi, *Norito*, p. 84, s. v. "Ara-matsuri-no-miya."

87. Takeuchi T., in *Nihon shakai minzoku jiten* (Social and folklore dictionary of Japan) (Tokyo: Nihon Minzoku Kenkyūkai, 1960), s.v. "Ebisu."

88. Cited by Philippi in *Kojiki*, p. 399 n. 4.

89. Ibid. This theory of Hiruko as the "sun child" has been most strongly maintained by the French scholar Jean Herbert. See his *Dieux and sectes populaires du Japon* (Paris: Éditions Albin Michel, 1967), p. 112, and *Les dieux nationaux du Japon* (Paris: Éditions Albin Michel, 1969), pp. 54.

90. See the creation myth of the Mande of Africa, recounted in Charles H. Long, *Alpha: Myths of Creation* (New York: George Braziller, 1963), p. 134. That the failed creation is abandoned seems to be a common theme in cosmogonic myths.

91. Cited in Ponsonby-Fane, *Vicissitudes of Shinto*, p. 70.

92. Cited in Namihira, *Kegare no kōzō*, pp. 341–342.

93. Ibid., p. 156. Namihira's discussion of the malevolent aspects of Ebisu is unconvincing (pp. 156–160).

94. Yoshii, *Ebisu Shinkō to Sono Fudo*, p. 137.

95. *Kojiki* 1:29, 3.

96. Ibid. 1:32, 1. References to this realm, which is the land of Japan, usually use simply "The Central Reed Plain," but in prayers various aspects of this long name are often used.

97. Ibid. 1:32; 1:33. Note that Philippi discusses the implications of these failed missions in his notes, p. 120f.

98. Another name for Koto shiro nushi no kami.

99. *Kojiki* 1:35, 9–13.

100. Ibid. 1:36, 10.

101. Ibid. 1:37, 3.

102. Ibid., p. 134f.

103. Izumo is the location where deities who were kicked out of the Imperial Line, such as Susano, are worshipped. It is understood that all the deities in Japan retire here for one month of the year.

104. *Kojiki*, p. 135f.

105. Aston, *Nihongi*, p. 225.

106. This point is made by Philippi in *Kojiki*, p. 131f.

107. *Kojiki* 1:37, 4.

108. Ibid. p. 412 n. 17.

109. Clearly the problem of Kotoshiro nushi's reprisal was of concern in myths at that time. According to Nihongi, a version of the Kotoshiro nushi myth has this

deity transformed into an eight-fathom-long bear sea monster, a menacing character. See Aston, *Nihongi*, p. 61.

110. These prayers have been translated, by Donald Philippi in *Norito: A Translation of Ancient Japanese Ritual Prayers* (Princeton: Princeton University Press, 1990). All wording of titles and translations are from Philippi's edition.

111. Ōkuni nushi and his kin.

112. Philippi, *Norito*, pp. 69–70.

113. The assimilation in this case is a meeting and blending of Buddhist and Shinto systems (*shimbutsu shūgō*), but it is important to keep in mind that other religious sources contributed to the history of Japanese religions.

114. The case of Hachiman is another example of a deity whose name does not appear in the chronicles being moved into mainstream religious worship, although in this case it is largely through identification with Buddhist figures.

115. It is difficult to identify all the diseases that ravaged Japan throughout history, in large part because local names for the same diseases varied, but mainly because historical descriptions of diseases frequently did not provide enough information to identify them. Smallpox, measles, dysentery, cholera, and venereal diseases are, however, readily identifiable from records of epidemics in Japan. Although some scholars argue that bubonic plague existed but was not adequately described in the records to be identified, Ann Bowman Janetta wisely points out that "such arguments are hardly convincing. The symptoms of bubonic epidemic are among the most graphic of diseases," so it is unlikely that anything as symptomatic as bubonic plague would have gone undocumented in Japanese history (*Epidemics and Mortality in Early Modern Japan* [Princeton: Princeton University Press], p. 191). Further supporting the view that Japan did not suffer from bubonic plague epidemics, she writes, "In Austria, a *cordon sanitaire* that was created in 1728 to keep the bubonic epidemic from entering from Turkey was successful, but the quarantine required an enormous effort on the part of the Austrian government. Unlike Austria, Japan had the advantage of being surrounded on all sides by a natural *cordon sanitaire* that was apparently able to keep the bubonic plague out of the country until the end of the nineteenth century" (p. 200).

116. See Hartmut O. Rotermund, *Hōsōgami: ou la petite vérole aisément: matériaux pour l'étude des épidémies dans le Japon des XVIIIe, XIXe siècles* (Paris: Maisonneuve et Larose, 1991) for a discussion of magical practices related to smallpox demons in medieval and early modern Japan. His study mentions Ebisu only in passing on p. 148, and he argues that many of the New Year's rituals of felicity and longevity should be understood within the larger context of epidemic control at a ritual level.

117. Nakajima Yōichirō, *Byōki nihon shi* Tokyo: Yūzankaku, 1988), p. 76, and Fujikawa Yū, *Nihon shippei shi* (Tokyo: Heibonsha, 1969), cited in Jannetta, *Epidemics and Mortality*, p. 68. Janetta points out that several of the intervals listed by Fujikawa were quite great, indicating that perhaps smaller epidemic in between these occurred but were not recorded. So, the number of smallpox epidemics in Japanese history is probably somewhere between fifty five and one hundred.

118. William McNeill, *Plagues and Peoples* (Garden City, N.Y.: Doubleday, 1976), pp. 139–141.

119. Technically, a *dōsōjin* is a spirit which protects travelers. Such spirits also have decidedly sexual overtones and may have been phallic deities. Depictions of *dōsōjin* are often phalli.

120. I have relied on Tsunoda's transcription of this text in *Ningyō geki no seiritsu ni kan suru kenkyū*, p. 399. Takano Tatsuyuki has suggested that the missing character in the quoted passage is "wood," which would give a reading of "the number of these they carve out of wood is in the hundred and thousands." Konishi Jin'ichi suggests, however, that the missing character was probably a comma, making the text read "People carve these by the hundreds and thousands" (ibid.).

121. This refers to the Leech Child.

122. Quoted in Yoshii, "Nishinomiya no kugutsu, p. 28

123. Ibid.

124. "Kōtaku o shinseki shukurin hōsō shugoshingo." The calligrapher referred to in this piece was Hosoi Kōtaku, a famous neo-Confucian scholar, famed calligrapher, and man of letters who lived from 1658 to 1735. For this translation, I have used the transcription in Tsunoda, *Ningyō geki no seiritsu ni kan suru kenkyū*, pp. 417–418.

125. One would hope that a sentence like this would serve as a reminder to contemporary historians and ethnographers never to assume that the obvious may be omitted from descriptions or discussions. Frequently the obvious that ties together many uncertain threads is the most vulnerable to omission in the historical record.

126. Yoshii, "Nishinomiya no kugutsu," pt. 1, p. 29.

127. Smallpox was largely a disease afflicting children. Janetta has documented and analyzed the records of infant and childhood deaths based on temple records (*kakochō*) during the Tokugawa period. See Jannetta, *Epidemics and Mortality*, pp. 61–107.

128. Bock, *Engi-Shiki*, p. 20.

129. Yoshii, "Nishinomiya no kugutsu," p. 30.

130. The play *Amida's Riven Breast* has been translated into English by C. J. Dunn in *Early Japanese Puppet Drama*, pp. 111–134.

131. Cited in Shinoda and Ningyō Butai-shi Kenkyūkai, *Ningyō jōruri butai-shi*, p. 195.

132. Yoshii, "Nishinomiya no kugutsu," pt. 1, p. 29. This record of the event at the Hyakudayū shrine is dated Shōtoku 4, the sixteenth day of the eighth month.

Chapter 4: A Dead Priest, an Angry Deity, a Fisherman, and a Puppet

1. Wakamori Tarō, ed., *Awajishima no minzoku* (Tokyo: Yoshikawa Kōbunkan, 1974), p. 3.

2. Miyamoto Tsuneichi, *Setonaikai no kenkyū* (Tokyo: Kadokawa Shoten, 1965), p. 104.

3. Umehara Takeshi, *Ama to tennō*, 2 vols. (Tokyo: Asahi Shinbunsha, 1991).

4. Nakano, *Hachiman shinkō-shi no kenkyū*. See in particular his discussion of the confederation of various tribes into the Usa clan.

5. See Niimi Kanji, *Awaji no ningyō shibai* (Tokyo: Kadokawa Shoten, 1974), p. 17, and Wakamori, *Awaji no minzoku*, 11–13. Although this hypothesis was credited to Wakamori, the bulk of the research was conducted by Handa Yasuo of Oita University. Professor Handa died before the research was published, and so it was published by Wakamori. Wakamori stated in his research reports that he wished credit for this hypothesis to go in part to Handa.

6. Tombs of amazoku were discovered on the tiny island of Okinoshima (about five hundred meters off the southwestern coast of Awaji and actually attached to Awaji during low tide), indicating that the island was settled by these maritime people. There is a curious story connected with this island, which appears to have some truth to it. It is believed that the amazoku buried on this island did not want their tombs to be bothered and that from a very ancient time this island was considered taboo. Oral tradition maintained that any fisherman who went too close to the island would crash on the rocks or drown, or some other terrible calamity would befall him or his family. In the 1950s, ignoring this local legend, a group of archaeologists from Tokyo Kyōiku Daigaku excavated the island, and within several months a number of them met tragic deaths. A year and a half later, according to many informants all of them had died. At the time I wrote my doctoral dissertation, no further research has been done on the tiny island of Okinoshima.

In the summer of 1990, the new owner of the island decided that it had great potential as a tourist attraction, and so he arranged to make it accessible. He hired some workers to clear brush and plant some wildflowers. Sunset cruises to see the tiny island where the amazoku were buried were offered to the public. That summer, I crossed over to the island to look at the tombs with a few other scholars, but we made sure that we were safe and took along elaborate offerings to the spirits of the amazoku in the form of salt, dried fish, rice and sake. When we arrived on the island, we discovered that the workers who had been there to clear brush had taken care of this before us, and a small appeasement stone had been erected for the amazoku. Nevertheless, we made our offerings in earnest before looking at the tombs.

Early in the fall of 1988 and again in the summer of 1990, I tried to follow up on the Usa hypothesis by tracing references to the deity Hyakudayū throughout the Inland Sea. My intent was to determine if the constellation of amazoku tombs, Sanjo districts, appeasement performances, women of pleasure, kugutsu, and epidemics spirits attached to this name might make it possible to suggest that there was a common tradition of ritual puppetry spreading with Hachiman belief of which both Nishinomiya and Awaji were representative centers. This research was both interesting and enjoyable, but in the end I abandoned it. Although still unproved, the hypothesis a bit further developed than when Handa left it. See my article "Of Plagues and Puppets" also Swanberg-Law, "Puppets of the Road," pp. 97–114, 121–148. I have come to the conclusion that we must satisfy ourselves with an inadequate history of ancient origins in the case of this tradition.

7. In her *Shintō minzoku geinō no genryū* Suzuka Chiyono attempts to construct a continuous tradition from the amazoku through Hachiman worship to various puppetry traditions (Tokyo, 1988).

8. This interpretation was mentioned in the early-nineteenth-century text *Awaji no kuni meisho zue*.

9. The reader is referred to chapter 2 and my discussion of the significance of Sanjo districts.

10. Other local versions also maintain that this figure is a *dōsojin*, a protector of travelers. In other locations Hyakudayū was also thought to be a dōsojin. I have suggested elsewhere that the female figure may be Tamayori Hime, or some other shaman.

11. Mihara-gun has several Hachiman shrines, but the major three are the Koda Hachiman shrine, the Kashu Hachiman shrine, and the Fukura Hachiman shrine. There are two main lineages in the Hachiman tradition: Usa, with head-quarters in Oita prefecture's Usa, and Iwashimizu, with headquarters in Kyoto. The Koda and Fukura shrines are in the Usa Hachiman lineage, and the Kashu shrine is in the Iwashimizu Hachiman lineage. Later, the Tsurugaoka, with head-quarters in Kamakura, became an important center of Hachiman belief through its connection with the military rule in Japan during the Kamakura and up through the Tokugawa period.

12. Niimi, *Awaji no ningyō shibai*, p. 18.

13. See a discussion of the phenomenon of *wakamiya* in Yanagita Kunio, "Hito wo Kami ni Matsuru Fūshū," *Yanagita Kunio zenshū* (Tokyo: Sōgeisha, 1968), 7:256–294.

14. The Genroku-era document from Awaji entitled *Awaji tsūki* (Records of a Passage through Awaji) does not mention any of these shrines, although descriptions of shrines and temples is one of the major features of the text. I examined the original text at the Awaji Rekishi Shiryōkan in Sumoto in the summer of 1988.

15. There are many offerings of statuary and structures presented around 1805 in both Koda and Omidō by the Sanjo-mura puppeteers, indicating that they perceived the relationship between these two sites.

16. Niimi, *Awaji no ningyō shibai*, pp. 18–19.

17. All three of these shrines were important in that oracles from them were combined to augment the authority of the imperial family through the religious constructions of Yoshida (Yui-itsu) Shinto.

18. The reader will recall that in chapter 2 we reviewed the significance of Sanjo districts and the meaning of attaching the name Sanjo to a performer's name.

19. Aston, *Nihongi*, pp. 13–17. Sometimes Awaji is counted among the islands and Onogorojima is the placenta. (Readers are encouraged to dust off their Latin for the coital scene in Aston's translation.)

20. About seven kilometers off the southeastern coast of Awajishima, there lies a small island measuring no more than three or four kilometers in length, called Nushima. This island also claims to have the site which is the original Onogo-rojima. On Nushima, one climbs up the steep mountain path and arrives at a small worship hall in which a painted picture depicting Izanami and Izanagi creating the world is hung. The people of Nushima, who numbered around three hundred in 1988, have frequent contact with the people of Awajishima. When questioned as to how there could be two Onogorojimas, an elder on the island of Nushima told me, "Who knows? Who cares? We have it and they have it. It's a pretty place on

Nushima, though, quite sacred, I think." It is likely that other places called Ono-gorojima probably exist throughout the Inland Sea, supporting the suggestion made to me by Joseph Kitagawa that Onogorojima probably denotes a type of sacred space and not an actual place. As this myth got redacted into the *Kojiki* and *Nihongi* narratives, its meaning was transformed.

21. Wakamori, *Awajishima no minzoku*, pp. 2–3.

22. de Poorter, *Motoyoshi's Sarugaku Dangi*, p. 159.

23. Gunji Masakiyo, "Kugutsu no Ki," in *Geinō ronshū*, ed. Honda Yasuji (Tokyo: Kinseisha, 1976), p. 619. Gunji's title is a pun on the title of the text by Ōe no Masafusa discussed in the previous chapter.

24. Goshiki Chō Kenkyūkai, *Goshiki chō shi* (Sumoto: Goshiki Chō Rekishi Kenkyūkai, 1986), p. 488.

25. This discovery was originally announced in *Habataki* (published by the Iwate Ken Bunka Shinkō Jigyō Dan [Iwate Cultural Promotion Group]), no. 6 (20 October 1987): 4. For a complete discussion of the discovery, see Kadoya Mitsuaki and Yamamoto Reiko, "Morioka han no ayatsuri shi suzue shirobē shiryō ni tsuite," *Iwate kenritsu hakubutsukan kenkyū hōkoku*, no. 6 (August 1988): 1–46.

26. The meaning of the suffix "tayū" in the names Hyakudayū and Kikudayū has shifted throughout Japanese history. Originally it was a sign of a court rank. By the late medieval period, it denoted that one was a principal member of a performing group (or that one had a shrine rank).

27. Some later texts say that Hyakudayū "fell in love with and was betrothed to the daughter," reflecting perhaps a concern with the sexual mores of later times.

28. The text uses the word *rinji*, which means "imperial order" and refers to documents such as the one mentioned above, dated 1570. It seems that as they traveled around Japan, puppeteers had to carry these documents stating their name (often granted them by an imperial person) and their business.

29. The text was reissued by Fukuura Kobundō in 1972.

30. Meisho zue frequently were geared to regions which were adjacent to, or part of, major pilgrimage routes, since a pilgrimage was a socially acceptable way to take a nice trip. Awaji is near the Shikoku pilgrimage route, and one could take a ferry from what is now Tokushima to the southern tip of Awaji. There were also miniature pilgrimages on Awaji, called *mame-junrei*, modeled on the larger routes such as Shikoku and Saikoku. See *Kodansha Encyclopedia of Japan*, s.v. "meisho zue."

31. Misumi Haruo notes that this motif of the supernatural stranger marrying a woman in the village is a common theme in performance traditions in Japan. He recounts the following storyline: One night a stranger appears in town and is allowed a night's lodging. That night, he has sex with a woman. In the morning, he goes to the beach, gets into a boat, and disappears on the sea. The girl becomes pregnant and later gives birth to a boy, who is named *Saburō*. He shows exceptional strength and growth, and is made chieftain of the village. This storyline has at least two motifs which have bearing on our discussion of the founder of Awaji puppetry. First, a stranger appears from nowhere and exhibits overt sexual behavior (i.e., gets a woman pregnant). Second, he disappears on the sea, indicating the maritime cosmology of powerful beings that come and go across the sea to the

other world. Third, the offspring has the name Saburō, often associated with Ebisu. These motifs recur in the text translated below, the *Dōkumbō Denki*. Misumi Haruo, "Sasuraibito no gikyoku," in *Geinō shi no minzoku teki kenkyū* (Tokyo: Tokyodō Shuppan, 1976), pp. 218–219.

32. I have looked for records of these litigations and have not been able to find them.

33. The text uses the word *shake*, which denotes a hereditary priest at a shrine. The word can also be used to refer to a *kannushi*, but since the text refers to Mori Kanedayū as a *shake* and to Mori Tango as a *kannushi*, we have to suggest that perhaps the word *shake* was used in a more general sense. Niimi interpolates *shake* as *shinshoku*, which means a shrine priest of lower rank. See Niimi, *Awaji no ningyō shibai*, 14.

34. The text says, "Settsu Amagasaki no Shōnenji to iu tera ni tayori," indicating that he perhaps had friends or family there whom he could "rely upon"—the nuance suggested by "ni tayori."

35. Wandering performers often sang the *Tales of Heike*, and standard narrative styles developed for presenting these stories. These ballad recitations became a broad source for jōruri recitations, which later became puppet plays.

36. A Japanese reader would perhaps understand that a member of the imperial family would not be allowed out of the imperial palace. To explain how the prince was able to see the performance, it was therefore necessary to indicate the circumstances.

37. The text uses the characters "dōjō dōge," which literally mean "those who go up (into the presence of the emperor) and those who stay down."

38. Cited in Niimi, *Awaji no ningyō shibai*, p. 16.

39. The text uses the expression *kido airaku*, which translates roughly as "rejoicing, anger, sorrow, and pleasure," a compound that refers to the range of emotions in jōruri recitation and performing arts in general.

40. Ibid., p. 16.

41. The family mentioned in these texts, the Hikida family, continues to be a powerful family on Awaji even today, and the puppetry group referred to in these texts became the largest and most successful of the jōruri troupes on the island.

42. See Edward Shils, *Tradition* (Chicago: University of Chicago Press, 1981).

43. In Shinoda, *Ningyō jōruri butai-shi*, p. 297.

44. See my discussion of the transformation of myths in the Usa Hōjō-e case in "Violence, Ritual Reenactment, and Ideology."

45. For a transcription of the Kanbun text, see Yamada Shijin, "*Dōkumbō Denki*: Awaji ningyō shibai no shison denshō," in *Dōshisha kokubungaku*, no. 13 (March 1978): 97. The report of Kadoya and Yamamoto, "Morioka han no ayatsuri shi suzue shirobe shiryō ni tsuite," also presents a transcription of the text.

46. The text is also referred to as the *Dōkumbō yurai* and the *Awaji hisho* (Awaji secret letter).

47. See Miyata Noboru, *Jisha engi* (Tokyo: Iwanami Shoten, 1975).

48. These scrolls have recently been relocated to the Mihara Municipal Archives.

49. See Nagata Kōkichi, *Ikite iru ningyō shibai* (Tokyo: Kinseisha, 1983), p. 195. Of these eight documents, I have personally examined all but that in Nagano Prefecture. It is apparent that these scrolls are all transcribed versions of an original document, since they are nearly identical. One version I examined at the Awaji Ningyō Jōruri Kan in Fukura is clearly a later copy of the text. It contains a number of mistakes in the characters and leaves out a few important characters in place-name compounds. These are merely transcription mistakes, not textual variants. Of the eight, two at the Awaji theater and those at the home of Toyota Hisae appear to be quite old. The Morioka text appears to have been recopied within the last one hundred years or so, most certainly from the document taken to Morioka in the middle of the seventeenth century by Suzue Shirobe.

50. The translation is my own. The division of the text into two parts is a device intended to highlight the appropriation of the *Nihongi* narrative as the opening of the document.

51. At this point in the text, Hyakudayū's name has the suffix "Dōkumbō."

52. Literally, the "world-opening island," the place from which the Japanese archipelago was created.

53. Niimi Kanji's discussion of the Awaji text makes the assumption that the Awaji reading of the name as Wakokuzaki rather than Wadazaki (or Wada hama) is an error. See his *Awaji no ningyō shibai*, p. 18.

Chapter 5: Puppets of the Road, Puppets of the Field

1. The term *ayatsuri* was also used to refer to puppeteers during the nineteenth century, but this term was not tied to ritual puppetry per se, whereas the term *Dōkumbō-mawashi* particularly meant a person who performed Ebisu or Sanbasō rites.

2. Numerous scholars in Japan have discussed the origins and development of the Sanbasō rite outside of the Noh tradition. I suggest that by looking at other rites which resembled the Sanbasō performance, it is easier to trace its history. Quite a number of references to *Senzu manzai hōshi* (probably human beings and not puppeteers) performing with Daikoku dancers (Daikoku being a deity coupled with Ebisu) from the fifteenth and sixteenth centuries suggest that these two types of performances were paired. The Sanbasō and Ebisu pair that we see in the Awaji tradition, I suggest, grows out of this earlier pairing of Senzu manzai and Daikoku.

3. Neary, *Political Protest*, p. 12.

4. Niimi, *Awaji no ningyō shibai*, pp. 169–170.

5. I was unable to interview people off Awaji, as it was not possible to find villages where one could be sure ritual puppeteers had performed. During the years I lived in the Kansai area, I encountered several elderly people who recalled Awaji puppeteers coming at the New Year. Performances in Kōbe, Osaka, and the area around Kyoto were common until the 1930s according to people on Awaji. Shikoku, particularly the Awa region, has large numbers of ningyō-mawashi.

6. Both were considered to be of lower status than puppeteers working in the theaters manipulating jōruri puppets.

7. It is possible that this distinction between locations of performance is based on the Tempō reforms (1830–44), designed to exacerbate the distinction between outcasts and the peasantry so as to increase the control of the shogunate over their peasants' tax base, upon which the shogunate was largely dependent for capital. One portion of these reforms forbade an outcast from stepping beyond the entryway to a peasant's home. Kobayashi Shigeru, "Kinsei ni okeru buraku kaihō tōsō," *Rekishi koron*, no. 6 (June 1977): 87–94.

8. Though common throughout the Japanese performing arts, it originated in the Sarugaku tradition and was originally presented by Shushi performers. This ritual performance was presented throughout Japan by itinerant performers from as early as the late eleventh century up through the postwar period, with, needless to say, considerable variation and development in its ritual context and performance style. The fundamental structure of the ritual, from the puppets and ritual chant used to the various symbols displayed during the rite, shows remarkable continuity throughout Japanese history.

9. Note the parallel between this conception of the characters in the rite and the perception of the performers as itinerant others, discussed below.

10. In these other performing arts, there is a strict distinction between the dance of Okina (*Okina-mai*) and the dance of Sanbasō (*Sanbasō-mai*). In the case of ritual puppetry, however, the Sanbasō performance has absorbed the dance of Okina and the terms are used interchangeably at times, leading to no small amount of confusion for scholars not familiar with puppetry rituals but aware of the ritual repertoire in other performing art forms in Japan. In the tradition of Sanbasō performance, Sanbasō is often closely identified with the Leech Child. Some variations of the oral tradition even equate the two, and thus the actions of this character in the performance, which are graceful and ritually potent, show the power of a failed creation (abandoned on the sea by his parents), a fine example of "negative capability."

11. This strategy was suggested to me by Karen Brazell.

12. This typology was explained to me by Umazume Masaru.

13. Nagata, *Nihon no ningyō Shibai*, p. 89.

14. This practice also sheds light on the role of Hyakudayū as an epidemic spirit at the Nishinomiya shrine, as seen in chapter 3.

15. Neary, *Political Protest*, p. 22.

16. Niimi, *Awaji no ningyō shibai*, pp. 179–180.

17. In versions of the Sanbasō rite in Kagura, Kabuki, and Noh, the dance of Sanbasō is largely seen as a humorous skit. This is probably a later interpretation of the earlier shamanic dance, perhaps to make fun of the frenzied gestures of shamans in trance. A number of other Sanbasō dances around Japan, however, are quite ribald. (For example, he is present at his own conception and crawls up between his parents as they are making love.)

18. Sometimes masks are put on two or even three of the puppets, and they all get possessed, although this seems to be a variation of the performance dependent largely on the number of performers available and the desire for real dramatic force.

19. This is my interpretation of the significance of the hat's design.

20. Maurice Bloch, "Symbols, Song, Dance and Features of Articulation: Is Religion an Extreme Form of Traditional Authority?" *European Journal of Sociology* 15 (1974): 55–87.

21. The implication here is that vomiting, unlike defecation, is beyond one's control, and hence he should not be seen as guilty of an offense.

22. Philippi, *Kojiki*, pp. 79–80; emphasis mine.

23. Ibid, pp. 80–81.

24. Laurel Rasplica Rodd, trans. *Kokinshū: A Collection of Poems Ancient and Modern* (Princeton: Princeton University Press, 1984), p. 35.

25. Konishi Jin'ichi, *A History of Japanese Literature*, vol. 2, *The Early Middle Ages*, trans. Aileen Gatten, ed. Earl Miner (Princeton: Princeton University Press, 1986), p. 113. Konishi sees the medieval Japanese perception of the spirit of words as influenced by another strain of magical language in Japanese religions, namely the concept of *dhāranī* from esoteric Buddhism.

26. Gary L. Ebersole, *Ritual Poetry and the Politics of Death in Early Japan* (Princeton: Princeton University Press, 1989), p. 19. In chapter 1, "Ritual Poetry in the Court," Ebersole discusses the ritual potency of song and poetry. See especially pp. 17–23.

27. Frank Hoff has translated a number of ritual chants used in related Okina rites. He correctly situates these poetic texts within their performance context to render the cryptic lines meaningful. Hoff, "The 'Evocation' and 'Blessing' of *Okina*: A Performance Version of Ritual Shamanism," *Alcheringa/Ethnopoetics*, n.s., 3, no. 1 (1977): 48–60.

28. The text of the Sanbasō rite is the Noh text of the Dance of Okina. In most puppet versions of Sanbasō, large parts of the performance have been rendered incomprehensible through what can only be regarded as a misunderstanding of the classical lines in the text by performers, who then handed down the variations to subsequent generations. I have found the meanings of using what could be considered a garbled text to be interesting, but for the purposes of this discussion, I have followed the advice of the Noh scholar Karen Brazell and have used the Noh yōkyoku to "reconstruct" the text.

29. I discuss the significance and possible meaning of these utterances below. Possible origins and meanings of these syllables have been suggested. The Russian linguist of Japanese and Ural Altaic languages, Sasha Vovin, has suggested that the words come from ancient Korean and may be references to the moon.

30. These images reinforce the visual imagery flashing into view on the puppet's costumes. References to the crane and turtle are twofold. The costume of Sanbasō has detailed drawings of both cranes and imaginary turtles. The colors of his costume—red, white, black, and gold—are colors used to depict the *senba zuru* (thousand-year crane), a white bird with a gold-colored beak, a red crest, and black under its wings. The turtle, in addition to the picture on Sanbasō's costume, is represented in the costume of Senzai by the six-sided motif. This shape is also stitched onto the bottom of Sanbasō's hat.

31. The line is from *Ryōjin hishō*.

32. Here, the meaningless syllables are transformed into onomatopoeia. "Dō dō dō" suggests the thundering sound of a waterfall.

33. The Japanese for "three songs" is *sankyoku*, and can refer to three styles of music in Noh, namely the *ryūsen*, which imitates the sounds of flowing water, the *takuboku*, which is a woodpecker, and the *yōshinsō*. Each type of refers to a different use of performed sound to imitate the natural world. Imitative magic in the ritual (described by the general term *nazoraeru*) implies in this case the ability of language, when performed in the proper ritual context, to create the realities to which it refers.

34. The "old men" are to Okina, Senzai, and Sanbasō, who have been summoned by the music, chanting, and felicitous imagery.

35. This is literally the "dance of ten thousand years," used widely in felicitous occasions in Japanese performing arts. Recall the discussion of the tōka dance and Senzu manzai in chapter 2.

36. It is interesting that in the puppet version of this performance, as opposed to the Noh version, masks are used to denote possession. It is possible that originally putting masks on puppets was a way that puppeteers imitated the Noh theater by doing *ayatsuri Noh*, discussed briefly in chapter 3.

37. The term *kami asobi* (deity play or playing with the sacred) refers to the aspect of a *matsuri* which is intended to entertain, and thus appease, the deity who has been invoked.

38. Genjōraku, literally "going to the capital music," refers also to a type of Gagaku dance, in which a snake is subdued by a person wearing a demon mask.

39. The Japanese line appears to leave the subject intentionally ambiguous. The line could also be read, "Together we enjoy the voice made by the pine trees and the wind." In this final line of the text, the ambiguity of the relational aspect of the language allows all the disparate threads of the text—the dancers, the imagery, and the audience—to be woven into one final moment.

40. One interpretation of these syllables, apparent in notes on the Noh versions of this piece, suggest that these syllables are intended to be the human voice imitating the musical instruments which are used to lure deities, namely the tsuzumi and fue (a small handheld drum and flute). *Yōkyoku zenshū*, vol. 12 of *Nihon ongaku zenshū* (Tokyo: Nihon Ongaku Zenshū Kikokai, 1948), p. 92 n. The entire Noh version of this chant, "Okina," is transcribed in this collection, although it differs from the puppet version on some points. The Noh version presents Okina as the *shite* (principle role), Senzai as the *tsure* (subordinate role), and Sanbasō as the Kyogen actor (a humorous acting position, vulgar in contrast to the refined Noh sensibilities).

41. A kalpa is defined by Sir Monier Monier-Williams' Sanskrit-English dictionary as "a fabulous period of time (a day of Brahmâ or one thousand Yugas, a period of four thousand, three hundred and twenty millions of years of mortals, measuring the duration of the world; a month of Brahmâ is supposed to contain thirty such kalpas; according to the *Mahâbharata*, twelve months of Brahmâ constitute his year, and one hundred such years his lifetime; fifty years of Brahmâ's are supposed to have elapsed, and we are now in the Svetavârâha-kalpa of the fifty first; at the end of a kalpa the world is annihilated. . . . with Buddhists, the kalpas are not of equal duration." Whether one accepts the orthodox Sanskrit definition of a kalpa or the reference to time or defines the term as the length of time needed to wear down a rock with a robe of feathers, the reference is to a very long time.

Since it is an incantation for longevity and fertility, it is optimistic indeed. Sir Monier Monier-Williams, *Sanskrit English Dictionary* (Oxford: Oxford University Press, 1979), s.v. "kalpa." (In a Pali narrative explaining a cognate term, *kappa*, the robe of feathers is a silk cloth.)

42. Across the Naruto Straits from Awaji there lived an Ebisu-kaki who continued to make rounds with his puppet until the early 1950s. A number of photographs in folklore books and studies of the Inland Sea show this puppeteer carrying his smiling puppet, which was about half his height. In many of the photographs, he is standing holding his puppet at the entrance to a house, dressed casually and with a bag on his back, as if going on a stroll. See for example the clear photograph in Kawajiri, *Nihon ningyō geki hattatsu shi—kō*, p. 90.

43. Gunji, "Kugutsu no Ki," p. 619.

44. This practice still continues, and all o-fuda, protective talismans (*o-mamori*), and other religious articles of this sort are taken to shrines during the New Year period and burnt in a receptacle for the disposal of sacred objects (*dondō-yaki*). It is understood that they are "exhausted" from the previous year. The cycle of purity and efficacy must be renewed for the coming year.

45. See the transcription of the Ebisu-mawashi's chant in *Tosa no minzoku geinō*. Niimi also transcribes a popular one from Awaji in *Awaji no ningyō shibai*, pp. 177–179.

46. In theater and ritual studies, there is a great deal of discussion about the issue of transforming rituals into theater. I discuss this issue in greater depth in Chapter 6. To a certain extent the performances by Ebisu- and *Sanbasō-mawashi* in this chapter already reflect the early stages of this process of transformation. This is not wholly a twentieth-century phenomenon, however. During the nineteenth century, when two-, three-, and four-day puppetry festivals (called *ningyō matsuri*) on Awaji became popular, there was great demand to have these itinerant arts made available. Both the Sanbasō and Ebisu pieces then underwent a great transformation and were elaborated into single pieces with several performers and a set script. In the case of Ebisu-mai, rather than the traditional *hitori-zukai* (single puppeteer) method of puppet manipulation, Ebisu is manipulated by three puppeteers. This performance absorbed many motifs and scenes from popular itinerant performances while also coming to resemble more a jōruri performance with chanters, multiple manipulators, and elaborate staging. A striking feature of the Ebisu rite was the addition of a scene at the beginning indicating the kadozuke origins of the rite. Ebisu would appear at a home asking for sake, and the householder would serve the deity with great style (perhaps some staged wishful thinking on the part of puppeteers, who were not always so well treated by hosts in the kadozuke context). This more formalized performance of Ebisu-mai could be presented at these festivals because there was more time to prepare an elaborate performance. The text and performance description of Ebisu-mai presented here reflects this transformation, in which we can see a number of individual scenes fused into one humorous performance. In the rite, since Ebisu catches the first fish of the season, the proper channels for a successful fishing year are acknowledged and a productive and safe year at sea is requested. We will use this stage context as the basis for our discussion because it is the most common, the most representative of the deity's character, and also the most lively. The rite, one of great merri-

ment and intoxication, clearly reveals the unity of performers and audience. The human audience is at once the host of the rite, the recipient of its efficacy, and a participant in its festivities.

47. Sakurai Tokutarō, *Minzoku girei no kenkyū* (Tokyo: Yoshikawa Kōbunkan, 1987), pp. 153–154.

48. Mura Torasuke, *Awaji nōgake jōruri shibai*, pp. 104–111.

49. This is the same collective that agreed to a "reenactment" of Ebisu-mai on the island of Susaki in Fukura harbor in 1990. See the discussion in chapter 6.

50. From photo in Mune, *Awaji nogake jōruri shibai*, p. 106.

51. Ibid.

52. Ibid., p. 107.

53. This is a recessed area in a home or office used to display pieces of artwork, flower arrangements, etc. See ibid., p. 105.

54. At the Ebisu festivals I attended during my studies on Awaji, when presenting oneself before the shrine, one drinks a small cup of sake with the deity. While this is also done in shrines dedicated to other kami, it is a very important part of the worship at an Ebisu festival, as this deity likes to drink.

55. Ibid., pp. 108–109.

56. A common feature of Ebisu festivals was the large amount of alcohol consumed. A village could usually afford to host only one of these festivals a year at best. Today on Awaji there has been a real effort to reduce the consumption of alcohol at these festivals, because local campaigns to address alcoholism have had far-reaching effects. But numerous people told me about how drunk people used to get at these festivals.

57. An important part of Ebisu-mai was the distribution of o-fuda depicting Ebisu to people in fishing villages. O-fuda were understood to embody the power and sacred authority of the central shrines (usually Nishinomiya) wherever they were hung. They were frequently put in the small kamidana in the cabin of a boat and invoked the presence of the deity. An o-fuda was sometimes understood to have magical abilities, as in the case of Hyakudayū o-fuda described in chapter 3. The central shrine for Ebisu worship in Japan, as we saw in chapter 1, was the Nishinomiya Ebisu Daimyōjin Shrine. Because puppeteers presenting the Ebisu-mai throughout Japan were technically sacred specialists representing this shrine, the o-fuda they distributed were those bearing the name Nishinomiya. For this reason, Ebisu-kaki presenting the Ebisu rite had to have prior approval of the Nishinomiya shrine. As we have noted, the relationship between these puppeteers and the ceremonial centers was often a strained one, because the puppeteers became popular and introduced their own popular interpretations of Ebisu worship into the performance. Nevertheless, the arrival of the Ebisu-kaki at New Year with the new and fresh o-fuda for the worship hall of the local Nishinomiya shrine served to revitalize the shrine and restore contact with the ceremonial center, no matter how far away. When the puppeteer brought with him the sacred power and authority of the ceremonial center and bestowed it on the small worship sites scattered around the Inland Sea, he was performing a service for people too busy to make annual pilgrimages to Nishinomiya to procure ritual implements such as o-fuda.

58. This translation is based upon the text used by the Awaji puppet theater and supplied to me by the theater director. An alternate version used by the Tosa Ebisu-mawashi (across the straits on Shikoku) can be found in Takagi Keio, ed., *Tosa no geinō: Kochi ken no minzoku geinō* (Kochi-shi, 1986), pp. 287, 288.

59. The Japanese is *inui no hō yori* (from the direction of *inui*). *Inui* corresponds to northwest and is a direction in the Taoist cosmology.

60. Literally, "the best god of luck in the three countries." The reference is to the three realms from Shinto and popular Japanese cosmology: the realm of human beings (Utsushiyo), the realm of the dead (yomo-tsu-kuni), and the realm of heaven (Takama ga hara).

61. O-mikki (sake for the gods), used for special ritual purposes.

62. A *sakazuki*, a small flat cup, is used for serving sake on ceremonial and polite occasions.

63. The name of the era in which he is said to be born is fictitious, written with the characters meaning "luck" and "virtue." To be born on the third day of the first year of an era, just before sunrise, is as felicitous a time of birth as one can imagine. A child born easily is also thought to be extra lucky.

64. *Ubuyu*. In Japan, there is the custom of giving a newborn baby a bath in ritually prepared water to remove the pollution of childbirth.

65. Ebisu is always depicted wearing a *kazaori eboshi,* a type of black hat carefully folded to flop over on one side.

66. Some people remember their family's giving sake ceremoniously to the *dōkumbō-mawashi* at New Year.

67. I have been told that in some versions of this performance, once the names of all actual fish have been given, Ebisu starts to make up names to get the chance to drink more. Sometimes, this rite is performed for occasions other than good fishing. In such a case, the event for which it is performed is inserted here. For example, if the piece is presented at a local school gathering, the wish may be for "good studies." At a home for the elderly, it may be for "good health." At a summer rural festival, for "a good harvest," etc. Again, if the event is other than a fishing rite, appropriate and frequently very clever wishes are inserted throughout this section, much to the amusement of the audience as the performers are able to second guess people's real intentions for participating in the rite. Performers can also interject comments about individuals in the audience, usually with a slight element of teasing.

68. These are place-names near Awaji, which can be changed to indicate any place from which fishermen set out.

69. At this point in the performance, the puppeteer may perform famous dances and skits from other Japanese traditions, showing off his prowess and knowledge. This extends the performance and creates an entertainment rite within the rite.

70. In the original these last lines are *"Oki wa tairyō, oka wa manzaku, shōbai hanjō, tsukisenu godai koso medetakere."*

71. *Eda mame* are soy beans in the pod, prepared by par boiling them in salt water. They are eaten cold as a snack.

72. Niimi, *Awaji no ningyō Shibai*, p. 165.

73. An excellent photographic record of the *nogake butai jōruri* was made by Mune Torasuke and published under the title *Awaji nōgake jōruri shibai* (Tokyo: Sogeisha, 1986).

74. See Hori, *Folk Religion in Japan*, p. 21. While I do not discuss them in any depth, there were also performances held all over this section of Japan on special stages in Hachiman and Ebisu shrines, called *nogakegoya*. These stages differ from their temporary counterparts in that they remain up all year round and tend to be used for a number of events. Kudō Takashi (*Awa to Awaji no ningyō shibai* [Tokushima: n.p., 1978], pp. 95–122) lists in detail the location and style of all the permanent nogakegoya in Tokushima Prefecture. The region of Japan that includes the lower half of Awaji and the adjacent province on Shikoku has the third highest number of "shrine stages."

75. Raz, *Audience and Actors*, p. 28.

76. See for example Izumi Fusako's discussion of Sanbasō in her *Kashira no keitō* (Miyazaki: n.p., 1984), pp. 364–371.

77. This is called in Japanese *kannigiwai*. See Sonoda Minoru, "The Religious Situation in Japan in Relation to Shinto," *Acta Asiatica* 51 (1987): 1–21, esp. 8–12.

78. This sort of performance was last presented at the National Theater by the Awaji troupe in 1960. This *nana-bake* was described to me by Umazume-san in the summer of 1988.

79. In 1988 I interviewed many elderly people concerning what they remembered about the annual performances. Without fail, everyone mentioned the dōgugaeshi as one of the more memorable features of the performances they had seen during the heyday of Awaji puppetry when outdoor performances were the norm.

80. See Mune, *Awaji nōgake jōruri shibai*.

81. For a brief general reference in English, see LaFleur, *Liquid Life*, pp. 144–145.

82. The reverse was also true. A common practice upon the death of a puppeteer was to have his puppets manipulated by other puppeteers to present his funerary rite. On September 1, 1988, the funeral of a famous puppeteer in the Bunraku theater in Japan was carried out in part by his puppets, manipulated by other members of the troupe. The female puppets were dressed in white, as were the unhooded puppeteers manipulating them.

83. My friend Uemura Yasuko gave me some suggestions and cases for this classification.

Chapter 6: Puppets and Whirlpools

1. This organization was founded in 1950 by the Ministry of Education, ostensibly to promote the recognition and preservation of local performance traditions throughout Japan. This new format, with government moneys, was a reformulation of the Kyōdo Buyō to Minyō no Kai (Local Dance and Folk Music Convention), which held annual performances from 1925 through 1936.

2. See, for example, the late 1980s film *MacArthur's Children* (a creative translation of "Setonaikai no Yakyū Kurabu"), set on Awaji during the Occupation. A

brief puppetry scene in the film shows performers from the theater presenting Shiki Sanbasō.

3. The nativist origins of Yanagita's enterprise are carefully set forth in Harootunian, *Things Seen and Unseen*, pp. 418–436. An excellent collection of essays critiquing the agendas of Yanagita's enterprise is J. Victor Koschman, Oiwa Keibō, and Yamashita Shinji, eds., *International Perspectives on Yanagita Kunio and Japanese Folklore Studies* (Ithaca: Cornell University Press, 1985). I also discuss this issue in Swanberg-Law "Puppets of the Road," chapter 1.

4. In his work *Zuroku Nihon no minzoku geinō* (Tokyo: Kinseisha, 1960), published in 1960, Honda established five categories into which folk performance traditions can be classified: *kagura* (performances within Shinto shrines or for Shinto *kami*); *dengaku* (performances connected with the cultivation of rice); *fūryū* (performances used to divert disasters and pestilence); *shukufukugei* (dances and performances presented on felicitous occasions and to bless events); and *gairaimyaku* (performances of foreign, largely Chinese, origin).

5. I would argue that the use of the term *shinkō* to demarcate Japanese religiosity already shows the influence of Western scholarship and conceptions of religiosity, where orthodoxic religion is viewed as normative.

6. A thorough discussion of this legislation and its ramifications over the last three decades in Japan is Barbara E. Thornbury's excellent article "The Cultural Properties Protection Law and Japan's Performing Arts," *Asian Folklore Studies* 53, no. 2 (1994): 211–227. The chronology of this discussion is drawn from her study.

7. I discuss this ritual in "Violence, Ritual Reenactment, and Ideology."

8. Many of the photographs of prewar and early postwar performances in this book were taken by Fudō Saiichi.

9. Fred Davis, *Yearning for Yesterday: A Sociology of Nostalgia* (New York: Free Press, 1979), pp. 1–2.

10. Ibid., p. 2f.

11. After surveying university students in the mid 1970s, Davis reports that while only half of the students associated the word nostalgia with homesickness, many more associated it with "warm, old times, childhood, yearning." Ibid., p. 4f.

12. Ibid., p. 6.

13. Stephen Nussbaum, introduction to Yanagita, "The Evolution of Japanese Festivals: From *Matsuri* to *Sairei*," in Koschmann, Oiwa, and Yamashita, *International Perspectives on Yanagita Kunio*, pp. 168–69.

14. Raymond Williams, *The Country and the City* (New York: Oxford University Press, 1973).

15. Fredric Jameson, "Postmodernism, or the Cultural Logic of Late Capitalism," *New Left Review*, no. 146 (September/October 1984): 53–92.

16. Ibid., p. 85.

17. Ibid., p. 66.

18. Ibid., p. 71.

19. Davis, *Yearning for Yesterday*, p. 31.

20. Jameson, "Postmodernism," p. 72.

21. Ibid., p. 73.

22. Harootunian argues that this feature of the contemporary folklore movement has its roots in the Tokugawa nativist movement (*kokugaku*). By the early nineteenth century, the kokugaku agenda had shifted from reclaiming a philosophically "authentic" Japanese spirit to the formulation of a theory of peasantry. Such a theory of peasants and peasant labor addressed a growing need for a coherent social discourse to maintain the social order in the face of the growing unrest with the rigid class system. This theory of peasantry, writes Harootunian, was most clearly formulated by Hirata Atsutane, who equated the *aohitogusa* (literally "blue grass people," his term for "the folk" who spring up everywhere and always grow back and bounce back from even the worst of conditions) with the landless peasants and the Ancient Way (*kodōron*) with agricultural labor. The outcome in this direction in kokugaku was that nativist discourse posited that the world of the peasant became the world of the real, and yet the public and external discourse of what the peasant was and what peasants did was set up not by peasants but by scholars such as Hirata Atsutane. See Harootunian, *Things Seen and Unseen*, pp. 23–25.

23. This thirty-three site pilgrimage route in western Japan (the literal meaning of the route's name) is dedicated to the bodhisattva Kannon (Avalokitesvara in Sanskrit) and is said to have been established in the ninth century. Pilgrimage is another good example of what has come to be considered an "exotic practice." Ian Reader suggests the recent popularity of pilgrimage reflects a nostalgic return to the past. See Ian Reader, "From Asceticism to the Package Tour—The Pilgrim's Progress in Japan," *Religion* 17 (April 1987): 140.

24. Interestingly, the first time I saw this scene performed was at the third puppetry summit in the fall of 1993. Although it was presented by the students from the local high school, it is a shattering piece of theater. Many of the theater enthusiasts with me that day were moved to tears and speechlessness by the scene.

25. This conversation occurred on July 22, 1988, in the theater in Fukura.

26. Renato Rosaldo, *Culture and Truth: The Remaking of Social Analysis* (Boston: Beacon Press, 1989), p. 70.

27. Ibid., p. 69; emphasis mine.

28. Marilyn Ivy, "Discourses of the Vanishing in Contemporary Japan" (Ph.D. diss., Cornell University, 1988), pp. 39–44.

29. I borrow the phrase "a past of things present," a reversal of the Augustinian dictum, from Joseph Kitagawa's article by that name, and I shall make the same point about the uses of history in Japan. See Kitagawa "'A Past of Things Present,'" pp. 43–58, esp. 53–58.

30. Richard Schechner, *Between Theater and Anthropology* (Philadelphia: University of Pennsylvania Press, 1985), p. 75.

31. Ibid., pp. 77–78.

32. See my article "The Puppet as Body Substitute," in *Religious Reflections on the Human Body*, ed. J. M. Law (Bloomington: Indiana University Press, 1995).

33. I attended this ritual performance with about thirty fishermen and my research assistant, Jirō Nakamura, to film the event. Nakamura was at the time a student in the Cornell College Scholar Program.

34. See my discussion of this center in chapter 4.

35. Again, my research assistant Jirō Nakamura was videotaping the performance.

36. Several years after this day, the performer who manipulated the puppets told me that throughout the entire rite and the repetition, tiny ants had crawled up inside his *haori hakama* and were driving him crazy. He said that because this event was being filmed, he did not want to jump up and scream, but had it "only been a real performance" (*honto no shibai dake dattara*), he would have probably done so.

37. Barbara Thornbury mentions the "summit" model being used in preservation of folk performing arts. See her article "From Festival Setting to Center Stage: Preserving Japan's Folk Performing Arts," *Asian Theater Journal* 10, no. 2 (fall 1993): 163–178. She briefly mentions the problems inherent in presenting rituals as stage entertainment.

38. I discuss below how my presence as a foreign Ph.D. was a scripted part of these trips.

39. For example, in the third summit, a new puppetry group from Kobe called "Ningyō Our Kobe" participated. Though strictly amateur, they are working on reviving jōruri in Kobe at a popular level.

40. See Thornbury, "Cultural Properties Protection Law," for a discussion of this view.

41. Sasahara Ryōji, "Kimyō na butai, bimyō na butai: Minzoku geinō taikai to minzoku geinō kenkyūsha," *Minzoku geinō kenkyū*, no. 12 (1990): 13–17.

42. Keir Elam, *The Semiotics of Theatre and Drama* (London: Methuen, 1980), p. 7.

43. Jiri Vetrusky, "Man and Object in the Theater," in *A Prague School Reader on Esthetics, Literary Structure and Style*, ed. Paul Garvin (Washington: Georgetown University Press, 1964), p. 84.

44. See the beautiful black-and-white photographs of farmers meeting to practice jōruri recitation in homes after leaving their muddy farming shoes at the doorstep in Mune Torasuke's collection of photographs, *Awaji nogake Jōruri shibai*, esp. pp. 28, 29. This book, a collection of photographs taken in the early 1960s, shows activities of Awaji puppeteers as they built their temporary stages in the countryside. The collection itself was part of a nostalgic process of "capturing the vanishing."

45. A related point, perhaps overemphasized in Japan these days, concerns the use of whalebone in the inner workings of puppet heads. As this is no longer allowed, puppet-head makers now use plastic, but they claim that one cannot make a puppet head properly without whalebone. This has become an issue in the environmental movement in Japan, as many traditional arts that use whale materials have had to substitute other materials. A return to the traditional is not always in line with a return to a more "eco-friendly" life.

46. I have also noticed this tendency to make the performance less a reenactment and more of a relevant performance among the high school groups performing it on Awaji. At the third ningyō summit in October 1993, the Mihara High School Puppetry Club presented the Ebisu performance. The tayū, a young girl of

only fourteen, was quite powerful, and the script included many references to teenage life and studying for exams, which drew many laughs from the audience.

47. Umazume Masaru, "Awaji ningyō shibai," in *Awaji ningyō kashira*, ed. Hyōgo Kenritsu Rekishi Hakubutsukan (Himeji: Hyōgo Kenritsu Hakubutsukan, 1985), pp. 21–22. My first research trip, after my initial introduction to the area in 1977, was in 1984, when I went to Fukura to set up the field research that began in 1987.

48. His reference, I assume, was to the problem of ritual puppeteers as purifiers and therefore as outcasts.

49. In Japan, unlike the United States, much scholarship on issues of regional interest gets done by high school teachers. Academia is not limited to universities, and frequently there is more exchange between local scholars and national universities than one sees in the United States.

50. Union Internationale des Marionettes, an international consortium of puppeteers and performers with representatives in several countries. The director of UNIMA in Japan is Takeda Shūnosuke, who directs puppet theater in Kanagawa.

Bibliography

Japanese Language Sources

Amano Fumio. "Okina Sarugaku no seiritsu: jōgyōdō shūshōe to no kanren." *Bungaku* 51, no. 7 (1983): 166–177.

Amino Yoshihiko. *Muen, kugai, raku: nihon chūsei no jiyū to heiwa.* Heibonsha Sensho 58. Tokyo: Heibonsha, 1978.

Amino Yoshihiko et al. *Chūsei no tsumi to batsu.* Tokyo: Tōkyō Daigaku Shuppankai, 1983.

Fudō Saiichi. *Awaji ningyō no yurai.* Mihara-gun: Awaji Ningyō Hōzon Kai, 1937.

Fujikawa Yū. *Nihon Shippei Shi.* Tokyo: Heibonsha, 1969.

Fujiwara Toshio. "Shin Sarugakki." In *Kodai seiji shakai shisō*, edited by Yamagishi Tokuhei et al., pp. 133–152. Tokyo: Iwanami Shoten 1979.

Goshiki Chō Kenkyū Kai. *Goshiki chō shi.* Sumoto: Gōshiki Chō Rekishi Kenkyūkai, 1986.

Hamagishi Kōichi. "Kishi tanabe no ebisu matsuri." *Matsuri*, no. 46 (spring 1986): 52–61.

Harada Tomohiko. "Danzaemon Yuishogaki kaidai." In *Nihon shomin seikatsu shiryō shūsei*, edited by Harada Tomohiko et al., pp. 427–428. Tokyo: Sanichi Shobō: 1971.

Hayashiya Tatsusaburō. *Chūsei bunka no kichō.* Tokyo: Tōkyō Daigaku Shuppankai

———. *Chūsei geinō shi no kenkyū: Kodai kara no keishō to sōzō.* Tokyo: Iwanami Shōten, 1960.

Honda Yasuji. *Minzoku geinō saihōroku.* Tokyo: Nihon Hōsō Shuppan Kyōkai, 1971.

———. "Nō no hassei: mikomai kara nō e." *Bungaku* (March 1977): 269–281.

Hori Ichirō. *Minkan shinkō.* Tokyo: Iwanami Shoten, 1951.

———. *Minkan shinkō shi no shomondai.* Tokyo: Miraisha, 1971.

———. *Nihon no shāmanizumu.* Tokyo: Kodansha, 1971.

———. *Wagakuni minkan shinkō shi no kenkyū.* 2 vols. Tokyo: Sōgensha, 1953–1955.

Hyōgo ken shi henshū senmon annai kai. *Hyōgo ken shi.* Tokyo: Kawakita Insatsu Kabushiki Kaisha, 1974.

Ishio Yoshihisa. *Minshu undo kara mita chūsei no hinin.* Tokyo: San'ichi Shobō, 1981.

Iwasaki Toshio. *Honpō shōshi no kenkyū.* Tokyo: Iwasaki Hakushi Gakui-ronbun Shuppan Kōenkai, 1963.

Iwate Ken Minzoku no Kai. *Oshira-sama: oshira-sama shimpojiumu kiroku.* Morioka: Iwate Kenritsu Hakubutsukan Shuppan, 1987.

Izumi Fusako. *Kashira no keitō.* Miyazaki: n.p., 1984.

Kadoya Mitsuaki and Yamamoto Reiko. *Awaji ningyō to Iwate no geinō shūdan.* Morioka: Shigunaru Sha, 1991.

———. "Morioka han no ayatsuri shi suzue shirobē shiryō ni tsuite." *Iwate kenritsu hakubutsukan kenkyū hōkoku,* no. 6 (August 1988).

Kawabata Yoshimizu. "Oita-ken ni okeru kugutsu keitō—geinō mura." Usa-shi, Oita, 1987.

Kawajiri Taiji. *Nihon ningyō geki hattatsu shi—kō.* Tokyo: Bansei Shobo, 1986.

Kimura Hideshirō, ed. *Awaji no kuni meisho zu e.* Vol. 3. Sumoto: Fukuura Bunzo Awaji, 1895.

Kita Keiji. *Hyōgo ken minzoku geinō shi.* Tokyo: Kinseisha, 1977.

Kita Teikichi. "Dōsojin to kaite sai no kami to yomu koto no kō." *Minzoku to rekishi* 1, no. 3 (1921): 297–303.

———. "Sanjo hōshi kō: Kodai shakai sōshiki no kenkyū." *Minzoku to rekishi* 1, no. 3 (1921): 123–126.

Kitahara Taisaku. "Sanjo hōshi kō: kodai shakai soshiki no kenkyū." *Minzoku to rekishi* 3, no. 4 (1921): 1–10.

———. *Senmin no kōei—waga kutsujoku to hankō no hansei.* Tokyo: Chikuma Shobō, 1974.

Kitamura Tetsurō. "Ningyō." *Nihon no bijutsu,* no. 11 (March 1967): 1–30.

Kobayashi Shigeru. "Kinsei ni okeru buraku kaihō tōsō." *Rekishi koron* no. 6 (June 1977): 87–94.

Kotaka Kyō, comp. *Chūsei geinō shi nenpyō.* Tokyo: Meicho Shuppan, 1987.

Kudō Takashi. *Awa to Awaji no ningyō shibai.* Tokushima, 1978.

———. *Nihon geinō no shigen teki kenkyū.* Tokyo: San'ichi Shobō, 1981.

Kuroda Toshio. "Chusei no mibunsei to hisen kannen." *Buraku mondai kenkyū* 33 (1984): 23–57.

Kyoto Buraku Shi Kenkyū Jo. *Chusei no minshū to geinō.* Kyoto: Aunsha, 1986.

Mihara Rekishi Kenkyūkai. *Mihara gun shi.* Mihara-gun: n.p., 1985.

Misumi Haruo. *Geinō shi no minzoku teki kenkyū.* Tokyo: Tōkyōdō Shuppan, 1975.

———. *Nihon minzoku geinō gairon.* Tokyo: Tōkyōdō Shuppan, 1974.

———. *Sasuraibito no geinō shi.* Tokyo: NHK Books, 1974.

Miyamoto Tsuneichi. *Setonaikai no kenkyū.* Tokyo: Kadokawa Shoten, 1965.

Miyata Noboru. *Jisha engi.* Tokyo: Iwanami Shoten, 1975.

———. *Onna no reiryoku to ie no kami.* Tokyo: Jinbunshoin, 1983.

Morita Yoshinori. *Chūsei senmin to zō geinō shi.* Tokyo: Yusankaku, 1981.

Moriya Takeshi. *Geinō to genzō.* Kyoto: Tankosha, 1985.

Mune Torasuke. *Awaji nogake jōruri shibai.* Tokyo: Sogeisha, 1986.

Nagahara Keiji. *Chūsei seiritsuki no shakai to shisō.* Tokyo: Yoshikawa Kōbunkan, 1977.

———. *Nihon no chūsei shakai.* Tokyo: Iwanami Shoten, 1973.

Nagata Kōkichi. *Ikite iru ningyō shibai.* Tokyo: Kinseisha, 1983.

———. *Nihon no ningyō shibai.* Tokyo: Kinseisha, 1974.

———. "Ningyō shibai no kigen shiryō." In *Geinō ronshū,* edited by Honda Yasuji. Tokyo: Kinseisha, 1976.

Nakajima Yōichirō. *Byōki nihon shi.* Tokyo: Yuzankaku, 1988.

Nakano Hatayoshi. *Hachiman shinkō-shi no kenkyū.* Tokyo: Yoshikawa Kōbun-kan, 1976.

Namihira Emiko. *Kegare no kōzō.* Tokyo: Seidōsha, 1992.

————. "Suishintai o Ebisu to shite matsuru shinkō: Sono imi to kaishaku." *Minzoku kenkyū* 42, no. 4 (March 1978): 335–368.

Niimi Kanji. *Awaji no ningyō shibai.* Tokyo: Kadokawa Shoten, 1974.

Niimi Tsuneyuki. "Umigami to Ebisu shinkō." *Matsuri,* no. 46 (spring 1986): 27–48.

————. "Awaji no ningyō jōruri shiryō." *Dentō engeki,* no. 13: 48–58.

Ōbayashi Tarō. *Nihon shinwa no kigen.* Tokyo: Kadokawa Shoten, 1961.

Ogura Manabu. "Noto no kuni hyōchakugami kō." *Kokugakuin zasshi* 15, no. 3 (1954): 30–43.

Oka Masao. *Nihon minzokugaku no rekishi to kadai.* Tokyo: n.p., 1958.

Okamura Akio. *Awaji no bunka.* Sumoto: Awaji Shin'yō Bijutsu Kan, 1960.

Okiura Kazuteru. *Nihon minshū bunka no genryū: hisabetsu buraku no minzoku to geinō.* Tokyo: Kaihō Shuppansha, 1984.

Origuchi Shinobu. "Okina." *Nihon geinōshi rokkō,* no. 2 (1944): 14–28.

————. "Okina no hassei." *Origuchi Shinobu zenshū.* Vol. 2. Tokyo: n.p., 1948.

————. "Okina no kenkyū." *Geinō* 4, no. 6 (summer 1972): 310–366.

————. "Tokoyo oyobi marebito." *Minzoku* 4, no. 1 (1948): 1–62.

Park Jon Yul. *Kadozuke no kōzō.* Tokyo: Kōbundō, 1989.

Sakurada Katsunori. "Noto no hyōchakugami no kenkyū." *Nihon minzokugaku* 1, no. 4 (1954): 91–94.

Sakurai Tokutarō. "Goryō shinkō no hassei to tenkai." In *Goryō shinkō,* edited by Sakurai Tokutarō and Shibata Minoru. Tokyo: Yūzankaku, 1984.

Sakurai Tokutarō and Shibata Minoru, eds. *Goryō shinkō.* Tokyo: Yūzankaku, 1984.

Sasahara Ryōji. "Kimyō na butai, bimyō na butai: Minzoku geinō taikai to minzoku geinō kenkyūsha" *Minzoku geinō kenkyū,* no. 12 (1990): 13–17.

Shinoda Jun'ichi and Ningyō Butai-shi Kenkyūkai, eds. *Ningyō jōruri butai-shi.* Tokyo: Yagi Shoten, 1992.

Suzuka Chiyono. *Shintō minzoku geinō no genruū.* Tokyo, 1988.

Takagi Keio, ed. *Tosa no geinō: Kōchi-ken no minzoku geinō.* Kōchi-shi: Kōchi-shi Bunka Shinkō Jigyōdan, 1986.

Takeda Seiichi. "Nishinomiya kugutsu shi to Awaji ningyō shibai." *Shiritsu Nishinomiya kōkōgakkō kiyō: "hyōron,"* no. 6 (1972): 1–11.

Takeda Shin'ichi and Tokuda Toshiharu, eds. *Awaji junrei.* Tokyo: Michō Shuppan, 1981.

Takeuchi, T. "Ebisu." In *Nihon shakai minzoku jiten* (Social and folklore dictionary of Japan). Tokyo: Nihon Minzoku Kenkyūkai, 1960.

Tsunoda Ichirō. *Ningyō geki no seiritsu ni kan suru kenkyū.* Osaka: Kuroya Shuppan, 1964.

Tsurumi Kazuko, ed. *Yanagita Kunio shū.* Kindai nihon shisō taikei 14. Tokyo: Chikuma Shobō, 1975.

Umazume Masaru. *Awaji ningyō shibai.* Fukura: Awaji ningyō za, 1975.

Umazume Masaru. "Awaji ningyō shibai." In *Awaji ningyō kashira*, edited by Hyōgo Kenritsu Rekishi Hakubutsukan. Himeji: Hyōgo Kenritsu Hakubutsukan, 1985.

Umehara Takeshi. *Ama to tennō*. 2 vols. Tokyo: Asahi Shinbunsha, 1991.

Wakamori Tarō, ed. *Awajishima no minzoku*. Tokyo: Yoshikawa Kōbunkan, 1974.

Watatani Kiyoshi. *Bunraku to awaji ningyō za*. Tokyo: Nara Shobō, 1956.

Yamada Shijin. "*Dōkumbō Denki:* Awaji ningyō shibai shison denshō." *Dōshisha kokubungaku*, no. 13 (March 1978): 91–101.

Yamagami Izumo. *Miko no rekishi*. Tokyo: Yūzankaku, 1984.

———. Nanase harai no genryū. *Kodai bunka* 22, no. 5 (August 1970): 124–151.

Yamaji Kōzō. "Kugutsu." In *Chūsei no minshū to geinō*, edited by Yamaji Kōzō, Mori Fumiko, and Kyoto Buraku Shi Kenkyūjo. Kyoto: Aunsha, 1986.

Yamaji Kōzō, Mori Fumiko, and Kyoto Buraku Shi Kenkyūkai, eds. *Chūsei no minshū to geinō*. Kyoto: Aunsha, 1986.

Yamaori Tetsurō. *Kami kara Okina e*. Tokyo: Seidōsha, 1984.

Yamamoto Shūnosuke. *Sado no ningyō shibai*. Niigata-ken, Sado-gun, Shinmachi: Sado Kyōdō Kenkyūkai, 1976.

Yanagita Kunio. "Hito o Kami ni Matsuru Fūshū." In *Yanagita Kunio zenshū*. Vol. 7. Tokyo: Sogeisha, 1968.

Yokoi Kiyoshi. *Chūsei minshū to seikatsu bunka*. Tokyo: Tokyo Daigaku Shuppan Kai, 1975.

Yoshii Sadatoshi. *Ebisu shinkō to sono fudō*. Tokyo: Kokushō Rikkōkai, 1989.

Yoshii Tarō. "Nishinomiya no kugutsu." *Minzoku to rekishi* 1, no. 1 (Taisho 8): 28–31.

Western Language Sources

Akazawa, Takeru. "Maritime Adaptation of Prehistoric Hunter-Gatherers and their Transition to Agriculture in Japan." In *The Affluent Foragers: Pacific Coasts East and West*, edited by S. Koyama and D. H. Thomas. Senri Ethnological Studies, no. 9, pp. 213–260. Osaka: National Museum of Ethnology, 1981.

Amino, Yoshihiko. "Some Problems Concerning the History of Popular Life in Medieval Japan." *Acta Asiatica* 44 (1983): 77–97.

Araki, James T. *The Ballad Drama of Medieval Japan*. Berkeley: University of California Press, 1973.

Aston, W. G., trans. *Nihongi: Chronicles of Japan from the Earliest Times to* A.D. **697**. Rutland, Vt.: Charles E. Tuttle, 1972.

Baird, Bil. *The Art of the Puppet Theater*. New York: Macmillan, 1965.

Barnes, Gina L. *Protohistoric Yamato: Archaeology of the First Japanese State*. University of Michigan Center for Japanese Studies, Michigan Papers in Japanese Studies, no. 17. Ann Arbor: University of Michigan Press, 1988.

Barnes, Gina L, and K. Hutterer, eds. *Windows on the Javanese Past: Studies in Archaeology and Prehistory*. Ann Arbor: University of Michigan Press, 1986.

Becker, Alton. "Text Building, Epistemology and Aesthetics in Japanese Shadow Theatre." In *The Imagination of Reality: Essays in Southeast Asian Coherence*

Systems, edited by A. L. Becker and Aram A. Yengoyan, pp. 221–242. Norwood, N. J.: Albex Publishing, 1979.

Bender, Ross. "The Hachiman Cult and the Dōkyō Incident." *Monumenta Nipponica* 24, no. 2 (summer 1979): 125–154.

—————. "Metamorphosis of a Deity: The Image of Hachiman in *Yumi Yawata*." *Monumenta Nipponica* 33, no. 2 (summer 1978): 165–178.

Bethe, Monica, and Karen Brazell. *Dance in the Nō Theater*. Ithaca: Cornell University Press, 1982.

Bettelheim, Bruno. *Freud and Man's Soul*. New York: Knopf, 1983.

Blacker, Carmen. *The Catalpa Bow: A Study of Shamanic Practices in Japan*. London: George Allen and Unwin, 1975.

Blau, Hagen. *Sarugaku und Shushi: Beiträge zur Ausbildung dramatischer Elemente im Weltlichen und religiösen Volkstheatre der Heian-Zeit under besonderer Berücksichtigung Seiner Sozialen Grundlagen*. Wiesbaden: Otto Harrassowitz, 1966.

Bock, Felicia. *Classical Learning and Taoist Practices in Early Japan with a Translation of Books XVI and XX of the Engi-Shiki*. Center for Asian Studies, Occasional Papers, no. 17. Tempe: Arizona State University, 1985.

Bourdieu, Pierre. *Outline of a Theory of Practice*. Translated by Richard Nice. Cambridge: Cambridge University Press, 1977.

Bowers, Faubion. *Japanese Theater*. New York: Hermitage House, 1952.

Corbey, Raymond, and Joep Leersen, eds. *Alterity, Identity, Image: Selves and Others in Society and Scholarship*. Atlanta and Amsterdam: Rodopi, 1991.

Cornell, John B. "From Caste Patron to Entrepreneur and Political Ideologue: Transformation in Nineteenth and Twentieth Century Outcaste Leadership Elites." In *Modern Japanese Leadership: Tradition and Change*, edited by Bernard S. Silberman and H. D. Harootunian, pp. 51–82. Tuscon: University of Arizona Press, 1966.

Craig, E. Gordon. "The Actor and the Übermarionette." In *Total Theater: A Critical Anthology*, edited by E. T. Kirby. New York: Dutton, 1969.

Davis, Fred. *Yearning for Yesterday: A Sociology of Nostalgia*. New York: Free Press, 1979.

de Coppet, Daniel, ed. *Understanding Rituals*. London: Routledge, 1992.

de Poorter, Erika Gerlinde, trans. *Motoyoshi's Sarugaku Dangi: A Description and Assessment with Annotated Translation*. Leiden, 1983.

DeVos, George, and H. Wagatsuma, eds. *Japan's Invisible Race: Caste in Culture and Personality*. Berkeley: University of California Press, 1966.

Dorson, Edward, ed. *Studies in Japanese Folklore*. Bloomington: Indiana University Press, 1963.

Douglas, Mary. *Purity and Danger: An Analysis of the Concepts of Pollution and Taboo*. London: Routledge and Kegan Paul, 1966.

Dumont, Louis. *Homo Hierarchicus: An Essay on the Caste System*. Chicago: University of Chicago Press, 1966.

Dunn, C. J. *The Early Japanese Puppet Drama*. London: Luzac, 1966.

Dykstra, Yoshiko Kurata. "Jizō, the Most Merciful: Tales from the *Jizō* Bosatsu Reigenki." *Monumenta Nipponica* 33, no. 2 (summer 1978): 179–201.

Ebersole, Gary L. *Ritual Poetry and the Politics of Death in Early Japan*. Princeton: Princeton University Press, 1989.

Egami, Namio. "Light on Ancient Japanese Cultural Origins from Historical Archaeology and Legend." In *Japanese Culture: Its Development and Characteristics,* edited by Robert J. Smith and Richard K. Beardsley, pp. 11–16. Viking Fund Publications in Anthropology, Wenner-Gren Foundation for Anthropological Research. Chicago: Aldine, 1962.

Eilberg-Schwartz, Howard. *The Savage in Judaism: An Anthropology of Israelite Religion and Ancient Judaism*. Bloomington: Indiana University Press, 1990.

Elam, Keir. *The Semiotics of Theatre and Drama*. London: Methuen, 1980.

Eliade, Mircea. *Shamanism: Archaic Techniques of Ecstasy*. Translated by Willard R. Trask. Bollingen Series, no. 76. Princeton: Princeton University Press, 1964.

Elisseeff, Vadime. *Archaeologia Mundi: Japan*. Translated by James Hogarth. Geneva: Nagel Publishers, 1973.

Feher, Michel, Ramona Naddaff, and Nadia Tazi. *Fragments for a History of the Human Body*. Part 1. New York: Zone, 1989.

Foucault, Michel. *Madness and Civilization: A History of Insanity in the Age of Reason*. New York: Pantheon Books, 1965.

Fustel de Coulanges. *The Ancient City: A Study on the Religion, Laws, and Institutions of Greece and Rome*. Translated by Willard Small. Garden City, N. Y.: Doubleday, 1956.

Garvin, Paul, ed. *A Prague School Reader on Esthetics, Literary Structure and Style*. Washington: George Washington University Press, 1964.

Geertz, Clifford. "Making Experiences, Authoring Selves." In *The Anthropology of Experience,* edited by Victor Turner and Edward Bruner, pp. 341–380. Champagne: University of Illinois Press, 1986.

Goodwin, Janet R. "Alms for Kasagi Temple." *Journal of Asian Studies* 46, no. 4 (November 1987): 827–841.

Grappard, Alan. "Lotus in the Mountain, Mountain in the Lotus: *Rokugō* Kaizan Nimmon Daibosatsu Hongi." *Monumenta Nipponica* 41, no. 1 (spring 1986): 21–50.

Harootunian, H. D. *Things Seen and Unseen: Discourse and Ideology in Tokugawa Nativism*. Chicago: University of Chicago Press, 1988.

Harris, William Wayne. *Population, Disease and Land in Early Japan: 645–900*. East Asian Papers. Cambridge: Harvard University Press, 1985.

Harrison, Bernard. *Form and Content*. New York: Harper and Row, 1973.

Harrison, John A., trans. "New Light on Early and Medieval Japanese Historiography." University of Florida Monographs, Social Sciences, no. 4 (fall 1959).

Havens, Norman, trans. *Matsuri: Festival and Rite in Japanese Life*. Institute for Japanese Culture and Classics, Contemporary Papers on Japanese Religion, no. 1. Tokyo: Kokugakuin University, 1988.

Herbert, Jean. *Dieux et sectes populaires du Japon*. Paris: Albin Michel, 1967.

———. *Les dieux nationaux du Japon*. Paris: Albin Michel, 1969.

Hoff, Frank. *Song, Dance, Storytelling: Aspects of the Performing Arts in Japan*. Cornell University East Asia Papers, no. 15. Ithaca: Cornell University Press, 1978.

Holtom, Daniel C. "The Meaning of Kami." *Monumenta Nipponica* 3 (1940): 2–27, 32–53.

———. *The National Faith of Japan: A Study in Modern Shinto.* 1938; reprint, New York: Paragon Books, 1965.

Hori, Ichirō. *Folk Religion in Japan: Continuity and Change.* Edited by Joseph M. Kitagawa and Allen Miller. Chicago: University of Chicago Press, 1968.

———. "Mysterious Visitors from the Harvest to the New Year." In *Studies in Japanese Folklore,* edited by Edward Dorson, pp. 76–103. Bloomington: Indiana State University Press, 1963.

Inoura, Yoshinobu, and Toshio Kawatake. *The Traditional Theatre of Japan.* Tokyo: The Japan Foundation, 1981.

Ishida, Eiichiro. "Nature and the Problem of Japanese Cultural Origins." In *Japanese Culture: Its Development and Characteristics,* eds. Robert J. Smith and Richard K. Beardsley. Viking Fund Publications in Anthropology, Wenner-Gren Foundation for Anthropological Research. Chicago: Aldine Publishers, 1962.

Ivy, Marilyn. *Discourses of the Vanishing in Contemporary Japan.* Ph.D. diss. Cornell University, 1988.

———. *Discourses of the Vanishing: Modernity, Phantasm, Japan.* Chicago: University of Chicago Press, 1995.

Jameson, Fredric. "Post-modernism, or the Cultural Logic of Late Capitalism." *New Left Review,* no. 146 (Sept./Oct. 1984): 53–92.

Janetta, Ann Bowman. *Epidemics and Mortality in Early Modern Japan.* Princeton: Princeton University Press, 19.

Kamata, Hisako. "Daughters of the Gods: Shaman Priestesses in Japan and Okinawa." In *Folk Cultures of Japan and East Asia.* Monumenta Nipponica Monographs, no. 25. Tokyo: Sophia University Press, 1966.

Kapferer, Bruce. "Performance and the Structure of Meaning and Experience." In *The Anthropology of Experience,* edited by Victor Turner and Edward Bruner. Champagne: University of Illinois Press, 1986.

Katō, Genchi. "A Study of the Development of Religious Ideas among the Japanese People as Illustrated by Japanese Phallicism." *Transactions of the Asiatic Society of Japan,* 2d ser., supp. to vol. 1 (December 1924): 5–70.

Kawatake, Shigetoshi. *Development of the Japanese Theatre Art.* Tokyo: Kokusai Bunka Shinkosai, 1935.

Keene, Donald. *Bunraku: The Art of the Japanese Puppet Theatre.* Tokyo: Kodansha International, 1973.

Kidder, J. E., Jr. *Early Japanese Art: The Great Tombs and Treasures.* Princeton: Von Nostrand, 1964.

———. *Japan Before Buddhism.* London: Praeger and Sons, 1966.

Kitagawa, J. M. *On Understanding Japanese Religion.* Princeton: Princeton University Press, 1987.

———. *Religion in Japanese History.* New York: Columbia University Press, 1966.

Koschmann, Victor J., Oiwa Keibō, and Yamashita Shinji, eds. *International Perspectives on Yanagita Kunio and Japanese Folklore Studies.* Cornell University East Asia Papers, no. 37. Ithaca: Cornell University Press, 1985.

Kristeva, Julia. *Powers of Horror: An Essay on Abjection.* Translated by Leon S. Roudiez. New York: Columbia University Press, 1982.

LaFleur, William. "Hungry Ghosts and Hungry People." In *Fragments for a History of the Human Body,* part 1, edited by Michel Feher, pp. 270–301. New York: Zone, 1989.

———. *The Karma of Words: Buddhism and the Literary Arts in Medieval Japan.* Berkeley: University of California Press, 1983.

———. *Liquid Life: Abortion and Buddhism in Contemporary Japan.* Princeton: Princeton University Press, 1992.

Law, Jane Marie. "Of Plagues and Puppets: On the Significance of the Name Hyakudayū in Japanese Religions." *Transactions of the Asiatic Society of Japan,* 4th ser., 8 (1993): 108–132.

———. "The Puppet as Body Substitute: *Ningyō* in the Japanese *Shiki Sanbasō* Performance." In *Religious Reflections on the Human Body,* edited by Jane Marie Law. Bloomington: Indiana University Press, 1995.

———. "Religious Authority and Ritual Puppetry: The Case of *Dōkumbō Denki.*" *Monumenta Nipponica* 27, no. 1 (spring 1992): 78–97.

———. "Violence, Ritual Reenactment, and Ideology: The Hōjō-e (Rite for Release of Living Beings) of the Usa Hachiman Shrine in Japan." *History of Religions* 33, no. 4 (May 1994): 325–357.

———, ed. *Religious Reflections on the Human Body.* Bloomington: Indiana University Press. 1995.

Ledyard, Gari. "Galloping Along with the Horseriders: Looking for the Founders of Japan." *Journal of Japanese Studies* 1, no. 2 (1975): 217–254.

Long, Charles H. *Significations: Signs, Symbols and Images in the Interpretation of Religion.* Philadelphia: Fortress Press, 1986.

Marra, Michel. *The Aesthetics of Discontent: Politics and Reclusion in Medieval Japanese Literature.* Honolulu: University of Hawaii Press, 1991.

———. *Representations of Power: The Literary Politics of Medieval Japan.* Honolulu: University of Hawaii Press, 1994.

Maruyama, Masao. *Studies in the Intellectual History of Tokugawa Japan.* Translated by Mikiso Hane. Princeton: Princeton University Press, 1989.

Mayer, Fanny Hagin. "The Yanagita Kunio Approach to Japanese Folklore Studies." *The Transactions of the Asiatic Society of Japan,* 3d ser., 13 (December 1976): 129–143.

McNeill, William. *Plagues and Peoples.* Garden City, N.Y.: Doubleday, 1976.

Mencher, Joan P., ed. *Social Anthropology of Peasantry.* Bombay: Somaiya, 1983.

Miki, Fumio. *Haniwa.* Tokyo: Weatherhill, Shibundo, 1974.

Miller, Richard J. *Japan's First Bureaucracy: A Study of Eighth Century Government.* China-Japan Program. Ithaca: Cornell University Press, 1978.

Miwa, Kimitada. "Toward a Rediscovery of Localism: Can the Yanagita School of Folklore Studies Overcome Japan's Modern Ills?" *Japan Quarterly* 23, no 1 (January-March 1976): 38–49.

Morse, Edward A. "Yanagita Kunio and the Modern Japanese Consciousness." In *International Perspectives on Yanagita Kunio and Japanese Folklore Studies,* edited by J. Victor Koschmann, Oiwa Keibō, and Yamashita Shinji, pp. 11–28. Cornell East Asia Papers, no. 37. Ithaca: Cornell University Press, 1985.

Nagahara, Keiji. "The Medieval Origins of *Eta-Hinin*." *Journal of Japanese Studies* 5, no. 2 (summer 1979): 385–404.

Nakamura, Hajime. *Ways of Thinking of Eastern Peoples: India—China—Japan.* Honolulu: University of Hawaii Press, 1978.

Nakane, Chie. *Japanese Society.* Harmondsworth: Penguin Books, 1973.

Narimitsu, Matsudaira. "The Concept of *Tamashii* in Japan." In *Studies in Japanese Folklore*, edited by Edward Dorson. Bloomington: Indiana University Press, 1963.

Neary, Ian. *Political Protest and Social Control in Pre-War Japan: The Origins of Buraku Liberation.* Atltantic Highlands, N.J.: Humanities Press International, 1989.

Niculescu, Margareta, ed. *The Puppet Theatre of the Modern World.* Transated by Ewald Osers and Elisabeth Strick. Boston: Plays, Inc., 1967.

Ninomiya, Shigeaki. "An Inquiry Concerning the Origin, Development, and Present Situation of the Eta in Relation to the History of Social Classes in Japan." *Transactions of the Asiatic Society of Japan*, 2d ser., 10 (December 1933): 47–152.

Ohnuki-Tierney, Emiko. *Illness and Culture in Contemporary Japan.* Cambridge: Cambridge University Press, 1984.

———. *Monkey as Mirror: Symbolic Transformations in Japanese History and Ritual.* Princeton: Princeton University Press, 1987.

Parker, Robert. *Miasma: Pollution and Purification in Early Greek Religion.* Oxford: Oxford University Press, 1983.

Philippi, Donald L. trans. *Kojiki.* Tokyo: University of Tokyo Press, 1968.

———. *Kojiki: Translated with an Introduction and Notes.* Princeton: Princeton University Press, 1969.

———. *Norito: A Translation of Ancient Japanese Ritual Prayers.* Princeton: Princeton University Press, 1990.

Ponsonby-Fane, Richard. *The Vicissitudes of Shinto.* Kyoto: Ponsonby-Fane Memorial Society, 1963.

———. *Visiting Famous Shrines in Japan.* Tokyo: The Ponsonby-Fane Memorial Society, 1964.

Raz, Jacob. *Audience and Actors: A Study of Their Interaction in the Japanese Theatre.* Leiden: E. J. Brill, 1984.

———. "Popular Entertainment and Politics: The Great *Dengaku* of 1096." *Monumenta Nipponica* 40, no. 3 (autumn 1985): 283–298.

Redfield, Robert. *The Little Community: Viewpoints for the Study of a Human Whole.* Ithaca: Cornell University Press, 1955.

———. *Tepoztlan: A Mexican Village.* Chicago: University of Chicago Press, 1930.

Reiniger, Lotte. *Shadow Theatre and Shadow Films.* London: B. T. Batsford, 1970.

Reischauer, Jean, and Robert Karl. *Early Japanese History (c. 40 B.C.—A.D. 1167).* Princeton: Princeton University Press, 1937.

Rickman, H.P., ed. and trans. *Dilthey: Selected Writings.* Cambridge: Cambridge University Press, 1976.

Ricoeur, Paul. *Hermeneutics and the Human Sciences.* Edited and translated by

John B. Thompson. Editions de la Maison des Sciences de l'Homme. Cambridge: Cambridge University Press, 1981.

Rotermund, Hartmut O. *Hōsōgami: ou la petite vérole aisément: matériaux pour l'étude des épidémies dans le Japon des XVIIIe, XIXe siècles*. Paris: Mai sonneuve et Larose, 1991.

Sahara, Makoto. "The Yayoi Culture." In *Recent Archaeological Findings in Japan*, pp. 37–54. Tokyo: Center for East Asian Cultural Studies, 1987.

Said, Edward. *Orientalism*. New York: Pantheon Books, 1978.

Sansom, Sir George. *A History of Japan*. Stanford: Stanford University Press, 1958.

Schaumann, Werner. "Leistet die Mythe vom Verlorenen Angelhaken *(Umisachi-Yamasachi no Shinwa)* Einen Beitrage zur Kalrung des Problems der Herkunft der Japanischen Kultur?" In *Beitrage zur Japanischen Ethnogenese: 100 Jahre nach Heinrich von Siebold*, pp. 129–147. Bonner Zeitschrift für Japanologie, vol. 2. Bonn, 1980.

Schechner, Richard. *Between Theater and Anthropology*. Philadelphia: University of Pennsylvania Press, 1985.

Scott, A. C. *The Puppet Theater of Japan*. Rutland, Vt.: Charles E. Tuttle, 1963.

Segawa, Kiyoko. "Menstrual Taboos Imposed upon Women." In *Studies in Japanese Folklore*, edited by Edward Dorson, pp. 239–250. Bloomington: Indiana University Press, 1963.

Simmen, Rene. *The World of Puppets*. New York: Thomas Y. Crowell, 1972.

Smith, Jonathan Z. *Map is Not Territory: Studies in the History of Religions*. Leiden: E. J. Brill, 1978.

Smith, Robert J. *Ancestor Worship in Contemporary Japan*. Stanford: Stanford University Press, 1974.

Smith, Robert J., and Richard K. Beardsley, eds. *Japanese Culture: Its Development and Characteristics*. Viking Fund Publications in Anthropology, Wenner-Gren Foundation for Anthropological Research. Chicago: Aldine, 1964.

Sonoda, Minoru. "The Religious Situation in Japan in Relation to Shinto." *Acta Asiatica* 51 (1987): 1–21.

Swanberg-Law, Jane Marie. "Puppets of the Road: Ritual Performance in Japanese Folk Religion." Ph.D. diss., University of Chicago, 1990.

Takayanagi, Shun'ichi. "Yanagita Kunio Survey Review." *Monumenta Nipponica* 24, no. 3 (autumn 1974): 329–335.

Tambiah, Stanley. "A Performative Approach to Ritual." In *Proceedings of the British Academy*, vol. 65. London: Oxford University Press, 1979.

Tanaka, Migaku. "The Early Historical Periods." *Recent Archaeological Discoveries in Japan*. Tokyo: Center for East Asian Cultural Studies, 1987.

Theunissen, Michael. *The Other: Studies in the Social Ontology of Husserl, Heidegger, Sartre and Buber*. Translated by C. Macann. Cambridge: MIT Press, 1984.

Todorov, Tzvetan. *Literature and Its Theorists: A Personal View of Twentieth Century Criticism*. Translated by Catherine Porter. Ithaca: Cornell University Press, 1988.

Tsuda, Sōkichi. "The Idea of Kami in Ancient Japanese Classics." *T'oung Pao*. Vol. 7, bks. 4–5. Leiden: 1966.

Tsude, Hiroshi. "The Kofun Period." In *Recent Archaeological Discoveries in Japan*. Tokyo: Center for East Asian Cultural Studies, 1987.

Tsunoda, Ryusaku, and L. Carrington Goodrich. *Japan in the Chinese Dynastic Histories*. Perkins Asiatic Monographs, no. 2. South Pasadena, Calif.: P. D. and Ione Perkins, 1951.

Tsunoda, Ryusaku, W. Theodore de Bary, and Donald Keene. *Sources of Japanese Tradition*. New York: Columbia University Press, 1958.

Turner, Victor W. *The Ritual Process: Structure and Anti-Structure*. Ithaca: Cornell University Press, 1969.

Turner, Victor W., and Edward M. Bruner, eds. *The Anthropology of Experience*. Champagne: University of Illinois Press, 1986.

Wakita, Haruko, and Susan B. Hanley. "Dimensions in Development of Cities in Fifteenth and Sixteenth Century Japan." In *Japan Before Tokugawa*, edited by John W. Hall, Nagahara Keiji, and Yamamura Kōzō, pp. 295–326. Princeton: Princeton University Press, 1981.

Walton, Michael J. *Craig on Theatre*. London: Methuen, 1983.

Williams, Raymond. *The Country and the City*. New York: Oxford University Press, 1973.

Wu Hung. "A Sanpan Shan Chariot Ornament and the Xiangrui Design in Western Art." *Archives of Asian Art* 37 (1984): 38–59.

Yamamoto, Yoshiko. *The Namahage: A Festival in the Northeast of Japan*. Philadelphia: Institute for the Study of Human Issues, 1978.

Yamashita, Shinji. "Ritual and Unconscious Tradition: A Note on Yanagita Kunio's *About Our Ancestors*." In *International Perspectives on Yanagita Kunio and Japanese Folklore Studies,* edited by J. Victor Koschmann, Oiwa Keibō, and Yamashita Shinji, pp. 55–64. Cornell East Asia Series, no. 37. Ithaca: Cornell University Press, 1985.

Yoneyama, Toshinao. "Yanagita and His Works." In *International Perspectives on Yanagita Kunio and Japanese Folklore Studies,* edited by J. Victor Koschmann, Oiwa Keibō, and Yamashita Shinji, pp. 29–52. East Asia Series, no. 37. Ithaca: Cornell University Press, 1985.

Yoshida, Teigo. "The Stranger as God: The Place of the Outsider in Japanese Folk Religion." *Ethnology* 20, no. 2 (1964): 87–99.

Young, John. *The Location of Yamatai: A Case Study in Japanese Historiography, 720–1945*. Johns Hopkins University Studies in Historical and Political Science, series 75, no. 2. Baltimore: Johns Hopkins University Press, 1958.

Index

ABOUT THE AUTHOR

Jane Marie Law is Assistant Professor of
Japanese Religions at Cornell University. She is editor of
Religious Reflections on the Human Body.